795
928296

SOVIET
MANAGEMENT

- **With Significant American Comparisons**

- **Barry M. Richman**
  University of California, Los Angeles

Prentice-Hall, Inc.   *Englewood Cliffs, New Jersey*

- **To Vivian and Viana**

PRENTICE-HALL INTERNATIONAL, INC., *London*
PRENTICE-HALL OF AUSTRALIA, PTY., LTD., *Sydney*
PRENTICE-HALL OF CANADA, LTD., *Toronto*
PRENTICE-HALL OF INDIA (PRIVATE), LTD., *New Delhi*
PRENTICE-HALL OF JAPAN, INC., *Tokyo*

- Library of Congress Catalog Card Number: 65-12169

- Printed in the United States of America   82385-C

• Preface

There are essentially two kinds of scholarly books about the economy of the Soviet Union. In the first group, the over-all views of the economy, are discussions of Russia's broad, aggregate problems, including such critical factors as strategic decision-making regarding resource allocation on the higest levels, the rate of economic growth, descriptions of the central planning apparatus, and similar factors. In the second type of work, the microcosmic view, problems concerning institutions and people of lower levels are discussed. Such studies often contain descriptions of the activities of various types of organizations or persons in Russia. These works occasionally deal with Soviet management, but only relatively few analyze the motives of managers, or even their behavior.

This book is intended to bridge the gap between these types of studies. The object is to examine those aspects of the over-all politico-economic-cultural environment which have a direct bearing on the critical Soviet management activities at the enterprise level, from whence production and wealth come. Hence, we examine the enterprise manager not only in isolation but also in regard to the forces above him which influence his behavior. Within this framework we focus on the processes and problems of Soviet industrial management and the role and significance of management in Russia's economic progress.

It is impossible to adequately understand broad movements of Russian economic development without knowing more about the nature of industrial management in the Soviet Union. Equally important, it is difficult to determine why managers act as they do without having considerable insight into the nature of the Soviet environment, which both influences and is influenced by industrial managers. Hence, both the large and the small become legitimate aims of analysis, although the prime focus of this book is on enterprise managers as a key group in the operation of Soviet economic activity.

The book has been written with both the nonspecialist and specialist of Soviet affairs in mind. The presentation will provide the nonspecialist with a vivid insight into how the Soviet economy works in general and the processes and problems of Soviet industrial management in particular. For the specialist, this study provides some original information about the Soviet system which has been obtained from personal interviews and research conducted in the U.S.S.R. by the author. This book will also provide the specialist with some original but worthwhile concepts and some new ways of looking at well-known problems. All readers may find the Soviet-American comparisons, which highlight major similarities and differences in the two systems, of particular interest.

This book has evolved with five years of intensive study, two research trips abroad, and a doctoral dissertation which was completed at Columbia University in 1962. Hence, it is not possible to acknowledge here all those persons and organizations who have contributed significantly to this study. I do wish to thank my financial benefactors: The Graduate School of Business of Columbia University; The Division of Research of the Graduate School of Business Administration at the University of California, Los Angeles; and the Bureau of Business and Economic Research at UCLA.

Numerous students of management and the Soviet economy in the U.S., Canada, Great Britain, and France have provided me with invaluable information, ideas, and assistance. I am particularly indebted to Professor William Newman of Columbia University, since this study would probably not have been completed if it were not for his assistance in every possible respect. I am also indebted to Professor Eli Ginzberg of Columbia and Dean Robert Senkier of Seton Hall University who have both rendered much advice and assistance. Professor Alexander Erlich of the Russian Institute of Columbia University and Professor Joseph Berliner of Brandeis University patiently and effectively helped me to understand the Soviet system when I was truly a novice in Soviet affairs. Letters of introduction provided by Professor Arthur F. Burns of Columbia University and the National Bureau of Economic Research, and Dr. Herbert Stein of the Committee on Economic Development, helped me obtain interviews with a number of Soviet economists and academicians. Dr. Benjamin Barg of the United Nations also rendered invaluable assistance at the pioneer stages of this study.

My colleague, Professor Richard Farmer of Indiana University, has been invaluable in helping me develop many of the ideas presented, in perusing and commenting on the manuscript, and in patiently putting up with my states of depression and elation during the book's preparation. My multilingual research assistant, Mr. Arman Shaffler, has done a remarkable job in searching out, obtaining, and translating a vast number of pertinent current Soviet sources, as well as those in a variety of other foreign languages. He has also provided much constructive criticism and many ideas in the preparation of this book. I am grateful to Dr. Ernest Dale, of Ernest Dale Associates and Cornell University, and Professor Holland Hunter, Chairman, Department of Economics, Haverford College, for their review of my manuscript. My appreciation is also extended to Professor Herbert Simon, whose interest at the early stages of this study was a major catalyst in its publication.

Finally, I wish to express my gratitude to the numerous Soviet, Czechoslovak, and Polish industrial officials, enterprise personnel, planners, economists, and academicians who were extremely helpful and kind to me during my trips abroad in 1960 and 1961. In this connection, the *Ekonomicheskaya Gazeta* in Moscow, Leningrad University, and the Czechoslovak Chamber of Commerce in Prague deserve a special note of thanks since they arranged for many of my personal interviews at industrial enterprises and various other organizations.

BARRY M. RICHMAN

• Contents

v

• Introduction

The nonspecialist who obtains his information about Soviet affairs primarily from the press, radio, television and other popular media may well be confused about what is actually happening to the Soviet economy. On the one hand, we hear about impressive Soviet economic growth and outstanding achievements in a limited number of strategic spheres of industrial activity; on the other hand, we hear about major industrial reforms and problems of extreme waste and inefficiency. Although national aggregate production targets are typically fulfilled and even overfulfilled, much of what is produced is unneeded, unsalable, unusable, or unused, and conditions of production are probably, more often than not, inefficient.

Such waste and inefficiency are due primarily to managerial shortcomings in the Soviet economic system. It has only been in recent years, as the Soviets entered a new stage of economic development, that shortcomings in their managerial apparatus have come to seriously hinder desired economic performance. It is rather paradoxical that Soviet economic success over time has rendered their economic system more and more unmanageable.

One can read with awe, disdain, or fear of production of eighty million tons of steel, Sputniks, million-pound thrust rockets, electronic gadgetry, 40-inch pipelines, vast mileage of electrified railways, and similar evidence of industrial development in the Soviet Union. No matter how the sometimes dubious statistics are analyzed, shifted, and changed, it is clear that in the past forty years the Soviets have built a vast industrial complex and that they are continuing to do so.[1] Their entire political and military power is built on this base.

However, outstanding accomplishments in a limited number of spheres of industrial activity and impressive aggregate results in industrial production are not enough in the Soviet economy of today. Efficient utilization of resources, cost and quality considerations, detailed specifications of the product-mix produced, and product and process innovation in all industrial sectors have become increasingly important in recent years. Only the managerial apparatus has not yet adjusted to the changing requirements and needs of the Soviet economy.

During the latter part of the 1950's the performance of industrial managers in the Soviet Union tended to deteriorate rather steadily. Desired

1

enterprise results were not being achieved, except possibly in aggregate output performance. But even in the case of aggregate production, numerous enterprises failed to achieve their targets. Poor managerial performance has continued into the 1960's. Ineffective performance at the operating level of the Soviet economy has been due to major defects in the over-all economic-cultural-institutional environment in which enterprise managers have operated. Typically, undesirable managerial behavior has not been primarily a question of incompetence, although many inept managers did and do exist. The basic problem has been that even an extremely able manager could not perform effectively within the system in which he has been required to operate.

The response to this type of problem has been to make significant changes in the system in an effort to encourage managerial behavior suited to changing conditions. This has proved difficult in a monolithic society which has been convinced of its possession of absolute answers to all questions of economic organization, but in spite of this ideological rigidity, changes have been made and are still being made at a rapid pace.

In this study we are chiefly concerned with the management of the Soviet industrial enterprise. Industrial enterprises are state owned in the Soviet Union, and the regime prescribes certain common ultimate objectives which are to be pursued by all enterprises. These ultimate objectives are translated into operating plans for each enterprise. The industrial enterprise is the key operating unit in the Soviet economy, since national industrial results for any given period are comprised of the aggregate of all enterprise results.

We are also interested in the management of the Soviet economy as a whole, but only as it bears on and influences the activities of enterprise management. It is the over-all Soviet organizational structure that sets forth the "rules of the game" within which enterprise managers must operate and which in large part determine their performance. In recent years a number of major reforms in the Soviet organizational structure have been undertaken in an attempt to improve managerial performance, and many proposals involving further changes are presently under study by the Soviet experts. We shall consider the recently implemented reforms that have a significant bearing on enterprise management, as well as the significant proposed changes.

This study focuses on the objectives and operating plan of the Soviet industrial enterprise and the relationship between enterprise management and the management of the economy as a whole. With this focus we can gain considerable insight into how the Soviet economic system functions, the major managerial processes entailed, the strengths and weaknesses of the system, and the type of reforms needed to improve managerial performance and national economic results.

In order to intelligently study Soviet industrial management, or management in any other country for that matter, it is best to first consider certain basic economic problems and critical productive functions common to all countries. Only then can we fully appreciate the role and significance of management in a given nation's economic progress. Since the economic systems in which enterprise managers operate differ rather dramatically in the U.S. and the Soviet Union, it is useful to explore the salient features of both systems. Therefore, as background for the nonspecialist in particular, Chapter 1 of this book presents a brief comparative discussion of the two systems, emphasizing the role of management.

In the second part of the book we shall consider how Soviet industry formally functions, focusing on the industrial enterprise and its management. Chapter 2 presents an evolutionary account of the organization of Soviet industry from the inception of the ministerial system in the early 1930's until the present. In Chapter 3 we examine the operations of the industrial enterprise, the specific nature of the ultimate enterprise objectives, and the content of the enterprise operating plan. Chapter 4 contains an analysis of the authority, independence, and influence of Soviet managers in running their enterprises. Of particular interest in both Chapters 4 and 5 is the role of enterprise management in the planning processes and in the execution of plans. Chapter 5 explores the processes by which enterprise plans are formulated, as well as the formulation of the national economic plan.

The third part of the book deals primarily with managerial problems in Soviet industry. In Chapter 6 we analyze in some depth the problem of efficiently allocating resources to industrial enterprises without using a competitive market price system. Chapter 7 explores the various incentives used to induce enterprise managers to act in the best interests of the state and society at large. The focus of Chapter 8 is on problems of managerial motivation and behavior resulting from two major factors, (1) the system of managerial incentives and (2) the deficient provision of resources to enterprises. Chapter 9 deals with innovation problems in Soviet industry, particularly emphasizing managerial opposition to product and technological innovation. In Chapter 10 we consider the management of personnel, focusing on employee motivation and behavior. Chapter 11 analyzes how effectively certain organizations and officials charged with the task of checking on and controlling the activities of enterprise management, carry out their control function.

The final part of the book analyzes the Soviet reforms, under study and underway, which have as their chief aim the improvement of managerial performance and national economic results. There is much debate among the Soviet experts on how best to change the system in order to derive the desired national results.

At various points throughout the study, comparisons between Soviet and American management will be presented for illustrative purposes and to highlight major similarities and differences.

The study is based on a comprehensive survey of available Western and Soviet sources, as well as on information obtained from personal interviews conducted by this author in the Soviet Union in 1960 and 1961. In total, approximately 100 Soviet planners, economists, academicians, workers, Communist party members, and trade union and industrial officials, including managerial personnel at 16 enterprises, were interviewed. Limited use is also made of data obtained from interviews with similar persons in Czechoslovakia and Poland in 1961. Appendix A discusses in more detail the sources of information utilized in this study.

References are cited by chapter at the end of the book. Liberal use is made of references so that the reader can follow up on various topics of interest not comprehensively dealt with in this book. In many instances pertinent Russian sources have been cited.

On January 1, 1961, the Soviet government revalued the ruble, ten old rubles equaling one new one. Unless otherwise noted, ruble figures given in this book are in new rubles. One ruble is roughly equivalent to $1.10, and 100 kopeks equal one ruble.

I · BACKGROUND

1 • Micromanagement, Macromanagement, and Economic Activity

Universal Economic Goals

In virtually all modern industrial societies (and most underdeveloped ones as well) the paramount economic goal is to obtain more production of usable goods and services.[1] In economic terms, what is wanted is steady and rapid economic growth in the gross national product of the country concerned. To be really effective, such growth should be in terms of increases in productivity per employee, although growth caused by expansion of the labor force is also acceptable.

Regardless of what is wanted by a society, be it atomic bombs, highways, consumer goods, steel mills, farm produce, or even art objects, the goal can be reached more easily if growth in productivity is sustained and if a high level of economic efficiency is achieved. To date, no modern country has expressed a serious desire to reduce the total flow of real goods or services, no matter what their precise goals may be. The Soviet Union has stated as official policy the desire—expressed in national production plans—for such sustained growth at the maximum feasible rate.

One important limitation on this process is that goods and services must be in usable form. It is not enough to produce things generally; production must be desired or needed by some person or organization. If output does not serve to fulfill the end or functional use intended—but rather rots in warehouses and stores—even though such output enters into statistics of national economic growth, it represents no real gain.

A second possible limitation might be that the work force be fully employed. Full employment does not necessarily mean that every person seeking work is always fully occupied; rather, a reasonable level of "full employment" is desired. Hence inputs should be used in a way which does not lead to mass unemployment (as does, for example, automation) since most societies would probably choose a slower rate of growth (but not an absolute decline in income) in order to keep most persons gainfully employed.[2]

Critical Economic Functions

Any type of economy must perform certain critical economic functions in some manner in order to survive at all. These economic functions will also be referred to as *productive* functions in this text.

5

First there is production. Land (including natural resources), labor, and capital must be combined to produce usable goods and services. Production can range from combining factors in the most automated factories to handicraft production in peasant huts; but unless a society can produce some minimum amount of goods to house, feed, and clothe its population, it cannot survive. A modern industrial state must produce far more than this minimum in order to maintain its advanced status.

In all cases, it must somehow be decided what is going to be produced, how much of each item is needed, and how production is to be done. Since production processes can be combined in unending variations, particularly in advanced economies, our choice is great, especially in the long run. For any given period, however, total production is limited. Increased production of one commodity means decreased production of another. Hence, directly related to the critical economic function of production is the problem of allocating scarce resources among competing ends for the achievement of maximum desired output. The proper quantity and quality of resources must be directed to those productive sectors which can deliver the needed goods and services.

The second critical economic function is distribution. Although the production function is concerned with the problems of what to produce and how much of each item, these problems are intimately linked to the distribution problem of for whom to produce. An economy must somehow distribute the commodities it produces to their intended destinations, regardless of whether the goods in question are processed materials, parts and components, machines, or consumer goods. Distribution, or marketing, is concerned with both the organization of distribution channels, involving the interrelationships between buyers and sellers, and physical distribution of goods, which involves warehousing, transportation, and inventory planning. Such distributive organizations and facilities can range from the most primitive barter systems to elaborate worldwide networks of trade.

Third, an economy must finance its production and distribution activities, and again, resource allocation in the form of capital is essential. This activity goes deeper than mere money financing, although the latter is extremely important. Real savings must somehow be accumulated in the form of stocks and capital if there is to be economic expansion in the future.

Fourth, a progressive society must engage in research and development to obtain new and improved products and processes. This research can range from activities in the most advanced, elaborate laboratories to mere observation and adoption of simple innovations emerging in the next village; but no society can make substantial advances without innovation in products and processes.

In addition to these critical functions, any economy, as well as each individual productive organization within a given economy, must keep track of its economic activities in order to plan for tomorrow. Statistics of every type perform this function, as do various systems of accounting. Without knowledge of what is going on at present, no meaningful pattern can be planned for the future.

Management and the Critical Economic Functions

In any economy human beings make the necessary economic decisions and human beings must carry them out. Since human beings do not react by biological instincts, they must somehow be induced to do the right things at the right time if the critical economic functions are to be carried out in a manner consistent with economic progress. The effective and efficient performance of the critical economic functions is the task of management in all its forms.

Management entails the coordination of human effort and material resources toward the achievement of organizational objectives, as well as the organization of the productive functions essential for achieving stated or accepted economic goals. Certain common functions of management must be performed whether productive enterprises are state or privately owned and whether resources are allocated through state planning or through a competitive market price system. Whether and to what degree self-interest is to be used in motivating managers is a most important practical question.

Micromanagement and Macromanagement

In discussing management in any country it is best to distinguish between macromanagement and micromanagement. The latter is the management of individual productive organizations on the lower operating levels of the economy. In any modern society there are thousands of productive units which contribute to and determine over-all national economic performance. Managers at this level coordinate human effort and material resources toward goal achievement in their respective organizations by the common managerial functions of planning (which includes decision-making), controlling, organizing, staffing, and directing.[3] In any complex productive organization plans must be established; activities must be controlled; duties must be assigned; departments must be set up; authority must be delegated and responsibility exacted; and personnel must be obtained, trained, appraised, motivated, supervised, and led. The administrators of a given organization must also devote some time to managing external relations with other organizations and persons with whom they must deal. Moreover, managers are generally expected to improve operations and results through innovation where feasible.

On the microlevel are found the production managers in factories, vice-presidents of finance, and all other persons concerned with the management of individual productive organizations, large and small. Such managers may be working in public or private organizations. A plant superintendent and a company sales manager are clearly micromanagers, as is a steel company president—until the one steel company, as is common in some smaller countries, is the only firm in the industry. In Communist countries micro- and macromanagement clearly represents a continuum of control. It is difficult to determine at times where one leaves off and the other begins.

The industrial enterprise is the key focal point of all the critical economic functions in the Soviet Union. Although production is the primary function of the enterprise, it is also involved in research and development and in distribution and financial activities. The enterprise also has a comprehensive statistical and accounting system which provides both its management and the government with pertinent information for decision-making.

Macromanagement denotes the management of an entire economy. In this study macromanagement is defined as that portion of the economic, political, legal, cultural, and social structure of a given country which bears on or influences the activities of micromanagers. Here the problem of interpretation can be quite vexing. In some countries, particularly Communist states, macromanagement is pervasive and detailed. All significant phases of economic activity are regulated through comprehensive national economic plans. In other countries, most typically those considered capitalistic, such management is often by law, tradition, or custom rather than by design. But in either case, the macromanagerial structure imposes various restraints on micromanagers. How well the critical economic functions are performed in a given society depends largely on the macromanagerial rules within which micromanagers must operate.

The U.S. Federal Reserve Board is practicing macromanagement when it alters interest rates; so is the U.S. government when it approves changes in corporate tax rates and antitrust laws. So, for that matter, is a Soviet central planner who makes investment or resource allocations for the steel industry.

Macromanagement is not normally considered management in the sense the word is used in business administration; but in fact it is since it involves decision-making and policy formulation. In the Soviet case it also involves the performance of the other basic managerial functions. The Soviet macromanagerial structure encompasses the entire governmental economic and planning apparatus apart from productive enterprises. Various governmental macroagencies play a significant role in planning, controlling, staffing, directing, and even organizing the activities of the tens of thousands of Soviet industrial enterprises. This is far from the case in privately owned American enterprises.

In general, societies have endless ways of organizing and performing their productive functions. In political terms, the possible range is from laissez-faire capitalism through monolithic totalitarian communism. In every case the over-all macromanagerial structure determines the rules for micromanagers at the operating level. Because the Soviet macromanagerial structure differs significantly from the typical capitalistic macrostructure, it is useful to examine briefly the distinguishing features of both. At the risk of some oversimplification, a brief comparative description of economic organization and the interaction of macro- and micromanagement in the U.S. and U.S.S.R. follows.[4]

Economic Organization and the Interaction of Macro- and Micromanagement: U.S.

In a basically capitalistic country, such as the U.S., it is common to find that there are few or no precisely stated national economic goals.[5] That is, the managers of individual productive organizations are generally quite free to produce whatever they wish, for whomever they wish, and however they wish. However, the American economy by no means resembles a pure laissez-faire capitalistic system. It is rather a mixed capitalistic enterprise system since there are many public enterprises, considerable governmental regulation and control, and various other elements that hinder the perfect functioning of objective market forces.[6] Nevertheless, the key automatic regulator of the system is market price competition in conjunction with the pursuit of profits. In contemporary times this twofold regulator tends to solve quite effectively the major economic problems common to all societies.[7]

In general, items in short supply which are wanted tend to be expensive, thus creating profitable opportunities for businessmen to supply the demand. No one seriously asks (in the economic sense) whether or not the desired items are useful, esthetic, or trivial—the critical feature of such a system is consumer sovereignty. Consumers, backing their wants with purchasing power, effectively determine the course of economic production, although government spending has become an increasingly significant determinant.[8] However, much of the government spending is done through contracts awarded to private firms on a competitive basis, and this factor tends to keep economic efficiency within reasonable bounds.

The rules in such a system tend to be constraints rather than positively stated national economic plans or goals. Hence a manager is not allowed to defraud anyone, nor can he sell poison to consumers for food, or float highly watered securities in financing his enterprise. He may be required to negotiate with unions, pay certain kinds of taxes, and subject his books to annual audits by suspicious tax collectors. These kind of rules basically tell a manager what he cannot do or what persons he must have precisely defined relationships with, but no law tells him what he must do or how to perform his managerial functions. General Motors, for instance, has a large legal staff to advise management on what is legal and what is not. But the idea of such a staff or anyone else telling management what it must do in the productive sense is alien to American thought. As pointed out above, management is generally quite free to produce what it chooses in accordance with the law, in the way it chooses; if it is wrong the market tends to correct quite quickly significant errors in judgment.[9]

It is true, however, that macromanagement in a capitalistic system can be active. Hence the central banking authorities' activities in a capitalistic economy influence supplies of money, interest rates, and foreign exchange rates. Such activities are designed to achieve vaguely defined national goals, such as the reduction of price inflation, the flows of foreign trade, and the rate of growth in the economy. To the individual manager, however, these activities appear as changes in prices, and he is free to select whatever options he chooses in planning his own operations. If interest rates rise, for example, no businessman is prevented from borrowing; nevertheless, the central authorities can be sure that such a price increase will in fact deter *some* businessmen from borrowing.

Such government policies as tax law can also be used in a capitalistic system to channel productive efforts into desirable roles. The high tax on the printing of national bank notes has effectively prevented private national banks from taking part in such activities, and the large depletion allowances available to mineral producers has encouraged such production. Again, to the individual manager, such macrocontrols are not necessarily absolute—he can, if in his judgment the price or tax is right, take part in any type of activity as long as legal requirements are met.

Management of productive enterprises in such an economy tends to be complex, full of risk, and quite rewarding to those farsighted enough to produce useful goods and services in demand. Much of management's task is the problem of seeing an opportunity and taking advantage of it by organizing to meet the expected need.

National economic performance and economic well-being in America are chiefly dependent on the activities of tens of thousands of productive organizations, each one devising its own plan of action and shaping its own destiny. Any person or group can establish any type of business unit as long as prescribed legal requirements are met. There are approximately 4.75 million business units in the U.S.,[10] and all but a small proportion of them are small-scale units owned by a single person. In terms of asset value, sales, payroll, employment, and economic power, a few hundred giant corporations occupy a strategically dominant position in the modern American economy. However, the myriad small-scale, privately owned, productive organizations play a crucial role in the American competitive system since they are often in a position to provide many goods and services in a more efficient manner than the giant corporations.

In such a society, the productive functions become diffused in all sorts of complex ways throughout the economy. There are many integrated firms that perform all the critical economic functions, and there are also numerous organizations performing only one or a few. For example, there are enterprises whose only basic function is to perform marketing activities for others on a commission basis; there are subcontracting firms concerned primarily with production; there are research and design organizations providing a service for manufacturing enterprises; and in the area of finance there are, not only traditional banks, but many other different kinds of financial institutions that provide capital to productive enterprises. No one can be sure what the activities, policies, and goals of the Little Nifty Company may be until after careful investigation. The name reveals nothing—the firm may in fact be involved in the distribution of export merchandise for another company, financing the activities of stockbrokers, or performing research and development in the hope of obtaining salable patents.

Although every productive enterprise formulates its own plans and policies and pursues its own objectives, no enterprise operates in a vacuum. If the enterprise is to survive it must fulfill some need in the economy; having initial capital is not enough. In the case of private enterprise the earning of profits is essential for survival. Various companies may not strive to maximize short-run profits, or even long-run profits.[11] This type of managerial behavior has become quite common as ownership and control have become divorced in large corporations.[12] Nevertheless, every company tends to pursue as a minimum the earning of adequate profits. Moreover, the notion of private property inherent in the American culture tends to instill in corporate management a sense of obligation to conserve corporate assets, even if management does not have an ownership interest.

The precise operational objectives an individual company establishes for itself, and the results actually achieved, are dependent on the expected and actual contributions of various parties both within and outside the company. These parties provide a flow of goods, services, and money crucial to the company's survival. For example, a large manufacturing company is usually dependent on suppliers, institutional customers, and/or the consuming public, transportation firms, investors, bankers, and often distributors. In addition, it may have to deal with labor unions, and it must also gain the cooperation and desired contributions from its own personnel.

The insiders and outsiders who contribute to the survival of the company have a direct interest in the company as long as they can be induced to cooperate and participate.[13] They may be thought of as *interest participants.* Each necessary participant, be it an individual or another organization, must find it advantageous to deal with the company, and the inducements offered must be feasible. That is, the goods, money, and satisfactions generated by the company must be at least equal to the combined demands of all participants. It is the task of management to strive for maximum contributions from participants with the inducements at its disposal in the face of complex competitive forces. How well this task is done will determine the size of company profits. If some key participants place too high a price on their contributions, there may not be enough inducements in the company kitty to go around, and the company fails. Management thus has the dual role of trying to increase the size of the company's surplus by devising ingenious way of running the business and of maintaining alliances with participants that will permit the company's survival and growth.

In such an environment a manager soon learns the meaning of economic efficiency, tolerance, flexibility, and cooperation. Since survival depends on one's customers, it would be disastrous not to carefully consider and satisfy their demands. A manager must worry, not only about what his customers want, but also about what his competitors are doing. Stark disaster faces any firm that fails to adjust over time to the changing whims and needs of his customers. Concerning personnel, firms cannot easily exploit labor, even if there is no union with which to contend. If the labor in question is skilled or in short supply, the payment of 10 per cent under the going wage rates quickly results in inferior performance as the more competent employees drift away to better paying opportunities. Considering another aspect, if the company tries to squeeze the last discount out of suppliers, it finds itself at the end of the line when special service is wanted or if a temporary shortage appears. In many instances, a given company is highly dependent on its suppliers, and the costs entailed in developing new dependable sources of supply are great. The company also cannot long ignore the wishes of investors and creditors, or the commitments to them, if it is to remain financially sound. The exploited, be they workers, investors, suppliers, or customers, also have the option of appealing, through the ballot box, to politicians who are quite sensitive to the grievances of large groups of downtrodden citizens.

The essence of the capitalistic enterprise system is mutual self-interest, cooperation, and interdependence through mutual consent and free choice. These mutual relationships are entered into in a competitive environment and are therefore subject to discontinuation if more favorable opportunities arise for either party. It is through this free but interdependent enterprise system, rather than a comprehensive national plan, that the critical productive functions are performed, coordinated, and integrated on a national scale. The interaction between the competitive price system and the pursuit of profits tends automatically to keep economic mistakes within reasonable limits. This joint economic regulator rather effectively solves the key economic problems of what and how to produce, how much of each item to produce, and for whom to produce. It tends to insure that needed and desired goods are produced at the right time and distributed to the right place and that production is carried on in a reasonably efficient manner. Moreover, it tends to encourage innovation in products and processes, since such activity often results in a competitive advantage for the innovating organization.

Effectively functioning enterprises require extensive feedback of knowledge about current operations so that management can plan for the future. In a capitalistic society, much pertinent information is obtained almost automatically through inventory levels, and from other organizations and parties that have a vested interest in the company in question. The company also can obtain various types of information from such organizations as chambers of commerce, trade journals, private publishing firms, trade unions, and various governmental agencies charged with accumulating relevant data for specific types of industries. Hence an American firm wanting to know about the market for nursery products in El Salvador can obtain needed market information from the Department of Commerce. A chemical company needing vital statistics can similarly get them from local and federal agencies. The individual enterprise may also have its own comprehensive statistical and accounting systems which enable it to keep track of current operations in order to plan and make decisions for the future.

There is no need for any one enterprise or the numerous governmental agencies to have at their disposal information about everything that is going on in the economy as a whole, or even in a particular region or industry. Governmental departments obtain and compile masses of statistical data, and the government also maintains a fairly comprehensive system of national accounting. However, these data are not used to comprehensively plan, coordinate, or control national economic activity. Rather they are used to assess national economic performance for a given period and to formulate broad economic policy.

Hence, in a capitalistic enterprise system one finds chaos oriented to precise organizational goals and economic efficiency. Literally billions of independent managerial decisions contribute to desirable economic performance on a national scale. Nothing seems logical at first glance; but the system works surprisingly well because the market is a regulator, capable of penalizing the lax and shortsighted and of rewarding those who can take advantage of existing opportunities.

Because of various imperfections, however, there are negative features inherent in such an economic system. For example, there can be disequilibrium, strikes, unemployment, monopoly, discrepancies between savings and investment, and distribution of income so unequal that the wants of many are not properly satisfied. In order to contain such problems within reasonable limits, governmental regulations, policies, and controls which often interfere with objective market forces are adopted. It is notable that the most serious economic problems and the biggest economic failures of capitalist countries arise when, for reasons of social welfare, national security, or venal self-interest, the law of supply and demand is violated. American agriculture, shipbuilding, and ocean shipping are cases in point.[14]

Capitalist economic systems in their pure form have no ethical content whatsoever beyond the general belief that ownership of private property is desirable and that if enterprises and individuals seek to maximize their individual monetary advantage, resource allocation and economic efficiency will be ideal. Efforts to inject ethics into the system—to aid underprivileged farmers, workers, or even capitalists—have generally resulted in substantial deviations from the efficient production of needed and desired goods and services.[15]

Capitalist systems also have the problem that they are typically democratic states, and the voters *do* inject substantial ethical content into the system, often at the expense of economic efficiency. Hence, the support of inept small businessmen by government loans, minimum wage bills, fair trade pricing laws, and protection from destructive competition by entry control laws, may have the effect of putting too many resources into a given industry, causing redundant capacity, higher than necessary prices, and general economic inefficiency. One is likely to find high taxes on whiskey and tobacco—reflecting the popular opinion that such commodities should be expensive—and this too distorts ideal resource allocation in accordance with consumer sovereignty. Moreover, some commodities, such as habit-forming narcotics, are not freely sold at all. Probably most of the macromanagerial rules that managers of a given productive enterprise *must* abide by are ethical rather than economic in nature.

Economic Organization and the Interaction of Macro- and Micromanagement: U.S.S.R.

Soviet communism came to power on the doctrines of Marx, following his notion of inevitable class conflict—notably the exploitation of labor —in the capitalist system. Marx said little about the future Communist economic system, and what he did say was vague. He did point to state ownership of productive resources and some sort of planned economy as being distinctive features of the future Communist society, but he left no blueprint or operational theory describing how the Communist economic system was to function.[16]

As the Soviet state evolved after 1917, it became clear to the Soviets that state ownership was the basic means by which the pure Communist state could be developed. By the end of the 1920's, the state takeover of all productive assets was well under way, and within a few years all major and most minor material means of production were in state hands. Today the Soviet government either owns outright or decisively controls all nonhuman factors of production, in agriculture as well as in industry.

The virtually complete state ownership of productive enterprises had the effect of destroying the market price system, since without competition among rival firms there could be no meaningful price competition. This in turn rendered the profit motive impotent as an automatic economic regulator. With the collapse of the competitive market price system, another means for solving the basic economic problems and performing the critical economic functions common to all societies had to be developed. The automatic regulators of economic activity inherent in a capitalist system, however imprecise they may be, were now gone.[17] To date there has been only one known, logically consistent economic system, that of general equilibrium developed by Walras and amplified by Leontief in his input-output analysis.[18] This system forms the basis for all capitalist and mixed economies.

The method of deciding key economic questions in the Soviet Union— that is, what should be produced, how much, how, for whom, when, where, and the allocation of resources necessary to achieve the production desired—was to be comprehensive national economic planning. Hence, what is done primarily by market forces in the U.S. must be consciously done by bureaucratic action in the U.S.S.R. In such a system there is a fusion of political and economic leadership, and all economic activity tends to be subordinate to the politically motivated decisions of the state. By the state is meant the highest party and governmental bodies in the land, namely, the Central Committee of the Communist Party and the Council of Ministers of the U.S.S.R., which are interlocked at the apex of the economy. At the top of the economy the central planners decide all major economic questions in the light of goals and values set forth by the leaders.

In a capitalist, price system economy, it is implicitly assumed that individual consumers will themselves determine whatever goals they desire, and their expressions, indicated by effective demand, will determine the course of economic activity. On the other hand, a society with specific ideas about the goals of the economy, be they rapid industrialization, growth in military power, or higher living standards, must plan in detail how economic resource allocations are to be made. The leaders must determine their important objectives and plan the economy to meet them.[19]

In such a system long-range economic planning is essentially investment planning, and annual planning is basically production planning. The annual national plan is the operational document for the individual Soviet productive organizations. The planners must decide how to divide production between consumer and producer goods, and the rate of accumulation (savings) necessary for desired future economic expansion must also be determined. Each production target must be limited so that the total of all targets does not exceed the productive power of the nation. The plan must also provide for allocations of economic factors into the necessary sectors in light of national objectives. In other words, the plan must be all-inclusive.

Although Marx never clearly indicated whether he was for or against consumer sovereignty, in this kind of economy it is not possible to have consumers determine the course of production. Such interference would tend to deflect scarce productive resources from other planned uses, thus upsetting the entire plan. Prices in such a system also have little guiding function; rather they are subservient to the plan.[20] Commodity prices are used chiefly for aggregation, control, and evaluation, although retail prices for consumer goods are used as a rather crude device of equating demand with supply (rather than vice versa). At the same time, wage differentials are needed to channel manpower resources into productive sectors in accordance with the requirements of the plan because some occupational choice, as well as a limited amount of labor mobility, is tolerated. Unequal income distribution also serves as an incentive for improving human capabilities and performance.

This type of planned system necessarily requires that central planners make a vast number of ethical decisions which in a free market economy are left to individuals. The stipulated national goals are in themselves value judgments. The volume of consumer goods production has traditionally been dependent on available resources after the resources required to achieve the other aims of the plan are accounted for. National production has been influenced by consumer demand only to a limited degree, and free consumer choice is limited to the goods the government decides to produce for the consuming public. Although the planners are not entirely insensitive to the desires and needs of the population, the planners' preferences do essentially take the place of the consumers' preferences—which implies that the planners know better than the public what is good for them. It was noted above that in a market economy, similar decisions about the propriety of certain commodities are made;

but these decisions are regarded as aberrations from the ideal rather than a necessary and critical part of the economic system.

In the planned state, it may be decided at the top that consumers should have more bread and less shoes than they would desire if they had free choice. Or certain highly desired commodities, such as chewing gum, rock-and-roll records, and automobiles, may be produced in negligible quantities or not at all. The setting of basic wage rates for different occupations also involves value judgments. Hence, if the national economic plan is really comprehensive and complete, as it must be to function properly, a very high degree of centralized ethical decision-making is built into the system.

Instead of the apparent chaos of the capitalist economic system, all is in order in the Soviet system—at least on paper. The macrorules for micromanagers, rather than being of the "thou shalt not" variety, are of the "thou shalt" type. In reality, the complexities and problems involved in planning the economic activities of an entire country, such as the Soviet Union, are beyond human imagination. The literally billions of planning decisions that must be made to achieve consistency result in a complex and complete interlocking of macro- and micromanagement. Predetermined tasks and resource allocations, rather than competitive buying and selling, regulate the activities of the myriad interdependent productive organizations on the basis of one comprehensive national plan. The number of planned interconnections called for increases more rapidly than the size of the economy, and since 1953 the Soviet economy has doubled in terms of national production. The job of planning, coordinating, and controlling national economic activity may be mathematically compared to the square of the number of the different commodities produced plus the number of productive units.[21]

A modern industrial society will produce perhaps 20,000 identifiable classes of output (that is, steel, bolts, shoes, radios, and so forth). Each class of output may have dozens of subcategories of products (that is, bolts of various sizes, made of various steels: brass, copper, and so forth). Even with the most sophisticated mathematical techniques and electronic computers, the task of interrelating demands and factor inputs for every possible item by every possible subcategory becomes impossible for the central planners alone. A gargantuan intermediate bureaucratic apparatus is needed, and the micromanagers themselves are called on to participate in the planning process and to make operating decisions.

The various types of productive organizations in the system are assigned to one or more of the critical economic functions, and their duties are spelled out in considerable detail. The state carefully guides the emergence and development of all productive units and consciously fashions their forms of organization. The result is a degree of homogeneity which is of doubtful pleasure to those who live in the society, but which nevertheless serves to greatly facilitate central planning and control. The American businessman who sets about establishing a new enterprise is limited only by his imagination and by his assessment of the advantages of the different types of opportunities open to him. By contrast, the Soviet administrator authorized to set up a new productive organization, or to manage an existing one, has the basic structure laid out for him in advance.

In the Soviet Union certain types of organizations are charged with the production function, others with distribution or finance, and still others with research and development. In addition certain agencies are charged with collecting detailed accounting and statistical data from all the productive organizations. Such data are crucial for macrodecision-making and control. The macromanagerial apparatus must have at its disposal information on all economic activity if the economy is to function properly.

Productive organizations in the Soviet Union do not deal with each other through mutual consent or free choice, but rather, by higher decree. Since all economic activities are assigned somewhere in the system, no competition is allowed; the organization which bears the responsibility need not worry about aggressive competition from outsiders. The system is orderly, neat, and horribly complex for the micromanagers charged with carrying out directives from above.

There are about two million separate organizations in the Soviet Union, each one of which has its own plan and objectives subordinate to the national plan.[22] A great many of these organizations are not directly involved in performing critical economic functions, for example, schools, hospitals, libraries, and so on.

Of major concern in this study are the more than 200,000 Soviet industrial enterprises engaged in the production of goods.[23] It was stated previously that the industrial enterprise is the key focal point for all the critical economic functions in the U.S.S.R. It is here that the key economic questions—what to produce, how much of each item, how and when to produce each item, and for whom—are translated into detailed enterprise operating plans in a manner which should be consistent with the national economic plan. The national plan must allocate to each enterprise adequate resources and funds if the desired production is to be forthcoming. It is from the industrial enterprise that goods are distributed to their intended destinations; and it is at the enterprise that new technical processes are introduced and new products are developed and produced. Moreover it is from the enterprise that the government obtains a major portion of the accounting and statistical information necessary for planning, coordinating, and controlling over-all economic activity.

The Soviet manager is not concerned with the survival of his enterprise since, as long as the state wants the enterprise in question to continue functioning, its future is provided for in the national plan. The earning of profits is not a requisite to survival, and 20 per cent of all Soviet industrial enterprises operate at a planned loss.[24]

The state prescribes the ultimate objectives to be pursued by all industrial establishments. Each enterprise is supposed to achieve as great a quantity of production as possible with given resources; or, given certain production targets, they should be achieved with minimum practical resources and costs. The production program is supposed to be carried out in accordance with a predetermined time schedule. Within the overall output targets and resource limits prescribed by the plan, the detailed product mix, including the quality of output, is supposed to conform to the requirements of customers. A balance between short-run and long-run considerations is also called for so that current decisions and activities should not endanger future operations, but rather, should enhance them and further the future needs of society.

In addition to these ultimate objectives or basic desiderata of enterprise performance, the state prescribes certain policies to be followed for their achievement, for example, the use of the most progressive utilization norms in planning and the constant improvement of technical processes, products, and quality.

Since the ultimate objectives to be pursued by the Soviet enterprise represent a high level of abstraction (in the same way that a profit maximization goal does in an American company), they must be translated into concrete operating terms. A system of interconnected plan indices which constitutes the annual enterprise operating plan, and which is directly linked to the national economic plan, is the device utilized for this purpose. Each Soviet industrial enterprise receives an annual plan having quarterly subdivisions. If the plan is sound, and if the managers do their jobs properly, the result should be the production of the right amount of goods and services, of the right assortment and quality, delivered to the right place at the right time. In theory, the proper design and execution of the plan means that resources are efficiently utilized and that nothing is wasted, since no unneeded excesses or shortages of goods would appear at any point. It is also hoped that enterprise managers would tend to innovate in both products and processes.

Although the micromanagers are narrowly confined by the targets and resource limits prescribed in the plan, their expert knowledge and participation are indispensable to its formulation and execution. It is physically impossible for superior authorities to plan in detail without close consultation with plant executives, or to exert instantaneous effective control over the execution of plans at the vast number of industrial establishments. The men on the spot are in the best position to determine the capabilities and resource needs of their enterprises and to adjust the plan to unforeseeable changing conditions. In addition, enterprise innovation depends greatly on what the micromanagers choose to do or not to do. Those who imagine the Soviet economy to be a pure "totalitarian command economy" in which enterprise managers merely carry out orders have no conception of reality.

Hence, in the absence of a competitive market price system, detailed directives and rules of behavior from above must guide managerial decision-making at Soviet industrial enterprises. Monetary incentives are also used in an attempt to achieve an identity between managerial self-interests and the interests of the state.

Management within the Soviet enterprise is quite similar to management within an American company, particularly an American factory. The same managerial functions are performed in many similar ways. However, the external relations that Soviet micromanagers engage in differ rather dramatically from those of their American counterparts. The capitalist enterprise is related to other organizations only through the market; it buys and sells according to price-cost relations and not to fulfill predetermined quotas; it expands and contracts as profit expectations dictate. In all these actions there is no red tape of the kind with which a Soviet executive must cope. The bureaucratic impediment lies primarily in the external relations of the Soviet industrial enterprise rather than in its internal structure.

The Soviet enterprise administrator is not charged with the major task of achieving desired contributions from other organizations by generating enough inducements to insure their participation. This delicate balancing job is, in the main, done for him. With very few exceptions, the plan prescribes the relationships among productive organizations, the contributions forthcoming from each, and the payments to be made for the contributions rendered. For example, a Kharkov enterprise engaged in the production of ventilation machinery had the following external relationships prescribed from above for 1961: It was to receive supplies from about 40 other producers; it was to produce goods for approximately 60 different assigned customers; it was to deal with 4 research and design institutes on a continual basis, as well as with various other institutes from time to time; it was to maintain accounts at 2 state bank branches; it was to deal with a number of transportation organizations; and its management was to have continuous contact with various higher authorities.

It will become clear during the course of this study that a system of prescribed relationships among productive organizations, rather than a system based on free choice and mutual consent, does not necessarily provide for mutual self-interest, cooperation, and interdependence.

Now that we have an insight into the distinguishing features of the Communist and capitalist economic systems and the nature and role of management in each system, we will examine the structure of Soviet industry and the place of the enterprise and its management in this structure.

2 • Organizational Structure of Soviet Industry

If the Soviet Union were a very small country, like Monaco, central authorities could perhaps directly plan, coordinate, and control the activities of all the nation's productive organizations in considerable detail and with tolerable effectiveness. But the Soviet Union is more than double the size of the entire U.S. in area and about 15 per cent greater in population. The activities of more than 200,000 industrial enterprises, as well as hundreds of thousands of other organizations, must be coordinated through one comprehensive state plan if the national objectives set forth by the top rulers are to be achieved.

Hence, the Soviet system seems to call for an all-seeing and all-knowing Planner, whose brain makes decisions in full awareness of all the relevant alternatives and all the consequences of his acts. But, alas, such a Planner cannot exist outside the imagination of model-builders and science-fiction writers; even the most ardent mathematician would probably concede that no electronic computer will *ever* be developed to fill such a job. Therefore, it is not surprising to find that a "huge" bureaucratic apparatus is required to plan and administer Soviet industry, and for that matter, the entire economy. The apparatus must be broken down into intermediate levels of authority, and each level in the industrial hierarchy should function within the objectives, policies, and other constraints prescribed by the central decision-makers. At the same time each level must be delegated authority to make certain kinds of decisions.

Political Structure

Before proceeding with a discussion of the Soviet industrial structure per se, a brief comment about the political structure is warranted. Soviet political organization is concerned basically with two major problems: first, the organization of what might be called the "traditional" political-governmental functions common to any country; and second, the organization of the productive and industrial sector of the economy which is basically Soviet or communistic in nature. The Soviet political-governmental apparatus extends from its acme, where the central government and Communist party interlock, down to local government administration. Traditional problems on the national level concern such critical matters as national defense, internal affairs, foreign affairs, and over-all social welfare. On the local level, the problems are concerned with police and fire protection, medical care, parks and recreational facilities, sanitation, and similar matters. The traditional sphere of governmental activity clearly interlocks with industrial activity at certain levels within the over-all hierarchy—notably at the national and republican levels. At lower levels the relationship becomes more obscure. Further complicating administration is the fact that the Communist party and governmental hierarchies are distinct entities; but in fact both are part of a single state system.

The supreme authority in all matters of state is the Central Committee of the Communist Party represented by its Presidium. The party Presidium, however, normally limits its role to the setting of major policy, and the chief executive and administrative body is the U.S.S.R. Council of Ministers. This Council consists of a chairman, ministers, deputy ministers, chairman of certain state committees and commissions (the best known probably being the State Planning Commission—*Gosplan* U.S.S.R.), and, ex officio, the chairman of the council of ministers of each union republic. The central or all-union governmental structure is almost wholly duplicated in each of the 15 republics which make up the country as a whole. There are also provincial, district, and municipal government bodies within each republic.

The relationship between the center and the republics in specific spheres of governmental activity varies, and it has given rise to three different types of ministry. First, there are the all-union ministries, headquartered in Moscow, which directly supervise the activities of subordinate units throughout the nation. These are similar to U.S. federal agencies. Secondly, there are union-republican ministries which exist both at the center and in the republics, in which case the republic ministry is simultaneously subordinate to its "big brother" in Moscow and to the council of ministers of the given republic. This is an example of dual subordination, a phenomenon commonly encountered in Soviet administration. Finally, there are purely republican ministries (like state agencies in the U.S.), which have no direct superior in Moscow but which have to conform to applicable policies and plans.

Some Soviet ministries are similar to governmental agencies functioning in any country, for example, health, culture, education, finance, foreign affairs, defense. Others are specifically Soviet in nature, created by the all-pervasive economic role of the Soviet state, for example, foreign trade, domestic trade (which pertains to consumer goods), and various industrial and construction ministries, most of which were abolished in 1957. The term "ministry" does not cover all organizations of ministerial status. As was pointed out above, there are a number of state committees and other bodies whose heads are members of the national or republican councils of ministers (for example, *Gosplan*).

The above institutions are part of the governmental hierarchy, and it is within this hierarchy that Soviet industry functions. Underlying the elaborate governmental structure at all levels is the Communist party of the Soviet Union, the engine driving the Soviet state. In a very real sense, government at all levels exists to carry out the policies and objectives set forth by the party, while the party itself guides and controls governmental activity. The party apparatus extends downward from its acme, the Presidium of the Central Committee, to the 15 republics, and within each republic to lower territorial units (provinces, districts, cities). There are also party "cells" (primary committees) within each industrial enterprise, state farms, and other types of organizations. The party agencies and committees at all levels are wholly subordinate to the central leadership in Moscow. At party headquarters there are departments which duplicate various governmental organs.

The Logic of Industrial Organization

How best to divide the tasks entailed in running the immense Soviet economy, and Soviet industry in particular, presents a problem of paramount importance. Each possible arrangement of planning and operational powers involves its own set of advantages and disadvantages, solving some difficulties and creating others—a fact familiar to the management of large American companies. Moreover, an organizational arrangement acceptable yesterday may no longer be suitable today. Factors such as growth and increasing complexity call for reorganization in the Soviet economy, just as they do in, say, General Electric or General Motors.

Certain forms of basic departmentalization have always been present in the Soviet industrial apparatus. In different periods one form or another has tended to predominate, but none has ever been present singularly in pure form. We should briefly note the major aspects of Soviet industrial organization or basic departmentalization, all of which are familiar in Western industry. The first lays stress on the industrial sector and is somewhat similar to product departmentalization in a giant multiplant corporation such as General Electric. Here the process of planning and control is based on the particular industry (entire product line)—for example, machine tools, textiles, coal, oil, metallurgy, armaments—with general coordination among industries at the governmental level. Second, there is the territorial principle, which would devolve planning and operational powers to regional authorities, in much the same way as is done in territorial divisions of American companies. Finally, there is functional departmentalization. Here powers are given to functional bodies, concerned on a national, republican, or even regional scale with supplies, distribution, labor, finance, investment, pricing, technical progress, and so on. These bodies undertake activities and make decisions which directly affect the operations of enterprises and other organizations within the industrial hierarchy. In many instances functional authority is exerted in much the same way that the corporate staff of General Electric issues directives and prescribes policies and/or procedures for divisional or operating department managers.

The logic of sound departmentalization rests on the same objective criteria in both Soviet and American industry. Each subdivision of the over-all organizational structure—be it a single company or an entire economy—should contribute effectively and efficiently to the achievement of over-all organizational objectives. Among the key criteria to be considered in organizing activities are the following: (1) facilitate planning, control, and coordination among interdependent and interrelated activities; (2) minimize costs and expenses without giving up efficiency; (3) take advantage of specialization; (4) secure adequate attention and provide for timely decisions concerning significant problems that may arise; (5) take into account local conditions in decision-making; (6) avoid unnecessary duplication and underemployment of facilities and resources.

In reality, balancing the over-all organizational structure to achieve all the above desired conditions is an extremely difficult task, more so, of course, for an entire economy than for a single giant corporation. In both cases the process tends to become one of "satisficing" rather than "optimizing." With respect to the Soviet economy, in any conceivable organizational arrangement, coordination among industries, between regions and functions, between output plans and investment, between production and resource allocations, and so forth, will present difficulties. These difficulties find their administrative expression in the creation of agencies and departments to deal with them. The basis of organization chosen at any point in time tends to make an appreciable difference to the chain of command, to the levels at which decision-making on various matters takes place, and to the weight given to various species of the problem within the over-all administrative machine.

The Soviet record is replete with minor organizational changes, and from time to time, major reorganizations involving the entire macro-apparatus. Authority relationships, as well as the degree of centralization or decentralization with respect to various issues, tend to be always in a state of flux within the industrial hierarchy. Organizational changes are undertaken primarily to improve performance at the industrial enterprise level. However, in spite of all the organizational changes undertaken, the macromanagerial rules for enterprise managers have not been significantly affected since the late 1950's. It is true that the superior organs and authorities with whom the enterprise manager must deal tend to change rather often. Nevertheless, for the manager looking upward, his own authority and the external bureaucratic environment have remained basically unchanged in recent years; and in running his enterprise the manager is doing essentially the same things in the same ways as he has been for several years.

Before we turn our attention to the topic of major concern—the industrial enterprise and its management—an investigation of trends in the organizational structure of Soviet industry over time is in order. In this manner, we can gain an insight into certain key macroproblems of Soviet industrial organization which will provide a frame of reference for later discussions. We can also derive an understanding as to how and why the present structure has evolved. We are chiefly interested in those aspects of the structure which have a significant bearing on the industrial enterprise and its management.

The Ministerial System

Centralized planning and control of the Soviet economy has induced the evolution of a ramified and cumbersome bureaucratic administrative apparatus. During the 1932-57 period, this structure had come to be typified by large and powerful all-union industrial ministries in Moscow which supervised and often directly intervened in management details of individual enterprises situated throughout the country. It was to these ministries and their departments that most of the important operational decisions were referred from the industrial enterprise. Each of the industrial ministries was in charge of an entire industrial sector, and the number of such ministries varied during this period from 3 in 1932 to a maximum of nearly 30 at the end of 1956, shortly before the ministerial system was abolished. The ministers themselves were subordinate to the highest rulers.

A typical ministry was divided into a number of main administrations (*glavki*). Some of the *glavki* were branch sudivisions of the given industrial sector (for example, textiles within the Ministry of Light Industry, certain types of machinery and components within the Ministry of Machine Building). These branch *glavki* were similar in nature to derivative product departments in giant Western companies. There were also functional *glavki* responsible for supplies, finance, planning, accounting, labor, and so forth. Within the branch *glavki* there were also functional departments.

Enterprises were, as a rule, subordinate to a branch *glavk* of their ministry. They received their plans from the *glavk,* and submitted applications for resources to the *glavk*. Each ministry had its own vast network of commodity supply and disposal (sales) organizations. The territorial system of administration was also present, but on a supplemental scale. For instance, the above-outlined powers were exercised in some cases through identically named republic-level industrial ministries (and their *glavki*), where the republican ministry was simultaneously subordinate to both its big brother in Moscow and the council of ministers of the given republic. Whether a given enterprise was directly subordinate to central, regional, or local authorities depended on its size and importance.

The existence of a large number of industrial ministries, each controlling their own national network of productive enterprises and supply and disposal agencies, naturally placed a heavy burden on the coordinating function. The power of coordinating national plans and operational decisions resided in the central government itself. The "staff" body which actually carried out the coordinating function and drafted plans was *Gosplan* U.S.S.R. This body had no authority to order any ministry to do anything, but its recommendations were usually the basis of top governmental and party economic decisions. Prior to 1955 *Gosplan* engaged in both current and long-range planning. In 1955 it was placed in charge of long-term planning only, and a new body, the State Economic Commission, was charged with current (annual) planning.

The ministerial system had proved itself effective in rapidly grafting advanced industries onto the backward Soviet economy. But as the economy expanded and grew more complex, the inefficiencies of the system became sufficiently obvious by the mid-1950's to call for some type of major reorganization. In general, all the key conditions inherent in sound organization, as discussed above, were being increasingly and severely violated.

The concentration of authority over enterprises scattered throughout the country caused bureaucratic delays in settling the numerous everyday questions which unavoidably arose. The geographical remoteness of the ministerial decision-makers from most of their subordinate enterprises led to numerous, and frequently serious, errors of planning and resource allocation within a given ministry. The ministry and its *glavki* were often ignorant about local conditions when establishing enterprise plans; and it was also extremely difficult to exert effective control over plan fulfillment at the numerous scattered plants.

Since the ministries themselves did not possess accurate information about the capabilities and resource needs of subordinate plants, they were in no position to provide the central planners with accurate data on the basis of which the latter could make rational choices in the allocation and use of national resources. When the relevant data were available to the central decision-makers and the various ministries, wrong decisions were frequently made because of the parochial interests of the individual ministries who participated in the final choice. Central authorities, *Gosplan* in particular, were generally too weak to keep the industrial ministries working together effectively.

Each industrial ministry exerted strong tendencies toward becoming a self-contained and self-sufficient economic empire, with its own self-interest taking precedence over the interests of the economy as a whole. This trait was referred to as "departmentalism" or *"autarky."* The desire for self-sufficiency was primarily due to the chronic uncertainties of supply from other ministers in conjunction with the fact that aggregate output performance was the key success indicator for the ministry as a whole and for each of its enterprises. This led to the establishment of one's "own" ministerial supply bases and ministerial factories to manufacture the necessary supplies and components. Because of the activities of each ministry in ensuring or producing materials and components for "its" enterprises, and also the tendency to make consumer goods out of by-products in many industrial sectors, the product coverage of ministries tended to be extremely heterogeneous.

High-cost production was often undertaken by enterprises to assure themselves of their own supplies even when the needed commodities were produced by nearby plants of another ministry. This practice resulted in small, relatively high-cost subsidiary operations attached to a given plant, while nearby, with unused capacity, specialized plants of other ministries might be producing the same item at much lower cost. For example, the Voronezh Agricultural Machinery Plant produced its own hardware articles (nuts, bolts, nails, screws) at a cost of 3,000 rubles a ton while nearby plants could supply these same items at 1,000 rubles a ton.

In the same vein, many plants made components for the nationwide ministerial empires and transported them to fraternal enterprises all over the country. There could be a plant in Siberia which supplied enterprises of the Ferrous Metallurgy Ministry in Moscow, Baku, and Kharkov, while other ministries had identical plants in these cities supplying, *inter alia,* these ministries' enterprises in Siberia. In general, both horizontal and vertical integration of plants was stimulated or limited by ministerial boundaries rather than by economic forces. This situation produced numerous instances of unnecessary cross-hauls on the already overloaded transportation system. Moreover, almost every enterprise had trucks assigned to it, ideally in sufficient capacity to satisfy the plant's peak needs. Since there was no effective regional coordinating authority, there could be no local truck-pooling arrangements to service enterprises within different ministries.

There were other significant shortcomings resulting from "departmentalism" and the desire for self-sufficiency. Enterprise managers, as well as the ministries and their *glavki,* attempted to put aside substantial stocks of buffer reserves of raw materials, semifabricated goods, equipment, and the like. These "reserves" exceeded the "legal norms" of inventories and were outside the officially designated state reserves. In cases where a given enterprise ran into difficulties in fulfilling its output targets because of inadequate resources, it frequently produced and delivered goods of poor quality or without the proper specifications to customers in other ministries, with the tacit or outright approval of its own ministry. In many instances enterprises failed to provide customers in other ministries with any of the supplies stipulated in the plan. Because of "departmental" barriers there was substantial waste of resources resulting from the failure to arrange for the utilization of by-products. For example, at many ore-processing plants, only zinc, lead, and copper were extracted, and many other elements, such as sulphur and tin, were discarded as waste because they were the responsibility of a different ministry. The large Gisichansk Chemical complex discarded carbon dioxide as a waste product while next door a soda plant was obliged to produce its own.

In pursuit of self-sufficiency, each ministerial empire maintained many supply and disposal organizations, as well as a vast number of other functional departments. This arrangement led to much organizational duplication and underemployed administrative staffs and facilities on a national scale. Duplication also resulted from the failure to integrate closely allied and adjacent plants of different ministries.

Moreover, there were serious problems in connection with capital investment. The ministries frequently used assigned investment resources for unintended uses, or they started an excessive number of projects instead of using the funds to complete projects already underway. An important motivation for diffusing investment funds among a great number of new projects was the desire of the ministry to be able to justify future requests for increased investment funds. The central planners, ignorant about local conditions, also made poor investment decisions and exerted ineffective control over investment projects. These faults often led to serious disproportions among various industrial sectors and within a given sector. A perennial problem of the Soviet economy has been the timeliness of completing new plant facilities within a given sector (for example, metallurgy) where, because of the nature of the production process, if new capacity in one branch (for example, blast furnaces) is to be utilized, new capacity in another branch is required (for example, iron ore). Because of "departmental barriers" within the ministry itself, disproportions also arose among the production capacities of its own *glavki*.

Finally, there was no effective authority responsible for regional planning, and this led to highly uneven economic development within different areas of the country. No one in any area had adequate authority to examine and act upon any assessment of the potentials of the given area from a viewpoint which transcended interindustrial boundaries.

Emergence of the Territorial System

In 1957, Khrushchev himself promoted the ostensibly sharp break with the ministerial system of industrial administration by establishing

105 regional economic councils (*sovnarkhozy*) along existing territorial-administrative boundaries with operational responsibility for the great majority of industrial enterprises located within their geographic confines.[1] The industrial ministries, both at the center and republican level, were almost completely abolished. Thus the previously existing pattern of nationwide subordination and administration according to the branch of industry was replaced by a territorial pattern of subordination with some simplification of detail in decision-making at the center. On page 31 is presented an organizational chart of Soviet industry immediately prior to the 1957 reorganization as compared to the structure in 1958.

The principle of "a single state plan" as the basis for Soviet economic management was not, however, repudiated. No serious erosion in central leadership and control resulted from the industrial reorganization. Although industrial and administrative authorities outside of Moscow were to play a larger role in planning and solving the day-to-day problems arising in the operations of enterprises, the central regime continued to reserve to itself decisions involving the definition of economic goals and appropriate policies for their attainment.

It is difficult to unravel the various motives for the industrial reorganization. Some Western students feel that a political struggle for power was the overriding cause; others contend that economic problems were the major basis for changes. Yet there was, clearly, no single cause for the reorganization. It occurred rather as an outgrowth of a complex pattern of motivations. On balance, the decision to reorganize and the nature of the principal changes themselves appear to have been based largely on economic grounds, but the timing of the reorganization and some of the measures finally detailed seem to have been politically influenced. In this latter connection the reorganization helped thrust Khrushchev to his supreme position of leadership through his defeat of the so-called "antiparty group"—Molotov, Malenkov, Bulganin, et al. —who were against it. Various strategic implications most certainly were also considered. In any event, a law embodying the basic features of Khrushchev's reorganization proposals was formally adopted in May 1957, and it came into operation in July of that year.

Organizational Structure

Under the new system of industrial management the chain of command now stretched from the central government in Moscow through the governments of the 15 republics to the *sovnarkhozy* within each republic and thence to the various enterprises within each *sovnarkhoz*.

With the reorganization *Gosplan* U.S.S.R. emerged clearly as the most "powerful" national economic agency. (Some of the other important central agencies will be discussed later in this chapter.) The central

ORGANIZATION OF SOVIET INDUSTRY, 1957 AND 1958

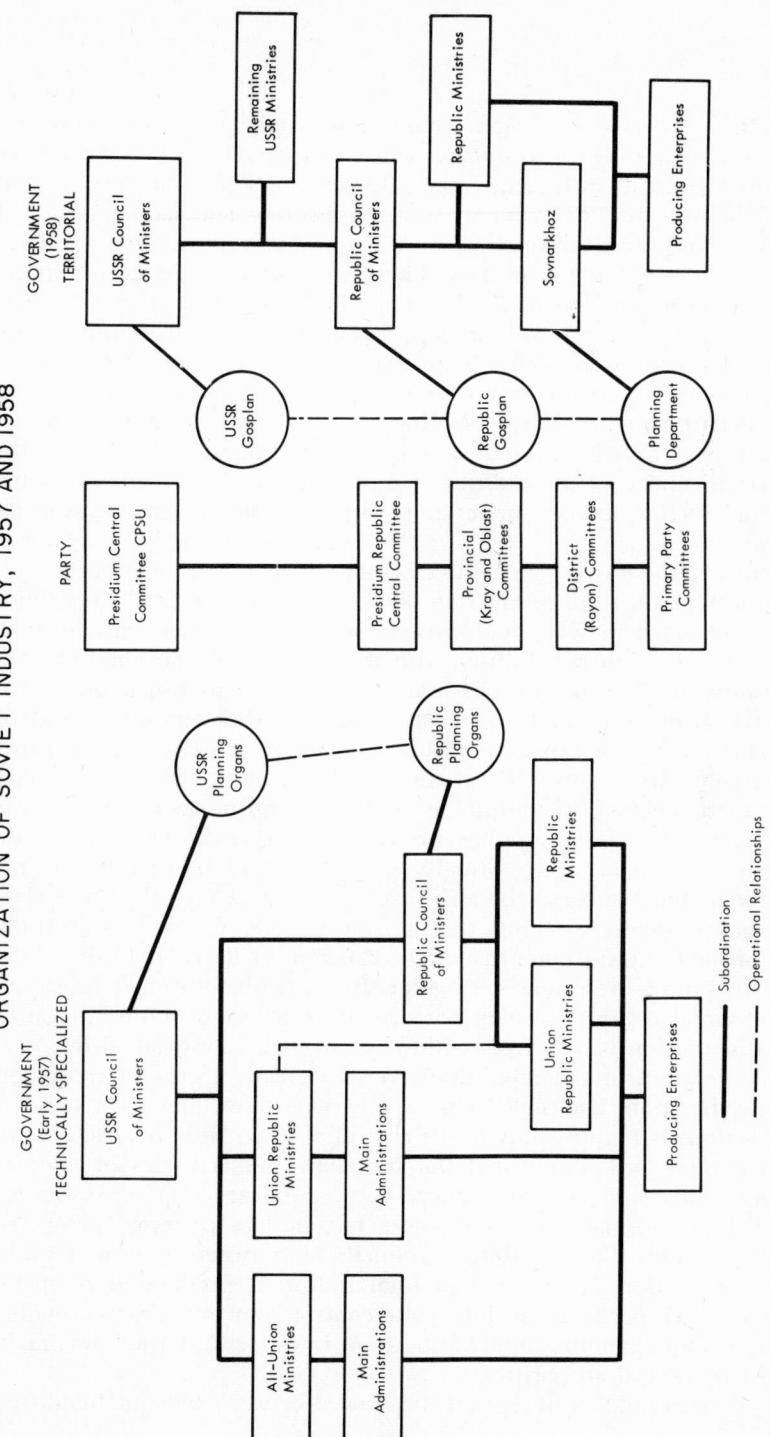

GOVERNMENT
(Early 1957)
TECHNICALLY SPECIALIZED

PARTY

GOVERNMENT
(1958)
TERRITORIAL

USSR Planning Organs

Republic Planning Organs

USSR Council of Ministers

Union Republic Ministries

Main Administrations

All-Union Ministries

Main Administrations

Republic Council of Ministers

Republic Ministries

Union Republic Ministries

Producing Enterprises

Presidium Central Committee CPSU

Presidium Republic Central Committee

Provincial (Kray and Oblast) Committees

District (Rayon) Committees

Primary Party Committees

USSR Gosplan

Republic Gosplan

Planning Department

USSR Council of Ministers

Remaining USSR Ministries

Republic Council of Ministers

Republic Ministries

Sovnarkhoz

Producing Enterprises

——— Subordination

– – – Operational Relationships

Unclassified United States government source.

planning apparatus was again changed to merge both long-term and short-term planning in *Gosplan,* which was greatly enlarged in both functions and staff. It became responsible for overseeing the development of all branches of the economy and for assuring adequate supplies of goods for industrial production. It acquired many of the activities performed by the defunct ministries. These activities were placed in "industrial" departments bearing designations similar to the former ministries (for example, chemicals, oil and gas, metallurgy, machine-building), and the departments were staffed with many former ministerial executives. In the process *Gosplan* took charge of a large number of supply and sales departments, each one dealing with a major commodity group, as well as many scientific research institutes formerly belonging to the industrial ministries. In addition, *Gosplan* contained several functional divisions such as finance, prices and costs, labor and wages, investment, and so forth.

Hence *Gosplan's* responsibilities became immense. It now coordinated and amended the draft production plans submitted to it by the republics. It had to make these plans consistent with one another, with over-all resource utilization possibilities, with the budget, with personal income, with innovation, and with the many other questions which must bear directly on planning and for which numerous other republican and regional agencies were now responsible. The task of allocating and controlling commodity supplies lies at the very heart of the planning process, since every decision on output at all levels requires factor inputs and simultaneously affects supplies for other enterprises. The powers extended to *Gosplan* were, formally speaking, small in that it was not the hierarchical superior of any plant, region, or republic. It had to act, again formally speaking, through the U.S.S.R. Council of Ministers and/or the Central Committee of the Communist Party. In reality, however, its powers were now very great. In particular, through its supply and disposal organs, *Gosplan* wielded great power over the allocation and distribution of resources within the over-all industrial sector.

The *gosplans* of the republics were also greatly increased in responsibility, function, and staff. (Unless otherwise noted the term *Gosplan* in this study will apply only to the central agency.) In effect, each republican *gosplan* now duplicated the functions and activities of *Gosplan* U.S.S.R. Like the central agency, the republican *gosplans* were not granted any formal executive power but in fact possessed great "informal" power. The republican councils of ministers now had under their jurisdiction 94 per cent of total industrial production compared with only 47 per cent in 1955, but control over numerous economic decisions—for example, supply allocation, investment, output—was maintained by central authorities.

The actual number of *sovnarkhozy* varied between 100 and 105 during the 1957-62 period. Each *sovnarkhoz* has been established by the related republican council of ministers and is responsible to it. (The present tense is used here since the *sovnarkhoz* system is still in existence in a modified form, as we shall see later.) The smaller republics—such as Armenia, Latvia and Georgia—become themselves one *sovnarkhoz*. By contrast the Russian Republic had 67 until 1963, the Ukraine 14, and Kazakhstan 9. The detailed internal structure of *sovnarkhozy* varies somewhat by region, but each has a governing body (council), an advisory technical-economic council, and branch of industry and functional subdivisions. An organization chart of the Moscow City *sovnarkhoz* in 1960 is presented below.

THE CITY OF MOSCOW ECONOMIC COUNCIL—1960

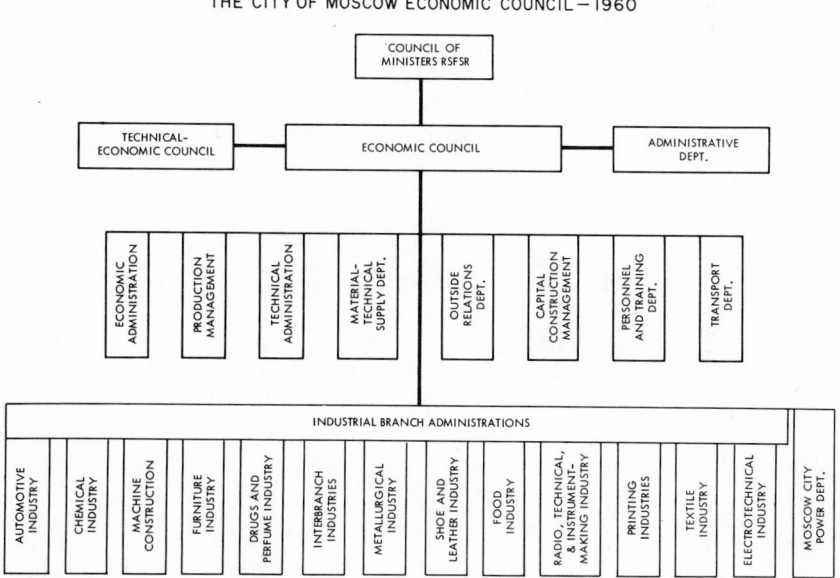

Translated from *Organizatsiia Upravlenii, i Planirovaniia, Promyshlennosti* (Moscow: Gosplanizdat, 1960), p. 17.

The functional departments deal with planning, commodity supply and sales, accounting, finance, and so forth. The type and number of industrial branch administrations or departments (*upravleniye*) within a given *sovnarkhoz* depend on the representation of enterprises within the region. In larger, more developed regions there are typically more than a dozen *upravleniye;* in small regions there are less. The branch administrations contain several functional subdepartments similar to those of the head office of the *sovnarkhoz*. With only few exceptions, the direct superior of the industrial enterprise is the appropriate *upra-*

vleniye of the *sovnarkhoz*.[2] (Unless otherwise noted the term *sovnarkhoz* refers to both the regional economic council as a whole and its individual departments.)

The *sovnarkhoz* apparatus is responsible for drafting plans for the region, organizing and controlling their fulfillment, supervising supply contracts and deliveries, and many other matters great and small—some covered by precise instructions and others left to their own initiative. More specifically, in its day-to-day operations the essential task of the *sovnarkhoz* and its subdivisions is to supervise the fulfillment of the plan approved by superior authorities, though it can decide details of the plan when they are not prescribed from above. It also approves the plans for each of its subordinate enterprises. Although the *sovnarkhoz* is guided in all important matters by the directives it receives from its superiors, it has a range of choices concerning how to carry them out, and it can decide on various matters independently. It may negotiate with other *sovnarkhozy* about matters of joint interest and make arrangements for mutual cooperation in supplies—subject to maintaining conformity with the centrally approved plan. The *sovnarkhoz* also has the duty to encourage new techniques, technological improvement, product innovation, and rational specialization within the region.

Therein lies a skeleton outline of Soviet industrial organization as it stood following the abolition of the ministerial system in 1957. Although the territorial principle became the dominant form of industrial organization, branch-of-industry departmentalization emerged at the central, republican, and regional levels. However, only the branch administrations of the *sovnarkhozy* exerted direct line authority over subordinate enterprises; branch departments at higher levels were concerned only with functional tasks pertaining to a given industrial sector (for example, the supply and sale of a given class of output, investment, technical development, and so forth). Various other types of functional departments also emerged at all levels.

Hoped for Improvements

The Soviet rulers hoped to eradicate, or at least greatly lessen, the growing deficiencies under the ministerial system by breaking down the economy into more manageable administrative units. The reorganization brought higher authorities closer to the enterprise level to reduce their ignorance about enterprise capabilities, resource needs, and over-all operations. It was hoped that by placing the direct superior agencies in close geographical proximity with their subordinate enterprises, and thereby taking into account local conditions, sounder plans would be established. In the same vein, it was felt that the reorganization would serve to reduce substantially bureaucratic delays, provide for more effective control and timely corrective action, and generally secure adequate attention to significant problems as they arose. Hence the new system was expected to provide more accurate information for decision-making purposes, at all levels in the industrial hierarchy, and better coordination of economic activity within a given region as well as on a national scale.

The leaders also hoped that much of the economic waste and inefficiency resulting from ministerial "departmentalism" would be eradicated. More rational supply and subcontracting relationships among producing enterprises would be established. Substantial economies would also be derived from greater specialization as well as amalgamations at the enterprise level on the basis of objective economic criteria. It was also anticipated that much more economical use would be made of transportation facilities through the elimination of unnecessary crosshauls, less transportation of goods from distant places, and better local truck-pooling arrangements. Moreover, there would be a better utilization of by-products since arrangements for their use could be facilitated, at least among plants within the same region. Through better planning, coordination, and control, much supply uncertainty was also expected to be eliminated, which, in turn, would significantly curtail hoarding practices as well as enterprise product-mix distortions.

Another intended effect of the reorganization was to reduce organizational duplication which was resulting in a substantial waste of human resources. In particular, it was anticipated that the widespread networks of supply and disposal organs under the ministerial system could be consolidated more efficiently and effectively under the new system. In general, a chief professed aim was to streamline the entire bureaucratic machine, thus reducing excessive overcentralization and improving communications throughout Soviet industry. Other economies would be achieved by amalgamating—both vertically and horizontally—closely allied plants in the same vicinity.

Finally, the reorganization was expected to lead to sounder investment decisions, better control over wasteful unfinished projects, and hence more balanced and proportionate industrial development within a given region and on a national scale.

Effects of the 1957 Reorganization: A Thumbnail Sketch

During the 1957-62 period, a long list of economic improvements were attributed by Soviet sources to the territorial system. These have included, in part, gains in output, reductions in costs, better utilization of materials and equipment, reductions in the average length of hauling railway freight, better investment decisions, reductions in the number of unfinished investment projects, more efficient combinations of technically related enterprises, reduction in the size of the administrative apparatus, ad infinitum. For the most part, it has not been conclusively demonstrated that these claims are products of the 1957 reorganization, and some of the claims themselves have not been adequately substantiated.

More important is the fact that Soviet criticisms about the *sovnarkhoz* system clearly began to outweigh plaudits within a few years after the reorganization. There were cetain definite, though mainly modest, gains in the first few years following the reorganization. These were essentially short-run windfall gains resulting from an accumulation of foregone opportunities and mistakes over many years.

Soon the stock of opportunities for improvement under the existing territorial system appeared to be exhausted. Many of the shortcomings of the ministerial systems emerged as serious problems under the territorial system in similar or modified form, and certain new problems also emerged. To overcome the problems that were getting seriously out of hand, a number of organizational changes evolved during the 1957-62 period. Finally, in November 1962 a major industrial reorganization was announced by Khrushchev and implemented in 1963.

Let us briefly sketch the more significant problems under the territorial system, focusing here on the 1957-62 period.[3] We will go into greater detail on the problems which directly affect the Soviet enterprise and its management in Part II.

Regional barriers of the territorial system have led to local distortions of the national interest, and campaigns to curb these localistic tendencies have no doubt inhibited the local initiative that the reorganization sought to promote. Each region has displayed strong tendencies toward self-sufficiency because undependable sources of supply from other regions have emerged as a crucial problem. (There are several reasons for supply deficiencies and they will be discussed in more detail in Part II.) Hence the ministerial problem of "departmentalism" has been replaced by the problem of "localism," and the desire for organizational self-sufficiency—which often leads to a distortion of the national interest— also remains as a major problem.

The ignorance of superior authorities directly above the enterprise about its operations has probably been somewhat reduced under the territorial system. These authorities tend to be in a better position than the former ministerial officials to assess the capabilities and resource needs of their subordinate plants and to approve plans for each enterprise, taking into account local conditions. However, even when the *sovnarkhoz* and its subdivisions have possessed fairly accurate and complete information about enterprise operations—and this has frequently not been the case—they have tended to provide republican and central authorities with deficient information, primarily to obtain "modest" or "easy" output plans for the region as a whole and thus to hedge against incessant supply uncertainties. Hence, the central planners continually have been required to establish national economic plans in the face of much ignorance about local conditions. In turn, deficient planning decisions at the center have been passed down through all levels of the industrial hierarchy.

Although the *sovnarkhoz* is in a better position to give prompter attention to local problems as they arise and to exert more effective control and timely corrective action over subordinate enterprises than the former ministries, this has often not been done in the national interest. Control over enterprise product-mix, output quality, and delivery distortions has tended to be reasonably effective where output has been destined for plants within the same region, but not where it has been destined for external customers.

There have been some definite, though mostly modest, gains in resource utilization under the territorial system. Some economic gains have been realized from better use of transportation facilities, fuller utilization of by-products by producers in the same region, improved local warehousing and selling operations, and amalgamations of plants within a given region. Following the 1957 reorganization, particularly in the initial years, *sovnarkhozy* have shifted excess resources from overstocked plants to more needy enterprises, but usually only within the same region. At the same time, hoarding practices at both the enterprise and regional levels have not subsided but in fact may have intensified.

There has been much evidence of the establishment of more rational supply lines, both in assigning closer suppliers to customer enterprises and in reducing the number of suppliers serving a single producer. There have also been numerous instances cited, where because of regional boundaries and the pursuit of self-sufficiency, opportunities for specialization and cooperation (subcontracting) have not been taken. The tendency of numerous enterprises to undertake uneconomical subsidiary operations to assure adequate supplies has remained a serious shortcoming. On balance there seems to have been only a modest improvement in specialization and cooperation in the supply of parts and semifabricates. Such improvements are largely confined within a given region rather than encompassing other regions. Within various regions there have also been examples of gains resulting from the shifting of production from high-cost to lower-cost producers.

In general, the achievement of the above-mentioned improvements has not been uniform in all regions. In many instances certain regions have clearly achieved improvements, whereas others have either not improved or have even retrogressed. The more fully developed and self-contained regions, which possess many plants representing all major branches of industry (for example, Moscow and Leningrad), have tended to realize the greatest economies and improvements. Their pursuit of self-sufficiency at the expense of the national interest has not been as intensive as in most underdeveloped and/or remote regions; nor have they felt the need to engage in "localistic" distortions to as great a degree.

Many of the shortcomings under the territorial system have clearly been caused by the small size of the regions, explicable only by administrative convenience (adaptations in most cases to existing provincial or district boundaries) rather than any attempt to relate the regions to an economic area. The vast majority of *sovnarkhozy* have not been of sufficient size or coverage to be economically rational or self-sufficient. In addition to the shortcomings outlined above, there has been a number of other adverse consequences resulting from this situation. There has been no planning or administrative organ on the spot responsible for examining the requirements of the natural economic areas divided among several *sovnarkhozy*. A given *sovnarkhoz* is in no position to assess the external economies or diseconomies resulting from its actions. Another practical difficulty of having small regions is that the large-scale specialized manufacture of various goods is more economical when supplying a larger area. But the *sovnarkhozy* have tended to adapt specialized production only to the needs of their own enterprises, limiting their links with other regions. Since production and various other economic decisions are based, not on directly economic criteria (for example, profitability), but on plans and directives, no *sovnarkhoz* can be expected to make rational decisions in terms of the needs of some larger area.

In several respects, the *sovnarkhozy* have been in a less favorable position to take into account the impact of their actions on the economy as a whole than were the former ministries. The latter were at least able, within their own industrial sectors, to think and calculate on a national scale. The specialized ministries, with their expert technical skills and know-how (and in spite of shortcomings cited earlier) were in a better position to aid the central decision-makers in both inter- and intraindustry investment planning. Abolition of these ministries, responsible for assuring "proportionality" in the development of their industries, has not been adequately compensated for by the mere assignment of members of their staffs to the industrial branch departments of *Gosplan* U.S.S.R. Disproportions within a given industrial sector and between sectors appear to have become more serious under the territorial system. Although there may have been some gains by having each *sovnarkhoz* warn of local disproportions in advance, there has been much evidence of serious deficiencies in planning and coordinating the total economic requirements within many regions. Moreover, because of "localism," the pursuit of self-sufficiency, and the resulting desire for increased investment funds, the problems of unfinished projects and misuse of allocated investment funds seem to have been intensified under the territorial system. Finally, as compared to the *sovnarkhozy*, the ministries were in a better position to introduce new technology and to undertake product innovation activities within their respective industrial sectors. The former typically have only relatively few plants in a given industry, and they lack the technical expertness and the extensive networks of research and development facilities that were at the disposal of the ministerial empires.

Even in the case of organizational duplication and wasteful human resources the territorial system has proved rather disappointing. A professed intention of the reorganization was to substantially cut down the size of the bureaucratic apparatus and streamline its functions. The abolishment of the ministerial system only reduced the over-all planning and industrial administrative staff by about 150,000—roughly 2.5 per cent of the total number in existence immediately prior to the 1957 reorganization.[4] Although there are no available figures, it is quite likely that this gain has been more than offset by the creation of new departments and agencies following the reorganization. Extensive networks of supply and sales organs soon emerged at all levels of the industrial hierarchy, from the center down to the branch administrations of the *sovnarkhozy*. In addition, as will be seen below, several new agencies have been established in an attempt to overcome the serious problems evolving under the territorial system.

Major Organizational Changes: 1957-1962

A series of organizational adjustments evolved during the 1957-62 period as the regime restlessly sought a more effective and efficient organizational arrangement. There were some clear advantages forthcoming under the territorial system. At the same time, built-in tendencies toward localism and self-sufficiency necessitated the preservation and reinforcement of strict centralization. Reforms undertaken to curb localistic tendencies have inhibited the local initiative that the reorganization sought to promote.

During the 1957-59 period, a considerable amount of administrative detail was decentralized. The republics, and to a lesser extent the *sovnarkhozy*, acquired certain decision-making powers over resource allocation, local investment projects, production, pricing, the maneuverability of working capital, and so forth. However, because of serious territorial distortions of the national interest, a recentralization trend began to emerge at the end of 1959, and this trend was intensified during the 1960-62 period.[5] (This did not have a significant effect on the decision-making powers of enterprise managers, as will be discussed in Chapter 4.)

In an attempt to strengthen central planning, long-term planning was taken from *Gosplan* in 1960 and placed in a relatively new central agency, the State Scientific-Economic Council (*Gosekonomsovet*). A move was also made in 1960 to strengthen planning and control at the republican level by relieving certain republican *gosplans* of the heavy administrative burden of handling inter*sovnarkhoz* production relationships as well as problems of supply and sales in those republics containing many *sovnarkhozy*. In the Russian, Ukrainian, and Kazakh Republics these administrative responsibilities were shifted to newly created republican "super*sovnarkhozy*" that were superimposed over the existing regional *sovnarkhoz* structure. The regional economic councils in these republics were now directly subordinate to both the new super*sovnarkhoz* and the Republic Council of Ministers. At the same time the five regional economic councils of the Uzbek Republic were replaced by a single *sovnarkhoz*.

In May 1961 a long-discussed scheme to further an old objective— the integrated development of "natural" economic regions broader in area than the regional *sovnarkhozy*—was put into operation with the division of the country into 17 large economic territories. Each region was to have a council for coordinating and planning the work of several *sovnarkhozy*. These councils were to be only advisory in nature; they were to study basic problems of complex regional economic development and work out recommendations for presentation to the republican *gosplans, Gosplan* U.S.S.R., and *Gosekonomsovet*. These 17 territorial councils were replaced by 18 new councils in 1963.

Many state committees organized on a branch-of-industry basis under the U.S.S.R. Council of Ministers were created during the 1957-62 period. These committees were not granted any operational powers, but they were to render advice on research, long-range planning, investment decisions, the development and introduction of new technology, and product innovation in their respective industrial sectors.[6] In 1957, following the reorganization, a small number of state committees—dealing chiefly with defense activities—were established to replace temporarily retained ministries. In 1958, a state committee for the chemical industry was created, since this industry had been undergoing a vast expansion program. In 1959 the State Committee for Automation and Machine-building was set up because of heightened emphasis on technology as an element of industrial growth in the 1959-65 Seven-Year Plan. During the 1961-62 period, state committees were also created for the metallurgy, fuel, and timber industries. These committees, staffed largely with former ministerial officials, have been created to improve the technical and proportionate development of key branches of industry, a task with which territorial authorities have not been able to cope.

An organization chart of Soviet industry, as it stood in late 1961, is presented on pages 42-43.

In spite of the above organizational changes the economic deficiencies inherent in the existing territorial system remained basically unchecked during the 1957-62 period. Both the ministerial and territorial systems have exhibited serious shortcomings which have evoked continuing adjustment and refinement, and each has presented certain problems which have defied solution. Either system, in practice, has owed part of its success to the incorporation of basic elements of the other. On the other hand, both systems have owed a large part of their inadequacy to their inability to encompass simultaneously and with equal effectiveness both branch-of-industry and regional considerations.

The 1957 reorganization replaced centralized industrial structures with a system supposedly territorial but in fact based on a multiplicity of central agencies. These agencies, working through territorial organizations, have been unable to delegate any effective authority over resource allocation. The central organizations have scarcely been able to do anything that has not impinged on other industrial organizations. The task of keeping all the units in the over-all structure in harmony is of such a nature that new organizations are frequently set up to coordinate and to be coordinated. But the basic problem remains: Who coordinates the coordinators who have been established to coordinate other coordinators?

In November 1962, Khrushchev announced another major reorganization of the industrial apparatus, and his proposed reforms were implemented in 1963.[7]

The Existing System

Before going into greater detail, let us briefly summarize the basic features of the 1963 industrial reorganization. First, the 100-odd *sovnarkhozy* have been reorganized into 47 new regional economic councils. Only a few of the more fully developed and self-sufficient *sovnarkhozy* remain essentially unaltered; the great majority have been merged into larger regions in an attempt to make them more economically rational.

Second, the entire central planning apparatus has been revamped in an effort to improve national economic planning, coordination, and control. *Gosplan* is once again responsible for long-term development planning, although most of its other functions have been given to a new central agency, the Council of the National Economy (or National Economic Council). This latter agency has been placed in charge of the details of short-run national planning, plan implementation, and control over plan fulfillment. In March 1963, the Supreme Council of the National Economy was formed under the U.S.S.R. Council of Ministers to supervise and coordinate the activities of *Gosplan,* the National Economic Council, and *Gostroy* (State Committee for Construction). This supreme agency

U.S.S.R.
ADMINISTRATIVE ORGANIZATION OF INDUSTRY AND CONSTRUCTION
JULY 1961

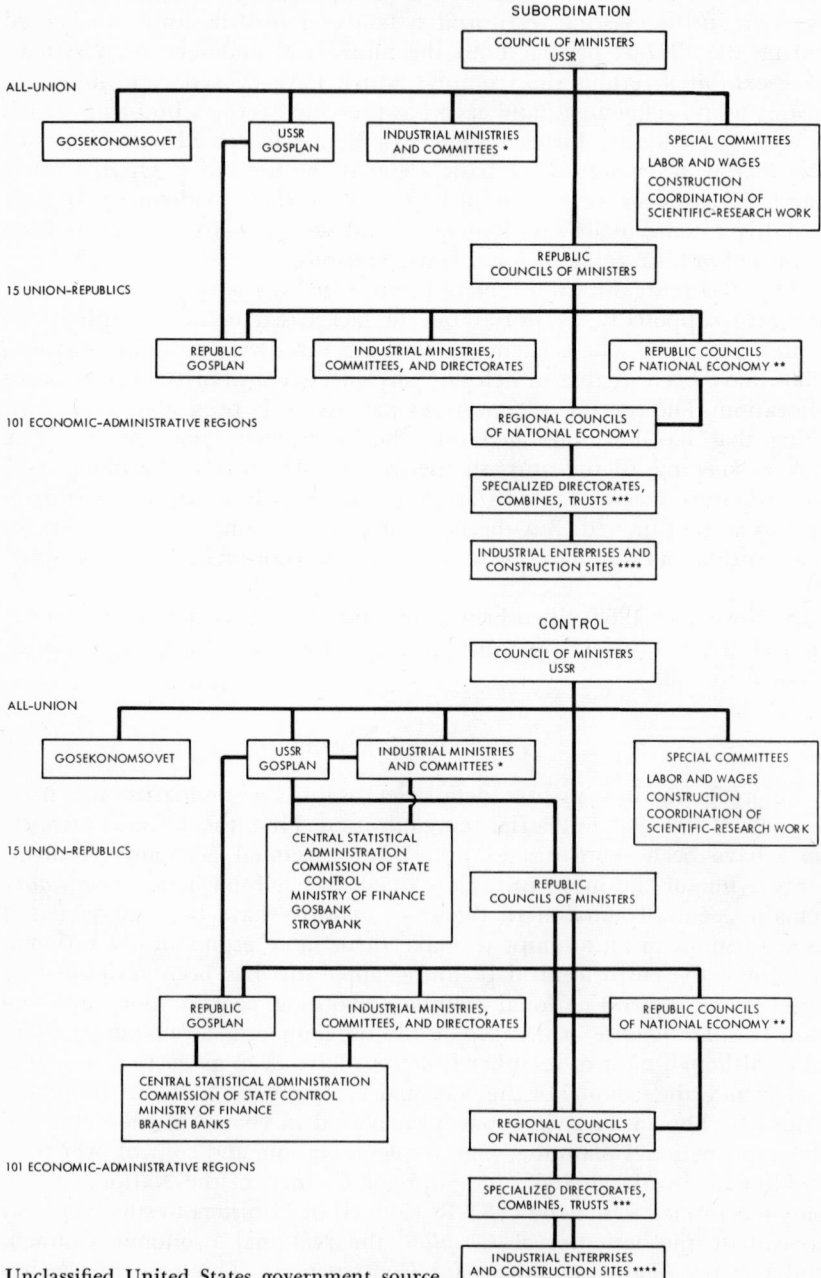

SUBORDINATION

COUNCIL OF MINISTERS USSR

ALL-UNION

GOSEKONOMSOVET

USSR GOSPLAN

INDUSTRIAL MINISTRIES AND COMMITTEES *

SPECIAL COMMITTEES
LABOR AND WAGES
CONSTRUCTION
COORDINATION OF
SCIENTIFIC-RESEARCH WORK

REPUBLIC COUNCILS OF MINISTERS

15 UNION-REPUBLICS

REPUBLIC GOSPLAN

INDUSTRIAL MINISTRIES, COMMITTEES, AND DIRECTORATES

REPUBLIC COUNCILS OF NATIONAL ECONOMY **

101 ECONOMIC-ADMINISTRATIVE REGIONS

REGIONAL COUNCILS OF NATIONAL ECONOMY

SPECIALIZED DIRECTORATES, COMBINES, TRUSTS ***

INDUSTRIAL ENTERPRISES AND CONSTRUCTION SITES ****

CONTROL

COUNCIL OF MINISTERS USSR

ALL-UNION

GOSEKONOMSOVET

USSR GOSPLAN

INDUSTRIAL MINISTRIES AND COMMITTEES *

SPECIAL COMMITTEES
LABOR AND WAGES
CONSTRUCTION
COORDINATION OF
SCIENTIFIC-RESEARCH WORK

CENTRAL STATISTICAL
ADMINISTRATION
COMMISSION OF STATE
CONTROL
MINISTRY OF FINANCE
GOSBANK
STROYBANK

15 UNION-REPUBLICS

REPUBLIC COUNCILS OF MINISTERS

REPUBLIC GOSPLAN

INDUSTRIAL MINISTRIES, COMMITTEES, AND DIRECTORATES

REPUBLIC COUNCILS OF NATIONAL ECONOMY **

CENTRAL STATISTICAL ADMINISTRATION
COMMISSION OF STATE CONTROL
MINISTRY OF FINANCE
BRANCH BANKS

101 ECONOMIC-ADMINISTRATIVE REGIONS

REGIONAL COUNCILS OF NATIONAL ECONOMY

SPECIALIZED DIRECTORATES, COMBINES, TRUSTS ***

INDUSTRIAL ENTERPRISES AND CONSTRUCTION SITES ****

Unclassified United States government source.

42

PLANNING

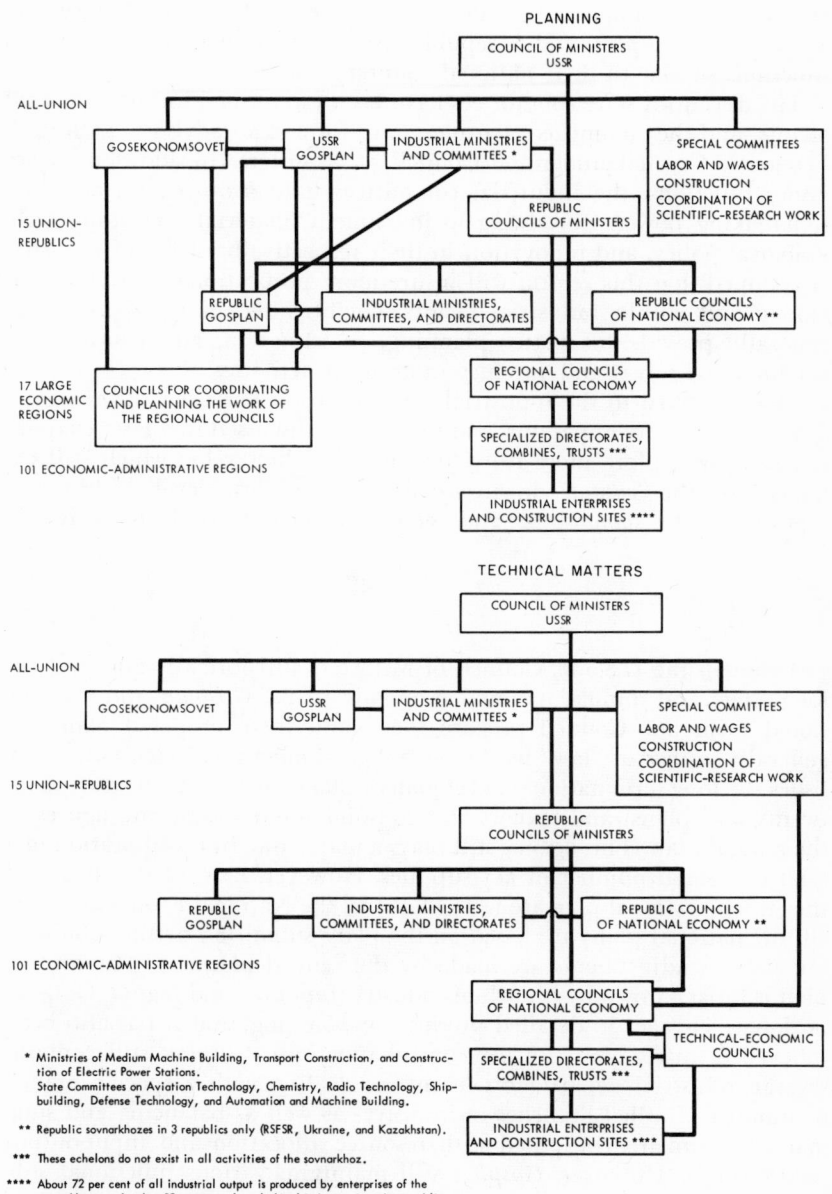

COUNCIL OF MINISTERS
USSR

ALL-UNION

GOSEKONOMSOVET

USSR
GOSPLAN

INDUSTRIAL MINISTRIES
AND COMMITTEES *

SPECIAL COMMITTEES
LABOR AND WAGES
CONSTRUCTION
COORDINATION OF
SCIENTIFIC-RESEARCH WORK

15 UNION-
REPUBLICS

REPUBLIC
COUNCILS OF MINISTERS

REPUBLIC
GOSPLAN

INDUSTRIAL MINISTRIES,
COMMITTEES, AND DIRECTORATES

REPUBLIC COUNCILS
OF NATIONAL ECONOMY **

17 LARGE
ECONOMIC
REGIONS

COUNCILS FOR COORDINATING
AND PLANNING THE WORK OF
THE REGIONAL COUNCILS

REGIONAL COUNCILS
OF NATIONAL ECONOMY

101 ECONOMIC-ADMINISTRATIVE REGIONS

SPECIALIZED DIRECTORATES,
COMBINES, TRUSTS ***

INDUSTRIAL ENTERPRISES
AND CONSTRUCTION SITES ****

TECHNICAL MATTERS

COUNCIL OF MINISTERS
USSR

ALL-UNION

GOSEKONOMSOVET

USSR
GOSPLAN

INDUSTRIAL MINISTRIES
AND COMMITTEES *

SPECIAL COMMITTEES
LABOR AND WAGES
CONSTRUCTION
COORDINATION OF
SCIENTIFIC-RESEARCH WORK

15 UNION-REPUBLICS

REPUBLIC
COUNCILS OF MINISTERS

REPUBLIC
GOSPLAN

INDUSTRIAL MINISTRIES,
COMMITTEES, AND DIRECTORATES

REPUBLIC COUNCILS
OF NATIONAL ECONOMY **

101 ECONOMIC-ADMINISTRATIVE REGIONS

REGIONAL COUNCILS
OF NATIONAL ECONOMY

TECHNICAL-ECONOMIC
COUNCILS

SPECIALIZED DIRECTORATES,
COMBINES, TRUSTS ***

INDUSTRIAL ENTERPRISES
AND CONSTRUCTION SITES ****

* Ministries of Medium Machine Building, Transport Construction, and Construction of Electric Power Stations.
State Committees on Aviation Technology, Chemistry, Radio Technology, Shipbuilding, Defense Technology, and Automation and Machine Building.

** Republic sovnarkhozes in 3 republics only (RSFSR, Ukraine, and Kazakhstan).

*** These echelons do not exist in all activities of the sovnarkhoz.

**** About 72 per cent of all industrial output is produced by enterprises of the
sovnarkhozy. Another 22 per cent, largely local industry, is under republican
ministries, committees, or directorates, and oblast or kray executive committees.
The remaining 6 per cent is under ministries and committees at the all-union level.

is the highest coordinating authority for Soviet industry and construction. It has both decision-making and control powers. Each republic now contains both a *gosplan* and a republic economic council, which perform functions similar to their national counterparts.

Third, central state committees have been established for all industrial sectors, and the committee chairmen have formed an advisory Technical-Economic Council under the Council of Ministers. In addition to advisory functions, the industrial committees have acquired certain decision-making powers pertaining to investment, material allocation, technological policy, and innovation in their respective branches of industry. It is hoped that this reform will insure more proportionate development among and within industrial sectors, heighten technical progress, and generally provide for better planning, coordination, and control over production process and product innovation activities.

Closely linked to the industrial reorganization has been the reorganization of the party apparatus, and this will be discussed in a later chapter. Let us now explore more fully the industrial hierarchy, which still extends from the "center" downward to the republican level, within each republic to the *sovnarkhoz,* and thence to the industrial enterprise.

Central Authorities [8]

Although the U.S.S.R. Council of Ministers still formally approves the long-range and annual national economic plans, *Gosplan* and the National Economic Council prepare them, and their proposed plans are generally ratified as "law" by the central government. *Gosplan* now establishes the long-term national development plans (five- or seven-year plans, twenty-year plans) and reviews and consolidates key aggregate figures of the annual plan. This agency still plays a major role in the allocation of a relatively small number of key supplies. However, most of the details of the annual national plan are worked out by the National Economic Council. All national plans are based on the plans submitted by the republics, but various adjustments are made by the central planners. The annual plan is broken down by branch of industry, republic, and region. *Gosplan* no longer engages in detailed production planning, and it has also been relieved of many of its former control functions. *Gosplan* still contains several industrial departments—each one dealing with a specific branch or number of allied branches of industry—as well as balancing and summary departments concerned with resource allocation and input-output relationships. Moreover, *Gosplan* still maintains various functional subdivisions dealing with pricing, investment, and the like.

The National Economic Council constructs the detailed annual economic plan and submits relevant data on past and projected national economic performance to *Gosplan* for long-term planning purposes. The former is also in charge of plan fulfillment. It carries out its activities through the republican councils of ministers, the republican economic councils, industrial state committees, and various other central bodies. It has the right to delve into matters at all levels of the industrial hierarchy, although it is supposed to issue directives through the formal chain of command. This agency is deeply involved in production decisions, resource allocation, and the establishment of supply and delivery relationships among republics, regions, and even enterprises. The control functions of the National Economic Council are many. It can revise both republican and regional plans within the limits of the over-all plans, as long as state budget interrelationships are not affected. It can make decisions on the redistribution and/or provision of additional resources for unplanned production and special projects; and it can change supply relationships among plants. The National Economic Council has many functional and branch-of-industry departments, including several supply and disposal administrations, each one dealing with a major commodity group.

Industrial state committees examine the branch-of-industry sections of the plans submitted by the republics. On this basis each committee prepares a national plan for its industrial sector. The committees work closely with *Gosplan* and the National Economic Council in the formulation of all national economic plans. There are about 11 specifically industrial state committees attached to *Gosplan,* and 1 attached to the National Economic Council. The committees concern themselves with all vital matters pertaining to their industrial sectors. Most of the industrial research and development institutes scattered throughout the country have been made subordinate to these state committees. The committees have been imbued with decision-making powers and authority over various matters that directly affect enterprise operations, but they are "formally" supposed to work through the industrial hierarchy so as not to violate the principle of unity of command. Among their major functions are the following: They formulate technological policies pertaining to automation and mechanization; they decide on dates for removing obsolete equipment and production processes from operation; they issue directives on product development, the production of new items, and the withdrawal of obsolete goods from production; they coordinate with the National Economic Council delivery dates for new goods; they distribute financial and material resources for the introduction of new technology, and in some cases, for product innovation activities; they are now working on the establishment of technical norms and standards in order to achieve a uniform technical policy in their respective branches of industry; they coordinate and control industrial research and experimental design and development projects within their sectors and with other sectors; and they play a major role in investment plans and decisions pertaining to their respective branches of industry.

In mid-1963, small planning commissions were set up in the 18 major (natural) economic regions mentioned earlier. Each of these territories contains a number of existing *sovnarkhozy*. The newly formed councils and commissions in these 18 territories serve as advisory staffs to *Gosplan* U.S.S.R., except for those of the Russian and Ukraine Republics, who are responsible to the republican *gosplans*.[9] The new bodies are to work on long-range territorial development plans, beginning with the 1966-70 national plan: They are to render advice on investment decisions, the location of new plants and industries, research activity, and various other matters having long-run implications. The planning commissions are to work jointly with *sovnarkhozy* in their area on proposals for drawing up capital construction and expansion plans, both for individual *sovnarkhozy* and for the larger area as a whole. In the past the major economic regions have not played a significant role in the Soviet economy. More will be said about the present territorial bodies in Chapter 12.

There are a few other central agencies worthy of mention here. The State Committee on Labor and Wages is responsible for working out basic and uniform salary and wage scales for all job occupations. The State Committee on Standards, Measures, and Measuring Instruments concerns itself with production quality, technical standards, and product standardization. The State Committee for the Coordination of Scientific Research has the task of coordinating and broadly defining the direction of basic and applied scientific research and development activity throughout the entire country. The Central Statistical Administration, with its nationwide branches, gathers and disseminates data for economic planning and control purposes. The State Bank (*Gosbank*) has numerous branches which control the financial transactions and expenditures of all industrial organizations through their checking accounts. The Ministry of Finance prepares the state budget, which serves to translate the over-all national plan into monetary terms, and with its army of inspectors audits the books of all industrial establishments.

If this brief discussion of the functions of important central agencies strikes the reader as confusing, in all sincerity it is not this author's fault. One thing remains vividly clear concerning the present organization of Soviet industry: To the Soviets themselves there remains much confusion about authority relationships, responsibilities, and the activities of the numerous planning and administrative agencies which make up the over-all structure. More will be said about this in Chapter 6.

On pages 47-48 are presented organization charts outlining the central planning and administrative apparatus, as of May 1963.

U.S.S.R. COUNCIL OF MINISTERS

PRESIDIUM

CHAIRMAN
● N. S. Khrushchev

FIRST DEPUTY CHAIRMAN
● A. N. Kosygin

FIRST DEPUTY CHAIRMAN
● D.F. Ustinov
(Chm. Supreme Economic Council)

FIRST DEPUTY CHAIRMAN
● A.I. Mikoyan

DEPUTY CHAIRMAN
● D.S. Polyansky

DEPUTY CHAIRMAN
● V.E. Dymshits
(Chm. of Sovnarkhoz)

DEPUTY CHAIRMAN
● P.F. Lomako
(Chm. of Gosplan)

DEPUTY CHAIRMAN
● I.T. Novikov
(Chm. of Gostroy)

DEPUTY CHAIRMAN
● L.V. Smirnov

DEPUTY CHAIRMAN
● M.A. Lesechko
(Chm. Presidium Commission for CEMA Questions)

DEPUTY CHAIRMAN
● K.N. Rudnev
(Chm. Scientific Research Coordination Committee)

DEPUTY CHAIRMAN
● A.N. Shelepin
(Chm. Party-State Control Committee)

"and individuals personally designated by the Councils of Ministers"

COMMISSIONS OF THE PRESIDIUM

CEMA*QUESTIONS
● M.A. Lesechko

CURRENT QUESTIONS
?

COSTS QUESTIONS
?

TRANSPORTATION COORDINATION
?

SERVICE UNIT

ADMINISTRATION OF AFFAIRS
(Housekeeping Functions)
G.S. Stepanov

MINISTRIES ALL UNION

FOREIGN TRADE
● N.S. Patolichev

RAILWAYS
● B.P. Beshchev

SEA FLEET
■ V.G. Bakayev

UNION-REPUBLICAN

AGRICULTURE
I.P. Volovchenko

FINANCE
● V.F. Garbuzov

COMMUNICATIONS
■ N.D. Psurtsev

FOREIGN AFFAIRS
● A.A. Gromyko

CULTURE
● Ye. A. Furtseva

HEALTH
■ S.V. Kurashov

DEFENSE
●R. Ya. Malinovsky

HIGHER & SPECIALIZED SECONDARY EDUCATION
● V.P. Yelyutin

OTHER MINISTERS
(without Portfolio)
A.A. Goreglyad   G.A. Karavayev
● V.N. Novikov

SUPREME COUNCIL OF NATIONAL ECONOMY

CHAIRMAN
● D.F. Ustinov

DEPUTY CHAIRMAN
■ A.M. Tarasov

COUNCIL OF NATIONAL ECONOMY (SOVNARKHOZ)
● V.E. Dymshits

STATE PLANNING COMMISSION (GOSPLAN)
● P.F. Lomako

STATE COMMITTEE FOR CONSTRUCTION (GOSTROY)
● I.T. Novikov

STATE COMMITTEE FOR COORDINATION OF SCIENTIFIC-RESEARCH WORK
● K.N. Rudnev

9 OTHER STATE COMMITTEES

3 STATE PRODUCTION COMMITTEES

STATE COMMITTEES

CINEMATOGRAPHY
■ A.V. Romanov

LABOR & WAGE MATTERS
● A.P. Volkov

CULTURAL RELATIONS WITH FOREIGN COUNTRIES
S.K. Romanovsky

RADIO BROADCASTING & TELEVISION
M.A. Kharlamov

FOREIGN ECONOMIC RELATIONS
■ S.A. Skachkov

PROCUREMENTS
■ L.R. Korniyets

OTHER COMMITTEES, ADMINISTRATIONS, ETC.

COMMITTEE OF PARTY-STATE CONTROL
● A.N. Shelepin

COMMITTEE OF STATE SECURITY
■ V. Ye. Semichastny

CENTRAL STATISTICAL ADMINISTRATION
▲ V.N. Starovsky

BOARD OF STATE BANK
A.N. Korovushkin

EX OFFICIO MEMBERS
(CHAIRMEN OF REPUBLIC COUNCILS OF MINISTERS)

■ A.Ye. Kochinyan (Armenian SSR)
E.N. Alikhanov (Azerbaydzhan SSR)
■ T.Ya. Kiselev (Belorussian SSR)
■ V.I. Klauson (Estonian SSR)
● G.D. Dzhavakhishvili (Georgian SSR)

● D.A. Kunayev (Kazakh SSR)
■ B. Mambetov (Kirgiz SSR)
V.P. Ruben (Latvian SSR)
■ M.Yu. Shumauskas (Lithuanian SSR)
■ A.F. Diorditsa (Moldavian SSR)

● G.I. Voronov (RSFSR)
■ A. Kakharov (Tadzhik SSR)
M. Gapurov (Turkmen SSR)
● V.V. Shcherbitsky (Ukrainian SSR)
● R. Kurbanov (Uzbek SSR)

● FULL MEMBER, CENTRAL COMMITTEE, CPSU   ■ CANDIDATE MEMBER, CENTRAL COMMITTEE, CPSU   ▲ MEMBER, CENTRAL AUDITING COMMISSION, CPSU

* CEMA: Council for Economic Mutual Assistance

From *Staffing Procedures and Problems in the Soviet Union* (Washington, D.C.: U.S. Government Printing Office, 1963).

SUPREME COUNCIL OF NATIONAL ECONOMY

CHAIRMAN
● D.F. Ustinov

DEPUTY CHAIRMAN
■ A.M. Tarasov

STATE PLANNING COMMISSION (Gosplan)

CHAIRMAN
● P.F. Lomako

STATE COMMITTEE FOR CONSTRUCTION (Gostroy)

CHAIRMAN
● I.T. Novikov

COUNCIL OF NATIONAL ECONOMY (Sovnarkhoz)

CHAIRMAN
● V.E. Dymshits

FIRST DEPUTY CHAIRMAN
■ V.F. Zhigalin

STATE COMMITTEES

FISH INDUSTRY
■ A.A. Ishkov

TRADE
■ A.I. Struyev

ALL-UNION ASSOCIATION

"Soyuzselkhoztekhnika"
A.A. Yezhevsky

STATE PRODUCTION COMMITTEES

MEDIUM MACHINE-BUILDING
● Ye.P. Slavsky

POWER & ELECTRIFICATION
P.S. Neporozhny

GAS INDUSTRY
■ A.K. Kortunov

FIRST DEPUTY CHAIRMAN
A.A. Etmekdzhiyan

FIRST DEPUTY CHAIRMAN
● V.M. Ryabikov

DEPUTY CHAIRMAN
■ N.A. Tikhonov

DEPUTY CHAIRMAN
■ V.P. Zotov

STATE COMMITTEES

AUTOMATION & MACHINE BUILDING
● A.I. Kostousov

CENTRAL ASIAN COTTON-GROWING
V.N. Kulikov

CHEMISTRY
N.K. Baybakov

ELECTRICAL ENGINEERING
N.A. Obolensky

FERROUS & NON-FERROUS METALLURGY
V.Ye. Boyko

FOOD INDUSTRY
P.V. Naumenko

FUEL INDUSTRY
N.V. Melnikov

HEAVY, POWER,& TRANSPORT MACHINE BUILDING
A.V. Topchiyev

INSTRUMENT-MAKING, MEANS OF AUTOMATION & CONTROL SYSTEMS
M.Ye. Rakovsky

LIGHT INDUSTRY
N.N. Tarasov

LUMBER, CELLULOSE-PAPER, & WOODWORKING INDUSTRY & FORESTRY
G.M. Orlov

MOTOR VEHICLE-TRACTOR & AGRICULTURAL MACHINE BUILDING
■ N.I. Strokin

PROFESSIONAL & TECHNICAL EDUCATION
G.I. Zelenko

FIRST DEPUTY CHAIRMAN
● I.G. Grishmanov

STATE COMMITTEES

BUILDING MATERIALS INDUSTRY
?

CIVIL CONSTRUCTION & ARCHITECTURE
M.V. Posokhin

CONSTRUCTION, ROAD, & COMMUNAL MACHINE-BUILDING
Ye.S. Novoselov

STATE PRODUCTION COMMITTEES

ASSEMBLY & SPECIAL CONSTRUCTION WORK
?

TRANSPORT CONSTRUCTION
● Ye.F. Kozhevnikov

CONSTRUCTION FOR THE CENTRAL-ASIAN ECONOMIC REGION
V.M. Gushchin

STATE COMMITTEE FOR THE COORDINATION OF SCIENTIFIC RESEARCH WORK
● K.N. Rudnev

STATE COMMITTEES

AVIATION TECHNOLOGY
● P.V. Dementyev

DEFENSE TECHNOLOGY
S.A. Zverev

ELECTRONIC TECHNOLOGY
■ A.I. Shokin

GEOLOGY
A.V. Sidorenko

INVENTIONS & DISCOVERIES
A.E. Vyatkin

RADIO ELECTRONICS
● V.D. Kalmykov

SHIPBUILDING
■ B.Ye. Butoma

STANDARDS, MEASURES, & MEASURING INSTRUMENTS
Yu.Ye. Maksarev

UTILIZATION OF ATOMIC ENERGY
A.M. Petrosyants

● FULL MEMBER, CENTRAL COMMITTEE, CPSU   ■ CANDIDATE MEMBER, CENTRAL COMMITTEE, CPSU

From *Staffing Procedures and Problems in the Soviet Union* (Washington, D.C.: U.S. Government Printing Office, 1963).

Republican Level

Each republic has its own *gosplan* and republic economic council, both agencies being directly subordinate to the Republic Council of Ministers; but at the same time both must carry out directives issued by their central counterparts. The internal organization and activities of both of these republican agencies are basically similar to those of their central counterparts. The republican or super*sovnarkhozy* that were set up in three republics in 1961 have maintained their staffs, but their functions have been enlarged with the 1963 reorganization.

Regional Economic Councils—Sovnarkhozy [10]

Instead of the 100-odd regional economic councils there are now 47. Where the Russian Republic formerly contained 67 it now has 14; likewise, the number in the Ukraine has been reduced from 14 to 7. Appendix B contains a map of the new *sovnarkhozy* and also presents data on the features of each region. Some of the more developed and self-sufficient regions (for example, Moscow, Leningrad, Kharkov, Kiev) have been basically unaffected by the reorganization, except for the absorption of some local counties. However, the large majority have been merged into larger *sovnarkhozy*.

A major rationale underlying the organization of the new enlarged regions has been the production principle; adjacent regions having similar leading branches of industry have been merged to enable more economical, large-scale specialized production. Another key consideration has been to provide for greater self-sufficiency within each region by providing a better combination of both complementary and supplementary industries. It is hoped that this reform will greatly reduce local distortions of the national interest. Soviet leaders have expressed a definite desire to extend greater decision-making powers to *sovnarkhozy,* and there are some indications that their authority and independence are being modestly broadened.

A few examples illustrating the nature of the regional mergers are in order. In the Northern Caucasus area, where oil is the leading branch of industry, four *sovnarkhozy* have been formed into one. Two *sovnarkhozy* having coal as their chief industry have been merged in the Donets Basin area. In the central Asian republics four *sovnarkhozy* have been combined into the Central Asian *sovnarkhoz* to provide for a better combination of different industrial sectors.

The internal structure of *sovnarkhozy* has remained basically intact with the 1963 reorganization. But, of course, the number and types of branch administrations (*upravleniye*) depend on the industrial representation of the newly formed regions. In some instances functional departments have been reorganized and/or new ones created. On page 51 is presented an organization chart of a typical *sovnarkhoz* as of September 1963.

There have been reports of reductions in administrative staffs resulting from the merger of regions. For example, the Dnieper *sovnarkhoz* now contains 3 former *sovnarkhozy*, and the total staff has been reduced from 1,718 to 1,300 personnel. Before the reorganization the 3 *sovnarkhozy* contained a total of 76 branch and functional departments. The unified *sovnarkhoz* now contains 23 branch departments and 16 functional divisions—a total of 39.[11]

The appropriate *upravleniye* of the *sovnarkhoz* remains the direct superior of the industrial enterprise. Although higher authorities at any level reserve the right to delve into the detailed affairs of the enterprise, it is the *upravleniye* that approves the over-all enterprise plan and controls its fulfillment.

Ministry of Trade—A Special Link for Consumer Goods Producers [12]

In the U.S.S.R., goods are distributed through two distinct networks: material-technical supply and trade. The bulk of producer goods are distributed through the former, and the planning, supply, and sales organs previously discussed perform this function. All consumer goods are distributed through the trade network, which encompasses both intermediary wholesale organizations and retail outlets.

Enterprises producing consumer goods have a relationship with Ministry of Trade organizations. In 1958 the All-Union Ministry of Trade was abolished, and its functions were taken over by *Gosplan*. At present there is a special state committee dealing with domestic trade problems of national importance. However, since 1958 the republican ministries of trade have played the major role in the country's trade activities. Within each republican trade ministry there are subordinate wholesale organizations for different groups of commodities. For example, there are separate organs dealing with footwear, clothing, textile fabrics, cultural goods (which includes watches and radios), and so forth. Each republic has its own combination of groupings, although there is not much variation among larger republics. Retail stores are also under the jurisdiction of the republican trade ministries.

The wholesale trade organizations, serving as the link between producers and retail outlets, perform distributive-warehousing activities. They are also responsible for analyzing and transmitting consumer demand—regarding varieties, styles, designs, colors, and sizes of products—to producers. The trade organ's relationship with the enterprise and its *upravleniye* concerns only the product-mix. They play a major role in planning the enterprise's detailed product-mix and can request revisions in the plan; but they have nothing to do with the setting of aggregate

STRUCTURE OF REGIONAL ECONOMIC COUNCIL (SOVNARKHOZ)

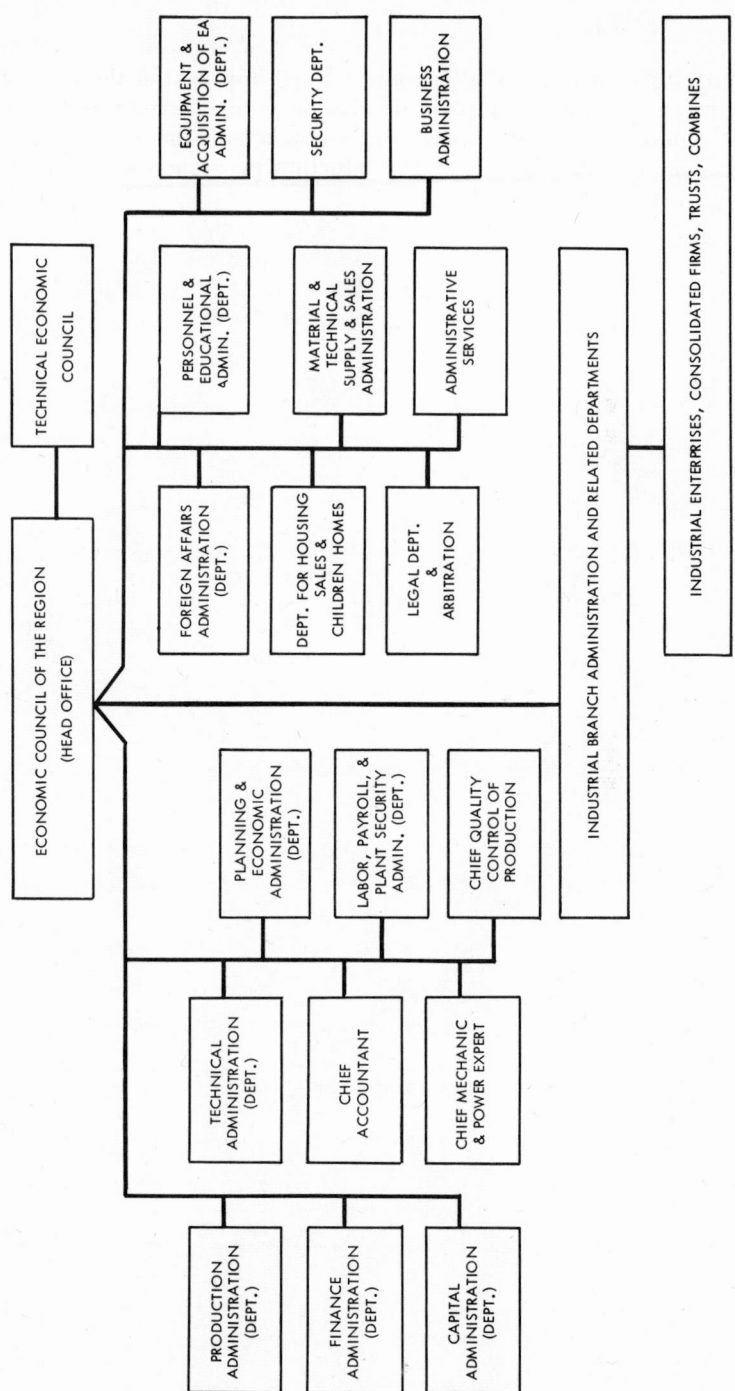

From *Ekonomicheskaya Gazeta* (September 14, 1963), p. 3.

output targets or resource allocation. Formal approval of the enterprise's assortment (product-mix) plan involves a joint decision between the trade organization and the *upravleniye*—the latter being concerned about consistency between the planned production program and resource allocations to the enterprise.

3 • The Soviet
Industrial Enterprise

The Soviet industrial enterprise is some hybrid of an American corporation and an American factory. In many respects it resembles an American firm producing almost entirely for one customer, such as the government, or a large mail-order company. Although production is the major function of the Soviet enterprise, it also undertakes accounting, procurement, finance, distribution (but not selling as such), and in most cases research and development. It operates as an autonomous financial entity having its own bank account(s); and it operates on a profit-and-loss basis, although the earning of profits is not a requisite to survival. Since the Soviet industrial enterprise is owned by the state, the state prescribes the ultimate objectives to be pursued by enterprise management.

In essence and law, the Soviet enterprise is the key unit for the administration of state property and productive resources. It is a juridical person—it can sue and be sued—but it owns none of its assets. The head of the enterprise is the director, and both he and his chief deputies are appointed by superior state organs (the *sovnarkhoz* with the consent and often active participation of local or even central party officials). There is no charge made for the use of the enterprise's capital (for example, interest, rent), since it belongs to the state anyhow. The state is entitled to transfer the enterprise's profits to the state budget except for that portion which the state's regulations or various *ad hoc* decisions permit the enterprise to retain. Moreover, it is within the power of appropriate superior state organs to expand or take away any of the enterprise's assets, if they see fit, without charge or financial compensation.

Enterprise Functions and the Managerial Environment:
An Introduction

If an American industrial manager could be transported magically to the Soviet Union—speaking Russian as well as he does English—and placed in charge of a Soviet enterprise, he would find both similarities and differences as compared to his accustomed environment. Our transplanted manager would engage in the same managerial functions as before, but his degree of authority and independence would be much more limited if he previously was a high-level executive in an American corporation. He would not be confronted with problems of uncertainty resulting from competition, or would he have nearly as much flexibility in running his enterprise. He would, however, be confronted with a great deal of uncertainty in obtaining needed resources to fulfill his production plan, and to overcome this problem our manager may have to assume an entrepreneurial role.

Our transplanted American would be in sole charge of his enterprise in the sense that he would be responsible to those who appoint him and should be obeyed by his subordinates. He would also find a formal chain of command within the enterprise managerial hierarchy. However, the principle of "unity of command" and the authority-level principle are subject in practice to significant limitations. Not only would the enterprise director's hierarchical superiors be liable to issue detailed orders and exert control on every conceivable matter, but he would also have to contend with a number of other inspection and control bodies. The most important of these is the Communist party, which also exercises a controlling influence over most other agencies. The director would be subject to inspection by external party agencies and to direct control by a party committee, headed by a secretary, within the enterprise. Although our director would probably be a party member he would hold no official position on the plant party committee. It would never be completely clear how much direct authority and power the party secretary would have, and the director and the party agent would have to work out their own modus vivendi.

There is also a trade union committee within the enterprise to which certain questions must be referred. Moreover, there are outside banking and financial agencies which inspect and control enterprise transactions.

If our transplanted manager was formerly employed by an American aerospace firm dealing extensively in government contracts he would perhaps adjust better to the Soviet environment of higher directives, capital allocations, inspections, and controls than if he had been a manager of, say, a textile company.

/ Probably the major similarities between the Russian and American managerial job would be in production. If the American were in charge of a ball bearing plant, for example, he would find that the same notions of quality control, intrafactory planning, budgeting, and production scheduling would exist in Russia as in the United States. Industrial products are inert objects responding to the same physical laws regardless of place of production. Such questions as the types of steel going into the final product, the production processes, and the statistical quality controls would be very similar./

The displaced American might also find that many personnel problems were the same. The technically oriented production personnel would tend to have much the same outlook about work. There would be problems of absenteeism, the sticky problem of who gets promoted to foreman, intricate problems of establishing labor utilization norms which would be equitable and would enable coordination among interdependent production processes, the endless problem of finding someone who is technically qualified to work on the new special multipurpose automatic screw machine, and so on.

The philosophy of personnel administration tends to vary somewhat by company in America, whereas it has always been a matter of government policy in the Soviet Union. This policy calls for the use of consultative direction by all managers. The managers, along with local party and union bodies, are supposed to stimulate employee participation and suggestions for improvement during the planning process. Numerous channels of appeal are open to unhappy enterprise employees, as well as plant party and union officials, and this tends to make the manager's job sensitive in terms of human relations. For example, a disgruntled worker or party secretary can complain to industrial, party, or union agencies above the enterprise, or he can even write a letter to newspapers stating his grievance. Hence, the formal chain of command is at times circumvented in Soviet industry, and the enterprise executive's authority may be undermined.

Labor relations would be a relatively simple matter for our transplanted American manager. All enterprise personnel belong to state unions, but strikes are illegal. The Communists argue that since the enterprise is owned by the population as a whole, it makes no sense for a worker to strike against himself. The plant union officials, as well as management, are supposed to be interested in increasing productivity and improving operations. Hence, cooperation between union representatives and management, where both types of leaders work for the state, would be relatively simple. The manager could not squeeze labor unduly, however, since workers have the right to complain or to leave on relatively short notice, and significantly worse labor conditions than the average could lead to extensive labor turnover.

The manager might find himself operating extensive housing developments, day nurseries, cafeterias, recreation facilities, and similar social services for enterprise personnel. Soviet labor typically lives much closer to the factory than in the U.S., often in enterprise controlled housing. This makes the on-the-job and off-the-job lives of Soviet enterprise personnel closely related. In a housing shortage, economy plants which succeed in providing the best housing and amenities for workers may be in a position to attract and maintain the best labor. The factory manager and party secretary might spend considerable time in trying to bargain with higher authorities to obtain still more and better housing for this reason.

Significant differences in management would be quite noticeable to any American who had worked in the marketing area. Instead of worrying about potential sales of the product, in the Soviet environment he would be chiefly concerned with meeting production quotas established in advance. The over-all production quotas, as well as quotas for each major item of the enterprise's product line, would be negotiated between management and appropriate superior authorities. Instead of trying to set as large a quota as possible, our manager would try to obtain an easy one, in order not to run into difficulties later with inability to produce the required quantity. The American would quickly learn that his bonuses and potential promotion possibilities depend largely on fulfilling and overfulfilling the production plan. Output produced would be delivered to the customers listed in the plan, and selling or sales promotion in the American sense would be virtually nonexistent.

/Our manager would find that obtaining needed resources would be a major problem. In his plan, he would indicate the types of materials, components, and equipment needed to fufill his production requirements, and these factor inputs would be produced according to plan by other enterprises. But even if our enterprise was allocated all the needed inputs—which is often not the case—it is likely that some of the supplying enterprises would either send too little, because they were having difficulties with production, or they would send the wrong items./

Since the manager is responsible for production, and since his income and prestige depend so greatly on gross or aggregate production, he would spend much time and energy trying to make sure that his supply sources provided the proper quantities and qualities of supplies. He may have some procurement expeditors on the payroll, who would not be adverse to wining and dining or even bribing suppliers in an effort to wheedle excess (or proper) supplies from them. It might be possible to bury all sorts of business sins in his accounts, and when the pressure was on, as it typically is, it would be tempting to pay off to obtain critical items.

Financial problems would be relatively simple compared to American situations. The plan would give production figures and costs for supplies and labor. Capital allocations from the state budget would be provided to carry out the plan. The only other available source of outside funds would be branches of the state bank. The bank would be willing to make a loan to the enterprise for any project which is expected to have a short-run payback period—usually for two or three years. If our manager was able to keep his costs in line, he would have little difficulty in financing his output. The exchange of funds resulting from the flow of goods among enterprises is controlled through state banking agencies by debiting and crediting the appropriate accounts. Surpluses generated within the enterprise would be turned over to the state, except for that portion (usually small) that the enterprise is entitled to retain. Lacking any form of public participation in ownership, the manager would not have to worry about stock options, fixed rates of profitability, stock market prices for company shares, or any of the types of public financial problems which are so important to American publicly held corporations.

Our manager would find a highly uniform accounting system at any Soviet enterprise he was charged to run. There would also be numerous standardized statistical, financial, and other reports to be compiled and forwarded regularly to appropriate superior agencies. The standardized nature of the data forthcoming from the enterprise level corresponds to the informational requirements of the monolithic Soviet economic system. The amount of paper work required by enterprises in the immense Soviet bureaucracy might at first overwhelm the American executive, unless he had previously worked for an extremely bureaucratic organization.

If our manager were to be placed in charge of a fairly large enterprise, he would likely have at his disposal a sizeable engineering staff and various facilities to be utilized for research and development. Such activities would include product development and improvement, the testing of new equipment and techniques to be introduced in the production process, and so on. The enterprise would also work jointly on research and development projects with one or more outside institutes.

Recessions and depressions would hold little fear for our manager. There would be none, given the tremendous expansionary efforts of the Soviet state. If, for certain reasons, the bearings produced were not needed in as extensive quantities as before, the planning authorities would transfer excess manpower and physical resources to other uses at this or some other enterprise.

Hence the transposed American would be likely to find many differences, as well as similarities, in managing a Soviet industrial enterprise as compared to an American firm. Managers trained as engineers and technicians would probably find the transition easier than those trained in marketing, finance, labor relations, purchasing, or personnel.

An American manager who worked through World War II in the United States would find the present Soviet environment somewhat similar. Resources are controlled in ways resembling the American experience during this period, although resource allocations and central planning are much more comprehensive and pervasive in the Soviet Union. The same kind of production pressure continues interminably in the Soviet economy, for much the same reasons—output is critical, given the Soviet goals, and the state planners are forced to adopt extreme resource allocation measures to expand it. With such pressure enterprise objectives other than total output often tend to be sacrificed.

Enterprise Organizational Structure and the Managerial Staff

Educational and Training Background of Soviet Managers

Soviet industrial enterprises are managed primarily by engineers. It is estimated that 90 per cent or more of all enterprise directors are engineers by training.[1] Other managerial positions within the Soviet enterprise are filled largely by engineers and highly specialized technicians and economists. The job classification of economist in Russia is much more inclusive than in America. A Soviet economist may be engaged in the supervision or performance of any one of a number of "white-collar," business administration activities, which include accounting, finance, planning and budgeting, distribution, procurement, labor and wages, and others.

The management staffs at industrial enterprises are referred to as Engineering-Managerial-Technical-Personnel or *ETMP*. The ETMP grouping encompasses all those persons who are managers regardless of level or type of job. There are nearly two million persons classified in this category.[2] The educational level of ETMP has risen sharply over time, and is well above the national average. Since 1950 the majority of enterprise managerial personnel have been recipients of higher and/or specialized secondary (semiprofessional) educations.[3]

Although Lenin advocated the adoption of F. W. Taylor's principles, techniques, and methods of scientific management in the early 1920's,[4] there is no equivalent to American schools of business or industrial administration. There were a number of schools of industrial management established in Russia after the Communist takeover, but all were closed down by Stalin in the early 1930's. Since that time management has not been perceived as an independent field of knowledge or application in the Soviet Union.

The great majority of Soviet managers possessing a higher education have attended engineering institutes, and to a much lesser extent engineering-economic or economic institutes, rather than universities. All the institutes offer only highly specialized training for the student. A growing number of these institutes are offering courses and specialties in accounting, statistics, finance, organization and planning of production, and various other industrial activities.[5] Such courses are highly descriptive in nature, and virtually no attention is given to management and organization theory, decision-making and problem-solving, human relations, or the behavioral sciences. This holds true, not only for the programs offered by these institutes, but for other types of industrial training programs as well.

It is only lately that the Soviets are again beginning to perceive management as an independent field of research, knowledge, and application. The managerial job in Soviet industry has grown increasingly complex as the economy has developed and expanded and as greater managerial decentralization has occurred. Hence, the Soviets have been forced to recognize that the absence of research and training in the field of management per se is a significant impediment to efficient managerial performance.[6] As a result, there is currently much talk of establishing special schools and programs for management development similar to those found in the U.S.[7] In fact, a team of Soviet experts was sent to study the Harvard Business School program in 1963. A member of this team has recently published a report which contains generally favorable comments about the Harvard program.[8]

Enterprise Organizational Structure

The size and complexity of the managerial apparatus vary, of course, with the extent and nature of enterprise operations. There are many Soviet enterprises having tens of thousands of personnel, such as the Likhachev Motor Works in Moscow. There are also a vast number having only a few dozen or a few hundred employees; for example, small food processing and pottery plants. In recent years there have been thousands of new large-scale enterprises established in the Soviet Union. The average number of personnel at the 16 enterprises in various branches of industry visited by this writer was about 4,000. On pages 60-61 are presented the organization charts of two of these enterprises.

For years Soviet industrial establishments have been organized on a highly standardized basis. The same basic structure has persisted from the early 1930's, when American administrators, engineers, and technicians played a major role in setting up and organizing Soviet factories. Hence, the typical Soviet enterprise even today closely resembles an American factory of the 1920's and early 1930's.

The Soviets have employed a highly monolithic form of organization throughout industry in order to facilitate central planning, control, and direction of economic activity. This organizational arrangement also facilitates the coordination of educational and manpower planning with economic planning. Greater standardization of policies, procedures, methods, and information is made possible by employing a system of parallel departmentalization [9] at all levels in the industrial hierarchy. (Compare, for example, enterprise departmentalization with the organization of regional economic councils indicated on the charts in Chapter 2.) Given this form of organization, it is much easier to derive uniformity of operations and information-reporting through the exertion of functional authority emanating from successively higher organizational lev-

ORGANIZATION CHART — KHARKOV BALL BEARING ENTERPRISE

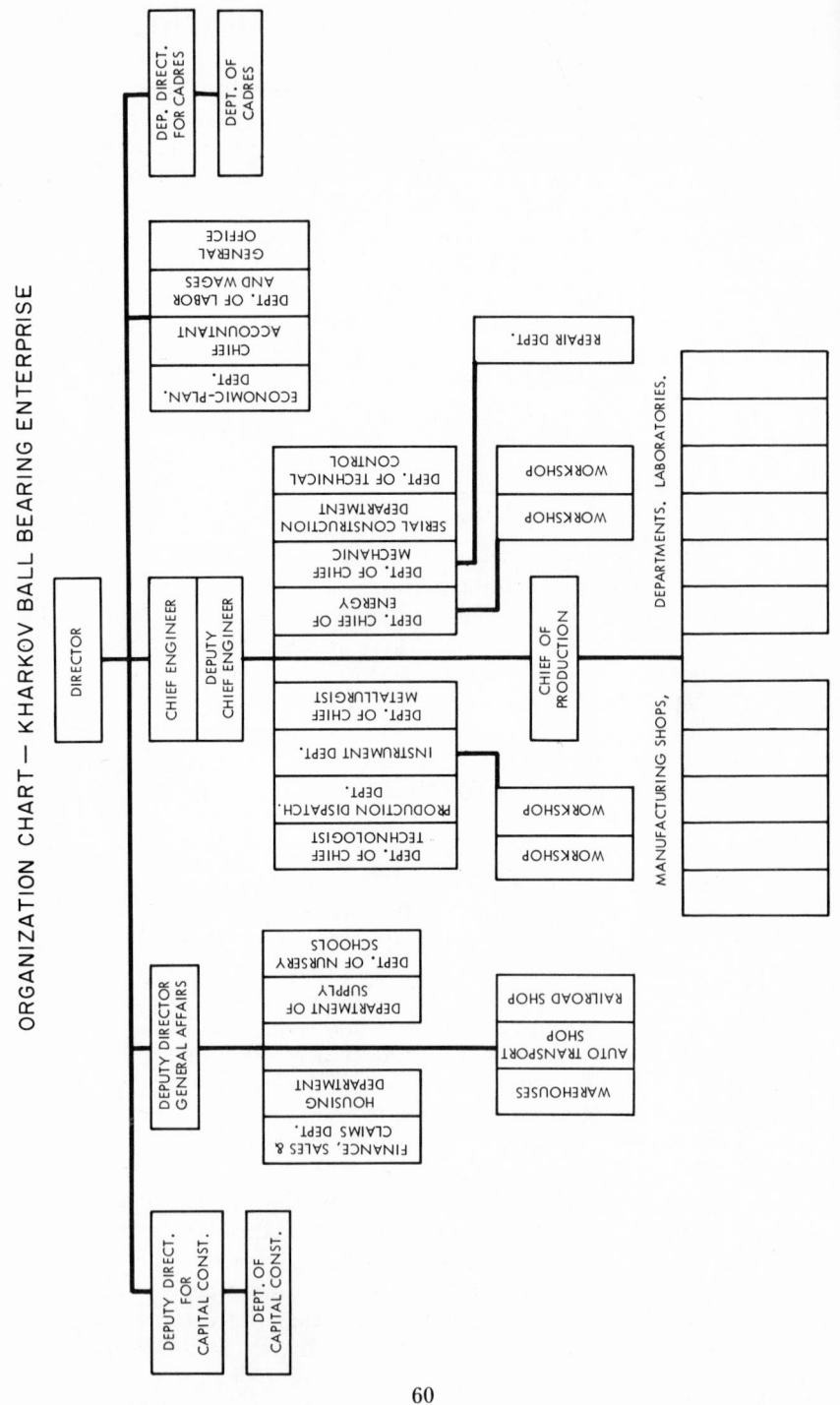

ORGANIZATION CHART— MOSCOW WATCH FACTORY

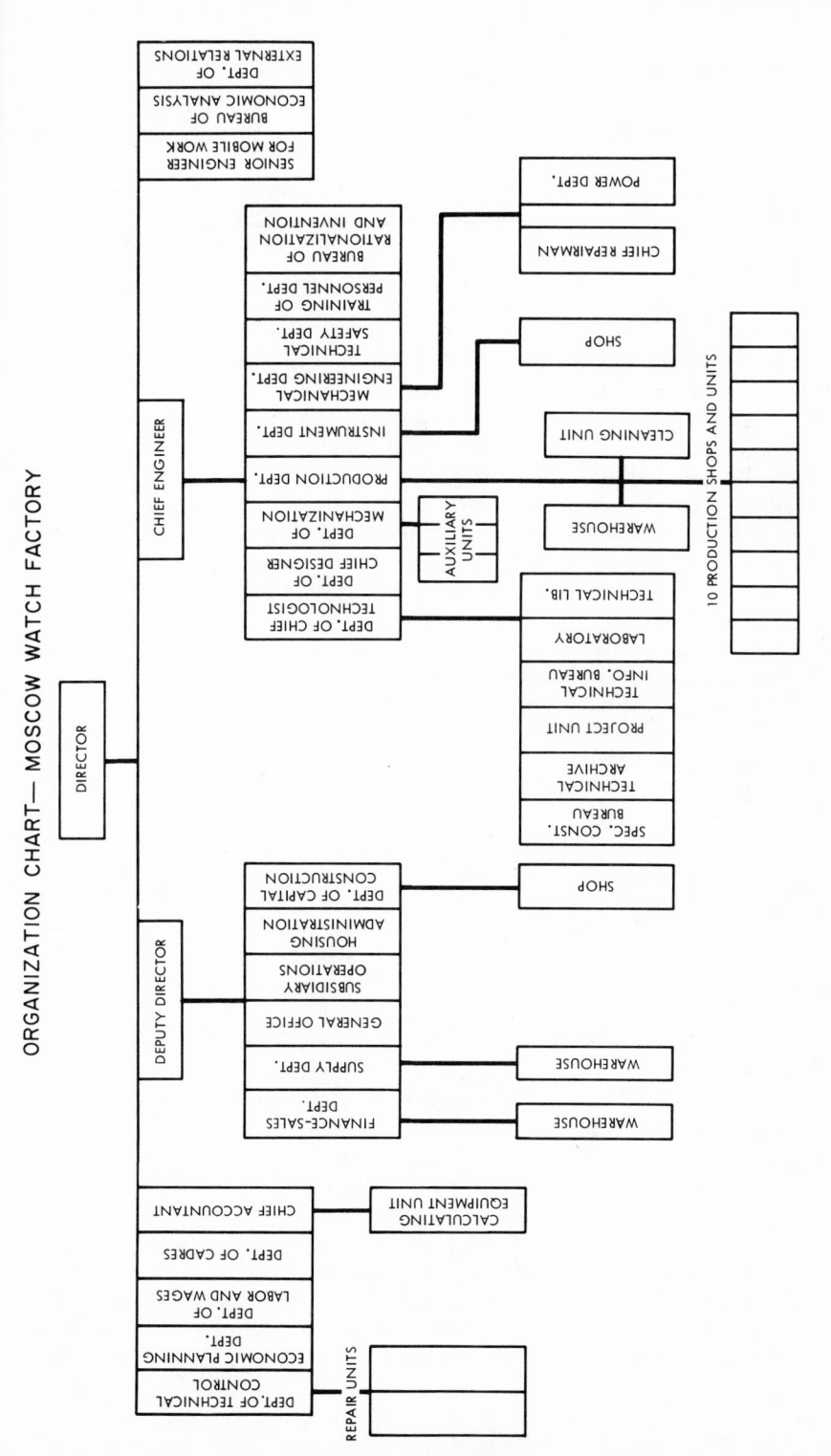

els.[10] Hence, the individual enterprise is subject to functional authority exerted by many higher bodies.

Functional authority and highly standardized organizational structures may yield certain benefits, but the Soviets have given little or no attention to the inefficiencies that are likely under such a system. For example, there tends to be a lack of adjustment to local needs, operating conditions, volume of activities, capacity of executives, and various other factors that vary from enterprise to enterprise. Yet the Soviets make virtually no use of organizational theory and related objective guidelines for organizing and grouping activities.[11]

What variations there have been traditionally in organizational structure among Soviet enterprises have stemmed chiefly from differences in size and technology. The latter point relates to whether a plant is engaged primarily in mass, serial, or custom-built production. Branch of industry as such has not been a significant determining factor. For example, this writer surveyed both a ball bearing and textile establishment engaged in mass production, and both had basically similar organizational structures. It has only been in the past few years that enterprise managers have been granted greater powers in organizing their activities; we shall return to this point in the next chapter.

Within the Soviet industrial enterprise there are several strata of managerial personnel. The same notions of line and staff, service departments, functional authority, and chain of command that exist in American firms exist in Soviet organization. As was pointed out earlier, the enterprise is headed by a director, and his key deputy is the chief engineer. The head of production generally reports to the chief engineer, and under him are the shop and section chiefs. Within the manufacturing shops and large sections there are assistant chiefs, foremen, assistant foremen, and the heads of work teams. In large multiplant enterprises, the heads of the various plants report to the director or chief engineer of the enterprise as a whole. If a given Soviet enterprise has more than one plant, rarely are they located in more than one city.

The organization of a subsidiary plant, shop, or large section is like a microcosm of the enterprise itself, with its head acting like a microcosm director. Even though it may appear that managerial authority is fairly decentralized at the subsidiary plant or shop level, the heads of these units are usually subject to a great deal of functional authority exerted by higher level administrators within the enterprise. For example, such authority is generally exerted over shop planners, labor normers, cost accountants, maintenance crews, and so forth.

Closely akin to production managers are those in charge of various other departments, bureaus, and servicing units, most of them common to American factories. For example, there are typically drafting, design, product development, quality control, fuel and power, and maintenance and repair units, laboratory facilities, technological departments, warehouses, and so on.

There are also a number of "white-collar" departments or units headed by managers—typically, planning, accounting, finance, personnel, labor and wages, sales and delivery, supply (purchasing), capital construction (investment), transportation, and housing. The managers of major "white-collar" departments report to the director or to a deputy director for economic or commercial affairs. The majority of these managers are recipients of higher or specialized secondary educations in economics and/or various business administration fields. However, in many instances these positions are filled by persons having engineering backgrounds.

Soviet enterprise managers spend a great deal of time in committee meetings and conferences within the enterprise; we will return to this subject in Chapter 10.

The success of the director and his enterprise is largely dependent on the chief engineer, the head of the planning and supply departments, and the chief accountant. The director is most likely to consult with and take with him on critical occasions these four executives.

The chief engineer is highly familiar with the over-all production operations and actual plant capacity. The head of planning is in the best position to negotiate for a "favorable" plan since his department serves as the coordinator and focal point for the flow and analysis of data during the planning process. His department also maintains a check over plan fulfillment, and its staff provides the current information on the basis of which management knows where it stands and what alternatives are open to it. Hence, the chief of planning is in a key position to detect incipient difficulties and to make recommendations for dealing with them.

The supply department prepares the crucial supply plan for the enterprise, engages in contract negotiations, and controls incoming deliveries. Failure to anticipate needs for materials and components may involve the enterprise in difficulties. Perhaps even more important is the task of seeing that needed supplies are actually delivered on time and in the proper quantities and qualities. The supply executive is often in the best position to press for additional resource allocations and to obtain critically needed items through various legal, semilegal, or illegal means.

The chief accountant prepares certain crucial quarterly and annual reports on which the fate of enterprise management depends in significant measure. He can shuffle his accounts in an attempt to make enterprise results appear more favorable. For this reason he is a close confidant of the director in matters that may involve a brush with the law.

In recent years art or assortment departments have been established at a great many enterprises engaged in the production of consumer goods. This department is comprised of designers, stylists, artists, and/or fashion experts who are responsible for initiating new products and improving old ones. Departmental personnel generally spend a few weeks each year on "creative leave" visiting retail outlets, special conferences, and the houses of fashion engaged in consumer demand analysis. Some of them go to other regions where the enterprise's products are sold and even to other countries to gather new product ideas. As a result of these activities, sample products are prepared. The head of this department generally reports to the director or chief engineer. Enterprises having a department of this type also usually have an artistic council subordinate to one of the above two executives. This council consists of key art department specialists, as well as various other enterprise personnel. The council makes recommendations to management on what new products should be produced.

Soviet enterprises have a department or bureau of technical information whose head reports to the director or chief engineer. This unit screens new ideas and employee suggestions relating to improvements in enterprise operations. It channels worthy proposals to the chief engineer for further study. It is also concerned with the exchange of information with other enterprises and obtains information from various domestic and foreign publications.

A May 1959 decree established a "bureau of rationalization and invention" at all Soviet industrial enterprises. The head of this bureau is subordinate to the chief engineer or his deputy, the chief technologist. The bureau estimates costs and savings that would result from the implementation of employee suggestions. Suggestions are first channeled to the chief engineer or chief technologist by the department of technical information. After they are properly screened, they are submitted to this bureau for further analysis before a decision regarding implementation is made by one of the above two managers.

Since 1961 a department or bureau of economic analysis has been established at most larger enterprises. It analyzes past performance, trying to find unutilized reserves and other areas of potential improvements in enterprise operations. At some establishments this unit is part of the economic planning department; at others, its head reports to the director or a deputy director for economic affairs.

Ultimate Enterprise Objectives: The Desiderata of Enterprise Performance [12]

The ultimate or highest objectives to be pursued by the Soviet industrial enterprise were briefly outlined in Chapter 1. These objectives can be broken down into a number of statements, each one representing a basic desideratum of enterprise performance. In this connection, enterprise operations should be planned and carried out in the following manner:

1. Quantity of output should be as large as possible.
2. This output should consist of items required by customers and should be of the highest possible quality in light of available resources.
3. Output should be delivered to customers in accordance with a predetermined time schedule.
4. Material, other supply, and labor inputs should be as small as possible.
5. Plant fixed assets should be utilized economically to the fullest practicable degree during a prescribed number of shifts.
6. Physical and monetary working capital should be as small as is practically possible but should allow for some flexibility in operations.
7. Cost of production, which consists of all factor inputs expressed in value terms and all other indirect production expenses, should be at the minimum necessary for fulfilling the production program.
8. Short-run activities and decisions should not be detrimental or lead to adverse consequences in the long run, but rather should enhance future operations and further the future needs of society.

Since the above objectives or desiderata are not operational, a system of interconnected indices (targets), which constitutes the enterprise operating plan, is utilized to translate them into concrete tasks. The indices are reduced, for the most part, to quantitative terms stated in physical, monetary, or time units of measure. The system of plan indices is also used for control and evaluation during the related operating period.

The enterprise plan should indicate the best over-all projected course of action for achieving the desiderata; an implicit condition is that the indices be mutually consistent in terms of factor inputs, costs, and product-mix. If the enterprise receives a substantially deficient plan in terms of actual capabilities and resource needs, the mere fulfillment of such a plan would not yield an over-all satisfactory level of desiderata attainment. If the over-all plan is sound and is adhered to during the related operating period, a favorable degree of desiderata attainment would result. An implicit condition here is that the enterprise be in timely possession of resources stipulated in the plan. Shortages or excess amounts of certain resources imply excesses or shortages of others, thus preventing the efficient or full utilization of the entire production input factor-mix. For example, if the enterprise finds itself short of certain new materials, some equipment and labor may stand idle; or if it has excess machine tools some may remain idle, even though manpower and materials are fully utilized.

How well Soviet industry as a whole functions and performs during a given period of time depends essentially on three paramount interrelated conditions:

1. How well the ultimate objectives of each enterprise are translated into operating plans;
2. how well the myriad enterprise plans are integrated into the comprehensive national economic plan;
3. how well the managers of each enterprise carry out their respective operating plans.

Let us now turn our attention to the individual enterprise plan, focusing on those indices which serve to translate the ultimate enterprise objectives into operational tasks.

The Enterprise Plan

Each Soviet enterprise, as well as the economy as a whole, has a long-range plan broken down into annual subdivisions. During the 1959-65 period there has been a seven-year plan, and for the 1966-70 period a five-year plan is to be compiled for the economy and for each industrial establishment.

The long-term enterprise plan contains targets for aggregate output, labor productivity, and cost reduction. The annual divisions of this plan indicate the targets in terms of percentage improvements over the preceding year. These targets are supposed to be arrived at by taking into account the measures outlined in the plan of technical development which is a major section of the long-range plan. The technical development plan indicates planned yearly capital investment allocations from the state budget. It also contains a list of measures to be undertaken during a given year, such as the introduction of new technology, increases in automation and mechanization, plant modernization, equipment replacement, and other major organizational and technical improvements. If the enterprise engages in product development, the plan may also contain certain directives in this area.

The targets and other measures stipulated in the related annual subdivision of the enterprise's long-term plan, in conjunction with adjustments for performance achieved to date, are supposed to serve as the framework for establishing the annual operating plan. In practice, however, the long-range plan is not operational and the formulation of the annual plan essentially starts from scratch each year, taking only past performance as the point of departure. Operational targets, other operating tasks, and resource allocations for a given enterprise are determined for the most part in the annual plan. The annual plan is then broken down into quarterly plans. At many enterprises it is the quarterly plan that is the true operating document, since the detailed product-mix is only spelled out on a quarterly basis.

The annual operating plan of the Soviet enterprise with its quarterly subdivisions is called the *tekhpromfinplan* (technical-industrial-financial plan). This document is comprised of a number of interrelated sectional plans which in total project the course of enterprise operations in great detail. Each sectional plan contains a number of subindices (building blocks) which culminate in aggregate indices or targets. The over-all plan is summarized by a cluster of basic aggregate targets which are common to all industrial enterprises. Below is presented the summary plan indices for two enterprises surveyed. These indices are similar from year to year.

Data on *Tekhpromfinplan* Indices

Actual basic plan indices—of the "Sverdlov" Moscow Silk Plant, 1961

Index	Unit of Measure
1. Output of main types of production in physical terms	thousand meters
2. New items first manufactured in the current plan (itemized by product)	" "
3. Marketable output in current wholesale prices of the enterprise	thousand rubles
a. Production in which the enterprise specializes	" "
b. Other production, manufactured for delivery to other (producing) enterprises	" "
4. Gross output in the enterprise's wholesale prices of July 1, 1955	" "
5. Total number of industrial personnel	persons
Number of workers (*rabochiye*)	"
6. Total fund of wages for industrial personnel	thousand rubles
Fund of wages for workers	" "
7. Average annual wage of industrial personnel	rubles
Average annual wage of workers	"
8. Output of gross production in the enterprise's wholesale prices of July 1, 1955, per one industrial employee	"
9. Total cost of production of all marketable output	thousand rubles
10. Outlay per one ruble of marketable production in current prices	kopeks
11. Unit-cost for basic items of production	rubles and kopeks
12. Profit from sale of marketable output	thousand rubles
13. Percentage of profitability	%
14. Prescribed working capital at year's end	thousand rubles
15. Speed of turnover of working capital	days
16. Technical production indices	
Coefficient of mechanization of the production processes	%
Coefficient of automation of the production processes	"
Coefficient of mechanical power of labor	"
Coefficient of shift work of the enterprise	"
Capital investment	thousand rubles

Data on *Tekhpromfinplan* Indices (*Cont.*)

Basic indices for enterprises under the machine-building branch administration of the Kharkov Economic Council 1960-1961 (obtained from a ball bearing plant)

Index	Unit of Measure
1. Gross output in (1955) wholesale prices	thousand rubles
2. Marketable output in (current) wholesale prices	" "
3. Number of total industrial personnel	persons
Number of workers (*rabochiye*)	"
4. Number of nonindustrial personnel	"
5. Total personnel of the enterprise	"
6. Fund of wages for all industrial personnel	thousand rubles
Fund of wages for workers	" "
7. Fund of wages for nonindustrial personnel	" "
8. Fund of wages for total personnel of the enterprise	" "
9. Gross output per one industrial employee	rubles
10. Shop overheads	thousand rubles
11. Shop overheads per 1,000 rubles of gross output	rubles
12. Shop overheads as % of wages in production	%
13. Enterprise overheads	thousand rubles
14. Enterprise overheads per 1,000 rubles of gross output	rubles
15. Enterprise overheads as % of wages in production	%
16. Total cost of production of all marketable output	thousand rubles
17. Expenditures per one ruble of marketable production	kopeks
18. Per cent cost reduction	%
19. Current repairs	thousand rubles
20. Capital repairs out of amortization fund	" "
21. Capital investment: total	" "
Capital investment for industrial construction	" "
22. Profit	" "
23. Turnover tax	" "

In addition to the above basic indices, each enterprise has certain physical assortment indices depending on the nature of its output. There are also usually a list of technical production indices similar to those at the silk factory. Each enterprise also formulates a plan of material and technical supplies and a detailed *orgtekhplan*.

The planning process within a Soviet enterprise closely resembles that of a typical American factory. The same problems of intraorganizational budgeting and bargaining for resources emerge, and many departmental conflicts are likely to arise, particularly when the enterprise as a whole is confronted with significant resource scarcities.

At this time a brief discussion of the content of the *tekhpromfinplan*, and the manner by which ultimate enterprise objectives are translated into plan indices, will be presented. The following chapter deals with the authority of enterprise management in the formulation and fulfillment of the plan, and Chapter 5 is concerned with the over-all planning process in Soviet industry.

Production Plan

The production plan is the keystone of the *tekhpromfinplan*. Total planned production is determined by taking into account estimated available plant capacity and the number of shifts during which equipment will be utilized. Aggregate planned output is summarized by two indices expressed in rubles—these are gross output and marketable output.

The index of gross output expresses the entire planned production program in constant wholesale prices. It includes completed production, subcontracting services performed for other organizations, the manufacture of auxiliary items used in the production of basic goods, and net changes in the value of goods in process for the period in question. The constant prices are set by the planners at infrequent intervals and are based on the average cost of production of all those enterprises producing the item in question plus a profit markup (typically 3 to 5 per cent). Most constant commodity prices were last established in 1955, although some price revisions have been undertaken during the 1962-63 period. Constant prices are not set for every specific item; rather they are based on representative items or units of measure corresponding to a given class of output. For example, a square meter of cloth, regardless of its actual specific attributes, is likely to have one constant price. The same would generally be true for many types of leather shoes, wool suits, a ton of steel, or a certain class of machinery. By using constant prices, time comparisons of the growth of output can be made, and this is deemed of prime importance to the Soviets. However, such comparisons may not be particularly meaningful if the enterprise's product-mix does not remain fairly stable over time.

The index of marketable production (also referred to as merchandise or commodity output) represents only finished production and completed services performed for customers. The index is expressed in "current" wholesale factory prices, also called transfer prices. This is the price the producer receives from customers, and the cost of production and profit are measured in terms of these prices. Constant and transfer prices may be identical at the beginning of a given base period, but they tend to diverge—often substantially—in level and internal structure over time. Transfer prices are supposed to be reduced at intervals, as and when related production costs are reduced, but this is seldom the case. The factory wholesale price and the retail price for a given consumer good are never the same, since a turnover tax plus distributor margins are included in the latter. Retail prices are of no concern to the producer. They are fixed to clear the market at the retail level both in aggregate terms and for each item.

Both aggregate gross and marketable output are expressed in value terms and as a percentage relationship to the preceding period. Marketable output may also be expressed in physical units of measure (for example, tons of coal, steel, machinery, or leather and square meters of cloth).

The physical assortment or product-mix of the enterprise is supposed to conform to customer needs. The production plan also contains a set of subtargets indicating the quantities of the different types of goods to be produced. The principal items or major product groups are usually expressed in physical and value indices. Other output may be expressed only in rubles. In such cases, the monetary figure may be arrived at by taking the price of a representative item or unit of measure for a given class of output and multiplying it by the total units.

The over-all production program is broken down into assortment classifications. The detailed specifications of the annual assortment plan vary according to the nature of the enterprise's product line. Certain major types of output such as standard machine tools or components may be specified in detail as to general size, type, or grade. This is the case at several of the machinery and ball bearing plants surveyed. Nonstandardized output and certain goods of lesser importance are indicated in tons, and in some cases only in rubles. The detailed product-mix is determined, for the most part, in the quarterly plans.

For most consumer goods producers, particularly where demand for their output is difficult to anticipate a year in advance, the annual plan would not contain a detailed product-mix breakdown in terms of varieties, styles, designs, colors, and so on. The physical indices are usually stated in broad terms. For example, a shoe factory has the total number of pairs of shoes to be produced during the planned year broken down only by men's, women's, and children's shoes; each broad assortment classification is summarized by total pairs. A silk producer has physical output targets in square meters by broad assortment classifications. At all the consumer goods enterprises, surveyed value indices are also used to summarize product groupings and output of lesser importance. The detailed product-mix at most consumer goods enterprises is determined on the basis of quarterly or semiannual contract orders established with trade officials. Hence, in such cases the annual plan would not really be operational.

Items to be produced for the first time by any enterprise would be assimilated into the production plan. They would usually be indicated by some physical unit of measure and by value indices. The wholesale factory price for a new product is initially established on a temporary basis, and this price becomes the constant price. Eventually a new transfer (current) price would also be established, and it would tend to be lower than the constant price since production costs tend to decrease over time.

The enterprise production to be sold during the planned period is tied to a series of delivery schedules. The quantities of the different items to be delivered, and the services to be completed by specific dates, are indicated by customer. The delivery schedules are actually part of the sales plan, which is sometimes referred to as the plan of cooperative deliveries.

A basic desideratum of enterprise performance calls for the production of the highest quality of goods possible with assigned resources. Most types of output are supposed to conform to prescribed standards of technical quality. Products are required to meet the minimum standards in order to gain the approval of quality control inspectors both within and outside the producing enterprise. Many producers of consumer goods, including most of those surveyed, have, in addition to technical standards governing many items, quality indices representing grades of output. In this connection the production program is divided into different grades of output—first, second, third—first grade being the highest quality. Higher grades are supposed to command a higher selling price; but, because of defective pricing, this is not always the case. Quality gradings take into account such factors as texture, durability, thickness, and flaws.

Plan of Utilization of Plant and Equipment

This sectional plan determines total estimated plant capacity, taking into account anticipated condition of existing equipment and capacity of new equipment to be installed for use during the planned period. In general, there is no target established by the planners which directly indicates utilization of plant capacity. If superior authorities desire that total planned output be established in accordance with maximum practicable planned utilization for a given number of shifts and if the production target is achieved with substantial idle capacity, this would imply shortcomings in the plan. It would also indicate that the desiderata relating to quantity of production and plant utilization have not been adequately achieved.

Plan of Labor and Wages

This plan indicates total manpower needs (excluding administrative personnel) required to carry out the production plan. Manpower needs are estimated by taking the planned production program as given and then applying labor utilization norms to all the functions necessary to fulfill the plan. The total work force is divided into a number of basic classifications according to occupations or activities performed. The corresponding plan of wages (payroll) is derived by utilizing average wage rates once the breakdown of the planned labor force is determined. The index of total manpower needs (in bodies) and the total related payroll figure are constraints within which the planned production program should be achieved. A basic desideratum is that the production program be fulfilled with a minimum of labor resources, and hence, at a minimum cost of manpower.

Index of Labor Productivity

This index is determined by dividing gross output by total number of industrial personnel to indicate gross output for one industrial employee. The labor productivity target is typically expressed as a percentage increase over the previous period.

Several Soviet industrial officials and economists interviewed asserted that the index of labor productivity is a meaningful measure of the utilization of fixed assets. Yet it is extremely difficult to isolate the impact of equipment utilization on labor productivity because labor productivity results are dependent on many other factors—for example, the introduction of new technology, improvements in production processes, organization, managerial and employee skills, and the actual product-mix produced.

Plan of Material and Technical Supply

This plan is also compiled by taking the planned production program as given. Quantities of basic and auxiliary materials as well as other supplies required to fulfill the production program are determined on the basis of input utilization norms. By applying input norms to the assortment plan and related required operations, the quantities of the different resources needed are categorized by commodity groups. This plan indicates not only supply inputs needed to fulfill the production plan but also planned inventories for flexibility. Inventory norms for most commodities are based on percentage relationships. Approved material and supply indices represent resource allocations to the enterprise for the planned year. They are in essence constraints within which the planned production program should be fulfilled. The direct supply inputs, as well as related physical working capital, should be at the minimum necessary to fulfill the production plan.

Cost of Production Plan

There is an index for total planned cost of production, which takes into account (1) total enterprise payroll, (2) total cost of materials and supplies used in production, and (3) general and overhead expenditures including administrative expenses and depreciation charges. A basic desideratum is that the production plan be achieved with minimum costs.

The most significant cost target for evaluation purposes is the cost of production per one ruble of marketable output. This index is derived by dividing the total cost of all marketable production by the total value of this production. The resulting target is expressed in kopeks (100 kopeks = 1 ruble) and as a percentage reduction relationship to the preceding period.

Plan of Technical Development and Orgtekhplan

The long-range plan of technical development, discussed briefly earlier, broadly indicates the direction of technical progress and product development for the enterprise. The technical and organizational improvement measures outlined in a given annual subdivision in this plan are incorporated into the annual *orgtekhplan* (plan of organizational and technical measures). The *orgtekhplan* is a basic section of the *tekhpromfinplan*. This plan takes into account anticipated capital investment, installation of new technology, and all other planned improvement measures, including employee suggestions, to be implemented during the planned year. The plan is supposed to estimate the impact that all of these measures will have on the basic *tekhpromfinplan* indices. Those measures requiring fairly sizeable capital expenditures or significant alterations in fixed assets are classified as major or large-scale innovations. Employee suggestions for the most part relate to improvements in existing operations and do not usually entail sizeable capital outlays; they are classified as minor innovations.

Until 1959 the *orgtekhplan* was typically worked out after the basic *tekhpromfinplan* indices were determined. The elaboration of the *orgtekhplan* was only undertaken in an attempt to obtain enough economies and other improvements to fulfill the key targets. Since 1959, state policy dictates that full account should be taken of all potential improvement measures at the same time that the basic plan indices are worked out. That is, the *orgtekhplan* measures should be integrated with the other sectional plans during the planning process rather than after the key targets are approved.

The annual plan of technical development may also include product development and/or improvement directives indicating research, design, or experimental tasks to be performed.

Short Run and Long Run

The measures incorporated into the technical development and *orgtekhplans* may have both short-term and long-run implications. Some of these measures may improve enterprise results and benefit society during the planned year, whereas others may not lead to significant internal or external benefits until future years. A basic desideratum requires that a balance between short- and long-run considerations be achieved during a given planned year. Therefore, innovation measures should be undertaken—even when there may not be any related short-term improvements—if they are likely to yield substantial future gains. It is difficult to translate this desideratum into concrete operating terms, except perhaps by stipulating time schedules for carrying out specific projects or tasks. But the enterprise plan should be established with this ultimate objective in mind.

Financial Plan

This plan translates all other sections of the *tekhpromfinplan* into monetary terms. It consists of a complete breakdown of revenues and expenses and also presents a breakdown of the sources and uses of funds for the planned year. The financial plan contains a number of summary indices.

There are total monetary working capital indices for each quarter, and at many enterprises working capital at the year's end is indicated as well. At any point in time, enterprising working capital may be held in several forms—cash on desposit in banks, finished goods, work in process, inventories of materials. When the total monetary figures are established, the various working capital needs are projected and aggregated. A basic desideratum states that monetary working capital should be at the practical minimum to carry out the *tekhpromfinplan*.

There is also a profit target which is determined by deducting all planned operating expenses from planned sales revenue. The index of profit may at times approximate a reverse expression of the cost per one ruble of marketable output index. However, the two rarely coincide since not all the marketable output may be for sale during the planned period, and there are likely to be certain revenues and expenses not related to marketable output. The profit target is expressed in total rubles and as a percentage relationship to the previous period. Enterprises operating at a planned loss would of course have loss rather than profit indices. The profit target is in essence a residual derived only after the other plan indices are established. Profit maximization cannot really be considered an ultimate objective because of the price structure. Moreover, profit results do not generally provide an effective measure of efficiency. Nevertheless, the state desires enterprises to earn as much profit as possible—by overfulfilling the profit target—since enterprise profits are a key source of funds for future industrial expansion.

The financial plan also contains an index of profitability. This index is determined by dividing total enterprise profit by total cost of production. Unlike the conventional Western rate-of-return computation, the Soviet profitability figure virtually ignores the cost of building and equipping the enterprise. The Soviet index of profitability does not provide a meaningful measure of capital utilization, nor, for that matter, any other meaningful measure of efficiency.

Plan Indices Requiring Higher Approval

Not all of the indices of the enterprise's annual and quarterly plans require higher approval. In most instances superior authorities approve only the following:

1. Total gross and marketable output.
2. Major items of the product-mix, the specificity in each case depending on the type of item. For a great many goods the detailed specifications per se are not subject to higher approval; but the over-all delivery contracts that indicate detailed product-mix are. In such instances the delivery dates and detailed specifications are negotiated between supplier and customer. Minor items are typically approved only in aggregate money terms. The enterprise's assortment plan is broken down by items according to the level of higher approval required—central, republican, or regional.
3. Quality grades of output by proportions require approval for certain types of consumer goods.
4. Total cost of production and cost per one ruble of marketable production.
5. Labor productivity.
6. Total wage fund.
7. Resource limit indices—capital investment, supplies by commodity groupings including planned inventories, total manpower, aggregate monetary working capital.
8. At times, certain technical development, product innovation, and/or other major improvement tasks.
9. Profit and profitability which are actually automatic once the other indices are approved.

The above indices, once formally approved by higher authorities, are referred to as "control figures."

Control Figures Considered as Maxima or Minima

The control figures are supposed to be considered as maxima and minima; hence the enterprise should try to better the operating targets with given resources. For example, if possible quantity of production targets should be exceeded, cost per one ruble of marketable output should be below plan and labor productivity should be greater than planned. The control figures should represent the minimum degree of desiderata attainment possible, based on an honest appraisal of enterprise capabilities. However, the state utilizes the device of maxima and minima control figures since precision planning is not possible. Unforeseen reserves may accumulate and possibilities may arise during the course of plan fulfillment enabling the enterprise to perform better than planned with assigned resources.

One may be inclined to conclude from the above discussion that the Soviet manager has little authority or independence over the operations of his enterprise. This may appear to be the situation in light of all the constraints placed on him by the plan; however, this is far from being the case, in reality, as we shall see in the next chapter.

4 • Authority and Independence
of Enterprise Management

The management of the Soviet industrial enterprise does not possess any ultimate authority per se, since its decisions are either subject to higher approval or can be rescinded by superior authorities. In practice, however, management, by delegating authority, can significantly influence the enterprise's plans, operations, and results. Moreover, Soviet enterprise managers tend to have more independence than one might expect.

Since the mid-1950's Soviet managers have acquired greater authority and independence over enterprise activities and, as will be discussed in Chapter 12, they will probably acquire even more in the future. As a result the managerial functions have taken on—and will continue to take on—greater significance at the industrial enterprise level. /

Functions and Authority of Management: An Historical Sketch [1]

The Managerial Job Until the Mid-1950's

Until the latter part of the 1950's planning at the Soviet enterprise was largely confined to implementing plans and policies prescribed in considerable detail by superior authorities. Enterprise management's planning job was essentially one of intrafactory planning—the distribution of planned tasks among subordinates and the undertaking of various technical computations—although it could often influence the content of the over-all plan by bargaining with higher authorities. A multitude of detailed plan indices—factor input and product prices, material, labor and equipment utilization norms, and so forth—were approved and often also established by superior agencies. Most of the materials, components, equipment, and other supplies allocated to the enterprise had their specifications spelled out in substantial detail by higher authorities. The same was true of the enterprise's product-mix. Moreover, product and process innovation tasks were, for the most part, initiated and prescribed by superior bodies.

Higher authorities controlled enterprise plan fulfillment in great detail. Most component elements of the enterprise's comprehensive system of accounts were subject to both higher approval and control, and management had little authority over sources and uses of funds.

The organizational structure of the enterprise was also prescribed in considerable detail; local managers had authority only over the organization of certain minor servicing activities and work brigades. Formal authority relationships within the enterprise hierarchy were rigidly dictated by the state.

The philosophy of personnel administration in Soviet industry has been and still is a matter of governmental policy. This policy calls for employee participation in planning and decision-making and for the use of consultative direction by all managers. For many years each enterprise has had a suggestion system enabling personnel to put forth proposals for improvement in operations and to be rewarded for those suggestions implemented. Enterprise managers are charged with motivating subordinates to act in the best interests of the state at all times and with constantly improving the skills and abilities of subordinates through careful appraisal and training. Moreover, they must be concerned with the general safety, welfare, and education of personnel.

In the past, particularly during the Stalin era, personnel problems, including staffing and direction, were not of significant concern to enterprise managers or the state. The labor force was in effect a captive audience; there was little freedom to change jobs. There was surplus manpower since the rate of capital investment had not yet outstripped the labor supply. Local managers needed to pay little attention to recruiting, selecting, appraising, or maintaining personnel. In most instances employees were assigned to enterprises by superior organs. Training was also not very important because the level of technology employed and the nature of enterprise operations were not yet very complex.

The government prescribed in detail the types of rewards and penalties to be used in motivating and disciplining personnel; local managers had only a modicum of leeway in their implementation. Monetary incentives served quite effectively as inducements since the physiological needs of the labor force were not being substantially fulfilled. In practice, there was a widespread tendency by managers to use autocratic direction techniques, not only because of their personality characteristics, but also because subordinates, with a relatively low level of education and skills, often had little worthwhile advice to offer.

Enlargement of the Managerial Job

By the mid-1950's it became increasingly obvious to the Soviet rulers that industrial overcentralization, resulting from the concentration of decision-making powers and initiative in the hands of relatively few high-level administrators, was leading to much inefficiency and waste, as well as to inadequate innovation, in the increasingly complex and expanding Soviet economy. New industries had evolved—chemical, electronics, various consumer goods, new types of machinery, and so on—output was now much more diverse; technology, production processes, and market requirements were all becoming increasingly complex. The problems of efficiently combining factor inputs and securing proper product specifications were becoming more severe. Innovation through local initiative relating to products and processes was now deemed essential in order to raise productivity and satisfy the wants of a population growing restless with shoddy consumer goods. In general, the task of planning, organizing, directing, and controlling national economic activity now required much greater precision. This in turn called for greater managerial initiative and ability at the enterprise level.

Since 1955 the authority and independence of enterprise management have been increased to meet changing conditions, and the manager's job has grown increasingly more difficult.

With a 1955 government decree extending the powers of enterprise directors, the micromanagerial job began to take on new significance. An April 1956 "liberalization" edict repealed an earlier law tying people to their jobs and also gave local managers more authority over the recruitment and selection of personnel (with the notable exception of new graduates from educational institutions). In May 1957, Soviet industry was reorganized from a highly centralized and concentrated branch-of-industry ministerial setup to a territorial system of industrial management. The reorganization served to deconcentrate and somewhat decentralize economic decision-making, authority, and initiative to lower levels in the industrial hierarchy. In this process, enterprise management also acquired greater authority and independence. At the end of 1957 it was decreed that local managers would thereafter take the initiative in proposing and compiling enterprise plans each year.

A number of economic reforms adopted in November 1962, which are discussed at various points in this book, have not significantly changed the enterprise manager's job, nor his authority.[2] However, since the end of 1962 a growing number of enterprises have been extended the right to experiment somewhat with their organizational structures and in the use of various incentives for motivating personnel. More will be said about this in later chapters.

All of these reforms have served to enlarge the micromanagerial job to its present scope. Before we go into greater detail about the authority of enterprise managers under present conditions, a general summary is warranted here.

The Managerial Job Under Present Conditions

Major decisions regarding what to produce, how much of each item, for whom to produce, and even how to produce are still made primarily by superior agencies. Higher authorities still approve a number of key enterprise plan indices. Most major types of supplies and equipment, as well as the bulk of financial resources, are still allocated to the enterprise, but now largely in aggregate terms. In general, the number of targets, tasks, and other plan indices subject to higher approval and control has been substantially reduced. At present the enterprise has greater authority and independence over the establishment of factor input utilization norms and cost estimates. Local managers can now also directly procure and sell many services and minor commodities independently. They also have somewhat greater independence over sources and uses of funds, prices, and the adjustment of the enterprise plan to unforeseen changing conditions.

In numerous instances enterprise managers now work out detailed product-mix specifications directly with customers and suppliers. In the consumer goods sector the industrial enterprise plays a much larger role in marketing research and demand analysis, although these activities are still primarily the responsibility of the Ministry of Trade organizations. The emphasis on marketing activities has been precipitated and intensified in recent years because of growing consumer resistance to shoddy goods. Having at least one pair of reasonably adequate shoes, the consumer is reluctant to buy an inferior product.

Local managers are also encouraged to initiate and implement product and process innovation measures to a much greater extent than in the past. As a result, research and development staffs, activities, and facilities have been significantly expanded at numerous enterprises. The complexity, quality, and quantity of information required for planning and control purposes has increased considerably in the past few years, making the Soviet manager's job more difficult.

In the sphere of organization, enterprise managers are now encouraged to reorganize shops, sections, and in some instances entire departments to derive greater operating efficiency. The work of a growing number of varied specialists and technicians must be assigned, integrated, and coordinated. These additional duties lead to new and greater organizational responsibilities for many micromanagers.

The managerial function of staffing has taken on new singificance with growing manpower shortages, greater labor mobility, and increased competition among enterprises for competent personnel. Recruiting, selection, appraisal, and training have become increasingly important activities for enterprise managers. In 1958, for example, direct hires constituted 84.1 per cent of all accessions to industrial establishments subordinate to regional economic councils. Direct hiring by individual enterprises from among the local labor supply includes outbidding other organizations by offering personnel substantial monetary and other inducements.[3] In order to attract and maintain competent personnel it is now more important to train them so that they can earn more pay and increase their status through upgrading, merit increases, and promotions. It is also more important to improve the over-all working environment, housing conditions under the control of the enterprise, welfare benefits, and the educational level of the labor force. Training has also become more significant and time-consuming with more difficult jobs to be done, and with the introduction of complex technology.

Because the Soviet labor force can no longer be considered a captive audience, it has placed new demands on the direction and leadership function. Enjoying greater freedom and independence, personnel no longer always listens and obeys. With somewhat better living standards, monetary incentives do not appear to be as potent a motivating force for many workers as they were previously. There is much evidence of high rates of employee turnover at numerous Soviet enterprises, and we will return to this point in Chapter 6. It is true that personnel change jobs in the majority of cases because they can obtain better pay and/or housing at other enterprises. However, in many instances personnel relocate because they are unhappy with their superiors and the existing "human" environment. It is evident that motivational and human relations problems have become more significant for enterprise managers, because mass indoctrination, slogans, and even monetary incentives are often no longer enough to induce employees to act as their superiors or the state wishes them to act.

In recent years local managers—the enterprise director in particular—have been given somewhat greater independence over the distribution of monetary incentives and other rewards among personnel. Several new types of employee participating bodies were established after 1957, and again during the 1962-63 period, at industrial enterprises. There is now increased emphasis on the elicitation of employees' proposals and advice on how to improve enterprise operations. With better education and greater skills, personnel is now in a much better position to contribute worthwhile suggestions than in the past. In general, leadership, communication, and supervision have taken on new dimensions with recent changes in the "human" environment in Soviet industry. In the final analysis, how well Soviet industrial personnel works depends in large part on the quality of interpersonal relations between superiors and subordinates.

It is significant to note here that a survey conducted at a number of Soviet chemical enterprises in 1963 reveals that department heads, shop chiefs, and even foremen are doing work that requires technical skill for only a minor part of their working day. The bulk of their time is spent on administrative problems. Managerial functions play an even greater role in the activities of the enterprise director and his deputies.[4]

It is now appropriate to focus our attention on the authority, independence, and influence of enterprise management in greater detail. We will concern ourselves with the enterprise plan; its formulation and fulfillment determine how well the ultimate enterprise objectives are achieved.

Enterprise management takes the initiative in preparing an over-all draft plan for the planned year. Managerial authority during the planning process can be divided into three categories: (1) initiation and implementation of planning proposals; (2) undertaking technical computations involving futurity estimates and intraenterprise planning; (3) the right to defend planning proposals to negotiate with higher authorities, suppliers, customers, and various other external organizations. The degree to which management can influence the content of the approved enterprise plan varies somewhat with the type of enterprise.

During the operating period the formal rights of enterprise managers are officially very limited. They have considerably less flexibility in fulfilling their plans or in running their enterprise than does a typical top-level American company manager, but probably not significantly less than a plant manager in a highly centralized U.S. firm. Soviet managers are, in principle, responsible for fulfilling the enterprise plan in its entirety. They do, however, have the right to request revisions in the plan.

Initiating and Implementing Planning Proposals

Product Planning

Enterprise managers can influence the content of the product assortment plan through their proposals. In this connection they may influence the types and related quantities of the output approved by higher authorities. Managers interviewed pointed out that this may entail convincing their superiors that the plant will not possess the necessary resources to carry out the desired production program. In most instances the assortment of goods approved by superior organs does not add up to the aggregate output indices, and the enterprise would usually establish independently about 5 to 10 per cent of its total planned output. This remaining capacity is used for subcontracting activities and/or the manufacture of various minor items. Most enterprises can also determine the detailed specifications of some types of output—for example, new or unstandardized goods—and they can initiate style and design changes in various products. Such activities are generally contingent upon customer agreement and at times upon higher approval.

The amount of detailed assortment planning undertaken by higher authorities depends chiefly on the nature and extent of the enterprise's product line. Enterprises producing a wide range of heterogeneous goods have more authority over their detailed product-mixes than those pro-

ducing a narrow line of homogeneous output. It is apparent from interviews with Soviet managers that, in general, consumer goods producers
play a greater role in product planning than do producer goods enterprises. The former typically participate and display their goods at trade
fairs and enterprise exhibitions. It was pointed out in Chapter 3 that
many consumer goods producers also send personnel to investigate demand and to interview employees and consumers at retail outlets where
their products are sold. Most consumer goods producers also study retail
inventory turnover and sales data which pertain to their products. Some
enterprises even send representatives to other countries to gather new
product ideas. In light of the above activities, the enterprise initiates
product-mix proposals and prepares samples of new items.

It may prove enlightening to briefly investigate the product planning
activities at a few of the consumer goods enterprises visited. All the enterprises, except a book factory, have an artistic council and an art, assortment or design department, and are considerably involved in product
planning.

A Leningrad shoe factory produces over twenty million pairs of shoes
each year in more than 100 different models or fashion groups. Within
each fashion group there are numerous varieties—different styles, colors,
and sizes. The enterprise has an assortment department comprised of
about 30 specialists, most of whom spend a few weeks each year on
"creative" leave going to retail outlets, fashion houses, conferences, con-
ventions, and the like. A few visit other countries (mostly Communist
ones, particularly Czechoslovakia). As a result of such activities, the
enterprise prepared 400 sample products in experimental shops during
1960 and the first half of 1961. On the basis of plant exhibits and the
opinions of the artistic council, about half of the samples were eliminated by management. The remainder were sent to a Russian Republic
footwear fair in 1961. At that time about 25 of the samples were selected
by customers, and tentative sales agreements were drawn up indicating
the amounts of each item to be supplied in future periods.

A Moscow silk and rayon factory and a Kharkov clothing manufac-
turer engage in product planning activities similar to those of the Leningrad shoe producer. A Moscow watch factory, which produces 9 basic
types of watches in more than 100 different styles, has the number of
watches to be produced annually set at a maximum of two million.
Unlike most other types of consumer goods, there is an abundance of
watches in Russia. However, the enterprise is encouraged to initiate and
develop new items that will command higher prices, since watch manufacture is largely an export industry. About 20 per cent of annual production consists of new varieties. The enterprise has several designers
who travel abroad—a few even to Switzerland.

By contrast to the above enterprises, a Kharkov book producer has little independent control over its product-mix. Customer publishing houses decide the content of the more than 450 million page sheets it produces annually. With remaining capacity the enterprise can independently manufacture calendars, writing pads, and various other items for local distribution.

The role played by most producer goods enterprises in demand analysis is confined to a study of customer needs for those goods or services produced independently. Unlike the consumer goods sector, there are seldom exhibits of producer goods, although some Soviet sources urge that they be organized on a widespread basis. At all the producer goods plants surveyed, except a Kharkov ball bearing factory, management can take the initiative in proposing new products to be incorporated into the production plan.

Of the producer goods enterprises visited, the ball bearing factory has the least independence concerning its detailed assortment since its output consists of a highly standardized product line having precise specifications. The chief of planning at a Moscow machine tool enterprise indicated that management can make specification changes in some types of output. It can also independently determine the output of some minor tools, parts and components which make up only a small portion of the total production program. This plant produces approximately 40 basic items; one of them—a mass-produced lathe—accounts for a major portion of total production. A Kiev machine tool plant had rights similar to those of the Moscow enterprise.

A Kharkov mining equipment plant produces about 20 major types of machinery, 4 of which require central approval. The other 16 or so are approved by either regional or republic-level authorities. The assistant chief engineer pointed out that management does at times influence the quantity targets for the noncentrally approved goods and can determine the detailed specifications for some. In addition, the plant can independently decide on the output of various minor items such as miners' lamps, flashlights, and certain small tools.

A Kharkov ventilation machinery enterprise produces nearly 1,600 types of equipment, about 400 of which require central approval. The chief engineer indicated that the enterprise could influence to some degree the breakdown of its assortment program, including at times even centrally approved output. It can also make specification changes in some products. This plant also produces some small pieces of equipment, as well as various parts and components, the assortment of which it can determine.

The above discussion illustrates that most enterprises play a fairly significant role in shaping their production programs. Management may influence, and in some cases actually determine, the quantities and types of planned production through its initiative and proposals. This in turn may have an impact on aggregate output, costs, resource utilization, and various other plan indices and results.

Cost-Plus Pricing

Enterprises have no authority over product prices which appear in the National Price List. These prices are centrally approved, and Soviet economists interviewed estimated that about 70 per cent of total industrial output relates to this price list. Republican and regional authorities also establish prices for many types of industrial output; nevertheless, enterprise management plays a key role in pricing under certain conditions. It can initiate price proposals for new, custom-built and other unstandardized goods, and in many instances where changes in product specifications are undertaken. The prices are proposed on a cost-plus basis—usually 3 to 6 per cent. Although an appropriate superior authority formally approves most of these prices, the price proposed by the producer is generally adopted. Such prices are wholesale factory transfer prices. In the case of new products they may also serve as constant prices in future periods. It is significant to note that wherever the enterprise's proposed prices are accepted, the related cost and resource input estimates would also be accepted. Let us briefly investigate enterprise pricing activities in more detail.

The pricing of custom-built output relates chiefly to producer goods. Several of the machinery enterprises surveyed indicated that a substantial proportion of their output is in this category. At four plants the proportions range from 20 to more than 50 per cent. All types of plants may produce certain nonstandardized items. Frequently, prices for such items do not even require higher approval.

Enterprises producing newly developed items initiate provisional (temporary) wholesale prices for them. Such prices are supposed to remain temporary transfer prices for only as long as it takes to perfect and produce the item in question on a large scale. (Depending on the type of product, the prescribed period would range from a few to 24 months.) At that time the price should be revised—almost always downward—and entered into the appropriate list as the official transfer price. The initial price would become the constant price used in determining gross output.

In cases where the plant undertakes significant product specification changes a price adjustment may be possible. If the producer obtains agreement from his customer(s), the proposed price is usually approved. Managers interviewed indicated that such agreement is almost always obtained, since price increases are provided for in the customer's plan.

Quality Technical Standards

Product quality standards can have an effect on the factor inputs required, and the processes to be used, in the production of the item in question. At a given enterprise there may be standards prescribed by central or other superior authorities, and others determined by the plant itself. Centrally established (all-union) standards are called *gosty* (singular *gost*). They are established by the State Committee on Standards, Measures and Measuring Instruments. The *gosty* relate to commodities which are centrally planned and/or consumed on a widespread basis throughout the economy. Each *gost* pertains to a given commodity, and it may have several indices specifying various physical attributes of the product (size, weight, shape, chemical composition, and so forth).

Most of the ball bearing plant's output is governed by *gosty*. The ventilation equipment producer has the ventilation systems of several products subject to *gosty*, although the frames are not governed by them. The air dynamic scheme, sizes of certain parts, and holes and openings are all indicated by *gosty*. At the mining equipment enterprise only the centrally approved output is subject to these standards. A Kharkov clothing factory determines the number of stitches per square centimeter for some products on the basis of *gosty*. There are also *gosty* pertaining to certain processes for treating fabrics. Most of the book factory's output is subject to *gosty*.

In general, many more producer goods are subject to *gosty* than consumer products. At most of the enterprises surveyed the majority of their product quality standards are not centrally determined. They are worked out by management, although many do require higher approval—usually by regional officials. Most technical standards for consumer goods are determined locally in light of the quality of production agreed upon with trade officials. Several enterprise managers indicated that quality standards in force, including *gosty*, may be revised at any time through their initiative. If management convinces higher authorities that established standards do not comply with local conditions or available resources, or that changes in inputs or processes will not significantly affect the quality of output, approval for revision is generally granted. Some Soviet managers and planners pointed out that enterprise requests for changes in technical standards are often approved because many standards, including *gosty*, are outdated and do not reflect existing technical conditions. In many instances changes in quality standards stem from a desire by management to substitute prescribed input materials.

Choice and Price of Input Materials

For most centrally planned output, and many other commodities requiring higher approval, the basic types of material inputs to be used are prescribed by superior authorities. In some instances, the specifications of certain input factors are dictated by quality technical standards, including *gosty*. However, most of the commodities allocated to the enterprise are allocated in aggregate terms—so many tons of coal, steel, or leather, so many meters of cloth, and so on—and the plant works out the detailed specifications with its suppliers. Moreover, management can apply for permission to use substitute input commodities, and such permission is often granted if superior authorities are convinced that desired output quality will not be adversely affected. For various commodities of minor importance, the enterprise has complete discretion over both the specifications and types of inputs to be used.

There is one definite way by which a given plant can wield considerable influence over the price of material inputs. This relates to decisions to make or buy. Two enterprise directors indicated that higher authorities often go along with their desire to make rather than buy certain commodities, providing that desired output quality does not suffer and other plant operations are not significantly disrupted.

Innovation Measures

Several managers stated that the great majority of the "innovations" incorporated into the plan and implemented during the operated period stem from initiative at the enterprise. For the most part these are relatively minor innovations resulting from employee suggestions. Management has the authority to accept and implement such suggestions as it sees fit. More will be said about employee suggestions in Chapter 10.

Enterprise management can also initiate major technological and product innovation measures, as well as various other large-scale improvement activities. However, managers at several plants indicated that in the majority of cases directives and approval are received from higher authorities for this type of innovation. Such directives may deal with automation, mechanization, modernization, new production processes, product development, and so forth. Enterprise product and technological innovation will be fully treated in Chapter 8.

Other Plan Indices and Resource Allocations

In general, management makes planning proposals pertaining to all the indices, including resource allotment limits, approved by superior authorities. These proposals are typically based on a myriad of technical computations, as well as certain other significant aspects of intraenterprise planning.

Technical Computations and Intraenterprise Planning

Plant Capacity and Capital Investment

It was pointed out earlier that total planned output is arrived at by estimating the amount of physical production that can be produced with expected plant capacity. Total output is related to plant capacity by using representative physical units of output, since the detailed product-mix would usually not yet be known. The representative units of output are translated into value indices by applying constant prices, and in this manner the gross output index is derived.

Management estimates plant capacity by calculating equipment utilization norms. Historical data on existing equipment are used for this purpose. The capacities of new machines to be provided during the planned year are prescribed in certificates (passports) established by the organization which originally designed the equipment in question. The directors and chief engineers of several plants indicated that in most instances the enterprise independently revises utilization norms for equipment already in use. Higher authorities are only likely to analyze the detailed equipment capacity calculations when there is an unresolved dispute about capital investment allocations or aggregate output targets. On the basis of its plant capacity calculations, management can, and often does, influence capital allocations and approved production targets.

Manpower Needs and Labor Utilization Norms

Managers at every plant visited pointed out that there are typically thousands of individual labor utilization norms used in preparing the plan of labor and wages. Most industrial establishments independently determine the large majority of these norms. There may be many norms established by higher authorities, even by the central planners, but even here the individual plant can often introduce "correction factors" in the light of local conditions. It is only when new equipment and/or highly standardized methods are used that the norm prescribed from above is accepted without modification.

The number of labor standards established independently at a given plant depends chiefly on the nature and diversity of its product line. An enterprise whose output consists of a small number of mass-produced, homogeneous items would establish considerably fewer norms than a plant manufacturing many different products with widely diverse specifications. Hence, a book page or oil producer would typically have much less independence and considerably fewer labor norms, than a plant producing custom-built equipment or a wide line of clothing. Most enterprises have much independence over the methods applied in calculating the labor norms they establish (that is, historical, statistical, technically calculated, or based on empirical studies).

In all probability, higher authorities analyze the plant's detailed labor standard calculations only when there is an unresolved dispute about the manpower needed to fulfill the production program. Management would then be required to justify its position on the basis of technical data and computations. In this manner, the managers may directly influence manpower allocations, payroll, and various other enterprise targets. They would influence labor productivity targets and results through their impact on manpower allotments and gross output.

The number of managerial and servicing personnel required by the enterprise to fulfill its plan is determined by rather crude methods. Records of past relationships between total number of workers, servicing personnel, and administrators are the major means used.

Payroll

Management has considerable independence, not only in classifying manpower according to occupations and professions, but also over the grading of personnel within each job classification on the basis of skills, abilities, and seniority. In most classifications there are roughly between 6 and 12 different gradings possible. Decisions in these areas are often contingent upon the approval of plant trade union officials, but several managers asserted that such approval is only rarely denied. Although basic wage rates and salary scales are established centrally—by the State Committee on Labor and Wages—management influences total enterprise payroll through its classification and grading of personnel. This would also be reflected in aggregate cost indices.

Supply Needs and Material Utilization Norms

There are hundreds, and frequently thousands, of utilization norms used in preparing the enterprise plan of material and technical supply. As is the case with labor norms, there may be certain supply input norms prescribed by superior authorities. These norms are typically based on a given set of technical conditions. Since conditions vary among plants, management can make adjustments in many of the norms prescribed from above. For the most part, management has considerable independence in establishing the majority of its norm in the light of local conditions. Moreover, the enterprise has much authority over the methods to be applied in material and supply norm setting (that is, historical, analogous, or estimates based on drawings). Analogy and drawings are frequently used for new products or operations not previously performed by the plant. Higher authorities are not likely to examine the numerous detailed input calculations closely, unless management is adamant in its desire for a greater allocation of supplies than these authorities wish to provide.

Working Capital Estimates

Management proposes working capital norms based on its estimates of the flexibility required to carry out the over-all plan. Inventory norms are prepared for basic and auxiliary supplies, spare parts, goods in process, and finished production. Physical working capital requirements are translated into value terms. Higher authorities approve the aggregate monetary working capital index as well as the physical norms for major commodities. The material and supply working capital limits constitute part of the plan of material and technical supply.

The enterprise may exert influence over its approved working capital limits, since numerous estimates and calculations are undertaken in compiling its working capital proposals. At the plants surveyed no precise formulae or techniques are used in estimating working capital needs, however, wide use is made of various qualitative factors based primarily on judgment. These include in part: distances from suppliers, the amount of material consumed per unit of output or time, frequency of deliveries, and operating conditions of the plant. In most cases, approved norms are based on past performance with some adjustment—usually arbitrary —for anticipated operations and conditions during the planned period.

Cost of Production Estimates

Management can influence the cost of production plan and subsequent cost results through its decisions and impact on all other sections of the enterprise plan. This, in turn, would have an impact on the cost per one ruble of marketable production index. The enterprise proposes an aggregate cost target, taking into account all factor costs of production as well as general overhead expenses. Managers indicated that overhead expense estimates are based on past relationships between these expenses and total production costs. Past relationships are also considered in allocating these general expenses among individual products and/or product groups. Some adjustments may be made in the light of anticipated conditions during the planned year. The plant is only likely to be required to justify its detailed cost calculations and estimates when there are unresolved disputes with superior authorities.

Financial Planning

Enterprise profit, profitability, and monetary working capital indices are derived automatically once the other plan indices are established. In essence, the financial plan is a translation of the over-all plan into monetary balances. The allocations of capital investment and working capital to the enterprise—whether they are from state budget grants or profits allowed to remain at the plant—are based on over-all planned operations.

Summary and Concluding Remarks

The amount of influence management can exert over approved enterprise operating targets and related resource limits tends to vary with the number and types of technical calculations undertaken independently. This, in turn, depends largely on the nature of the product line, production processes, and general technological features of the enterprise. In addition, the stability of enterprise operations over time, in terms of operating methods and procedures, is also a significant determinant. Enterprises producing homogeneous output on a mass-production basis would tend to exert less influence on their approved plans than those plants producing a broad and varied product line of, say, consumer goods or custom-built equipment.

Defense of Planning Proposals and External Negotiations

Enterprise managers have the right to defend all of their planning proposals through negotiations with higher authorities. They also partake in negotiations with customers in connection with the detailed specifications of their enterprise's assortment plan, with suppliers on the detailed specifications of the plant's material and supply requirements, and with various other organizations, such as transportation firms, which provide the enterprise with a service. In this latter connection, enterprises can independently obtain modest short-term bank loans for seasonal needs which bear interest of 1 to 2 per cent. Since 1955, they can also obtain bank loans—at interest rates of 1 to 3 per cent—for the introduction of new technology and various other improvements in operations. These loans are typically of two or three years duration, and are usually amortized, in large part, by derived economies.

Officials at several enterprises pointed out that "protocols" (petitions) are sometimes prepared by the enterprise during the planning process. These protocols are essentially a list of grievances—typically dealing with resource allocation deficiencies and other problems pertaining to the enterprise's capabilities and needs—where there is a point of significant dispute with higher authorities. Whenever these disputes cannot readily be resolved, the management, other employees, and even party and trade union officials at the enterprise may compile a list of grievances and attach their signatures to this "petition." This document may be forwarded to officials at any level in the industrial hierarchy, or even to higher party agencies, at any time. It was indicated in interviews that in some cases the enterprise's grievances are accepted and appropriate action taken.

Plan Fulfillment

Revisions in the Approved Production Plan

There are frequent revisions in the assortment plans of many enterprises during the operating period and this topic will be pursued further
in other chapters. We are interested here only in the role of enterprise
management in revising the planned production program. Managers at
the enterprises surveyed indicated that at times they initiate changes in
their assortment plans. However, such action would only be considered
official or "legal" if the proper procedures for ratificaton and formal
approval were adhered to. This would entail the approval of the superior
body responsible for planning the output of the item in question. Frequently, where changes relate to product specifications rather than the
total number of products of a given class, the producer can undertake
such changes independently with the consent of the customer. In cases
where the items are not subject to higher approval, management would
also undertake changes independently in this manner. Enterprise managers may also initiate substitutions of some material inputs during the
operating period, as well as changes in quality standards.

Aggregate output targets are revised much less frequently than the
product-mix plan. If management requests a downward revision in the
gross or marketable output target, approval would be forthcoming only
by forcefully convincing higher authorities that resources are inadequate
to fulfill the target.

Above Plan Output

All the enterprises surveyed, except the watch factory, indicated that
they have considerable independence and a fairly wide range of choice
over the above plan items they can produce. Most of the consumer goods
producers have almost unlimited discretion in this respect, since, as one
director stated, "everything can readily be disposed of due to shortages."
As will be seen in Part II, this statement is no longer always true. The
producer goods enterprises indicated that there are a number of items
they cannot produce above plan, but this does not greatly limit their
range of choice.

In recent years, there has been a growing number of commodities
which cannot be produced above plan because they are no longer in
critically short supply. In 1960 the central planners issued a list of more
than 1,000 types of goods that cannot be produced in excess of planned
quantities. One regional economic council official pointed out that the
appropriate branch-of-industry administration may also provide subordinate enterprises with lists of items requiring republican or regional-level
approval, which cannot be produced above plan.

Independence Over Sources and Uses of Funds

Although managers are supposed to use specific portions of allocated capital investment and working capital funds for earmarked purposes, they have some leeway to shuffle funds within the total allotment during the operating period in order to carry out the plan. Assigned funds, particularly state budget allocations, constitute by far the greatest source of funds for most enterprises. At the same time, the enterprise is likely to have independence over the sources and uses of a limited amount of funds. This may include in part, bank loans, fines or damages collected from delinquent suppliers, and revenue from the sale of unneeded assets.

Plants having an Enterprise Fund formed from profits kept by the enterprise, can use such funds independently within broadly prescribed limits. These funds are used for the payment of bonuses to employees, housing improvements, welfare benefits, and various other purposes. The Enterprise Fund will be discussed in more detail in Chapter 7. It will suffice to point out here that at most plants the amount of funds from this source is very small compared to the funds allocated by higher authorities.

At many enterprises there is another separate fund over which management has virtually complete authority. This fund is formed from the sale of products made from waste materials, and the plant keeps 95 per cent of the profits earned from such output. At the enterprises visited, this fund is quite small and is relatively unimportant in terms of over-all operations.

Management would also have control over funds derived from unplanned economies during the operating period. Often such funds are utilized for overfulfilling production plans.

5 • The Planning Process

The process by which the Soviet state estimates available resources and determines what use it wishes to make of them during a given period is extremely complex. Only a small portion of the whole process involves the enterprise, but this is a very crucial part of the process since each enterprise provides pertinent information to the planners. Although the economic "ends" to be achieved involve central decisions, the top planners must seriously consider the "means" available for accomplishing the desired objectives, and information concerning the means comes largely from industrial enterprises. It is the enterprise's role in the planning process that is of primary interest here. However, some general background information on Soviet economic planning would be in order.

Nature of National Plans and Planning Decisions

The Soviet Union has a 1960-80 Twenty-Year Plan for national economic expansion. This is a very general plan merely laying out the tentative sequence of major projects to be undertaken in leading industries considered strategic for both defense and economic growth. There was also a 1959-65 Seven-Year Plan, but it was abandoned in mid-1963, and a new Five-Year plan for 1966-70 is being drawn up. A two-year interim plan for 1964-65 has been prepared. The long-term five- or seven-year plans are essentially investment plans, and are not operational. They do not order any enterprise to do anything.

The annual national plan is the operational document for the Soviet economy; it is the basis for actual resource allocations, supply relationships, and the contracts which express them. This plan is related to the long-range plans only in the sense of being a practical expression of the same economic policy. But even economic policy may be amended during the course of a given long-term plan. This is precisely what happened in 1961 when defense spending was greatly increased, and again in 1963 when it was decided to allocate more resources to the chemical and electronic industries at the expense of steel while providing more resources for agriculture and consumer goods. In general, investment plans must be geared to current operating plans to provide machinery, materials, and other resources needed to continue or complete the planned investment projects.

The starting point for all Soviet planning is the formulation of political directives by top party and government authorities indicating their priorities and preferences with respect to economic activity (for example, relative emphasis on heavy and light industry, agriculture, defense, and chemicals). These directives are based largely on an achievement balance for the entire economy and each of its major sectors.

The decisions on "what to produce" are essentially political decisions. Typically, capital formation through the expansion of heavy industry and defense production are pushed hard, with leftover resources going for consumer goods. Whether a true and significant change in policy regarding consumer goods has taken place in 1963 remains to be seen. Similar pronouncements have been made in the past without substantial results. In any case, what is to be produced, and how much of each item, would have to be worked out according to the aims of the plan, the available resources, and the need for proper balance and integration of interdependent production processes.

With regard to decisions "for whom to produce," the Soviet economy works to a considerable degree for the state and the future. The Soviet rulers can push economic growth since they can enforce a restriction in consumption contrary to the wishes of the consuming public, not because their system is superior to the capitalistic system.

The question "how to produce" is answered by resource allocations rather than by market possibilities. The problem of how to produce most economically cannot be properly answered without a competitive price system. Prices set by the Soviet planners have little or no guiding function. Since factors of production are substitutable within limits, the production program must be drawn up with reference to the given technical possibilities. By trial and error a modicum of technical integration evolves. However, gradual achievement of a workable technical integration is not sufficient if we want to make the "best" economic use of the factors of production. At best, technological integration may guarantee that the system will function without breakdown and that resources will be fully utilized, but it does not guarantee the best combination of factors in an economic sense.

Hence, the observer finds production operations in the Soviet economy curiously uneven: on the one hand, he may see a top priority (in terms of resource allocations) military ballistic plant which has achieved a precision of ball bearings and gyroscopes rivaling the best in the world; on the other hand, he may visit a consumer goods plant where things are being done in an almost unbelievably primitive way, with the quality of output almost worthless by American standards. Since enterprises are typically allocated the bulk of their physical resources, we can talk about "efficient" resource utilization only in terms of the most economical and fullest use of given resources within a given plant. On a national scale we can talk about efficiency only in terms of the proper matching of factors of production, so that all factors are fully utilized in the accomplishment of desired objectives. Hence, economic efficiency in the Soviet system cannot have the same full meaning as in a capitalistic system where the "best" combination of factors is also a relevant problem, given market forces and the profit motive.

Soviet Planning Methodology

It is obvious that the Soviet planning process must be fantastically complex. There must be a flow of operational directives to each of the tens of thousands of enterprises. Plans must be devised for various sectors and coordinated with those of other sectors, since the outputs of one industry are the inputs of other industries. The plans approved for enterprises prescribing what to produce must be backed by necessary resources, and the outputs must, of course, be related to planned inputs. Every economic decision is interconnected with numerous other decisions or involves a number of necessary consequential effects. It is not possible to let each micromanager freely pick and choose his own product-mix, resource combinations, and suppliers. The plan must provide for such problems if the various phases of the over-all plan are to be interrelated in a mutually consistent manner. But how is this done without the competitive market price system which we take for granted?

There is no elaborate formalized structure of Soviet planning so that one could write a treatise on pure communistic economics that would equal in length a treatise on the general equilibrium of purely competitive market systems. Soviet planning decisions depend on a mixture of purely technical considerations and adaptations to the scarcities of various economic resources. A continuous process of trial and error exists. One eminent American economist describes Soviet economic planning as follows: "They [the planners] rely pragmatically on a mixture of physical, accounting, and economic planning, make some use of pricing and costing, and take some recognition of the various scarcity of economic resources; but there is no reliance on systematic theory." [1]

While the Soviets are showing an increasing interest in Leontief's system of input-output and Kantorovich's techniques of linear programming, this methodology is not relied on significantly in basic planning. There is so far only a highly aggregated (83×83) input-output matrix available for relating sector inputs and outputs. The available matrix techniques require an extremely high level of aggregation and deal only with broad categories of commodities. The rather ineffective statistical reporting system, the serious deficiencies in available planning data, and the limitations inherent in the matrix techniques themselves all hamper the operational validity of these techniques in practice.

At present the planners do make modest use of computers, mathematical techniques, and econometrics, but mainly on an experimental basis.[2] Thus far, "advanced scientific" planning methodology is being utilized chiefly at the national level, and only to a very limited extent in the republics and regions. Some experiments in the use of the above techniques and tools are also being conducted at a few large industrial enterprises. It is hoped that in the not too distant future regional computing centers will be set up to service local plants. It is also hoped that *eventually* mathematical methods, operations research, dynamic programming, and the like, will be used for production planning at all levels of the economy.

The whole process of Soviet planing is often referred to by the Soviets as "planning by material balances." It involves a simplified and rather crude form of input-output procedure, carried out largely in physical terms.[3] A "balance" in physical terms presents the current, or intended, relations between certain supplies and their allocation for specific commodities or groups of commodities. The total bill of goods to be produced during a given planned year is determined centrally, although the breadth and detail prescribed for different classes of commodities vary at this level. To secure this bill the central planners allocate major supplies primarily in physical terms, by establishing product requirements on the basis of technical coefficients (production functions), and by using the physical balances to equate sources and uses of intermediate and final products. Because of the enormous multiplicity of products in an industrialized economy, goods are grouped into certain conventional classifications by using technical conversion factors, such as steel content, horsepower, or some other physical common denominator. The entire plan is built around national output goals and the expansion of capacity needed for major industrial sectors.

Fixing physical output targets for key commodities and classified goods may be crude but it does have substantial validity, since the most common combinations are reducible, as in chemistry, to a relatively small group of elements (such as iron, coal, steel, cement, rolled metals, fuels, electricity, various fabrics, rubber, leather, and the principal nonferrous metals). The physical balancing process is based on technical coefficients linking various factor inputs to various commodity outputs (for example, w tons of coal to produce x tons of steel; y tons of steel to produce z number of lathes). These coefficients are derived by crudely aggregating and averaging past input-output relationships at enterprises, although at times adjustments are made for anticipated improvements. The central allocation of supplies depends on the input schedules for each industry, given its output targets. Resource allocations must also necessarily be subdivided and further elaborated by republics, regions, and individual plants.

The national plan also includes, as basic components, a manpower balance and a balance of capital construction. The latter indicates sectoral production capacities, and it details volume, location, and structure of capital installations. It also specifies in itemized lists the main projects and the timetable for their completion.

Central authorities typically utilize from 7,000 to 12,000 physical balances in preparing the annual national plan; some 700 to 1,200 major commodity groups are used for supply planning. In practice, the central planners must devote their attention chiefly to certain key industrial sectors. This is so because enormous practical difficulties are involved in going beyond first-order inputs for the determination of technical coefficients even for key products, and also because the price system is distorted. Monetary balances, which supplement physical balances, are needed as a common denominator because of physical dissimilarities among materials, equipment, output, and labor.

In short, there is no theory of planning that can unite all the physical balances into a single system and integrate them with the financial balances. The key balance of raw materials, equipment, fuel and power, manpower and capital installations are based on planned outputs for leading industries. These outputs, in turn, have been established by taking into account the past and potential growth of the key industries and related branches under the assumption of full employment of all available resources. Actually, the balancing process is a never-ending one, always attempting to make the balances balance in order to provide for technical consistency in light of national economic objectives.

It is clear that Soviet planning at the top level deals primarily in aggregates, expressed as so many tons of steel, for example. But as the plan works down to the operating level, increasingly complex details must be included: What kinds of steel? where produced? with what specific resources? These and numerous other questions become relevant for administrators further down the industrial hierarchy. The process is far from being one-sided. If the national plan is to be realistic and consistent, enterprise managers must tell the planners above them what can realistically be expected from each plant in terms of production, and what types of resources are necessary to meet the production targets.

In order to tie the myriad component parts of the national plan into a unified whole, a common classification of planning indices is utilized at all levels. Several of the key indices of the enterprise plan, discussed in Chapter 3, are common to all levels. These include aggregate gross and marketable output, physical output targets for important commodities, labor productivity, cost of production and cost reduction, and profit that is calculated only for state budget purposes. There are also aggregate resource limits established for major commodities used as factor inputs by various plants and industries: capital investment, working capital, manpower, and total payroll. Upon formal approval these plan indices become the control figures for guiding the activities at each level. Additional directives and instructions are issued during the planning process and during the related operating period, but the preceding group of indices serves as the basis for economic management each year.

Let us now briefly examine the process entailed in formulating the annual economic plan.

Annual Planning

The actual process, sequence, and timing entailed in constructing the annual national plan and all of its derivative plans vary from year to year.[4] Since the macroorganizations engaged in planning, as well as their activities, also change frequently, the authority relationship at different levels in the industrial hierarchy is also subject to change. Moreover, the number and types of commodities centrally planned and distributed vary somewhat from year to year. Following the 1957 reorganization, much of the planning and resource allocation detail was pushed down to lower levels. During the 1960-62 period, there was a recentralization involving the number of commodities and some of the detail planned and distributed below the center.[5] This was due to localistic tendencies, commodity scarcities, and disproportions which became intensified under the territorial system of administration. There are some indications that with the 1963 reorganization, there will once again be somewhat greater decentralization of planning, resource allocation, and decision-making. In recent years, the enterprise's role in the planning process has not changed significantly in spite of the many changes taking place at higher levels.[6]

With this background in mind, let us try to construct a representative picture of the annual planning process. We will briefly outline the process here and give greater descriptive detail in the next section; the problems entailed will be discussed in the next chapter.

The annual planning process comprises stages of proposals, counterproposals, and reconciliations. The enterprise prepares a preliminary draft plan and submits its planning proposals, in the form of indices, to the branch administration (*upravleniye*) of the *sovnarkhoz*. In some years preliminary directives may be received from higher authorities by a given enterprise regarding the draft plan prior to its preparation; in other years there may be none. During this stage, however, some preliminary directives usually flow from the center to the republic, and, at times, to the regional levels. At each level draft plans of subordinate units are aggregated and channeled upward until they reach the center. Negotiations—usually in the form of hard bargaining—take place between superiors and subordinates at each level during this time, and a tentative agreement is reached regarding the basic plan indices of each administrative unit. In reality, directives and counterproposals continuously flow up and down the hierarchy during the draft planning stage.

At about the same time that enterprises are preparing their preliminary draft plans, central planners are working out the achievement balances and preliminary balance projections for the economy as a whole. After the national level receives the aggregated draft plans from republican planning agencies, the national plan is completed and approved by the government. The national output targets and resource allocation limits are disaggregated down the hierarchy. Once again there are negotiations between superior and subordinate organizations. However, the central control figures are generally taken as given at this stage.

The total national "pie" of planned outputs and resource allocations requires a subdivision of production assignments and resources among enterprises. The indices approved for each plant are arrived at primarily through negotiations between enterprise management and the *upravleniye*. But republic-level and/or central authorities in some instances directly decide the allocation of certain goods and/or the assignment of certain tasks for a given plant.

In general, central authorities plan the output and allocation of a long list of goods which are deemed of paramount importance, in critically short supply, and various others that are consumed by several republics.[7] Typically this includes, in part, various types of machinery and equipment, ferrous and nonferrous metals, fuels, rubber, leather, and selected chemicals. Much of the detailed allocation work regarding centrally planned goods is done by the republican planning agencies. These agencies also independently plan and distribute various commodities consumed largely by regions within the same republic. For some items the *sovnarkhozy* themselves allocate and distribute to plants or maintain warehouses from which enterprises may freely buy what they need. The enterprise itself may also be permitted to independently acquire subcontracting services and certain locally produced supplies such as sand and gravel, or office supplies.

Process and Chronology of Enterprise Annual Plan Formulation

The enterprise prepares its annual operating plan (*tekhpromfinplan*) twice: the first time as a preliminary draft plan and the second time as a formally approved operating document. It was pointed out in Chapter 3 that the long-range plan of the enterprise, in conjunction with results achieved to date, is supposed to serve as the point of departure for the formulation of the annual plan. In reality, the long-term plan has little significance, and annual planning starts from scratch taking into account only performance to date.

The annual plan is summarized by a cluster of indices (see Chapter 3) requiring higher approval. Enterprise managers interviewed indicated, however, that negotiations during the planning process focus almost entirely on output, cost of production, labor productivity indices, and on resource needs. Apparently other approved indices usually entail automatic "rubber-stamp" approval. The enterprise officials who negotiate with superior authorities are, in most cases, the director, chief of supply, chief of planning, chief engineer, and chief of production. It should be noted that the process of planning for enterprise product and technological innovation will be dealt with in Chapter 9.

Preliminary Stage: Initial Tekhpromfinplan

This stage covers the period from the time initial planning begins at the enterprise in the spring until final approved indices are received from higher authorities toward the end of the planning year. Following the 1957 industrial reorganization, enterprises have usually taken the initiative in preparing their draft plans before any preliminary central figures have been received from above. There are reports that as of 1963, many enterprises may receive preliminary directives concerning anticipated capital investment, increases in output, and cost reduction. The preparation of the enterprise draft plan usually begins in April or May, and it is therefore necessary to estimate performance for the balance of the current year, as well as for the planned year. Enterprises that do not produce a substantial amount of centrally allocated goods or require a substantial amount of centrally allocated supplies submit summary draft indices to the *upravleniye* the beginning of June. For those plants producing or requiring significant amounts of centrally planned commodities, the submission of their draft plans may be preceded by preliminary propsals, counterproposals, and negotiations.

Since there are some basic differences in the process of planning between producer and consumer goods enterprises during the draft plan stage, they are treated separately.

PRODUCER GOODS ENTERPRISES.   At producer goods plants surveyed, at least half of the total output and supplies of each plant consists of centrally planned and allocated goods; at the ball bearing factory this figure is about 90 per cent. In late April or early May these enterprises make preliminary proposals dealing with the quantities of different classes of centrally distributed output that they would be able to produce during the planned year. Preliminary directives are received from the central planners early in June indicating the quantities of these classes of output desired. The enterprises do not prepare an actual material and supplies plan until June. However, they make proposals and prepare some broad estimates of their requirements of centrally allocated supplies prior to June. The enterprise receives by early June, at about the same time preliminary directives on output are received, an indication of certain important types of supply (for example, metal) that it may expect for the planned year.

Before and after receipt of these output and supply directives, negotiations are conducted between the enterprise and superior officials. There does not appear to be any common pattern as to whether the plant negotiates directly with central planners or whether *sovnarkhoz* officials serve as intermediaries. For example, two of the enterprises surveyed—the ball bearing plant and a ventilation equipment producer—receive their preliminary directives directly from the center with copies going to their other superior agencies. On many occasions these two enterprises negotiate directly with central authorities. The chief engineer of the ventilation plant pointed out that much direct contact with central planners was required in 1960 and 1961 because a substantial portion of new products was adopted in the enterprise plan (about 40 to 50 per cent of the plant's centrally planned production consisted of new products for 1961). Furthermore, central authorities were more familiar with these new items than the *sovnarkhoz* and therefore direct negotiations were more beneficial. The deputy director of the ball bearing factory gave no specific reasons for direct negotiations other than "it is a matter of expediency."

Interviews show that the enterprise plays a greater part in the planning of its output than in the planning of its supply. The republican agencies, and, to a lesser extent, the *sovnarkhoz*, appear to play the major role in matters of supply. The negotiations concerning centrally allocated outputs and inputs are most intensive in May and June and then begin to taper off. By August changes in figures for centrally allocated outputs are usually only minor in nature.

It is important to note that several enterprise managers indicated that *sovnarkhoz* officials often support and even defend enterprise views and proposals during negotiations with central authorities. More will be said about this in Chapter 11.

The enterprises prepare their over-all draft *tekhpromfinplan* in early June, and this compilation includes both centrally and noncentrally allocated outputs and supplies. At this time all basic indices and major proposals for the *orgtekhplan* (plan of organizational and technical measures) and for resource needs are prepared.

The form that summarizes the plants' estimated material and supply requirements is called a *zayavka*, which means statement of requirements. The *zayavka* encompasses all supplies allocated by and requiring the approval of higher authorities. The classes of commodities are presented in similar grouping each year to facilitate comparisons of planned and past needs. The *zayavka* is usually prepared twice by the enterprise, once during the preliminary drafting stage, and again after the plant receives its formally approved control figures. The draft plan is always completed by the end of June, and summary indices and related proposals are submitted to the *upravleniye*.

Sometime in July, after the *upravleniye* has worked out its own preliminary plan, it submits counterproposals to the enterprise. This usually entails adjustments (typically upward) in some or all of the enterprise's draft indices, and sometimes various other directives relating to *orgtekhplan* measures, technical development, resource limits, and so forth. In July and August many proposals and counterproposals pass between the enterprise and its *upravleniye,* and extensive negotiations are conducted. Normally, by the end of August some mutual understanding is reached with regard to the refined enterprise draft plan.

CONSUMER GOODS PRODUCERS.   None of the consumer goods enterprises negotiated with central authorities in connection with their output plans. Their assortment plan (product-mix) is negotiated with trade officials. A shoe factory was the only enterprise to receive a preliminary directive concerning supply before the initial compilation of the draft *tekhpromfinplan*. Around May this plant generally receives an indication of the amount of leather—a centrally allocated item—to be expected for the planned year.

Apparently the consumer goods plants do not participate in supply planning to the same extent as producer goods enterprises. The head of the planning department at a silk fabric factory stated that the nature of their final assortment plan is directly dependent on the availability of materials. The enterprise evidently can do little in the way of negotiating for centrally, and even various noncentrally, allocated supplies. This strongly suggests that this enterprise, and probably many other consumer goods producers, have a low priority rank in resource allocation. They may well receive "leftovers" after high priority sectors are accounted for. More will be said about this matter in Part II.

At five of the plants surveyed, planning begins in early May. At this time the enterprise prepares assortment proposals based on past demand for its products and the total estimated volume of production for the planned year and negotiates with trade officials concerning the preliminary assortment plan. Existing and new products, styles, designs, patterns, varieties, and sizes are discussed, with the *upravleniye* often participating in these negotiations. In the case of the watch factory, which exports more than half of its output, there is some direct contact with foreign trade officials and the USSR Chamber of Commerce as well. During preliminary negotiations the enterprise often displays samples of its goods, especially new items and varieties. For example, the shoe factory holds a formal exhibition around May, attended by trade and *upravleniye* officials, retail personnel among others.

With the exception of a Kharkov clothing plant, all the enterprises surveyed submit their draft plan indices to their *upravleniye* by early June, when preliminary *zayavki* are also submitted. The *upravleniye* then examines the indices with respect to available resources. The clothing enterprise does not submit its draft plan to the *upravleniye* until after the Ukraine Republic Wholesale Clothing Fair in July. In addition, this enterprise does not prepare any *zayavki* until after its approved control figures are received around October; then it prepares its detailed *zayavka*. It was not made entirely clear why the chronology and pattern of planning differ at this plant. Apparently, because it distributes output to, and is supplied by, organizations almost entirely within the republic, negotiations and contracts are of a local nature and this may permit a later elaboration of plans and less initial detail or coordination with respect to material needs. (The other enterprises distribute output to, and receive supplies from, other republics.)

During June and July there are continuous negotiations between the consumer goods enterprise and its *upravleniye* as well as with trade officials, the latter being concerned only with the assortment of production. Interviews revealed that there is at times some direct contact with republican agencies, but rarely with central authorities.

Some time during the summer, after the adjusted indices are received by the enterprise, there is usually a republic and in some cases a national exhibition for each consumer goods branch of industry. Each enterprise sends representatives with samples of its products to the appropriate exhibition. Other participants include trade and retail personnel and various regional and republic officials. At these exhibitions tentative assortment contracts are arranged between producers and customers.

Enterprise managers indicated that the major portion of their planned production program is accounted for in tentative contractual agreements entered into at these exhibitions. Some types of output are specified in rather broad physical terms, whereas other classes, including many standardized items produced in the past, are specified in detail regarding style, variety, color, size, and so on. Some producers may also exhibit in November or December after their approved control figures are received. At that time detailed assortment contracts covering all items to be produced during the first quarter, six months, or during the whole planned year are established. In general, the over-all detailed product-mix for most consumer goods producers is determined on the basis of half-yearly, and in some instances quarterly, contract orders with trade officials. In such cases the annual plan would not have true over-all operational significance. Nevertheless, aggregate output, cost and labor productivity targets, as well as resource allocations, are determined in the annual plan.

The coordinating body for the distribution, sale, and delivery of goods to other republics is the republic economic council.

Final Stage: The Plan as Law

In most respects the process at this stage is similar for both producer and consumer goods enterprises and they are considered together.

The final stage of enterprise annual plan formulation commences with the receipt of formally approved control figures, resource limits, and sometimes with various other directives from above. The enterprise receives its approved control figures sometime after the national plan is approved in September or October, and it is supposed to receive its approved indices by the end of October. In reality they are often forwarded several weeks, and occasionally several months, late; in fact, in some years, not until January or February of the planned year. All supply limits are indicated with centrally allocated commodities listed separately. A special acquisition document (called *fond*) is required by the enterprise for the procurement of various centrally allocated supplies. In most instances the *sovnarkhoz* divides these *fondy* among subordinate plants, but apparently some may be specifically earmarked for certain plants by the central planners.

The *fondy* typically indicate material limits by categories in broad rather than specific terms. For example, the enterprises may be allocated so many tons of iron, metal or leather, or so many meters of certain fabrics. The detailed specifications regarding sizes, grades, shapes, colors, and the like, would not usually be indicated. The names of suppliers, the total quantities to be supplied by each, and the delivery dates for centrally allocated commodities are submitted to the enterprise.

Each enterprise is in a sense both a buyer and a seller; hence certain horizontal negotiations with suppliers and customers are generally required. On the basis of all its broadly stated supply limits, the plant negotiates with suppliers on the detailed specifications of its needs, as well as delivery dates, if they have not yet been prescribed. In some cases there may be various combinations of intermediary links and superior agencies involved in contract negotiations, particularly in the signing of contracts. This is especially true with centrally allocated goods.

For consumer goods plants in their roles as sellers, there are typically at least three parties to each contract: the producer; the wholesale trade organization; and the actual customer, either another enterprise or a retail outlet. For example, the Moscow Silk Fabric Factory distributes about 70 per cent of its output to other plants manufacturing finished consumer goods and 30 per cent to the trade organization for retail shops. In both cases the trade organ is the intermediary. If consumer goods are destined for other republics, there may be more than three parties involved in the contract. In some instances, usually where goods are only of local importance, contract orders may be established directly between retail stores (generally large ones) and producers.

On the basis of detailed contracts with suppliers, each enterprise constructs its final *zayavki,* this time specifying itemized supply requirements. These *zayavki* are forwarded to higher authorities where they are processed along with contract agreements. Then delivery assignments and enterprise-to-enterprise ties are formally established. Depending on the type of commodity, supply and delivery contracts may be drawn up on a quarterly, semiannual or annual basis.

By mid-December the enterprise is supposed to receive warrants (*naryady*), which indicate specific supply needs and the conditions of individual procurement agreements with suppliers. These *naryady* serve as the basis for the conclusion of supply contracts signed by producers and their customers. Directives and *naryady* relating to the conditions of delivery and supply are received by both supplier and customer enterprises. Conflicts arising over details and conditions of the contract may be resolved by state arbitration commissions at various levels (regional, republican, central), the level depending on the nature of the conflict.

There may be some negotiations with higher authorities during the fourth quarter, after receipt of the approved control figures, in an attempt to change various enterprise plan indices, including resource limits. Depending on the nature of the adjustment, approval may be required from republican and/or central authorities as well as the *sovnarkhoz* and its *upravleniye.* Enterprise managers interviewed asserted that adjustments at this stage are generally of a minor nature and under the jurisdiction of the *sovnarkhoz.* In some instances, adjustments may be made in the enterprise plan. This may compel the *upravleniye* to adjust the indices of certain other enterprises in order to keep its own approval plan intact.

After receipt of all final approved indices, the enterprise completes its annual *tekhpromfinplan* with quarterly subdivisions. At this stage all shop plans are worked out in great detail with monthly breakdowns for the first and sometimes the first two quarters of the planned year. This is the point when the enterprise emerges from technical-economic planning into operating-production planning.

Revisions in the Enterprise Plan During the Operating Period

Many revisions are needed in the plans of numerous enterprises during the operating period, and more will be said about this in the next chapter. Changes in plans pertain mostly to the product-mix and in some instances to allocated supplies, rather than to adjustments in aggregate operating targets. Aggregrate targets may at times be revised downward, but only if the enterprise is faced with severe unanticipated resource deficiencies.

Changes in the assortment plans of consumer goods producers in particular are common "because of changing consumer tastes and demand," as one chief engineer stated. Climatic conditions was another reason given by one enterprise director. Such changes are negotiated with the trade organization.

Several enterprise managers stated that changes in the product-mix are generally made without altering the aggregate output, cost, profit or labor productivity targets, or resource limits. The major reason given was that it is usually very difficult and time-consuming to calculate the effect of product-mix changes on other plan indices.

The watch factory revised its assortment plan for 1961 during the first quarter of that year. The trade organization received a communication from retail outlets in January indicating an unanticipated change in consumer demand for certain watches. Within 30 days a change in the enterprise's assortment plan was worked out and approved without adjusting aggregate targets or resource limits. The deputy chief of planning at this enterprise said that the change in the product-mix could have had some impact on various other indices, but it was probably only minor in nature and therefore the *upravleniye* allowed the existing indices to prevail.

Managers at both consumer and producer goods enterprises indicated that revisions in plans are sometimes achieved through the initiative of the enterprise, as discussed in the preceding chapter.

III · PROBLEMS

6 • Resource Uncertainty

Introduction

For many years, the most salient fact of economic life for the Soviet manager has been the inadequate provision of resources necessary to fulfill the enterprise production plan. In spite of the many organizational changes and other reforms introduced in the Soviet economy during the past decade, resource uncertainty stubbornly persists as the most critical problem for enterprise management.

As the Soviet economy has expanded and grown more complex, the interrelationships among factors of production have become a more delicate and crucial problem. The problem of supplying enterprises with proper materials, machinery, and components becomes increasingly critical as production rises and requires higher tolerances in quality, detailed specifications, and delivery times.

The deficient provision of supplies to enterprises has been and is still due to a number of conditions present in the Soviet economy. Briefly, the most significant conditions can be summarized as follows:

1. Central authorities have followed a policy of overcommitting national resources, particularly materials, when establishing the annual national economic plan. This results in strained (that is, unbalanced) national plans in terms of output targets and available factor inputs, and this strain is passed down through the industrial hierarchy, directly affecting a great number of producing enterprises.
2. Traditionally, the central planners have focused their attention on a few high priority sectors of the economy, thus assuring the provision of needed resources to these sectors. The priority principle of resource allocation has proved quite effective for economic growth and development as long as the regime single-mindedly concentrated on a few easily defined objectives—notably, the expansion of basic heavy industries at any cost. In the present day Soviet economy there are a growing number of pressing commitments for scarce resources; there is less flexibility in maneuvering resources among different industries; and the economic objectives deemed of high priority by the state have become more numerous and more difficult to define clearly and enforce.
3. Because of the overcentralized, bureaucratic organization of industry, there are numerous unintentional errors in resource allocation—primarily due to

poor communication—affecting enterprises during the planning process. Overcentralization and red tape also make it extremely difficult to rectify planning errors during the related operating period. For this reason many producers underfulfill their production plans, thus causing a chain reaction at dependent customer enterprises.

4. The most highly valued goal that Soviet managers pursue in running their enterprises has been, and still is, the attainment of short-term monetary premiums (bonuses). The receipt and actual size of these premiums is dependent on the fulfillment and degree of overfulfillment of certain enterprise targets—notably, gross output, and, in recent years, on cost reduction and labor productivity also. The deficient provision of resources has long been the major obstacle to premium attainment at most enterprises. In their efforts to overcome this obstacle, enterprise managers engage in a variety of undesirable practices which greatly aggravate and further compound supply problems in Soviet industry.

5. Although the state has adopted various penalties in order to induce enterprises, in their roles as suppliers, to fulfill their contractual commitments with customers, such penalties have not proved very effective to date for a variety of reasons. In this connection superior authorities—ministry officials in the past and *sovnarkhoz* officials at present—have been inclined to condone violations of enterprise supply contracts as long as other plants within their area of responsibility have not been adversely affected. Such behavior on the part of superior authorities has been labeled "departmentalism" and "localism."

Of major concern in this chapter are the first three sets of conditions as chief causes of enterprise resource uncertainty and supply problems in Soviet industry. We shall also explore the latter two sets of conditions here, but a more comprehensive analysis will be presented in later chapters.

The actual examples of resource allocation deficiencies in Soviet industry discussed in this chapter should not be misconstrued. To the surprise of nonspecialists and many specialists of Soviet affairs, the Soviet economy does work; the punctual arrival of proper supplies is not news and would seldom be reported in the Soviet press. Nonetheless, the problems to be discussed here are real and serious—probably more serious than ever—not only because they are attracting widespread critical attention by the Soviets themselves, but also because they are built into the system.

Overcommitment of National Resources

The Soviet leaders have long desired to make full use of national resources in order to maximize economic growth. In fact, central authorities have traditionally followed a policy of overcommitting national resources when establishing the annual national economic plan. This, it has been felt, leads to high managerial aspiration levels at industrial enterprises, thus inducing management to work at peak performance and under constant pressure. To insure maximum effort enterprise managers have long been entitled to lucrative bonuses for fulfilling and overfulfilling aggregate output plans, and more will be said about this in the next chapter.

The policy of overcommitting resources, particularly materials, has continually resulted in strained (that is, unbalanced) national plans in terms of output targets and available factor inputs. This strain has been passed down through the industrial hierarchy, directly affecting a vast number of producing enterprises. In fact, this overcommitment policy has been one of the most significant causes of the dominant market power of the enterprise in its role as a supplier and "seller."

During the 1952-62 period, an average of 30 per cent of the annual gross national product of the country was used for investment projects. In 1960, for example, 31.3 per cent of the GNP was utilized for capital investment, 40 per cent of all new capital being used for industrial expansion, of which the producer goods industries received 88 per cent.[1] In the past decade the Soviet stock of fixed capital has grown by 11 per cent per year, faster than the average annual increase in output, and at the same time outstripping both available working capital and manpower. Hence, the high rate of capital formation, in conjunction with the desire of the Soviet rulers to make maximum use of fixed assets as well as all other resources, has caused numerous plants to underfulfill their production plans.

Prior to 1957, on the average 25 to 40 per cent of all industrial enterprises did not fulfill their annual production plans.[2] (It is very important to note that fulfillment of the production plan pertains only to gross output and tells us nothing of the quality of output or the detailed product-mix actually produced.) The 1956-60 sixth Five-Year Plan was terminated abortively in 1957, when it became blatantly obvious that the output goals were too ambitious. After an interval of about one year, the 1959-65 Seven-Year Plan was introduced. Khrushchev stated in 1957 that the policy of overcommitting national resources would be rectified. In this connection he said, "The Seven-Year Plan is being drawn up in such a way that it can be carried out without overstrain." The average annual growth of total industrial production (including defense industries) for the seven-year plan period was set at 8.6 per cent compared with 10.5 per cent for the sixth Five-Year Plan, and at 11.3 per cent for the fifth. The actual annual growth of civilian production during 1950-55 was 10.1 per cent; for 1955-61 the figure was 8.7 per cent; and for 1960-61, 6.6 per cent.[3]

There are indications that, after 1957, somewhat more "realistic" annual national plans were established. In the first half of 1958, "only" 19 per cent of all enterprises did not fulfill their production plans.[4]

In 1959 the figure was 11 per cent.[5] However, these figures represent national averages and tell us nothing about actual performance in different regions or different industrial sectors; nor do they tell us whether the product-mix actually produced served the functional or end use intended. Evidence of this type will be presented shortly.

In spite of the apparent improvement on a national scale, continued complaints have been voiced in Soviet sources claiming that strained national output targets have not been sufficiently eradicated, particularly in certain branches of industry. There are indications that the 1959-65 long-range plan has been scrapped not only because of a basic change in the priority emphasis of different economic sectors, but also because various output goals have been too ambitious in terms of available resources.

The Priority Principle in Resource Allocation

Even though a greater proportion of enterprises have been fulfilling their aggregate output targets than in the past, Soviet sources complain that this represents "uneven performance and development in different branches of industry." Typically, heavy industry and defense-related sectors fulfill and even overfulfill their output targets, whereas the production targets for the consumer goods and agricultural sectors are underfulfilled. In 1961, for example, although the plan called for an increase in producer goods output of 9.5 per cent as compared to 1961, the actual increase was 10 per cent. The consumer goods sector's planned increase was 6.9 per cent, but the actual increase was only 6.6 per cent.[6]

The underfulfillment of various sectoral targets probably serves as a good indication of what goals are considered expendable by central authorities, and which are deemed top priority. It is quite clear from national production results that the central planners still adhere to the priority principle in supply allocation. This means that attempts are made to allocate adequate resources to high priority sectors, frequently at the expense of low priority setcors. In the same vein, as bottlenecks arise in carrying out the national plan, attempts are made to shift assigned resources from low priority to higher priority branches of industry.

For many years, particularly during the Stalin era, the priority principle of resource allocation proved effective because the regime could single-mindedly concentrate on a few easily defined tasks—notably the expansion of heavy industry at any cost. Moreover, centralized planning and control in connection with heavy industry was not an unmanageable task since the bulk of the output and related inputs were of a fairly homogeneous nature (for example, coal, oil, gas, pig iron, electricity, cement, aluminum, and to a lesser degree, steel).

In the present day Soviet economy there are a growing number of pressing commitments for scarce resources; there is less flexibility in maneuvering resources among different industries; and the economic objectives deemed of high priority by the state have become more numerous and more difficult to enforce and define clearly. It is no longer possible to make fast or desirable headway by concentrating on a few relatively easy tasks. Yet the system is still basically geared to the production of more of the same thing. Khrushchev has clearly pointed this out in his recent statement about steel production when he said, "The production of steel is like a well-traveled road with deep ruts; here even blind horses will not run off because the wheels will break. Similarly, some officials have put on steel blinkers; they do everything as they were taught in their day. A material appears which is superior to steel and is cheaper but they keep on shouting 'steel, steel.' " [7]

Priority emphasis is now being given to the chemical and electronic industries, and the regime hopes to triple the output of the former by 1970. The Soviet leaders are also attempting to allocate substantially more resources to the failing agriculture sector. At the same time, it cannot be ignored that the population has long been clamoring for more and better consumer goods and housing. Although consumers have found their lot improving since Stalin's death, such improvement has been very modest in the last few years, and there is much pressure on the rulers to further ameliorate this situation considerably. They may have little choice but to do so, for fear that higher pay for higher productivity will be an impotent incentive if there is little that is worthwhile for the "state employee" to buy. All of these factors are reflected in the stated change in Soviet economic policy in 1963, at the time the 1959-65 plan was scrapped.[8]

As if these pressures were not enough, the regime has seen fit to increase space and defense spending about 50 per cent during the 1961-63 period, although a cutback has been announced at the end of 1963. Moreover, foreign trade and economic activity both within and outside the Soviet bloc are expanding and becoming more complex. With emphasis placed on all the above sectors of the economy by the Soviet leaders, and with each sector placed in a seemingly high priority position, what is the enterprise manager to do when confronted with an either-or production decision?

When a given manager runs into difficulty in fulfilling his enterprise's production plan, he has only two subjective compasses to guide him: his evaluation of those products that are most beneficial in terms of aggregate performance, since he is evaluated and rewarded on the basis of aggregate results; and his assessment of what his superiors consider to be of highest priority. In the past, when priorities were clearly defined and easy to enforce, it was obvious to the management of a multi-product machinery plant that the machinery for their steel mill customer should be produced and delivered on time, whereas the textile and agricultural machinery was of secondary importance. What is the manager to do today in this situation?

He knows that his planned output for customers in the metallurgical, chemical, coal mining, and defense-related industries is deemed very important by the regime; he also knows that the top leaders are strongly emphasizing greatly improved agricultural performance, and hence his farm machinery production also seems to be of high priority; moreover, he may now run into serious trouble if he fails to deliver ordered equipment to certain stipulated consumer goods plants, housing construction organizations, and various foreign customers in Poland, Rumania, and Africa. Manufacturers of chemicals, ball bearings, parts and components, rubber, leather, cloth fabrics, various metals, and numerous other commodities are likely to find themselves in a similar dilemma.

As breakdowns in the plan arise, the central planners are also faced with serious problems in shifting resources among sectors. Because of modern technology and because many branches of industry are technologically unique, there is much less leeway to maneuver allocated resources from low priority to high priority sectors to remove bottlenecks. A given producer can no longer make do with just any supplies if his own production plan is to be properly fulfilled. Because of more varied inputs and outputs, all calling for more delicate tolerances and specifications, breakdowns in production now tend to spread even to high priority industrial sectors. Defense and missile production may be the one significant exception, since central authorities can still effectively plan and control activities pertaining to a limited number of highly strategic projects.

In spite of all these problems, the priority principle in resource allocation is still adhered to by the Soviet central planners where possible. This is not only evident from national production results, but also from concrete specific examples and from personal interviews with Soviet managers. For example, in one Soviet source the director of the Liberated Labor Textile Mill complains bitterly about deficient supply allocations for 1963. He claims that his enterprise has only been allocated 20 per cent of the indigo dyes, 10 per cent of the active dyes, 25 per cent of the acid dyes, and about 25 per cent of certain other chemicals needed to fulfill the production plan.[9] Managers interviewed at a silk factory and a clothing enterprise indicated that failure to fulfill their production plans in various quarters of 1960 was due to the lack of suitable materials and equipment. They also pointed out that they have little influence on resource allocation during the planning process, and that bargaining sessions with higher authorities deal mainly with quantity of production and cost targets.

On the other hand, managers at a Moscow watch factory asserted that they are allocated adequate supplies since theirs is a high priority plant, producing largely for export in competitive world markets. This may be generally true since the enterprise fulfilled its production plan in every quarter in 1960. Managers at three, apparently high priority, machinery and ball bearing plants claimed that inadequate allocation of supplies was in no way responsible for the failure to fulfill their production plans in various quarters of 1960. Rather, the blame was placed primarily on inadequate skilled manpower; but at the same time it was revealed at two of these enterprises, that, although adequate supplies had been allocated, some required materials were not received on time. Hence, allocation of adequate resources is clearly not enough for even a high priority producer; it must also be in timely possession of these resources if its production plan is to be properly fulfilled.

Deficiencies in the Planning and Allocation of Supplies

Even granting that the regime does not overcommit national resources to as great a degree as in the past, and in spite of the priority principle— blurred as it may now be—an individual enterprise, be it of low or high priority, may still be faced with a deficient allocation of supplies. There are numerous, and often serious, unintentional errors in supply allocation throughout the system. In a very real sense the Soviet planning process is one in which the "blind lead the blind." Greatly aggravating the supply problem is the enterprise manager's tendency to provide higher level planners with deficient information about their production capabilities and resource needs, thus making the "blind who lead the blind" even more blind.

Overcentralization and Organizational Confusion

In our descriptive presentation of the planning process in the preceding chapter, we talked merely of central, republican, and regional agencies. In reality, the sheer volume of planning work requires it to be divided among literally hundreds of different offices, departments, and subdepartments at each level. There are separate departments dealing with the allocation of a given class of supply, others with the sale and/or delivery of a certain type of commodity, and still others with investment, production planning, financial planning, labor and wages, technical development, product innovation, and so forth.

In theory, the *sovnarkhoz* and its branch administrations are supposed to be the direct superiors of subordinate enterprises in all matters. They are supposed to disaggregate among their plants, supply allocations, production targets, and various other tasks emanating from the republican and central planning agencies. In practice, the formal chain of command is constantly being short-circuited. Although the *sovnarkhoz* apparatus is responsible for controlling subordinate enterprises, it has little effective authority over resource allocation. Literally millions of allocation certificates are issued by different supply offices in Moscow and in the republics. Each represents, in essence, a portion of the production of the enterprise which must deliver the allocated commodity. Yet not only are there many supply departments which raise difficulties of coordination (for example, where several different commodities must be allocated to one factory), but since 1957 the supply departments have been separated organizationally from production planning. Even within the *sovnarkhozy* there are often conflicts and confusion between the supply, sales, production, and other functional departments of branch administrations and the head office.

A given enterprise is likely to receive supply allocations, production assignments, and various other directives from many different central and republic-level departments, in addition to those received from the *sovnarkhoz* and its subdivisions. This was the case at most of the enterprises surveyed by this writer. As the draft plan emerges from the *sovnarkhoz*, both *sovnarkhoz* officials and enterprise managers find themselves in a bureaucratic maze. The Soviets themselves are inclined to ridicule the bureaucratic confusion built into the system of supply allocation. The satirical Soviet publication *Krokodil* has published a cartoon illustrating the statement of a Moscow party official to the effect that to receive ball bearings from the First Moscow State Ball Bearing Plant, the neighboring Likhachev Automobile Factory's requests for an allocation make a long journey, through 14 republican and central supply, sales, and planning departments.[10] In another source a *sovnarkhoz* executive points out that in the case of electrical equipment and related components alone, one central department allocates 30 different items, a second 1,397, and a third 1,776. Ball bearings required by plants in his region are assigned in aggregate quantities in one agency, whereas specific types and sizes are processed and approved in another.[11]

Hence, the approved operating plan for a given enterprise is very likely to consist of a number of different production targets, other tasks, and supply allocations emanating from various higher level offices which are ill-informed about each other's doings, and which adopt different—often conflicting—criteria. Therefore it is not surprising to find a great many accounts in Soviet sources of enterprises receiving production and delivery plans that are inconsistent with allocated supplies, capital investment plans that are not properly geared into either the production or supply plans, or financial and cost plans that are incompatible with all the other sections of the plan.

Because the functions, powers, and responsibilities of the numerous departments and agencies in the system change somewhat from year to year and are never clearly spelled out, matters are complicated further. In their attempt to clarify the rights and activities of various planning and administrative agencies, following the November 1962 reorganization of industry, Soviet sources have had great difficulty. Thus we get the following typical statement in one highly authoritative source about various joint planning decisions that are rendered by *"Gosplan in cooperation with* the National Economic Council, the planning agencies of the individual republics, and the industrial state committees, *Gostroy* U.S.S.R., and other appropriate central organizations." [12] In the light of this reorganization, it appears that some of the most basic features of overcentralization, organizational duplication, and general bureaucratic confusion not only remain, but may even have been intensified.[13]

An article in a leading Soviet economic journal strongly advocates that clear laws regarding the functions, powers, and responsibilities of all planning and administrative organizations should be established in view of the recent industrial reorganization. The source goes on to condemn severely the organizational confusion that persists throughout the system, citing actual examples.[14] But how can meaningful, clear laws be established if the over-all organizational apparatus is in a constant state of flux?

Hence, it is no wonder that there are many reports to the effect that enterprises cannot obtain needed items from suppliers beacuse no department in the system had been clearly granted the power to allocate the item in question or to enforce the supplier to accept and fulfill the customer's order. This is frequently the case with nonstandardized components, or materials. For example, one Soviet source tells of an oil refining plant in the Caucasus that tried to get three different suppliers, in three different regions, to provide it with certain parts, but to no avail. When the enterprise managers appealed to various higher authorities for help, they were told that neither the National Economic Council nor the industrial state committees nor the republican planners had the right to take any action in this case. The *sovnarkhoz* officials involved in this situation also pointed out that they could do nothing to compel their subordinate plants to provide the parts.[15]

In a very real sense, some enterprises, particularly those of high priority, may have been better off under the ministerial system. At least then the plant had to deal only with one superior agency which had the authority to make virtually all production, resource allocation, and other decisions involving the enterprises. The enterprise also had a high level defender who could bargain for resources on an equal basis with other republic-level or central authorities. Under the *sovnarkhoz* system, this is far from being the case. On the other hand, it should be noted that many enterprise managers interviewed expressed a strong perference for the *sovnarkhoz* system nevertheless. Their chief reason was that *sovnarkhoz* officials have a better understanding of, and greater concern about, the problems and resource needs of the enterprise, whereas the ministerial officials tended to operate in a "vacuum," assigning unrealistic tasks without considering local conditions.

Lack of Parity Between Administrative Authority and Responsibility

The enterprise manager, now as before, is held responsible for fulfilling his production plan, although he has little if any authority over the acquisition of required supplies—at least in the aggregate sense. Thus we read that the Tula Combine Factory, responsible for delivering 394,000 hinges to customer plants in 1962, was not able to produce more than 250,000 because it lacked the necessary supplies. In view of this situation the factory director stated, "Neither our requests, nor the danger of breakdown in supply cooperation, bothers the planning organs. In the last analysis, we will be held responsible for the underfulfillment of the hinges plan, while the planning organs will be out of the line of fire." [16] This is analogous to holding the sales manager of an American firm responsible for not fulfilling the sales plan because of a serious breakdown or strike in his company's or in a supplier's plant.

The lack of parity between authority and responsibility is a major organizational defect in the Soviet system. Superior organs have the power to allocate supplies and to make numerous other decisions directly affecting industrial enterprises; yet the enterprise is held responsible for failures beyond its control. Since responsibility for negligent, or even intentional, supply allocation deficiencies is hard to trace through the bureaucratic maze, there is usually no penalty to pay by those actually responsible. One can read almost daily in Soviet sources of supplies being allocated from unbuilt plants or uncompleted workshops, and of various other types of resource allocation irregularities. In most instances no attempt is made to trace the person or department who is actually responsible for such gross deficiencies. Even when there is an earnest attempt to do so, it turns out to be a very complex and time-consuming, if not impossible, task. One concrete representative example will suffice to highlight this point.[17]

One Soviet official describes his efforts to discover why—among a myriad of other supply complaints—the allocation certificates for phenol (carbolic acid) issued by the Department of Chemicals and Rubber of the Russian Republic *Gosplan* were not honored, why deliveries could not be made, output was halted at user plants, and so forth. The head of this department, besieged by representatives of *sovnarkhozy* and enterprises, complained that he did not know this year, or in the previous

year, what proportions of his allocations would be covered by actual production. He admitted that a Saratov plant was to have delivered phenol
which it was not able to produce, and referred complaints to *Rosglav-
khimsnagsbyt*—another supply and sales administration duplicating in
some measure the other department cited above. Here a planner admitted that they knowingly allocated nonexistent Saratov production of
phenol and blamed *Soyuzglavkhim*—a division of *Gosplan* U.S.S.R. There,
in turn, it was stated that they knew of the situation, and in fact had
reported the need to reduce the national output plan of some chemicals
in which phenol is used—this they reported to the Department of Aggregate Balances and Material Requirement of *Gosplan* U.S.S.R. They also
blamed the Russian Republic *Gosplan* for planning "fictional deliveries."
The next step was to blame the Production Department of the Chemical
Industry of *Gosplan* U.S.S.R. The official there declared, "You will never
find the actual guilty person. I can assure you that if anyone said he was
responsible for the muddle and should be punished, no one would believe him."

Finally, the head of the Production Department of the Chemical Industry of *Gosplan* U.S.S.R. blamed the Russian *Gosplan*. There it was
confirmed that the Saratov plant should have been producing phenol
back in 1960. The necessary shop should have been started in 1957, but
the State Committee for the Chemical Industry altered the investment
project, and building did not begin until the end of 1960. Errors in
investment plans led to further delays. Then it was found difficult to
place the necessary orders for equipment, and by the end of 1961 only
35 per cent of the projected work had been completed. Enterprises located in 12 *sovnarkhozy* failed to obtain the phenol provided for in the
supplies plan. And so on.

The Soviet author makes it quite clear that phenol is one small
example "taken at random."

Information Distortion and Arbitrary Allocation Decisions

Various planning departments, even when making an earnest effort
to allocate supplies in an efficient manner, are severely handicapped by
the deficient information about supply needs emanating from the enterprise level. The whole planning process is somewhat like a guessing
game: the enterprise attempts to pad its supply requests to protect itself
against failures in the system, while the central planners, desiring maximum results, try to pare down the requests channeled up from the
bottom. This is typified in one Soviet source which has posed the following question to an enterprise director, "Why do enterprises pad their
plan proposals and requests?" and the answer was, "Because the central

planners (*Gosplan* in this case) cut our requests." *Gosplan* was then asked, "Why are enterprises' requests cut?" and the answer was, "The requests are padded." [18]

This type of process must necessarily result in numerous planning errors and rather arbitrary resource allocation decisions. Faced with such a dilemma, a given planning office may have no choice but to base its supply allocations on what was allocated to a given republic, region, or enterprise in the past. But this kind of planning can result in serious adverse consequences if the quantity of supplies actually required during the planned year differs significantly from past allocations. This may happen if a substantial change in inventory levels has occurred, if operations requiring the commodity in question are significantly expanded or contracted, and for a variety of other reasons. Let us cite a concrete example to drive home the point.

The Estonian region requested 7.6 tons of semihard rubber for 1960, but it was allocated only .6 tons—the same amount as the previous year. Enterprises in the region requiring this rubber understandably ran into trouble. For 1961 the region requested 21.5 tons of this same rubber, but were only allotted 1.45 tons. When the regional officials protested to the central planners, they were told that this was a "generous" allocation since it was more than double that of the previous year. On the other hand, this same region did not require any measuring gauges of a certain type in 1960, yet they were allocated a slight increase over 1959. [19]

The Time Problem

As if all of the above problems in supply allocation were not enough, there are still others. The enterprise usually must estimate its over-all supply needs before its production plan is formally approved, and the formal approval for both the production plan and supply allocations is frequently late in arriving. It is perhaps more serious that in most instances the enterprise's detailed product-mix is not spelled out in the annual plan; yet supplies are allocated on an annual basis. These problems contribute to the inconsistencies that frequently arise between the production program, supply allocations, and delivery schedules at a given enterprise.

Contractual Negotiations and Disputes

Even after supply allocations are received by the enterprise, much detail remains to be worked out with the suppliers regarding commodity specifications and quality. Naturally, this results in many delays and conflicts. Suppliers desire to produce those items that are most beneficial for their aggregate results, whereas the product specifications stipulated in contracts are often not for products in customer demand. (More will be said about this situation in Chapter 8.) At times attempts are made to iron out disputes in contracts between suppliers and customers through state arbitration commissions. It seems that more often than not, the producer wins his case; he may convince the commissions that he will not possess adequate resources to produce goods with the desired specifications.

Enterprise Supply Ties

With the emergence of the territorial system in 1957, it was hoped that direct supply relationships between producer and customer enterprises would be established on a more rational and permanent basis and would alleviate the time-consuming task of having superior agencies work out the detailed specifications of supply and delivery contracts. We noted in Chapter 2 that such improvements have been forthcoming, although not to as great an extent as had been anticipated. There are still many complaints that irrational arrays of supplies are being assigned to a given customer because the superior organs, responsible for determining these relationships, are ignorant about local conditions, and often because they are concerned only with the production problems of the producers rather than with the interests of the consumers. For essentially the same reasons, suppliers are frequently changed—even from quarter to quarter within a given year.

At 12 enterprises surveyed, there was some changeover to suppliers of a more local nature following the 1957 reorganization; however, this changeover did not appear to be on a widespread scale. Several of these enterprises had more than 100 different suppliers, and all but the ball bearing factory had at least 25. Many of their suppliers were located in other regions, and even in other republics. While some of the enterprises claimed slight reductions in the total number of suppliers in recent years, others claimed slight increases due to extended subcontracting and specialization.

One of the aims of the 1963 reorganization is to further provide for more rational and direct supplier-customer relationships. Since most of the newly created *sovnarkhozy* are considerably larger, and apparently somewhat more self-sufficient than the earlier ones, such an improvement may be realized—at least to some degree. If this be the case, this may well lead to better cooperation and understanding regarding detailed supply requirements, at least among enterprises in the same region. However, this largely depends on whether the *sovnarkhoz* can keep a close check on contractual activities, thus counteracting the bargaining power of enterprises in their role as sellers. The span of control could possibly serve as a constraint in this connection, given larger regions.

Changes in Plans

Numerous *ad hoc* decisions are required to cope with planning errors and disequilibria discovered, once the plan is implemented. It may be found that the requirements for various commodities cannot be met within the period in question. This often leads to the assignment of different and/or additional production tasks to enterprises without proper provisions being made for new or additional supplies that may be needed. Because of the rather crude system of annual aggregate planning, the detailed product-mix determined in the quarterly plans may well be inconsistent with allotted supplies. In addition, changes in the assortment plan may call for changes in factor inputs.

The director of a Kharkov clothing factory told this author that in 1960 he received a directive to change the assortment plan to provide for more production of a certain kind of suit. This meant that the enterprise would need more of a certain fabric from its Kiev supplier. It turned out that the Kiev plant could not process enough of the needed fabric on time because it did not have adequate equipment. Perhaps if the situation were traced further it would be found that, in order to obtain additional equipment of the proper type, the production plan of the Kiev's machinery supplier would have had to change his plan. In turn, this may well have called for additional components from the machinery plant's suppliers, thus causing changes in their plans, and so on through the interrelated industrial chain.

There is substantial evidence of myriad changes in plans throughout the system. For example, we read that the Moscow Province *Sovnarkhoz* made about 1,500 changes in the plans of subordinate enterprises in 1962. The Electrostat Heavy Machinery Plant alone had its plan changed 94 times.[20] These changes included output, delivery, supply, and capital investment, as well as new directives dealing with technical development, product innovation, and various other matters.

Some American administrators and project engineers at various large West Coast aerospace firms find themselves in situations similar to those confronting the Soviet manager. When working on government contracts they receive numerous directives calling for changes in plans and work schedules; priorities given to different projects are often shifted in midstream; requests for additional funds—even modest amounts—or even requests to maneuver the allocation of funds among different uses, typically require filling out numerous forms, and processing these forms through a time-consuming bureaucratic apparatus. Here, as in the Soviet case, the macromanagerial rules of the game are more of the "Thou Shalt" variety, rather than the "Thou Shalt Not" type. American company personnel tend to be disrupted and even resentful in such an environment. Even in our competitive market economy, suppliers cannot always promptly provide the items needed when frequent changes in plans are undertaken, particularly if the items are of a highly complex technical nature.

Receipt of Adequate Supplies During the Operating Period

Even if a given enterprise is allocated adequate supplies and enters into favorable contracts with suppliers, management is still faced with the very real possibility of not receiving supplies on time or according to specification. As one enterprise director aptly puts it: "To defend the requested resource is only half of the work. The actual receipt of the goods is the other half." [21]

Supply Failures and Chain Reactions

Many enterprises obtain unrealistic production plans, thus preventing them from properly fulfilling their supply and delivery commitments. As will be discussed more fully in later chapters, violations in supply contracts are also greatly compounded by the system of managerial incentives. Supply failures during the operating period set off chain reactions throughout the system, often upsetting the operations even of enterprises that have been allocated adequate resources during the planning process.

A manager of a Soviet ball bearing factory told this author about the breakdown of an automated production line at his enterprise involving 14 workers. Some of the workers' equipment remained idle for about a week because the necessary parts that had been ordered from the supplier were late in arriving, nor were they available at the regional warehouse. Consequently, the enterprise could not fulfill its delivery schedules for a number of customers. The manager indicated that this may well have caused a chain reaction adversely affecting many other plants. At the same time his own supplier was not blamed, because he in turn had not received the metals necessary to produce the required parts.

There are numerous examples of supply failures even at very high priority plants. For instance, at the high priority Kirovakan Chemical enterprise, which began operations at the end of 1962, eight machines stood idle during 1963 because of supply failures involving raw materials.[22] This caused the enterprise to substantially underfulfill its assortment and delivery plans, thus upsetting operations at several customer plants. A steel mill in the Perm *Sovnarkhoz,* which was supposed to begin operating in the third quarter of 1963, could not do so because it had no smoke stacks. The allocated materials for these stacks had not arrived. In fact, of the 450,000 pieces of concrete needed in the construction of this plant during 1962 and 1963, only 80,000 have been provided, and many of these are classified as "junk." Yet, other enterprises have been allocated output from this plant for the remainder of 1963.[23]

The Byelorussian Tractor Factory, which has 227 suppliers, had its production line stopped 19 times in 1962 because of the lack of rubber parts, 18 times because of ball bearings, and 8 times because of transmission components. The pattern of breakdowns continued in 1963. During the first quarter of 1963 only about one-half of the plant's ball bearing and rubber needs were satisfied, and only half of the required batteries were available. One supplier shipped 19,000 less wheels than called for in the contract. In total, they were short of 27 different items.[24] Similar, and even more plentiful, examples regarding supply deficiencies at consumer goods plants could be cited.[25]

It is not surprising that 90 enterprises out of 100 surveyed in the Chelyabinsk region blamed their underfulfillment of production plans in 1962 on supply deficiencies.[26] It is unlikely that a similar survey in 1963 or 1964 would show a substantial improvement.

The above examples are by no means mere aberrations or isolated incidents. Similar, and often more serious, examples of supply failures are reported in many issues of *Pravda, Izvestia,* and in Soviet economic publications, particularly the party economic publication *Ekonomicheskaya Gazeta.*

Inadequate Reserve Stocks for Flexibility

In an attempt to guard against failures in the supply system, reserve stocks of raw materials, equipment, and components are maintained at the national, republican, and regional levels. Warehouses supply enterprises requiring odd-lot shipments of goods and also provide "emergency" reserves required to fulfill the plan. They also keep on hand items which can supposedly be freely purchased by producers. One eminent Soviet economist interviewed indicated that such planned reserves of the *sovnarkhoz* level are roughly equivalent to 3 to 5 per cent of the total planned output of the region.

There are also many complaints that there are not nearly enough local stores and warehouses of this type, and that existing warehouses do not carry nearly enough different items, and many that are stocked are obsolete. For this reason enterprises have little confidence in this source of supply. For example, the Chief Ferrous Metals Supply Warehouse of the Russian Republic annually receives requests for more than 4,000 different items, but it carries only about 1,300, many of which are obsolete.[27] It also appears that significant red tape is often involved in obtaining even "free goods" from the warehouses. No doubt, personal relationships and politics tend to play an important role regarding who gets what and how fast.

Localism

The most crucial problem in connection with the timely receipt of proper supplies is clearly that of "localism." It is natural for a given *sovnarkhoz* to strive for the timely delivery of required items among subordinate enterprises before giving due consideration to "external" customers. For enterprise management, this situation blurs even further the regime's priority system regarding different sectors of the economy. A given manager may have to decide whether to fulfill his supply commitments for a high priority enterprise in another region or one of lower priority in his region. Adoption of the former course of action will almost surely bring wrath and perhaps penalties from his direct *sovnarkhoz* superiors; if he adopts the latter, it is more difficult to predict what will happen, since reaction would come from further removed superior agencies. The big question for him then would be, "Will there be adverse consequences emerging from the high-level bureaucratic maze?" Although there are numerous examples of enterprises not fulfilling supply contracts to plants in the same region, there are strong indications that management tends to sacrifice external commitments before intraregional commitments.

The customer enterprise would generally have no high level defender to act effectively against the power of sellers in other regions, and particularly in other republics. If the abused customer is of very high priority, republic-level or central authorities may well take action, but by then it would usually be too late to rectify this particular situation— the customer would still not receive the proper supplies on time. Soviet sources are filled with reports of *sovnarkhozy* and republics fulfilling and even overfulfilling their supply delivery plans within their own areas, although underfulfilling plans to other areas at the same time.

Enlarging the *sovnarkhozy* in 1963 was an attempt to create better balanced and more economically self-sufficient regions. Shortly after the 1963 reorganization, Khrushchev disclosed that, in the past, only 2 to 8 per cent of the enterprises in the highly developed and more self-sufficient *sovnarkhozy* (such as Moscow and Leningrad) failed to fulfill their quarterly and annual production plans. At the same time, in many less self-sufficient and/or isolated regions, 20 to 65 per cent, and, at times, even a greater proportion of the enterprises failed to fulfill their output plans.[28] This is understandable, but what Khrushchev failed to point out was that even in those regions where most enterprises have fulfilled their plans, the product-mix and quality of output have frequently not been according to specifications.

It is quite likely that the enlarged *sovnarkhozy* will at least improve the supply situation to some degree. If a greater portion of requested supplies are available within a given region, there will be less need to engage in localistic practices. However, future improvements will depend largely on how well the *sovnarkhozy* can control and how closely they can watch the activities of subordinate plants. In this connection some large *sovnarkhozy* may possibly find that their span of control is overburdened.

The Soviets realize that even with the 1963 reorganization, localism will not disappear overnight. They are apparently resigned to the fact that it will remain a very serious problem for some time to come. However, they foresee the day when, through the construction of new plants and the location of new industries, highly developed and relatively self-sufficient economic regions will evolve throughout the nation. It is with this aim in mind that councils and planning commissions have been set up in the 18 newly created major economic regions (natural territories). More will be said about this in Chapter 12.

Localism still remains a highly critical problem in spite of the reorganization of *sovnarkhozy*. Hence, we read that the Misherskii Steel Frame Plant refuses to produce badly needed components for an enterprise in another region; and comrade Avilov, the vice-chairman of the steel plant's *sovnarkhoz,* declines to break the "obstinacy" of his subordinate enterprise. The same enterprise is then turned away by two other suppliers in two other "foreign" regions who claim that they lack the tools necessary to produce the needed components.[29]

We also learn that the metallurgy enterprises in the Russian Republic have shipped 33,000 tons of above plan orders to customers in this republic, but have failed to ship below plan orders to plants in other republics.[30] Similarly, the Uzbekistan chemical machinery plants have failed to supply 162 units of equipment to other regions during the first quarter of 1963, because they have been "busy" fulfilling nonplanned orders from their own *sovnarkhoz.*[31]

During 1963, a large enterprise in the Moscow region produced 900 cranes that are not needed by anybody in this region. These cranes are not being used although there is a great need for them in other regions. This source also points out that the Moscow *Sovnarkhoz* officials have implied that as long as their region is satisfactorily supplied they are happy, but they have little or no concern for other regions.[32]

Soviet sources are not completely without humor in their condemnations of localism. For instance, one source presents a cartoon showing a man (presumably an enterprise representative) entering the office of either a *sovnarkhoz* or another enterprise, where two loafing bureaucrats are sitting at their desks. The man says, "Will you, at last, give us the bolts and shovels?" On the desk of one of the bureaucrats there is a huge sign stating, "Do not enter if you are from another *sovnarkhoz*." [33]

Ineffective Penalties for Supply Violations

The regime administers certain penalties in an attempt to induce producers to fulfill their product-mix and delivery commitments in accordance with contractual agreements. Customers—whether they be other plants or trade organizations—can legally press for fines and damages from delinquent suppliers. Larger fines can be levied where customer enterprises are in other regions. We will come back to this subject in later chapters, but it is important to note here that such penalties tend to be rather ineffective.[34]

There is much evidence that arbitration commissions responsible for determining whether, and how much, in the way of fines and/or damages should be levied, either do not take any action or fail to enforce their decisions. This is understandable, since it is likely to be extremely difficult and time consuming to clearly attribute blame to the delinquent supplier. The supplier in question may not have been allocated adequate resources; he may not have received proper supplies from his own suppliers; or his plan may have been disrupted by revisions. Damages are harder to collect than fines, and it appears they are seldom awarded.

In general, abused customers are reluctant to file claims for fear of alienating suppliers, thus upsetting future relations. This is often referred to by the Soviets as "the rotten practice of mutual amnesties." One enterprise director in an interview with an *Ekonomicheskaya Gazeta* correspondent told about his supply woes. But he urged the correspondent not to name the delinquent suppliers because "they are not happy with our complaints, and if they get mad, things will get worse." [35]

Should the customer be awarded fines and/or damages, it entails a lengthy, complex, bureaucratic process—meanwhile he is still without the needed items. Even when fines are paid they are often small. And finally, in cases where monetary penalties are substantial, the major portion is actually paid by the state since they are paid out of the enterprises' total profits before deductions and are credited to the Enterprise Fund.[36]

Supply Uncertainty and High-Cost Subsidiary Operations

Because of this environment of chronic supply uncertainty, enterprises continue to engage in high-cost subsidiary operations to assure themselves adequate supplies. This significantly hinders rational and economical specialization. There are widespread complaints that *sovnar-khozy* fail to take advantage of many opportunities for specialization among subordinate plants, and some sources urge that incentives be provided to *sovnarkhozy* for doing so.[37] The lack of specialization is most serious in connection with small hardware items (fasteners, nuts, screws, bolts, parts, components, and so forth). Fasteners are made at 1,350 plants of which only 18 are specialized. Welding electrodes are produced at several hundred enterprises of which only 11 are specialized.[38]

The cost of one ton of small screws produced at the Magnitogorst Metal Products Plant of the Southern Urals *Sovnarkhoz* is 303 rubles, whereas at the Miass Electrical Apparatus Plant in the same region the same items cost 1,540 rubles. In this connection Khrushchev has quipped, "Well, frankly, the comrades at this plant must be making gold screws.[39]

We also read that castings and forgings are being produced in small shops by highly uneconomical semihandicraft methods using obsolete equipment. At enterprises in the Russian Republic, small casting shops with capacities of less than 1,000 tons a year account for more than 50 per cent of iron castings and more than 60 per cent of steel castings. The average production cost of a ton of iron castings manufactured in these shops is more than 170 rubles, compared to 90 rubles per ton in large shops.[40]

It should be pointed out, however, that in some regions an enterprise merger movement—involving both vertical and horizontal integration—is underway. These mergers are being undertaken to achieve economies of scale, and in the case of vertical integration, to provide for greater dependability of supply. We will explore this situation more fully in Chapter 12.

Illegal Procurement Practices

Perhaps one of the best barometers for gauging the seriousness and pervasiveness of the supply problem in Soviet industry is the extent of illegal procurement activity. This pertains to the use of "fixers," "push-ers," or "expediters" (*tolkachi*), personal influence, bribes, and special favors (*blat*) in obtaining supplies illegally through informal channels.[41] Unfortunately, it is difficult to estimate accurately how extensive these activities are, since they are in fact illegal. However, Soviet sources disclose incidents that suggest that these practices are prevalent.

Officials of the Dnepropetrovsk *Sovnarkhoz* estimated that their metals and chemical factories were visited by 4,000 *tolkachi* in 1959, while 3,000 more descended on machinery enterprises, and 1,000 besieged the supply and sales department of the *Sovnarkhoz* itself.[42] The business manager of another *Sovnarkhoz* stated recently, "We are overrun with expediters. They fill all the hotels in the city—expediters spend millions of rubles of state money and bring disorder to the work of enterprises and supply bases.[43] One Minsk enterprise sent 32 representatives to the same Leningrad supplier in 1962 to expedite the shipment of goods at any cost. A total of 400 days were spent in the city and a 10,000 ruble hotel bill was charged to travel expenses. The director of this enterprise points out how he must obtain required supplies: "There comes in the *tolkach!* It is the same man against whom, year in and year out, they pronounce all kinds of curses, but who continues to live, flourish, and occupy a large amount of hotel rooms." [44]

In a July 1962 issue of *Izvestia*—the official government paper—comrade Zhebrak, the supply manager of a leather factory, made the following confession in a letter to the editors: "We expedite strenuously, using all legitimate and illegal means to justify our existence and to push through the next shipment of materials that at times are desperately needed by the organization that sent us." [45] Moreover, he reveals that expediters are at work at all levels in industry. The editors sympathetically commented that comrade Zhebrak is an expediter against his will and that they can understand why he behaves in this manner, in view of the supply situation. Other sources suggest that many, if not all, *sovnarkhozy* find it necessary to undertake various illegal and semilegal procurement activities.

The director of one machinery plant stated in an interview that illegal procurement activities are "a necessary evil." Understandably, he did not say whether his own enterprise engages in such activity. In early 1962, a central decree pertaining to economic crimes was issued: bribery, embezzlement, black-market operations, pilfering, and the like, could bring capital punishment for repeated and very serious offenses. A rash of executions ensued during 1962 and 1963. However, none of the executions reported were for enterprise illegal procurement activity per se, and such activity was not singled out in the decree.[46] In spite of the decree there is much evidence that illegal procurement is still a widespread phenomenon in the Soviet system, particularly at the enterprise level.

Another facet of illegal procurement activity is the informal "barter" system among enterprises. We read that the director of the Fomashina enterprise has illegally exchanged 50 tons of rolled black metal for another metal not needed by his plant but by another plant. Another enterprise has swapped 20 barrels of ammonia for 2 tons of coal. And still another enterprise director claims that he had to give up some of his metal to get urgently needed spare parts from another plant.[47] And so on.

Since there are few prosecutions reported for illegal procurement of supplies, this suggests that the rulers tolerate such behavior—at least to some degree—because it aids the over-all supply system. This improvement would be the result if supplies were deflected from low priority to high priority plants; but there is little evidence to this effect. The "informal" markets and supply relations give the enterprise manager some illegal independence and provide for shortcuts in the bureaucratic apparatus. No doubt, higher quality goods are obtained, in numerous instances, through this informal network rather than through regular channels. In the process, various enterprises (and probably individuals) reap undisclosed profits. In a very real sense there is a black-market system.

Some Western observers infer that extra-legal markets, of various shades of gray and black, are tolerated by the regime since the system could not function otherwise.[48] In effect, they are actually questioning whether there is in fact central planning in the Soviet economy. This, however, is probably overstressing the importance of extra-legal markets; yet it cannot be doubted that such markets are extensive and offer both advantages and disadvantages for the regime.

Manpower Problems

Soviet sources clearly indicate that the labor force, in terms of total numbers and required skills, is not keeping pace with increasing industrial expansion or growing technological complexity. In an earlier, simpler day, surplus labor provided for much flexibility in Soviet industry. If a given plant or industry did not possess adequate equipment or materials to fulfill the production plan, chances were that this could be overcome by adding more labor as a factor input. However, this is no longer the case and growing manpower shortages are being felt throughout Soviet industry.[49]

Several reasons explain this situation: first, there was the great loss of life during World War II; second, underemployed peasant labor from the agricultural sector has been virtually completely absorbed and, in fact, there has been renewed emphasis on the expansion of agricultural activity recently; third, there is the high rate of formation of industrial capital, coupled in 1961 with a reduction in the workweek from 46 to 41 hours; fourth, lagging technological innovation has hampered sufficient increases in labor productivity to offset manpower shortages. (More will be said about this point in Chapter 9.) At the same time, however, increased technological complexity and the technological uniqueness among different branches of industry require more highly trained and specialized manpower, thus deterring interindustry manpower mobility.

Labor shortages are most severe in remote regions or those areas with unfavorable living conditions. Shortages are also a serious problem in low priority industrial sectors—the educational system is not geared to provide these sectors with ample properly trained personnel. There is also much evidence of insufficient numbers of skilled personnel in industries undergoing rapid technological change (for example, chemicals and electronics). In general, no industry, except perhaps strategic defense projects, is totally unaffected by scarce manpower.

None of the enterprises surveyed in the Moscow or Leningrad regions attributed the nonfulfillment of their plans to labor shortages. Yet, a ball bearing plant and a mining equipment enterprise, two high priority plants in the Kharkov region—a relatively favorable area in terms of living conditions—attributed nonfulfillment of plans in 1960 to the lack of suitable skilled labor.

In addition to genuine manpower shortages that might exist at a given enterprise, the enterprise may well be confronted with the additional problem of labor turnover. Since the 1956 decree allowing workers greater freedom in changing jobs, labor turnover has become a very significant problem. Let us cite two concrete examples of labor turnover, one dealing with a high priority plant, the other with a relatively low priority enterprise. According to the Soviet trade union publication *Trud,* about 1,000 employees left the Dnieper Heavy Machinery enterprise in 1962.[50] According to the newspaper *Soviet Russia,* one Leningrad clothing factory lost 17 per cent of its production workers in 1962.[51] Although there are no over-all figures on labor turnover in Soviet industry available, Khrushchev has conceded that "turnover of personnel is causing great injury to the national economy." [52]

Some Comments on Resource Allocation in American Industry

Those who have managed companies under Western wartime conditions have probably had a "taste" of the resource problems that confront the Soviet manager daily. But this would no doubt have been merely a "taste," because in Soviet industry supply allocation is all-pervasive and virtually all-inclusive, whereas in the American World War II economy, physical allocation and stringent controls focused chiefly on a limited number of strategic commodities (for example, steel, copper, and aluminum).[53] Allocation certificates were not required for many goods, and our system allowed a substantial amount of freedom in the selection of suppliers. The major resource problem was the labor shortage that grew more severe toward the war's end.

Very significant psychological force also enabled the American wartime economy to function much more smoothly than the present day Soviet system: first, the American economy was basically a "single-purpose" economy geared to winning the war; whereas the Soviet economy has now evolved into a multiobjective system, with the priority rank of objectives becoming more and more blurred; second, the wartime controls in the American system were accepted by all concerned to be only temporary. Thus, suppliers were not inclined to blatantly disregard customer interests; the majority probably rather cooperated with customers, since the "sellers' " market could well turn into a "buyers' " market once the war was over. In the Soviet system, because of its very nature, the enterprise manager still does not foresee the day when he will find himself in a "buyers' " market.

In the American economy, under normal conditions the competitive market price system—in spite of various imperfections—serves quite effectively as a mechanism for efficient resource allocation in most instances. It is true that one finds evidence of supply "foul ups," in American industry—particularly in the speeches and writing of NASA, the military, and defense industry personnel. For instance, in one highly publicized speech Admiral Rickover stated that in the manufacture of the atomic submarine, 90 per cent of the subcontracted parts arrived late, 50 per cent were late more than six months, and 40 per cent were deficient. However, such serious deficiencies are only likely to occur where the supplier or subcontractor is in a monopolistic position and there is no alternate source to turn to, where there is a strong sellers' market, and/or where the production of a highly complex, new technical product is entailed.

In the everyday American economy, rather than having supply expediters, we have salesmen who wine, dine, and at times give "kickbacks" and bribes to purchasing agents in order to secure their business. It is therefore surprising to many Soviet citizens that American sales personnel and not purchasing agents spend their time—much of it unproductive —traveling and trying to secure commitments from other organizations and individuals. They just do not understand how the abundant and rather affluent American economy works.

7 • Managerial Incentives

The Soviet regime encourages capable, intelligent persons to pursue managerial careers by providing basic salaries well above the national average, and by providing those who reach the top rungs of the managerial ladder with fringe benefits such as a company car and favored housing. The regime also deems it necessary to provide additional incentive compensation to spur managers to maximum effort in the "best interests" of the state. Managers at all levels within the Soviet enterprise, as well as virtually all other enterprise personnel, can potentially earn some kind of monetary reward in addition to basic pay. In fact, the Soviets rely on monetary incentives to a greater extent than any other industrial nation.

It has been found that all men require motivation to perform adequately in their working lives. The Western behavioral studies of the past 25 years have made abundantly clear that such motivations are not necessarily monetary, although monetary gain may prove highly effective in many instances. The Soviets have given little attention to the impact of nonmaterial factors on human motivation in industry. This in itself strongly suggests that they believe that material incentives are more potent than any other motivational factor in the Soviet industrial culture.

The early zeal of communism was a powerful force historically in motivating persons in the Soviet Union, but even at the outset, it was recognized that nonmonetary incentives would prove inadequate when applied on a nationwide scale. There are simply not enough true believers and pure altruists in any system to make such a system work properly. Even Lenin realized that self-interest—the desire for personal gain—is a universal phenomenon—at least until the state had "withered away" and "full-scale communism" had evolved. A typical Leninist tenet makes this clear: "Production should be organized so as not to depend on moral stimuli alone, but these moral stimuli should be bolstered by material incentives."

Stalin, and later Khrushchev, have insisted on an operational emphasis of monetary incentives in Soviet industry. On many occasions Khrushchev has made pronouncements such as the following: "It is completely wrong to oppose material incentives to moral ones—the development of moral stimuli, of material self-interest, are indissolublely linked." [1]

Hence, a major problem facing the regime has been to devise a system of monetary incentives that would encourage all managers to produce good results and to act in the best interests of the state. But before an effective incentive system can be set up, the problem of defining "good results," and "best interests of the state," must be faced. As we shall see in due course, this is a vexing issue in a Marxist economy. In a market economy, profit, at least in theory, serves as an all-embracing criterion in this connection. In fact, the capitalistic concept of profitability is the only truly objective performance standard *anywhere* in terms of economic efficiency. But profit has little, if any, meaning in an economic sense in a communist system where cost-price relationships, and hence marginal analysis, do not serve as effective guidelines for managerial decision-making.

Philosophy of Monetary Incentives: U.S.S.R. vs. U.S.

The Soviet philosophy of monetary incentives is basically similar to the philosophy prevailing in American industry. In both cases the aim of a given incentive scheme in use at a particular time is to harness the satisfaction of individual goals to the attainment of formal organizational objectives. In practice, this process of harmonizing objectives may result in several hierarchical links. An attempt may be made to link individual goals to group and/or departmental objectives and in turn, departmental objectives to those of the organization as a whole. If ownership and management are divorced within a given organization, an attempt may also be made to link the personal goals of top management to the objectives of the owners. The actions of management are sure to have a very significant impact on the attainment of the ultimate organizational objectives, and this, of course, relates directly to the interests of the owners. This is the case not only in the Soviet Union where the owner of the enterprise is the state, but also in American corporations where ownership is widely dispersed. In both cases there is the danger that managerial self-interest will be in conflict with the ownership interest.

In American industry there are objective criteria that serve as fairly effective guidelines for managerial decision-making—notably the competitive market price system and the profit motive. Yet even these objective guidelines do not necessarily insure that management will act in the best interest of the owners. Hence, in many American corporations we find stock-option plans, bonuses linked to various measures of profitability, and a variety of other incentive schemes to induce management to act in the stockholders' interest. The scheme has a fairly good chance of being effective if it can be linked to some meaningful measure of profitability. At lower levels in the company, where meaningful measures of profitability are more difficult to ascertain, the problem of designing an effective monetary incentive scheme tends to become more difficult. But even here cost-price relationships and marginal analysis may provide an effective framework for devising a beneficial incentive system.

But what about Soviet industry? How can an effective incentive system be designed to induce managers to pursue the ultimate objectives of their enterprises, as prescribed by the state? In absence of objective criteria, plans and directives from above in conjunction with "rules of behavior" must be relied upon to guide managerial decision-making. The state sees fit to buttress the system of plans, directives, and rules with a system of monetary incentives. Yet there is no all-embracing criterion, such as profitability, to which an effective system of managerial incentives can be linked. This is acknowledged by an eminent Soviet economist: "Analysis shows that at least for the time being, there is still no index usable as a universal criterion for appraising the performance of enterprises in the various branches of industry. As a result, conflicting and independent indices are used simultaneously in an effort to evaluate enterprise and managerial success." [2]

Premiums, Success Indicators, and Managerial Goals

The key managers of the Soviet enterprise have traditionally received premiums (bonuses) in addition to their basic salaries for fullfilling and/or overfulfilling those enterprise targets which the state deems most important. The targets linked to the payment of premiums are often referred to as "success indicators." It is the premium, the size of which is linked to success indicator performance, that is the fundamental operational goal of management. Executives who consistently obtain premiums are judged competent managers and are those most likely to be promoted; laggards remain in the same capacity or may be demoted. Hence, the premium is the primary goal for managerial action for two reasons: First, it provides for lucrative additional compensation; second, it serves as a means for attaining recognition, prestige, promotion, and greater power.

Monetary Significance of Premiums

In most branches of industry, managers can potentially receive quarterly premiums equivalent to 40 to 60 per cent of their basic salaries, depending on the type of enterprise. Although these premium payments are clearly substantial, we must consider whether managers do in fact reap significant payments. For premiums must be attainable if they are to be a potent motivating factor. There are indications that lately premiums actually awarded to managers have averaged 25 to 33 per cent of basic salaries.[3] Table I indicates the amount of premiums received by management in 1960-61 at ten enterprises surveyed. The figures reveal that at about half of the enterprises, maximum or near maximum premiums were received for a majority of quarters during this period.

TABLE I • *Enterprise performance—administrative premiums received as per cent of basic salary*

Enterprise	1960—Quarters—Per Cent				1961—Quarters—Per Cent	
	1	2	3	4	1	2
Leningrad Machine Building	40	40	30	40	40	
Moscow Machine Tool	50	50	0	50		
Kharkov Mining Equipment	40	0	0	0		
Kharkov Air Conditioning & Ventilation	40	40	40	40		
Kharkov Ball Bearing	0	0	0	0		
Kharkov Clothing	0	0	20	40		
Moscow Silk Fabric	0	38	20	30	0	
Moscow Watch	25	40	40	30		
Leningrad Shoe	40	20	0	0	0	
Kharkov Book *					40	40 (expected)

* The book factory has been rewarded on the basis of the cost criterion only since January 1, 1961.

Possibly, incentive compensation is generally a more potent tool for managerial motivation in Soviet industry than in American industry. The Soviets have a much lower standard of living; aside from basic necessities, many goods are so highly priced that they cannot be purchased without the additional income provided by premiums. Moreover, the tax bite even on the highest incomes in the Soviet Union is only about 13 per cent.

Symbolic Significance of Premiums

Although it is his salary which serves as a measure of the importance of the manager's enterprise, the size of his premium is a measure of the skill with which he is running the enterprise, and the receipt of premiums often helps him to obtain his personal goals.

Joseph Berliner has probably made the greatest contribution to an understanding of managerial motivation in Soviet industry.[4] In light of his numerous interviews with former Soviet citizens—many of them former managers—Berliner contends that premium payments to Soviet managers constitute the major personal goal that these officials strive for in operating their enterprises. Although Berliner's interviewees had left Russia in the 1940's, there is no doubt that his contention about premiums is still valid. This is clear from present day Soviet sources as well as from interviews conducted by this writer in the Soviet Union. The consensus among Soviet managers and many other officials pointed to enterprise success indicator performance—reflected by earned premiums—as being a key criterion in judging managerial success. Several enterprise managers indicated that premiums received constitute a significant yardstick in determining whether an administrator is to be promoted. This is true, as one plant director asserted, "since it [the premium] represents socially desirable behavior and results."

Operational Significance of Premiums

In his 1957 study, Berliner pointed out that premiums available to enterprise management are both operational and concrete; therefore, they directly affect the choice of alternatives undertaken by managers.[5] The desire for premiums was frequently given as the reason by his respondents for taking one course of action as opposed to another. Obviously, the efforts to attain premiums were directly associated with day-to-day operating decisions in concrete situations. In this vein Berliner has stated, "Given the specific conditions of the economic milieu, the observed practices of managers are logical corollaries of the goals they strive to attain." [6]

As we will see shortly, the premium-success-indicator system has been changed in 1959, but the above statement still holds true. Soviet managers still tend to act in a way best designed to maximize their personal advantage; and this usually boils down to the maximization of premiums. The behavior patterns of Soviet managers investigated fully in Chapters 8 and 9, are still clearly the logical corollaries of the pursuit of premiums, given the macromanagerial structure within which they must operate.

Emphasis on Short-Run Results

Premium payments to management are linked to short-run success indicator results. Before 1959, awards were made monthly, and since then they have been paid quarterly. It is understandable that there still is incessant pressure on enterprise managers to fulfill the short-term success indicator targets. This short-run pressure is further augmented by frequent relocations of managerial personnel, particularly directors. At 16 enterprises surveyed, 9 had directors who had been there less than 4 years. Some of the new directors stated that their current jobs were promotions, and indicated that they had had good premium records in their previous positions.

Since premiums, promotions, transfers, and demotions depend largely on short-run performance, we can expect that enterprise managers are not inclined to give much, if any, weight to the long-run implications of their actions. This is, in fact, the case as will be seen in Chapter 9 where enterprise innovation is discussed.

The Premium-Success-Indicator System

The size of premiums awarded to management has always been dependent on the fulfillment and/or degree of overfulfillment of certain targets, with 100 per cent fulfillment being necessary to derive any premiums. For example, if the success indicator target is stated as 2 million rubles of output and this amount is realized, the target is considered 100 per cent fulfilled; if 2.2 million rubles of output is produced the target is considered overfulfilled by 10 per cent. The same reasoning would be applied if the output target is stated in some physical unit that lends itself to aggregation (tons, square meters, and so forth). If labor productivity is a success indicator, the 100 per cent target would be stated as, say, 10,000 rubles or 1 ton of output per enterprise employee. Similarly, given cost of production as a success indicator, the 100 per cent target would be stated, for example, as 80 kopeks per 1 ruble of marketable output; if actual performance is 76 kopeks, the cost reduction plan is considered overfulfilled by 5 per cent.

If such an incentive system is to prove effective in practice, the 100 per cent targets should represent an accurate projection of enterprise potential. For the targets are merely operational expressions of various ultimate objectives that the enterprise is supposed to pursue; hence, deficient targets, in terms of true potential, are not likely to lead to a favorable degree of desiderata attainment.

Historical Perspective

Until 1959, gross output was the dominant success indicator in Soviet industry and premiums were awarded monthly. Various other success indicators were tried on a piecemeal basis from time to time in different branches of industry, but gross output prevailed as the key target for virtually all industrial enterprises. The gross-output-premium system precipitated a variety of undesirable managerial practices throughout Soviet industry. (This is not to say that similar practices do not prevail today.) The overemphasis on gross output is often referred to by Soviet sources as the "cult of the gross."

In pursuit of premiums, plant executives strove for gross output targets that could easily be exceeded. They usually hoarded resources, concealed productive capacity, overstated supply needs, and generally concealed pertinent facts from higher authorities. The environment of chronic supply uncertainty greatly intensified this type of behavior. By following these practices during the planning process, managers had a much better

chance of getting gross production targets which could readily be fulfilled and even overfulfilled. Managers who were either honest or poor
bargainers in their dealings with higher authorities unfortunately were
stuck with impossibly high production goals.

It seems that Evsey Liberman, a Soviet economist, was the first Soviet
citizen to publicly condemn the impact of the premium system on the
formulation of enterprise plans. (Liberman has received much attention
in Western sources during 1962 and 1963 for his profit motive proposals
and more will be said about this in Chapter 12.) He pointed out in 1955
that if premiums are paid for fulfilling and overfulfilling certain "100
per cent" targets, enterprise managers will naturally desire easy targets.[7]
The stress on 100 per cent success indicator targets has since been referred to by various Communist writers as the "fetish of 100 per cent."

Because of the state's great emphasis on gross output results, enterprise managers and even their direct superiors, in their efforts to fulfill
and exceed gross output targets, frequently failed to fulfill other targets
and tasks set down in their plans. This was most pronounced at enterprises that received difficult production plans, and a great many did.
The fulfillment of cost of production, labor productivity, profit and
various other targets were frequently sacrificed. The emphasis on aggregate output led to a widespread disregard for quality and proper
product-mix.

Many managers engaged in a variety of simulation practices, as well
as outright cheating in reporting, in order to present favorable gross
results. Since premiums were awarded monthly, the inability to deliver
goods at the proper time was also relevant. Usually there was a mad
rush at numerous plants at the end of the month to fulfill the gross output target: raw materials were dumped into production, items lacking
proper specifications were produced, and in haste orders were at times
shipped to wrong destinations. As a rule, this rush was followed by a
period of disorganized slack during the first weeks of the next month,
and as the end of the month neared, the same drive to fulfill the output
plan emerged again. Such activity greatly compounded the supply
crisis. Innovation, in both products and processes, also lagged since more
often than not, innovation activities hindered monthly aggregate output
results.

Given the gross-output-premium system and the uncertainty of supply,
it is understandable that managers would do all in their power to get
modest aggregate output targets, and if necessary to fulfill them in
undesirable ways. The distortions and supply problems created and
aggravated by imperfect managerial incentives led to poor enterprise,
and hence, poor national results.

When the Soviet Union was less complex industrially, output without
regard to other considerations could have been a meaningful goal.

Pressure for forced industrialization meant shortages of every type of goal; hence, most anything produced could be used somewhere or by someone in the nation. But as the economy grew more complicated, as the interrelationships among steadily expanding industries became more delicate, and as a somewhat wider choice of consumer goods improved the standard of living, the aggregate gross output indicators of success became less meaningful.

The Current System

In view of the serious defects and growing inefficiencies resulting from overemphasis on gross output as the dominant success indicator, the state introduced a new premium system in 1959.[8] The new scheme applies to most branches of industry. A few branches where centralized planning and control over operations are relatively easy tasks because homogeneous output is entailed (for example, coal and oil) have not been significantly affected.

The 1959 reform shifted primary emphasis for awarding premiums from gross output to cost of production (represented by cost per one ruble of marketable output). The advantage of this cost index is that improved cost results need not be in conflict with greater output. At most enterprises both gross output and labor productivity targets are supposed to be fulfilled for any premiums to be paid. Also the total size of premium awards now depends on the degree of overfulfillment of the cost target (that is, above plan cost reduction). At some plants, notably various consumer goods producers, additional premiums can still be earned by overfulfilling the gross output target as well. Here both gross output and cost reduction results are given about equal weight. Premiums are now awarded quarterly rather than monthly in most cases. The emphasis on cost performance and to a lesser degree on labor productivity was a logical move in view of the growing pressures on the economy for more efficient resource utilization. The change from monthly to quarterly premium payments has been an attempt to encourage more even operations and more deference for longer run considerations at industrial enterprises.

The success indicator reform also sought to give emphasis to certain other aspects of enterprise performance. In this connection the reform stipulated that various other conditions, in addition to those cited above, must be fulfilled for management to receive any premiums. These conditions depend on the branch of industry and type of enterprise and may include certain physical output indices, total marketable output, quality, product delivery schedules to customer plants in other regions, and major technical and product innovation measures.

The 1959 reform placed a maximum limit—which did not exist previously in most cases—on the amount of premiums that could be awarded to enterprise management. The limit varies from 40 to 60 per cent of basic salary depending on the type of enterprise. It should be noted that the premium limits serve as limits for total incentive compensation to management for any one quarter, with the exception of bonuses from socialist competition (to be discussed shortly). Management may be entitled to bonuses from the Enterprise Fund and/or for various innovation results. The point is that if maximum premiums are not earned, the other bonuses may be awarded up to the maximum limit, but if maximum premiums are realized the other bonus payments cannot be made.

Conditions for Premium Payments at Enterprises Surveyed

Surveys at 12 enterprises show that the conditions for premium payments vary somewhat between branches of industry, and to a lesser extent even among plants in the same branch. There are no indications that the information obtained from these enterprises is obsolete.

Variations in the conditions for premium payments are apparently based on the following criteria:

1. The importance the state attaches to the fulfillment and overfulfillment of certain targets at a given type of plant.
2. The difficulty involved in the overfulfillment of the key success indicators by a specific enterprise, and the magnitude of resulting benefits to the state.
3. The feasibility of using a given success indicator as a meaningful measure of enterprise efficiency.
4. The desirability of maintaining highly qualified personnel in important enterprises by the use of large potential monetary incentives.

At all the enterprises, gross output expressed in rubles, cost reduction, labor productivity, and certain physical production targets are supposed to be fulfilled within the approved resource limits for any premiums to be awarded. If these targets are fulfilled, a basic premium varying from 8 per cent of basic salary at a Kharkov book factory to 15 per cent at several machinery plants is awarded to management. At each enterprise additional premiums are paid for every 1/10 per cent overfulfillment of the cost reduction target; for example, 2 per cent additional premiums for every .1 per cent of above plan cost savings. The additional premium factors were greater at the producer goods enterprises than at the consumer goods plants. At a Moscow silk fabric plant and a Kharkov clothing factory, additional premiums are also awarded for each percentage of overfulfillment of the gross output target. Managers at these enterprises claimed that this is the case due to major shortages of their outputs.

The nature of physical output success indicators depends, of course, on a given enterprise's product line. For example, at a shoe factory this target is expressed as x million pairs of shoes, broken down only by men's, women's and children's shoes. The silk plant's target is expressed as x million square meters of fabric subdivided into a number of broad groups by type and quality. The clothing factory also has a target in millions of square meters subdivided by suits and coats for men, women, and children. Before 1958, the physical output at the clothing enterprise was indicated in linear meters. The book factory has a physical target reflecting x million page sheets. These printed pages are subdivided into black and white on the one hand, and colored on the other, because of differences in production costs.

At the producer goods enterprises, physical success indicators for certain standardized items, particularly those requiring central approval, are expressed as total number of units. Weight indices (tons) are used as physical success indicators for most other types of output.

It is evident that physical output indices which are supposed to be fulfilled if premiums are to be awarded, tend to be stated in rather broad terms at most enterprises. This seems to be necessary if some flexibility regarding the detailed product needs of customers is to be provided for in the plan. This is particularly important in connection with consumer goods, because assortment plans prescribed in rigid detail would be insensitive to changes in consumer demand. Hence, in the final analysis, penalties in the form of fines and damages must be used in an attempt to induce managers to produce those detailed items needed and demanded by customers. And we have seen in the previous chapter that this system of punishment leaves much to be desired.

Only some of the enterprises surveyed have total value of marketable production as a success indicator. The reasons given for having the fulfillment of this target obligatory for the receipt of premiums at some plants, and not at others, were not entirely clear. It seems that if a given enterprise has a heterogeneous, constantly changing detailed product-mix from one period to the next, marketable output would not be an obligatory condition since it would not enable meaningful comparison of enterprise production efficiency over time. The gross output index serves as a better check on actual increases in output over time because it is based on representative items and fixed prices. However, at all enterprises marketable output is used in computing both cost reduction targets and results. If the marketable output index is established on the basis of a broad rather than a detailed assortment plan, this would be reflected in the cost reduction target. Output need not be delivered to customers for it to be credited toward the fulfillment of the marketable output target; goods need only be fully processed and not rejected by local quality control inspectors.

Quality indices representing the allowable proportions of different grades of output are success indicators for only some of the consumer goods plants surveyed. However, in all cases where items are supposed to possess stipulated quality technical standards, the minimum standards are supposed to be attained if this output is to be credited toward the fulfillment of the enterprise production plan.

The Kharkov Ball Bearing Factory is the only enterprise surveyed to have the fulfillment of its delivery schedules to customers in other regions as a necessary condition for premium payments. The factory's assistant director indicated that management did not receive any premiums in 1960 because this condition was not met. But no legal action involving fines or damages was undertaken; the only sanction imposed was the loss of premiums. Evidently, the ball bearing factory is subject to this condition because it supplies plants in every region of the country, and because it is urgent that this type of output be delivered on time. Although many of the other enterprises visited also have customers in other regions, it appears from interviews and Soviet sources that the fulfillment of these delivery schedules is required for premium awards at relatively few enterprises. When asked why meeting interregional deliveries is not necessary for the receipt of premiums, managers at some plants claimed that by fulfilling the assortment plan, the timely delivery of goods to customers is assured. It was revealed, however, that this does not necessarily insure delivery on a specific predetermined date; but rather that, if goods are shipped within a specified quarter, the plan is generally considered fulfilled.

The Moscow Watch Factory is the only enterprise surveyed to have the fulfillment of certain innovation tasks as a necessary condition for the payment of premiums, and even here this is not the case every quarter. Obligatory innovation tasks with regard to premiums typically involve stipulated style and design changes in certain products, but only in those quarters where specific measures are spelled out in the plan. This type of condition is evidently found at the watch factory because the regime exports the bulk of this enterprise's output not only to other Communist countries, but also to about 30 capitalist nations. Hence, watches that can fare well in competitive world markets must be produced. It is not clear what precise criteria are used in determining whether product innovation tasks have been satisfactorily fulfilled to justify the payment of premiums.

In general, innovation measures seem to be obligatory conditions for the payment of premiums at only very few Soviet enterprises. At most enterprises, including all those surveyed, there are certain bonuses available to management for various innovation accomplishments. However, innovation bonuses rarely take precedence over the pursuit of premiums as the primary managerial goal. Innovation activity and related bonuses are treated in Chapter 9.

According to interviews and some secondary Soviet sources, various other success indicators have been used in certain branches of industry in recent years. For example, in the clothing industry indices of processing costs or value-added cost (the cost of working up materials irrespective of their original cost) have been established at some plants. However, these various other success indicators are not important to this study since they have only been tried on a very limited experimental basis in connection with premium payments. Yet it is interesting to note that each one has precipitated a variety of undesirable management practices.[9]

It should be mentioned here that managers at some of the enterprises surveyed indicated that premiums may at times be awarded even if certain obligatory conditions are not fulfilled. They explained that this may happen if management can justify such nonfulfillment by convincing superiors that it was due to conditions beyond the enterprise's control, or due to actions in the best interests of the state. It was made clear, however, that premiums would very rarely, if ever, be awarded if the gross output target is not fulfilled.

Profit and the Enterprise Fund

Profit performance does not normally serve as a success indicator at Soviet enterprises, nor is it significant in evaluating or rewarding management. Profit does not serve as a meaningful efficiency measure because of the system of artificial fixed prices. Only in certain extractive industries, (for example, oil, coal, iron ore) where comparable homogeneous output is produced from year to year, can profit serve as a crude measure of efficiency; but even here it is just as well to use the cost reduction target for this purpose. At enterprises producing a varied and/or changing product-mix, profit has no meaning in terms of economic efficiency. In fact, earned profits vary significantly even among enterprises in the same branch of industry. For example, in 1961 the level of profitability at Leningrad machine-building enterprises ranged from 10 to 122 per cent.[10]

This is not to say that the regime is not interested in the size of enterprise profits. At present, profit earned by enterprises constitutes the single largest source of state revenue, and in turn, capital investment. If total profits increase significantly, turnover taxes may be cut on consumer goods, thus providing for lower retail prices for selected items. In 1963, the total planned profit figure for Soviet industry was 35.7 billion rubles, while the turnover tax figure was 33.8 billion.[11]

Any interest that management may have regarding the enterprise's profit target and its profit results stems from a fund at its disposal called the Enterprise Fund. This fund is fed by a small portion of total profits earned by the enterprise and may be of some interest to management and other plant personnel, since certain benefits may be forthcoming. The extent of such benefits depends on the nature of profit performance: greatly increased benefits are realized from above plan profits. In cases where enterprises operate at planned losses, and about 20 per cent do, the size of deductions to this fund is determined by performance in relation to the cost reduction target.

Each enterprise deducts a portion of planned and above plan profits earned each quarter into its Enterprise Fund, and the balance is turned over to the state. The rates of deduction vary from 1 to 6 per cent of planned profits and 20 to 50 per cent of above plan profits, depending on the type of enterprise. The maximum allowable deduction at a given enterprise in a given year can not exceed 5.5 per cent of its total annual payroll. It is felt that such a deduction limit is necessary to prevent plants with relatively small labor forces, producing output with large profit margins, from receiving excessive deductions. Such deductions would not be based on economic efficiency, but rather on factors beyond the enterprise's control. But are not all deductions, in varying degrees, dependent on factors beyond the enterprise's control? [12]

Within broadly prescribed limits, the director has authority over the use of the Enterprise Fund, subject to formal approval by the factory trade union committee. Table II indicates the conditions for forming and using this fund at 12 enterprises surveyed.[13]

It should be noted that a July 1960 government decree advocated a new system of deductions for the Enterprise Fund at machine-building and metal-working plants producing new products. This new scheme was not yet in use at applicable enterprises surveyed in mid-1961. In general, the decree, even if fully implemented, is likely to have little bearing on managerial motivation and behavior. This topic is discussed further in Chapter 9.

Since part of the Enterprise Fund can be used by the director to pay bonuses, it is a convenient source for rewarding personnel for various accomplishments, or even for personal reasons. However, the bonuses to management, or for that matter to other personnel, are negligible in most instances. Soviet sources reveal that bonuses from this fund average annually about two rubles per employee—less than .25 per cent of average basic pay.[14] At those enterprises surveyed that disclosed this type of information, the average available bonus was less than 1 per cent of average basic pay at 3 plants, and slightly more than 1 per cent at a fourth.

The Enterprise Fund may also serve as an incentive because it provides management with some independent funds which it can use for a variety of other purposes, (perhaps even illegal procurement). The enterprise typically confines its expenditures from this fund to minor uses not fully provided for by allocations from the state budget. For example, managers

TABLE II • *Rate of deductions from profit to the enterprise fund 1960-1961*

Enterprise	Planned Profit Per Cent Deductions	Above Plan Per Cent Profit Deductions	Use of Allocated Funds—Per Cent		
			Bonuses, Premiums, and Social Benefit Payments	Expanding and Improving Enterprise Operations	Housing, Cultural and Communal Services
Leningrad Machine Building	4	40	40	40	20
Moscow Machine Tool	4	50	40	30	30
Kiev Machine Tool	4	50	not reported		
Kharkov Mining Equipment	6	30	50	50 divided between these two classes	
Leningrad Electrical Equipment	4	40	not reported		
Kharkov Air Conditioning Equipment	4	40	not reported		
Kharkov Ball Bearing	4	50	40	30	30
Moscow Silk Fabric	2	20	50	50 divided between these two classes	
Kharkov Clothing	2	30	40	30	30
Moscow Watch	4	50	40	20	40
Leningrad Shoe	1	30	30	40	30
Kharkov Book	1	20	40	20	40

indicated that portions of this fund are used for expansion of working capital, housing improvements, children's camps, canteens, recreation facilities, holiday centers, to subsidize cultural activities, and for various other employee fringe benefits. Hence the size of the fund may have some bearing on employee morale and the attraction of new personnel. Though, it is important to note that the bulk of the enterprise's capital is derived from allocations from the state budget. Moreover, budgetary allocations have little, if any, relationship to the size of enterprise profits or the Enterprise Fund. While roughly one-third of total profits earned remain at Soviet enterprises, the bulk of this retained profit is assigned by higher authorities and has nothing to do with the Enterprise Fund.

Western studies, current Soviet sources, and personal interviews clearly show that, generally, neither profit nor the Enterprise Fund are significant factors in managerial motivation. A desire to maximize profit or the size of this fund seldom takes precedence over the pursuit of premiums, nor is the Enterprise Fund invariably a significant motivating factor for nonmanagerial personnel.

Management would, of course, prefer an easy profit target since the deductions into the Enterprise Fund from above plan profits would be much greater. But the profit target is merely a residual index evolving with the approval of the other operating targets. If management succeeds in obtaining easy cost and output targets, this would tend to be compatible with an easy profit target; but profit performance would depend on the actual product-mix produced. Increased profits may be incidental to the overfulfillment of the cost reduction target, although this need not be the case given the price structure. Product choices are probably made, in most instances, in view of their impact on success indicator performance, and not profit results. In 1959, for instance, the enterprises in the Tambov region exceeded the regional cost reduction target by 6.5 million rubles, while profits fell 3.8 million rubles short of the plan.[15] For three quarters of 1962, 37 per cent of all industrial enterprises failed to fulfill their profit plans, whereas for the whole of 1962 only about 20 per cent did not fulfill their cost reduction targets.[16]

In recent years Soviet sources have been calling for expanded use of profit as a managerial incentive. During the 1962-63 period, the adoption of a profit motive in Soviet industry was the subject of widespread discussion and great debate by leading Soviet experts and influential Soviet publications. But how can a meaningful profit motive be introduced in a Marxist economy? This topic of great concern will be dealt with in Chapter 12.

Incentives Arising from Socialist Competition

Socialist competition involves quarterly or semiannual competitions among enterprises within the same branch of industry for best results achieved.[17] Both regional and all-union (national) awards are given to those plants placing first, second, or third. The winners are selected in light of the degree of overfulfillment of those targets that superior authorities wish to have overfulfilled, the degree of fulfillment of all other tasks stipulated in the plan, and various other improvements realized such as safety record, better working conditions, and the like. All in all, an assessment of over-all enterprise operations is entailed. At each competing plant pledges are signed to fulfill and, where possible, to overfulfill the entire plan.

Socialist competition is essentially a form of nonmaterial incentive, though material rewards are usually given to the winners. The moral stimulus is that considerable publicity and prestige is typically accorded for their achievements: the plant is given a red banner to fly from the roof; management and leading workers may get their pictures, or at least their names, into the paper; medals may be awarded, and so forth. All of this may also, at times, increase the chances for promotion, particularly for management.

The size of the monetary awards depends on (1) branch of industry, (2) the number of competing plants, (3) rank (first, second, third), and (4) number of employees at the victorious enterprises. Awards under 20,000 rubles all go toward bonus payments to enterprise personnel. Of awards exceeding 20,000 rubles, 70 per cent goes toward bonus payments and the balance toward improving social insurance benefits.

From the monetary awards, top management is entitled to bonuses of 50 per cent of basic monthly salary for first place, 40 per cent for second place, and 30 per cent for third place. Even if management has succeeded in maximizing its quarterly premiums, these additional payments may still be received. The director also pays out premiums to individual employees in proportion to basic wages.

The assistant head of the planning department of the watch factory indicated that his enterprise won first place in the regional competition in the first quarter of 1961. The enterprise has 6,300 employees and the size of the award was 20,000 rubles. This constitutes an average award per individual employee of about three rubles even before administrative awards are accounted for, and is well under one per cent of basic monthly wages.

The assistant chief engineer of the mining equipment plant said that his plant is entitled to 40,000 rubles for first place, 30,000 rubles for second place, and 20,000 rubles for third place. From 1949 to 1955 this enterprise, with few exceptions, continuously placed first in the branch-of-industry competition. Since 1955 it placed only once—third—in the first quarter of 1960 and was awarded 20,000 rubles to be divided among 5,000 plant employees.

The book factory, which has 2,000 employees, placed first in the first quarter of 1961 and received 8,750 rubles. In 1960 it placed second in three quarters and received 6,000 rubles each time.

The assistant director of the ball bearing plant, with 5,000 workers, indicated that his plant had not won for several years, although it used to win frequently in the past. At present, if it should win the first place, the enterprise is entitled to 15,000 rubles, and for second place 12,000 rubles. The head of the planning department at the silk factory disclosed that his enterprise, with 2,000 employees, is entitled to up to 20,000 rubles for first place, since there are many competing enterprises in this *upravleniye*.

If one takes some Soviet sources—primarily textbooks—at face value, it would appear that socialist competition is a significant motivating force. Lenin described it as "one of the most important forces of drawing the working masses into the management of production." However, none of the enterprise personnel interviewed seem to view socialist competition as being a very significant factor of motivation. Managers at a few enterprises did take some pride in casually pointing out that they had recently been awarded a red banner for placing in socialist competition.

Victory is clearly not an easy task. There are a considerable number of directly competing plants within a given region, and hundreds more compete for the national awards. For example, the enterprises surveyed have from 37 to 60 directly competing plants in their regions. If a given enterprise is to compete seriously, it may have to refrain from maximizing premiums in order to fulfill all the necessary conditions for winning, unless of course it has obtained an "easy" operating plan. There are some indications that many of the same enterprises are victorious from one period to the next. This suggests that easy plans are obtained, and the plant can go on winning until its excess resources and capacity are in some way eliminated. The next chapter will clearly show that socialist competition generally has little, if any, conscious bearing on managerial behavior.

It should be pointed out here that since 1962, Soviet leaders have given certain new forms of socialist competition much stress, affording nonmanagerial personnel considerable publicity. More will be said about this in Chapter 10.

Analysis and Concluding Remarks

In absence of objective criteria, plans, directives, and "rules of behavior" are relied upon in the Soviet system to guide managerial decision-making at the enterprise level. The regime sees fit to buttress the system of plans, rules, and directives with a system of monetary incentives for enterprise managers in an attempt to spur them to maximum effort in the "best interests" of the state. In theory, management is supposed to design and obtain a plan for its enterprise that reflects balanced and favorable degree of over-all desiderata attainment. Again, in theory, this plan is supposed to be fulfilled in its entirety. Yet the system of managerial incentives does not correspond to this theory.

The discussion in this chapter makes it quite clear that the attainment of premiums is the primary operational goal of enterprise management. Although there are various other managerial incentive schemes, it can be expected that managerial action in pursuit of premiums will generally take precedence over any effort to derive other forms of monetary rewards.

The 1959 premium-success-indicator reform has somewhat narrowed the range of choices open to management in its quest for premiums by imposing some new conditions for the payment of these premiums. However, these conditions are still of an aggregate nature. Moreover, the basic principle of awarding premiums for the fulfillment and over-fulfillment of aggregate targets stated in terms of 100 per cent has not changed. Given the pervasive environment of resource uncertainty, there is every reason to expect that managers still strive for easy targets. If the system of managerial incentives is to be effective in terms of ultimate enterprise objectives, the 100 per cent targets should represent an accurate, or at least an honest, projection of enterprise potential. Another necessary condition is that resources must be available in accordance with the plan.

Once the enterprise plan is put into effect, the premium system would focus managerial effort on the fulfillment and overfulfillment of the key aggregate success indicators. Yet these success indicators pertain to only a few ultimate enterprise objectives—notably total production and cost of production. However, even aggregate production and cost results do not necessarily yield a favorable degree of desiderata attainment in these spheres, particularly if the targets themselves were set too low. Nor are labor productivity and cost reduction results necessarily a meaningful reflection of how well the different classes of enterprise resources (material, equipment, manpower) have been utilized. The degree of desiderata attainment in all these spheres of performance depends on how consistent and sound the over-all plan has been.

No incentives are available to management in connection with proper product-mix (in terms of customer requirements), output quality, and product delivery results. Yet each of these spheres of performance is linked to various ultimate enterprise objectives. In order to induce managers to give proper attention to customer requirements, quality of production, and the timely fulfillment of delivery schedules, the state must resort to a system of penalties. But we have already seen that such penalties leave much to be desired in terms of effectiveness. Therefore, one would expect a tendency on the part of Soviet managers to sacrifice, within limits, those desiderata not linked to the payment of premiums, if this is deemed necessary to derive premiums. This would also include innovation tasks and other measures that may be beneficial to society and the enterprise itself in the future, but which would have an adverse impact on short-run success indicator results. Even though there are certain bonuses available for various product and technological innovation accomplishments, they tend to be rather impotent in their impact on positive managerial action. As we shall see later, the vexing problem of balancing long-term and short-term goals is also present in capitalist enterprises; the success criterion of profitability does not adequately resolve this problem.

8 • Managerial Behavior

It is evident, even without extensive first-hand knowledge, that there are clear patterns of undesirable managerial behavior throughout Soviet industry. They are undesirable with regard to ultimate enterprise objectives, and hence, the interests of the regime. It is not possible to gauge accurately the intensity of these practices, or what their impact is on the objectives of a given enterprise or on a national scale. We will, however, present some evidence that suggests answers to these questions.

If we accept the following three conditions, it is safe to conclude that the undesirable practices are built into the existing Soviet economic system. (1) With very few exceptions, the macromanagerial environment is basically the same for all enterprise managers. (2) Soviet managers generally tend to pursue the same priority operational goal in running their enterprises—the attainments of premiums. (3) Enterprise managers generally strive to overcome the same paramount obstacle to premium attainment—resource uncertainty and the deficient provision of supplies.

The practices to be discussed are clearly not mere aberrations; nor are they due to a lack of patriotism or dedication to the managerial job. Rather, they are due to defects in the over-all macromanagerial structure within which the micromanagers must function. If an American manager were to be placed in a similar structure, he would undoubtedly behave in much the same way as his Soviet counterpart. This is evident from what is known about managerial behavior under American wartime conditions. In such an environment the manager was faced with considerable resource uncertainty, a sellers' market for numerous commodities, and pressure for more and more output. But even then, undesirable managerial practices were not as pervasive or intensive as in the everyday Soviet economy, for reasons discussed in Chapter 6. However, as we shall see in due course, even under normal conditions American managers are inclined to behave in much the same way as Soviet managers when certain similar environmental conditions exist.

In this chapter we shall first explore the nature of undesirable managerial practices at Soviet industrial enterprises. Then we will analyze the impact of such practices on ultimate enterprise objectives. Finally, we shall consider certain significant implications for the Soviet economy as a whole.

Behavior During the Planning Process

Desire for Easy Plans

The Soviet enterprise manager learns quickly that the key to his success is the attainment of an easy plan. If the success indicator targets are set a few feet from the firing line, bull's-eyes are much easier to hit. Managers who are optimistic in their planning proposals, or who have little persuasive ability with superior authorities, are likely to find themselves with unattainable targets. The director of planning at one *sovnarkhoz* vividly describes managerial behavior during the planning process: "No manager will go to the *sovnarkhoz* and ask for a bigger production program with lower material and labor expenditures. On the contrary, enterprise managers strive to obtain easy plans that allow them to spend more and produce less." [1]

Search for Organizational Slack

Managerial behavior during the planning process is typified by a constant search for "organizational slack" [2]—that is, the difference between stated potential and the best honest estimate of true potential. The pursuit of slack involves the incorporation of "safety factors" and other deficiencies into the enterprise draft plan. In plan fulfillment the degree of organizational slack—assuming it can be measured—is represented by the difference between actual and potential performance. This would not, however, adequately reflect any misdirection of resources, only the degree of resource utilization.

Virtually all Soviet enterprise managers are likely to search for slack as the plan is being formulated, but with varying degrees of intensity. The degree may depend largely on their assessment of the chances of obtaining an easy approved plan. In turn, this may depend on how successful the enterprise has been in accumulating slack to date (for example, hoarded resources, excess reserves), and whether superior authorities appear to be aware of the magnitude of this slack.

In general, the search for organizational slack would become more active with greater resource uncertainty, with greater inflexibility in revising plans as serious planning errors are discovered, or because assigned resources are not available. Hence, a top priority enterprise, such as an armaments factory, may feel less need to strive for considerable slack than, say, a clothing plant. The actual amount of slack that a given enterprise can incorporate into its approved plan might be influenced by the amount of authority and independence management possesses during the planning process. It is evident from our discussion in Chapter 4 that a plant producing standardized homogeneous output would probably have less influence than an enterprise producing a wide, heterogeneous product-mix, which changes somewhat from year to year.

The quest for organizational slack in planning is typically accompanied by the provision of inaccurate and/or incomplete information to higher authorities. Since superior authorities are aware of the type of biases that enterprise managers tend to present in their planning proposals, some attempt is usually made to correct them when approving the plan. This results in hard bargaining between the plant managers and their superiors until some settlement is reached. The words of the director of a Leningrad machinery enterprise vividly portray the essence of the Soviet planning process:

> How are plans drafted at present? The planning agencies argue vigorously with the managers of enterprises to induce them to accept a higher plan. The enterprise representatives on the other hand, argue with equal energy that the high assignments are unrealistic.[3]

This quest for slack, and the resulting bargaining between superiors and subordinates, are not unique to Soviet industry; they are also common in American companies, as will be discussed later in this chapter.

Let us now explore in some detail Soviet managerial behavior during the planning process, indicating the motives behind such behavior, where appropriate.

Safety Factors in Productive Capacity

Management strives for modest aggregate output targets by understating plant capacity because the fulfillment of aggregate production quotas remains a necessary condition for the payment of premiums. Easy output targets could mean easy labor productivity targets as well. Moreover, "favorable" cost reduction results, and perhaps sizeable above plan profits, may be realized with management's choices regarding above plan production. Concealed productive capacity can also be used as a bargaining lever to obtain more capital investment.

Managers engage in two kinds of practices regarding "safety factors" in plant capacity. First, there is much evidence that they establish deficient equipment utilization norms. These norms are frequently adjusted downward—more than is warranted—by the claim that the productivity of machinery is on the decline. Even when improvements in equipment productivity are undertaken through modernization and repair they are frequently not reflected in the plan.

Second, managers hoard and overorder fixed assets. There is no interest charge on capital nor a depreciation charge on uninstalled equipment. Even if a given plant is quite certain of being provided with proper machinery and spare parts, it still pays to overorder and hoard equipment in order to derive easy plans. Moreover, excess fixed assets serve an additional purpose for managers—they can independently dispose of unneeded equipment and use derived funds for various activities, such as illegal procurement.

Many plants are evidently successful in hoarding and maintaining overabundant quantities of fixed assets. For example, the Kramatorsk Machinery Plant frequently complains about shortages of fixed capital; yet a careful check at this enterprise disclosed that of 72 machines, about one-quarter were completely idle during the first shift. The figures for the second and third shifts were much higher.[4] A check at the Khabarovsk Chemical enterprise in 1961 revealed about one million rubles of uninstalled equipment.[5] Another source reveals that an entire glass-treating shop in a bottling factory remained virtually idle for eleven years. This factory received a document to transfer an expensive overhead crane to another enterprise in 1957, but by mid-1961 no action had yet been taken. This source gives several similar examples and goes on to exclaim "a whole shop may become a moribund treasure." [6]

Distortions in the Planning of Supplies and Working Capital

Evidentally, managers at virtually every type of enterprise hoard materials, overstate supply and working capital needs, and establish deficient material utilization norms. These are natural tendencies given the existing supply situation. Some Soviet sources suggest that the adoption of cost reduction as a success indicator may have intensified management's efforts—even at high priority plants—to obtain overabundant supplies (and expense budgets) to get easy cost of production targets.

Unjustified "correction factors" are often applied to material input norms. Norms are frequently not tightened with improved technical conditions, or where less inputs may be needed because of product specification changes. To cite a concrete example of material norm practice: the Kharkov Piston Plant established an input norm of 6.4 kilograms of aluminum alloy for product #202 for 1960. In the previous year only 5.16 kilograms were actually consumed in the same product, yet technical conditions were no better.[7] Supply norms for auxiliary activities, such as repair and maintenance, are in numerous cases extremely uneconomical due to intentional distortions by enterprise personnel.

Widespread criticism is voiced in Soviet sources that managers grossly overstate working capital requirements by basing estimates on nonapplicable historical data. Because adequate techniques for estimating working capital inventory norms are lacking, enterprises often are successful in obtaining excessive amounts of working capital. Apart from intentional biases, efficient working capital estimates are also hindered by deficient accounting methods.

Management may well obtain excessive allotments of supplies and working capital through its hoarding practices, and many plants conceal supplies substantially in excess of legal reserves. For example, a thorough investigation at the enterprises in the small Chelyabinsk region at the end of 1962 and beginning of 1963 revealed three million rubles of hoarded materials stacked in plant warehouses.[8] One enterprise director states that mountains of parts and other supplies are stored in the warehouses of his plant. This source explains why this is done, as follows:

> Well, in the first place, because the director has no faith in the supply apparatus; and in the second place, because at a difficult moment, when fulfillment of the plan is jeopardized, he can order increased deliveries of various items from the warehouse, enter them in the books as output, and the gross will be fulfilled.[9]

In spite of all the recent industrial reforms, hoarding remains a pervasive and serious problem in Soviet industry.

Distortions in Manpower and Payroll Planning

Managers tend to overstate manpower needs, establish deficient labor norms, and distort the related plan of wages (payroll) since this may lead to easy labor productivity, output and cost targets. No doubt, growing labor shortages and increased labor mobility have intensified such practices.

There is substantial evidence in Soviet sources that deficient labor utilization norms are established at enterprises throughout Soviet industry. Management frequently avoids establishing technically based ("scientific") norms in favor of norms based on obsolete historical data, even when the former should clearly be used. When technically calculated norms are used, they are typically adjusted downward by correction factors "in view of local conditions."

Several Soviet economists and three enterprise officials interviewed said that labor norms could stand improvement at many plants, and that such norms are "at times" not tightened from year to year even with improved technical conditions. An editor of a leading Soviet economic publication stated that deficient labor norms are a major problem in Soviet industry.

The greatest deficiencies in labor norms relate to auxiliary and servicing activities. This leads to excessive numbers of servicing and auxiliary personnel at numerous plants, many of whom are ordered into direct production activities by management if there is trouble in fulfilling the plan.[10] Such excesses of this type of personnel are also partially attributed to management's lack of interest in improving the organization of shops and departments. Many enterprises have considerably more "white collar" employees and auxiliary workers than production personnel.

Khrushchev recounts in *Pravda* that one Kiev enterprise has no many auxiliary workers that the director told them to hide when he [Khrushchev] visited the plant. He states further that Russia purchased several cinder block plants from the U.S. after World War II. One that, in America, required 16 people to operate has required 100 in the Ukraine. This situation he attributes largely to excessive numbers of auxiliary workers.[11] According to Soviet figures, 45 per cent of all Soviet plant workers were engaged in auxiliary operations in 1958, compared with 32.3 per cent in the U.S. The proportion of those auxiliary workers engaged in internal plant transport and warehousing operations was nearly twice as high as in the U.S.[12]

When new technology is introduced at a given plant, management frequently maintains unneeded production personnel rather than having them transferred to more needy enterprises. Soviet sources complain that on numerous occasions management's claims of labor shortages are "bluffs" rather than expressions of true need. For example, many enterprises in the Leningrad region complained of severe labor shortages in 1960 and 1961. Yet it was found in April 1961 that enterprises in this region had 11,600 more employees than the total number specified in the over-all 1961 labor plan of the Leningrad *Sovnarkhoz*.[13] Most of the enterprises in the relatively small Upper Volga *Sovnarkhoz* claimed to have labor shortages during 1963. But a careful check in the fall of 1963 revealed an excess number of employees at plants in this region totaling 8,000, and an excessive total payroll figure of 7.5 million rubles.[14]

According to many reports, enterprise managers improperly classify and upgrade workers in terms of occupations, skills, various other qualifications, and seniority. One source reveals that many plants have no personnel listed in the lower gradings within various classifications, though many of them are clearly untrained and highly unskilled.[15] Through such practices the enterprise may receive an easier cost target because of a larger planned wage fund. Management would then obtain undisclosed funds from payroll differentials arising from the difference between actual wage payments and the planned level of wages reflecting higher job ratings. Savings derived from this source may be shuffled among other enterprise accounts, thus providing for favorable cost reduction results.

No doubt managers also pursue such practices in order to maintain various personnel by actually providing them with higher wages. It is often difficult for higher authorities or other control officials to check on such activities if they desire to do so. The labor record books maintained for all employees—which indicate skills, education, length of service, and so forth—are frequently outdated and/or impossible to decipher.[16]

Padding Cost and Expense Estimates

Any slack that management can incorporate into other sections of the over-all plan would also affect the cost plan. There are also a large number of accounts pertaining to general, overhead, and nonproductive expenditures which constitute the enterprise's cost plan. Managers tend to pad virtually all expense categories in the cost plan—this includes everything from travel to telephone and postage expense estimates.[17] Since there are no suitable techniques for determining what relationships should exist between the various elements of the cost plan and the planned production program, this may be the subject of much bargaining.

It is evident that even the determination of direct production cost estimates typically involves a rather crude process. For example, where enterprises do not produce a narrow line of homogeneous output, production cost estimates are usually based on "representative" items of similar classes of output. In general, the target representing cost per one ruble of marketable output is established before the detailed product-mix is known at most enterprises.

Product Planning Distortions

It has been pointed out earlier that the detailed product-mix to be produced is usually worked out between suppliers and customers, and for consumer goods between the producer and wholesale trade officials.

The Soviet press gives numerous examples of supplier enterprises compelling customers to agree to contractual terms in which many of the items are not those most needed by users or in demand.

In the past, management desired to produce high priced goods, often with little concern about unit costs, since this led to favorable gross output results. At present, with cost reduction a success indicator, managers are probably more inclined to try to compel customers to agree to terms where the assortment provides for large price-cost gaps (profit margins), preferably where the actual size of such gaps is not apparent to higher authorities.

There seems to be a tendency for most every type of enterprise to influence their assortment plans at the expense of customers, although this type of behavior is most intensive in connection with consumer goods and customers in other regions. Only if the customer enterprise is of very high priority in the eyes of the state, is it likely to possess adequate bargaining power to fully counteract the "personal" motives of suppliers.

The leading Soviet aircraft designer, Antonov, aptly describes the dilemma of supplier-customer negotiations during the planning process:

The influence of customers on their suppliers and on the suppliers' production plans is extremely limited, while the central and higher level planners are not in a position to plan in detail the work of each enterprise in harmony with all the others.[18]

He also reveals nostalgia for the role of feedback in a market economy:

In the system of capitalist production the role of feedback is played by selling, by the market, by competition. It is these factors that force the capitalist to make better, more durable and cheaper goods, which are in demand.

The highly influential *Ekonomicheskaya Gazeta* points out a basic flaw in the Soviet system regarding the product-mix problem:

The present organization of supply is not capable of promoting and enforcing the socialist principle of mutual cooperation between producers and users. There is a lack of effective levers on which users could bring pressure to bear on the items to be supplied conforming to the needs and requirements of production. . . . In order to improve supply there is a need to provide for an incentive which would make the suppliers take an interest in the success of their customers.[19]

Although enterprises producing consumer goods are playing an increasing role in demand analysis, evidence strongly suggests that they do not take such activities seriously. One Soviet source discloses that management frequently vetoes items that have been selected for production by the enterprise's artistic council, and which are desired by trade officials and apparently in great demand.[20] A Moscow trade official has exclaimed in frustration, "For the past ten years we have not been able to settle the assortment of goods with a single factory properly or in good time." [21] Managerial personnel at three retail stores (shoes, clothing, and hoisery) in Moscow and Leningrad indicated during personal interviews that there is often much trouble in getting producers to accept desired trade orders.

In general, the supplier enterprise, probably more often than not, has its wishes upheld when arbitration commissions are called upon to settle contract disputes, because it is difficult to disprove that the supplier will not have adequate materials and other resources to produce the specific items desired by the customer. Trade officials, in particular, are in a very disadvantageous position in this connection, since the trade hierarchy is divorced from the industrial hierarchy. Disputes must be processed through a bureaucratic maze of red tape extending upward to the republic, and at times, the national level. However, all of the shortcomings in product planning concerning consumer goods, cannot be blamed on the producers. Trade organizations responsible for analyzing consumer demand frequently make gross miscalculations which are transmitted to producers. Moreover, the wholesale trade officials, themselves, may not be very concerned about satisfying consumer demand since their success indicators and related rewards are not based on retail sales.[22]

Pricing Distortions

Managers engage in price inflation in cases where they have the authority to recommend provisional wholesale prices (see Chapter 4). They also frequently succeed—often for many years—in extending these prices beyond the allowable time period. Prices are inflated by padding related cost-plus estimates, and this often enables management to derive excess resources, as well as easy success indicator targets. Evidence suggests that the emphasis on cost reduction as a key success indicator has intensified management's efforts to engage in pricing distortions. Price inflation is most prevalent at enterprises producing unstandardized output, new products, and where specification changes in products are often undertaken.

A manager of a Moscow ball bearing factory complains that his machinery suppliers often introduce many new specifications in their products. At times this enables as much as a fourfold price increase even though the machine may be only slightly more productive. He then cites actual examples: one machine that formerly cost his enterprise 4,600 rubles, presently costs 19,000 rubles, yet it is only 25 to 30 per cent more productive, and the customer has little say in such matters.[23]

Stifling of Innovation

The absence of operational long-range plans in conjunction with the existing success indicator system discourages managers from incorporating product and technological innovation tasks into the operating plan. There are many indications that the emphasis on cost reduction in the payment of premiums has further intensified management's efforts to avoid such assignments. Managers would seldom initiate or desire innovation tasks unless it were felt that they will have a favorable effect on short-run (quarterly) results. The underlying causes for the conflict between innovation and premium attainment are dealt with more fully in Chapter 9.

In addition to avoiding major innovation obligations, managers, when formulating the enterprise plan, usually do not reveal all economies that could be derived by implementing employee "innovation" proposals. If all available proposals were taken into account in the draft plan, a more difficult approved plan would be established. Hence, there is a tendency to shelve many worthwhile employee suggestions until related economies are more advantageous for success indicator performance. Evidence of this is presented in Chapter 10.

In general, Soviet sources complain extensively that resource needs and operating targets are formulated by management without properly accounting for all potential improvements in operation. There are many criticisms that managers relegate *orgtekhplan* improvement measures to a secondary role, considering them only during the operating period when there is difficulty in fulfilling the plan, rather than when the plan is drawn up. One source states, "Many *orgtekhplan* measures are left hanging in mid-air." [24] A second source states, "Such measures are not considered to be important and are lost in the computation of production plans." [25] Managers at several enterprises surveyed indicated that the *orgtekhplan* is not usually completed until after the receipt of the approved plan indices.

Falsification of Records

Many of the practices discussed do not entail an outright falsification of records since they involve futurity estimates. There are varying shades and degrees of legality attached to deficient information reporting. In large part this type of behavior is accepted as "part of the game" by higher authorities. However, outright falsification of records is branded as clearly illegal. It was apparently getting so out of hand that in mid-1961 a government decree made it a criminal offense, punishable by up to three years in jail.[26] Since then, however, there have only been rare reports in the Soviet press of penalties being imposed on enterprise managers for such offenses. It appears that managers still engage in outright falsification practices, in both plan formulation and plan fulfillment, on a fairly widespread scale.

Khrushchev, himself, has acknowledged the implications of the falsification of data and the widespread use of inflated figures. On one occasion he exclaimed, "If we don't restore order the plans will be statistically fulfilled, but there won't be enough products. As is known, you can't make pancakes out of statistics." [27]

Point-of-Departure Planning and the Approved Enterprise Plan

It should not be concluded that the formulation of enterprise plans is an entirely chaotic process—although it clearly leaves much to be desired. A major stabilizing factor concerning enterprise planning over time is the practice of point-of-departure planning. It is fully understood by enterprise managers that higher authorities would usually show great displeasure if they proposed plans that do not represent at least some improvement over results achieved previously. But the practice of point-of-departure planning has many weaknesses.

It does nothing to deter management from adversely affecting the enterprise assortment plan, or from the practice of not initiating or stifling beneficial innovation tasks. Even small changes in the product-mix and production process can have a significant cumulative effect over time. The introduction of new technology and substantial capital outlays can, of course, have a major effect on enterprise operations. Moreover, if easy plans have been approved for a given enterprise in the past, and it continues to maintain excess resources and capacity, point-of-departure planning does not assure sound plans.

Some, but not necessarily all, excess reserves may be flushed out during the course of overfulfilling success indicators—the system of premiums serves as an upper limit in this connection. For this reason many plants can and do maintain excess reserves, by hoarding and not revealing improvements in operations for long periods. Hence, a substantial tightening of enterprise draft plans and/or an intensive investigation of enterprise activities may be required to eliminate excessive organizational slack.

On the other hand, enterprises that, for legitimate reasons, have not been fulfilling their plans are liable to end up with unreasonably difficult plans—given the principle of point-of-departure planning. One plant director indicated with a smile that lower targets for the planned year may be approved in the event of a *vsesozhzhenie*—a holocaust. The chief of planning of another enterprise stated that such an approval may be given in the event of major disruptions—a fire or plant reconstruction. He said that his enterprise received a reduction in targets—compared to the previous period—only once in the past ten years. Hence, an enterprise having difficulty in fulfilling its plans would usually have to bargain very convincingly for a reduction in targets and/or more resources for the same targets.

If we think of a sound planning system as one in which the state and enterprise management both strive for objectively realistic targets and resource allocations, then it is clear that a system where one systematically overshoots and the other undershoots must lead to serious and widespread inaccuracies. On the one hand, enterprise managers strive for easy plans, not only because of resource uncertainty, but also because of the premium-success-indicator system. On the other hand, central authorities, desiring maximum national economic performance, must tighten the planning proposals channeled upward in the industrial hierarchy in the face of much ignorance.

The conflict of interests between the state and enterprise managers in the planning process breeds a vicious circle of distrust. In turn, this results in a system of arbitrary planning. Much time, effort, and expense is expended in calculations, information gathering, and bargaining because enterprise plans tend to be established with little regard for data and proposals submitted by managers.

Lower level organizations generally take for granted that the higher level planners will tighten their draft plans. An actual example of this tightening process can be seen from the experience of the enterprises under the Sverdlovsk *Sovnarkhoz*. The draft plans of the enterprises showed a 3 per cent increase in total production for 1958 as compared to actual performance anticipated in 1957. The branch administrations of the *Sovnarkhoz* raised this figure to 4.4 per cent, the *Sovnarkhoz* itself to 5 per cent, and the Republic planners increased it to 5.5 per cent which was acceptable to the central planners.[28]

It is interesting to compare the initially proposed and formally approved success indicator targets for four enterprises surveyed. The figures are for the 1961 operating period and were arrived at during the 1960 planning process.

Enterprise	Gross Output (Per Cent)		Labor Productivity (Per Cent)		Cost of Production (Kopeks)	
	Draft	Approved	Draft	Approved	Draft	Approved
Machine Tool	5.0	5.5	5.0	7.0	95.7	95.0
Ball Bearing	5.5	6.5	6.0	9.0	82.0	80.0
Silk	4.0	7.5	6.5	7.5	92.0	90.0
Clothing	3.0	6.5	5.0	6.5	91.6	90.3

Gross output and labor productivity are the percentage increases over 1960. Cost of production is the cost in kopeks per one ruble of marketable output. (100 kopeks = 1 ruble.)

It appears from these figures that higher authorities were more concerned about "squeezing" additional output from consumer goods producers than from the producer goods enterprises. Managers at the ball bearing plant explained that the high planned increase in labor productivity was primarily due to modernization and the addition of some new equipment.

It is evident that the planning process in Soviet industry is rather like a strategic bargaining game. Past performance and arbitrary upward adjustment in lower level proposals are at the heart of the process. The suspense-filled question for enterprise management is, "Will higher authorities cut away significant portions of meat as they attempt to cut away the fat?" In most instances it would be virtually impossible for a *sovnarkhoz* and other control authorities to have full knowledge of enterprise capabilities and resource needs. Enterprise managers typically prepare thousands of documents and tens of thousands of technical calculations during the planning process.[29] Higher level planners cannot possibly analyze such mountains of data carefully—no doubt this is a major reason why the state advocates enterprise participation in planning.

In the final analysis, there is a widespread tendency for *sovnarkhozy* to disaggregate their plans among subordinate enterprises rather arbitrarily by using results achieved to date as their only compass. The rules used by the *sovnarkhoz* (including its branch departments) for such dis-aggregation tend to remain basically unchanged for fairly long periods; in effect, these rules seek to maintain the relative positions of subordinate enterprises. If a given *sovnarkhoz* succeeds in deriving considerable slack in its own plan, subordinate enterprises also stand a better chance of obtaining easy, or at least realistic, plans. (That the *sovnarkhoz* is inclined to aid its enterprises in their pursuit of organizational slack—at least until its own plan is approved from above—is discussed in Chapter 11.)

Evidence suggests that the higher level planners, confronted with defective information, proceed to establish plans that are too difficult or too easy for probably a large majority of enterprises. This means that many enterprises will either underfulfill or overfulfill their production plans—and it would be a rare coincidence indeed, if the latter compensated for the former in terms of product-mix. Underfulfillment of plans would clearly have a ramifying snowball effect, often leading to adverse consequences even at enterprises which have obtained realistic plans.

Undesirable Practices and Subjective Forces in Planning
as Keys to Managerial Success

Whether a given enterprise obtains an easy or difficult plan is largely dependent on management's ability to capitalize on various undesirable practices. Management's skill in gamesmanship and bargaining strategy, as well as the interaction of personalities, are all of utmost importance. Soviet sources clearly reveal that these factors are frequently the major determinants of the "looseness" or "tightness" of the approved enterprise plan.

For example, one Soviet source reflects the significance of subjective forces in planning decisions by citing an actual case involving a newly appointed shipbuilding enterprise director, named Mairov:

> Not for nothing do they say at the shipyard that Mairov began to increase the per cent of plan fulfillment before he reached Astrakhan. Indeed, as soon as he was appointed the annual plan was reduced and the enterprise's output was revalued at higher prices. This cost the state much, but the enterprise climbed to a leading place in plan fulfillment.[30]

There are numerous examples where the plans for different enterprises provide for substantial differences in production costs, labor productivity, equipment utilization, and so forth, even though the enterprises have nearly identical technical conditions and produce essentially the same items. Then again, comparable plants achieve widely different results. For instance, a Kiev machine tool plant produces a six-spindle automatic tool at a cost of 4,160 rubles, while a Moscow plant produces an almost identical model, except for minor design differences, at a cost of 10,278 rubles.[31] The productivity of spinning equipment at the Kineshma Weaving Factory is 18 per cent lower than at the Ufa Cotton Mill—yet both possess the same equipment and produce nearly identical items.[32]

One Soviet source gives a concrete example showing that premium attainment, and hence managerial success, is not necessarily due to economic efficiency, but rather to an easy plan. The performance and related bonus payments for two evidently comparable enterprises in the Gorky *Sovnarkhoz* during three quarters of 1960 are presented here.[33] The figures are in rubles, and they speak for themselves.

	Enterprise A	Enterprise B
Cost Per One Ruble of Marketable Output	91.1 kopeks	85.9 kopeks
Total profit	1,556,200	2,156,300
Output per worker	4,798	8,847
Nonproductive expenditures	242,600	17,600
Total bonuses awarded to enterprise	174,600	30,100

Situations such as those cited here are attributed mainly to management's ability—or lack of ability—in getting an easy enterprise plan. Any deficiencies incorporated into the approved plan have the state's blessing, as does management's failure to include beneficial tasks in the plan. If management is successful in obtaining an easy plan, there would be less need to engage in undesirable—sometimes risky—practices in fulfilling the plan in order to derive premiums.

Behavior in Plan Fulfillment

Some undesirable managerial practices in plan fulfillment do not clearly violate any rule or planned obligation, others involve an outright disregard for rules and plans. No doubt most enterprises follow most of the lines laid down in the plan—but in many instances substantial portions of the plan are violated. The extent of such violations may vary according to the difficulty the enterprise encounters in fulfilling its success indicators, and is probably most intensive at the margin where management is striving for the few extra percentage points that spell the difference between nonfulfillment and overfulfillment.

In general, formal rules and regulations, as well as the plan itself, do serve as constraints over the intensity of undesirable practices. A ruthless disregard for the over-all "rules of the game" may result in rather severe penalties, as well as the forfeiture of premiums. Hence, the Soviet manager must, in reality, walk a tightrope. When he finds it necessary to engage in various undesirable practices, he must be fairly subtle and shrewd, or the roof may well cave in on all his aspirations. All in all the Soviet manager plays the "law of averages" in much the same way that the Western businessman may stretch or violate the law when filing tax returns to the government.

As we shall see shortly, each enterprise success indicator precipitates its own distortions and unintended effects. Attempts to close up one undesirable loophole induces an intensive search for other loopholes which, when discovered, lead to intensified distortions in new directions. The Soviets have come to realize that slogans, rules, instructions, plans, rewards, and penalties are not sufficient to deter undesirable managerial behavior—undesirable loopholes are always found if this is necessary for managers to achieve their personal goals. This is acknowledged by the eminent Soviet economist and administrator Evsey Liberman who states: "Personnel [of enterprises] capable of squaring things and pushing things through, more often than not, get around the barriers." [34]

Product-Mix Distortions

The assortment of production (product-mix) has been a perennial problem in Soviet industry which manifests itself in various forms. In an effort to fulfill their success indicators, enterprise managers frequently disregard products and product specifications stipulated in their plans, often substituting less desired, unrequired, or unsalable items. Such behavior is facilitated by the imprecise and aggregate nature of planning and control. Resource limits and aggregate operating targets are typically established before the detailed product-mix is determined. Depending on the actual product-mix produced, this would have different effects on aggregate results and resource inputs. Even subtle deviations from the assortment plan can spell the difference between success or failure. At the same time, it is an extremely difficult and time-consuming task for superior authorities to compare planned with actual performance for each element stipulated in the plan—especially if the product-mix is heterogeneous.

In its product choices the enterprise has no incentive to satisfy consumer requirements or demand, but every incentive to fulfill its aggregate success indicators. If machine A is more productive and/or durable than machine B, but for various reasons machine B is more beneficial for success indicator performance, the enterprise may substitute more production of B in place of A. The same would be true for material or shoe type x and material or shoe type y, where x is in greater demand, but y is more beneficial.

The nature of the product-mix distortions are patterned by the statistics which express the achievements of the enterprise by reference to its various success indicators.[35] If the aggregate output target is expressed in total number of bolts, or tons of bolts, and the cost of making bolts varies among different sizes and types, management is encouraged to manufacture a product-mix consisting of the largest number of lowest cost items. The aggregate success indicators may be fulfilled, and indeed overfulfilled, but customers may find themselves with an abundance of unneeded 2-centimeter bolts and a shortage of 1-centimeter bolts. Similarly, if the aggregate production target is expressed in square meters of clothing, or even total number of items, consumers may be confronted with an oversupply of black suits with wide pants and relatively few other styles to choose from.

In general, aggregate production quotas expressed in weight (for example, tons) typically leads to the production of large, heavy and/or bulky equipment, cement blocks, steel pipe, chandeliers, cardboard, and so forth. In the case of machinery, equipment, and durable consumer goods—whatever the output-success-indicator measure—producers are usually discouraged from making critically needed spare parts. Various types of metals output (for example, roofing), too heavy when the success indicator was in tons, becomes too thin when expressed in square meters. One humorous Soviet publication shows a cartoon of a plant which fulfilled its output program for nails in tons by the manufacture of one gigantic nail, hanging on one overhead crane and taking up the entire length of the workshop.

For many years textile and clothing output was measured in linear meters. This led to long, narrow production runs. One Soviet source has published a cartoon where the output of a textile factory was one centimeter wide and stretched down the highway from Ivanova to Moscow—management gleefully pronouncing that the plan had been fulfilled. Today, square meters, and in some cases total number of items produced (for example, shoes), are used as output-success-indicators for many types of consumer goods. This may limit management's range of choices in meeting the plan, but it does nothing to insure that output will be in harmony with consumer demand. Hence, we learn from the Soviet press that a clothing factory has fulfilled its plan and obtained premiums by producing a plethora of kerchiefs; another plant has done so by overproducing items of the same color and style; and numerous cases are reported where enterprises fail to produce enough children's articles since this is not beneficial for success indicator results. Where either consumer or producer goods output is expressed only in rubles, management has even greater leeway for distortion.

If management is having difficulty in meeting its cost reduction targets, this would encourage the manufacture of items having low-cost and/or low quality variants. While this would discourage the use of high-cost materials and possibly adversely affect aggregate production results, this need not always be so. Because of the price structure, low-cost material inputs can often be substituted for higher cost inputs without affecting the price of the finished item.

Since cost reduction results vary with the breakdown of the product-mix produced, the cost reduction target can be fulfilled and overfulfilled without any improvement in the unit costs of the individual items produced. The emphasis on cost reduction as a success indicator also seems to have further discouraged management from developing and producing new products according to plan. Better cost results can usually be realized by producing old, familiar items, as discussed further in the next chapter.

Cases where the enterprise overfulfills its production plan indicate that more often than not the above plan items are unneeded or unsalable.[36] Evidence also suggests that where management desires to overfulfill the profit plan—usually only when attention is no longer focused on success indicators—product choices frequently result in unsalable or unneeded output.

Thorough investigations to compare the actual product-mix produced with the planned assortment stipulated in contracts, disclose that many enterprises that fall short of their assortment "obligations" by 10 per cent, 20 per cent, and even more, fulfill their success indicators and are awarded premiums. This is often the case at ball bearing factories, steel mills, equipment producers, chemical plants—in fact, at most every type of producer goods enterprise.[37]

Product-mix distortions appear to be even more pronounced in the consumer goods sector. For example, an investigation in 1961, covering all types of consumer goods revealed that there is little correlation between planned orders and actual output. In fact, the range of consumer goods orders fulfilled by producers ranged from 30 to 250 per cent.[38] Unplanned consumer products produced in 1961 totaled about two billion rubles.[39] The manager of a large Moscow retail store stated, "Last year we selected 67 dress models of stylish fabrics at the All-Union Fashion House Exhibition and sent orders to factories in Moscow, but we have received dresses for only two kinds of models." [40] Personnel interviewed at three Soviet retail stores attributed much of their unsalable merchandise to the violation of contract orders by producers.

In view of managerial behavior regarding the enterprise's product-mix one Soviet source states:

> This is why warehouses are sometimes filled with tens of millions of rubles worth of goods for which there is no demand or need. This is why many enterprises cannot obtain needed supplies, instruments, tools, and semimanu-factures from their suppliers, and why consumers cannot obtain shoes and clothing of fashionable styles and colors.[41]

Output Quality Distortions

Just as serious as the product-mix problem is the problem of poor quality output. In a vast planned economy it is impossible for the higher planners to establish precise quality technical standards governing all output specifications, or to revise standards promptly with changes in the production process. Enterprise managers rarely initiate higher quality standards—if anything, they tend to strive for lower standards.

Quality control remains minimal in such a system. It is possible in numerous instances to specify minimum standards, but enterprises pressed to fulfill their aggregate targets can and do find ways around stipulated quality standards. Product inputs are skimped on and processes are left out in an effort to fulfill and overfulfill enterprise success indicators. Often this is done in ways not readily detectable by external quality control officials and customers. Defects resulting from such methods may only become apparent once the product is in use, but then it is too late to penalize the producer.

Equipment breakdowns, unusable materials, unsalable consumer goods, and the constant need to repair consumer durables (appliances and so forth), are attributed chiefly to poor quality output at producing enterprises. The emphasis on cost reduction as a success indicator has greatly intensified output quality distortions.

In the first six months of 1962 as compared with 1961, output of all kinds in Soviet industry classified as useless spoilage increased by 13.6 per cent.[42] At the enterprises in the Upper Volga *Sovnarkhoz* losses from output spoilage amounted to 6.2 million rubles during the first nine months of 1963—a sharp increase over 1962.[43] There are numerous complaints about low quality industrial materials and equipment. For example, we read that during 1963 one-third of the output of the Minsk Machinery Plant is virtually useless.[44]

While substandard output is a critical problem concerning producer goods, it is even more critical with regard to consumer goods. In 1962, 36.2 per cent of the men's suits produced by the Novosibirsk Clothing Factory was labeled substandard by trade quality control inspectors. At the Baku Textile Plant 20 per cent of its output during the first half of 1963 was classified as "junk, unfit for sale or commercial processing." [45] *Izvestia* reports that about 50 per cent of the output of a large shoe factory has been classified as "junk" by trade inspectors during the first half of 1963.[46] In Moscow there are about 1.3 million registered television sets, and 1.2 million needed repair in 1962. The great majority of these repairs were attributed to poor quality, defective manufacturing rather than old age.[47]

During 1961 the trade agencies of the Russian Republic Ministry of

Trade classified as spoilage and significantly substandard more than one-third of all dresses, shoes, and knitted garments inspected, and about 50 per cent of the hosiery.[48] During 1963 quality control inspectors of the same trade ministry examined 16.5 million products, of which 7.7 million were considered to be "junk." [49] The bulk of this figure represented nondurables, but a large proportion of consumer durables—especially refrigerators, washing machines, furniture, television sets, cameras, and the small number of cars produced—were also of highly defective quality. Rather surprisingly, in all of these cases, the bulk of the defective output was allowed to proceed to the wholesale warehouses and retail counters, where much of it is apparently rotting for the lack of buyers.

In general, customers—whether they be other producers or trade organizations—frequently have no choice but to accept inferior goods. To refuse them would make their own plan fulfillment even more difficult since usually no other source of supply is readily available. Trade officials do not evaluate consumer goods in terms of retail sales. Moreover, the trade organizations to which the goods are shipped are often not those responsible for the contractual agreement. For these and various other reasons the trade agencies frequently close their eyes to substandard merchandise.[50]

It was pointed out earlier that customers can legally press for fines and damages from delinquent suppliers, but more often than not they do not press charges because of a lengthy and complex bureaucratic process and fear of upsetting future relations. Furthermore, blame for improper and defective goods often cannot be attributed to the supplier since he may not have had adequate supplies. We shall see in Chapter 11 that higher authorities and local party officials charged with the task of controlling enterprise output distortions tend to shut their eyes to such practices. Where fines and damages are paid by producers, Soviet sources acknowledge that this usually does not make amends for one-hundredth of the harm done on a national scale.[51]

There are numerous examples of enterprises engaging in fairly extensive quality distortions and still obtaining premiums. There are also many examples of enterprises paying out tens of thousands of rubles in fines, incurring hundreds of thousands of rubles in unproductive expenditures from spoilage, but fulfilling their success indicators and receiving premiums.[52] Such enterprises have no doubt obtained easy plans and successfully accumulated substantial organizational slack to withstand such expenditures and still derive premiums.

In spite of the threat of fines and the costly system of checks and controls, poor quality output continues to grow more serious in Soviet industry. Beginning in 1960, the regime has undertaken a vigorous campaign against substandard goods, particularly consumer goods. *Pravda* and *Izvestia* have urged their readers to report cases of defective merchandise, and most enterprises must now put their name or trademark on their products for identification. Occasionally, enterprise directors are discharged and even imprisoned because of poor quality output.[53] But all of these penalties, campaigns, and measures have had no noticeable effect.

The Soviets have come to realize that effective incentives are drastically needed if enterprises are to produce high quality goods. As one Soviet source aptly points out:

> Quality tends to depend on the conscience and desires of workers, managers, designers, and controllers on the spot. . . . The reason for poor quality goods is the absence of a system to ensure the production of high quality output. Indeed, one cannot seriously suppose that this task can be solved by agencies of technical quality control, which, after all, actually do nothing more than put the "defective" tag on output and try to influence the production process through slogans and chants.[54]

The big question is what kind of incentive system can one devise to encourage high quality output given the basic features of the Soviet economic system?

Storming

Where the enterprise is striving to fulfill its aggregate production targets, we typically get "storming" practices—a mad rush to fulfill the production plan in the final days of the month or quarter. There are numerous accounts of enterprises which produce 50 to 60 per cent, and often more, of their output during the last ten days of the month.[55] This type of behavior is a major cause of substandard output, the production of items not according to specification, and disruption of delivery schedules to customers. The enterprise is accredited with a sale as long as the output is shipped by the end of the given month or quarter, even if the goods are needed earlier. Enterprises that engage in storming practices have been dubbed the "Heroes of the 29th Day" because they ship their output during the final hours of the month.[56] But as long as the enterprise's success indicators are fulfilled management still obtains premiums.

Aggregate Output Distortions

The gross output measure of success results in additional undesirable actions. Because net changes in uncompleted production count in gross output statistics, goods are dumped into production at the end of the quarter. There is a tendency to start work on production which will not be completed for some time to come, or which is not even undertaken for customers. Hence, we read that in 1963 the Irkuts Aluminum Plant melted finished ingots and reworked them in order to fulfill the gross plan and obtain premiums.[57] Similarly, a Moscow machine tool enterprise casted massive steel plates to cover its workshop floors in order to fulfill the tonnage plan—the source goes on to point out that such flooring costs more than Persian rugs.[58]

If marketable output were used as a success indicator instead of gross output, this would not give credit to the enterprise for genuinely unfinished production. Where management is concerned about fulfilling the marketable output target, semiprocessed goods are often pulled off the production line and the machines are loaded with products that are easy to complete before the end of the month or quarter.

Enterprise managers often order nonproduction personnel—maintenance crews, shipping clerks, research and development staffs—into production in an attempt to fulfill aggregate output and, at times, labor productivity targets. This, of course, leads to neglect of nonproduction areas.

Ignoring Planned Assignments

Managers—particularly those at enterprises which have not obtained easy plans—in their efforts to fulfill and overfulfill success indicators, frequently fail to introduce new technology, changes in production process, and organizational improvement measures according to plan. They also ignore plant modernization, equipment maintenance and repairs, training of personnel, and various other planned "obligations" which would result in better enterprise performance. For such activities divert time, effort, and resources from short-run success indicator performance. Moreover, management would not normally derive any future benefits from these activities since subsequent enterprise plans would be tightened to reflect much or all of the resulting improvements.

Falsification of Results

It is not surprising to come across many reports of managers falsifying enterprise results in a system where 99.9 per cent plan fulfillment spells failure, and 100 per cent spells success. Cost figures are juggled to simulate fulfillment of the cost reduction targets. Output that will occur in the following quarter is credited with being produced in the current quarter—if things go well the following period, the "borrowed" output is repaid. These are but some of the ways by which management "fudges" figures to fulfill success indicators and obtain premiums.

Illegal Procurement Activities

Managers at plants lacking adequate supplies to fulfill production targets would be the ones most likely to engage in extensive illegal procurement activities, but even enterprises allocated adequate resources may find it necessary to engage in such activities if proper supplies are not received. There are reports that the directors and administrative staffs of various enterprises spend half of their time, or more, trying to obtain critically needed commodities through both legal and illegal means.[59] This, of course, diverts their attention from other important duties.

Organizational Slack and Plan Fulfillment

Managers at enterprises with easy plans would rarely overfulfill success indicators beyond the point where allowable quarterly incentive compensation is maximized, as this would lead to more difficult plans in the future. Thus many enterprises that overfulfill plans are still in possession of excess capacity and resources which provide them with organizational slack for the future.[60] No cost or penalty is entailed for maintaining excess fixed and working capital. There would be little need for enterprises not having difficulty in fulfilling their plans to search actively for improvements in operations; in fact, many worthwhile employee innovation proposals may be shelved until a more auspicious time for management.

Enterprises with easy plans would probably not engage in substantial product-mix or quality distortions. They would most likely carry out the major innovation measures stipulated in the plan; and to try earnestly to be victorious in socialist competition. Once assured that their success indicators will be sufficiently overfulfilled, they may then turn their attention to profit performance and the maximization of the Enterprise Fund.

There are some indications that, when managers feel success indicators cannot be fulfilled during a given quarter, they may try to derive premiums in subsequent quarters by accumulating reserves. This would be done by underfulfilling the plan more than necessary during one or more quarters. Apparently this practice is quite common in Hungarian industry,[61] and various Czech and Polish officials interviewed stated that enterprise managers in their countries sometimes follow it. Data presented in Table I, Chapter 7 suggest that this practice may also exist in Soviet industry. The table shows that the Moscow Machine Tool, Moscow Silk Fabric, and Kharkov Clothing enterprises received substantial premiums for some quarters during 1960, and none in others.

At enterprises which obtain unreasonably difficult plans, management may well succumb to the "psychology of losing hope," and rather than engage in extremely risky distortion in an attempt to fulfill success indicators, management may act to underfulfill plans to a greater degree than is necessary. In this manner, because of the practice of point of departure planning, the enterprise would improve its chances of obtaining an easier plan in subsequent periods. According to a Hungarian economist, such behavior is commonly encountered in Hungarian industry. He points out that where enterprises could fulfill their plan by 95 per cent, they may in fact only fulfill them by 90 per cent or even less.[62] No doubt a similar tendency exists at Soviet enterprises.

Inflexibility as a Barrier to Rational Managerial Behavior

Because of the inflexibility of the enterprise plan, management is often prevented from acting rationally and desirably. For example, the Soviet economist, Liberman, relates a personal experience which highlights the inflexible nature of Soviet planning:

> Some foundry workers complained they had no chaplets, posts, or hooks for holding cores in place—that they had all got lost in the casting process. They said they used to be allocated metal from which they made chaplets, but no metal was now available for them, and hence, there were no chaplets. They asked that a few women workers be assigned to recover and sort the chaplets, but it turned out that this was impossible because the wage fund would not stand it. And so we lose 10,000 rubles worth of metal by saving 2,000 rubles in wages.[63]

Inflexibility also leads to many relinquished opportunities which arise during the course of plan fulfillment. If, for example, the enterprise discovers a new cost reduction device that would improve short-run as well as long-term results, chances are that funds and other resources required to introduce this device could not be obtained.

Impact of Managerial Behavior on Ultimate Enterprise Objectives

It is difficult to isolate clearly the impact of managerial behavior on ultimate enterprise objectives from other factors that also have a significant impact—in particular, planning errors made by external authorities and failures in the supply system. Of these factors, managerial behavior appears to be the most potent, and managerial practices in both the planning process and plan fulfillment must be considered. Depending on the easiness or difficulty of the approved enterprise plan, managerial practices in plan fulfillment would affect the ultimate enterprise objectives in different ways and degrees.

It is apparent that probably a majority of enterprises do not obtain approved plans that are well-balanced and internally consistent. If the plan is too easy, this would indicate that management has successfully capitalized on its undesirable practices and has displayed much skill in gamesmanship with superior authorities. If the plan is too difficult, this is also in large part due to undesirable behavior. When management provides defective information, higher authorities cannot approve sound enterprise plans.

Managerial behavior during the planning process is possibly a more potent cause of mutual distrust than state planning policy and higher level planning errors. If management were to provide higher authorities with accurate planning information, the element of distrust could be lessened considerably, and superior authorities would probably consider management's planning proposals more seriously. If these proposals represented an honest appraisal of enterprise capabilities and resource needs, sounder plans could result.

Under the present system, managerial behavior during the planning process clearly hinders the chances of a favorable over-all degree of enterprise objective attainment because the plan does not effectively translate the ultimate objectives into operating terms. This shortcoming is most evident with regard to innovation and the enterprise's assortment plan.

No doubt a major portion of the assortment plan does conform to the requirements and wishes of customers. But management frequently incorporates a significant number of items into the plan that are not in accordance with the interests of customers. Most enterprises can and undoubtedly do stifle the inclusion of at least some innovation measures in their plans, which would not only be beneficial for future operations but for society as well. That such behavior is in conflict with the desideratum calling for a balance between short-term and long-run considerations is obvious.

By providing deficient information to superior authorities, managers adversely affect the approved enterprise resource limits and related operating targets. An inconsistent plan hinders the effective utilization of the over-all production input factor-mix once the plan is implemented. If the various classes of assigned resources (supplies, manpower, fixed and working capital) are not in balance, at least some of the desiderata pertaining to maximum resource utilization are not likely to be favorably achieved.

It should be pointed out, however, that if a given enterprise succeeds in incorporating organizational slack into its approved plan, this can at times have favorable effects. If the plant does not receive all of its allocated supplies on time or in kind, such slack may prevent breakdowns and the underfulfillment of the production plan provided that the excess supplies on hand are substitutable for those not received. In the event of unanticipated labor turnover or equipment breakdowns, excess reserves may enable a fuller over-all utilization of resources and more output than would be the case without such reserves. Slack arising from an easy plan may encourage the enterprise to fulfill various innovation assignments that would otherwise be ignored and enable it to fulfill its plan with a minimum of product-mix, delivery, and quality distortions.

During the operating period enterprises with easy plans would probably achieve the most favorable degree of desiderata attainment in output quality, product-mix in accordance with customer wishes and needs, timely delivery of goods, and balance between short-run and long-term considerations. However, they would probably not make full use of their resources, maximize production, or minimize costs if incentive compensation can be maximized without doing so. In the event that above plan output is produced, much of it may be unneeded by customers.

Enterprises with unrealistic, difficult plans would also be inclined not to make full use of resources, maximize output, or minimize costs in order to obtain easier plans in subsequent periods.

At those enterprises with tight but realistic plans, the desiderata calling for maximum output, minimization of costs, and full utilization of resources may be favorably achieved. The fact that the total size of premiums depends not only on the fulfillment, but also on the overfulfillment of certain success indicators, may well induce managers to engage in product-mix, delivery, and quality distortions, and this would represent a misdirection of resources. Various planned "obligations" that are beneficial for future operations but would hinder short-run success indicator performance would probably be ignored.

Enterprises with difficult but not entirely unreasonable plans would tend to engage most extensively in such distortions in an effort to fulfill their success indicators and would also be inclined to sacrifice many innovations and other long-run measures in pursuit of premiums. While the objectives—maximum output and the minimization of costs—may be favorably achieved, full use may not be made of all classes of resources because of imbalances among them.

Illegal procurement practices can often have a favorable effect on the ultimate objectives at a given enterprise—although they can upset performance at other enterprises where earmarked supplies are deflected. Such practices may serve to correct planning errors, thus bringing the various classes of resources into better balance in plan fulfillment. If adequate supplies are obtained illegally, plant capacity and manpower are likely to be utilized more fully than would otherwise be the case. Consequently, more output would be achieved, more delivery schedules would be met, and perhaps there would be less misdirection of resources arising from quality and product-mix distortions.

It is evident that the reforms undertaken by the Soviets to eliminate undesirable managerial behavior and improve enterprise results have not been effective. Undesirable managerial practices and poor results are not due to mere idiosyncrasies or a lack of patriotism but rather to shortcomings in the rules of the game by which the Soviet enterprise manager must operate. The principal shortcomings remain: the system of success indicators on the one hand, and the deficient provision of resources to enterprises on the other. The two interact creating a vicious circle that significantly hinders managerial performance and enterprise results.

The Soviets have not been able to design an incentive system that encourages managers to pursue with equal effort and effectiveness all of the objectives of their enterprises. Each incentive scheme tried has had the unintended consequence of inducing managers to engage in a wide variety of practices contrary to the state's interest; each has precipitated its own types of distortions and patterns of undesirable behavior. In every case, there have been dysfunctional consequences relating to some or all of the ultimate enterprise objectives—some desiderata have been maximized while others have been sacrificed substantially.

Impact of Undesirable Managerial Practices on the Soviet Economy

Perhaps the best way to assess the impact of undesirable managerial practices on the Soviet economy as a whole, is in terms of inefficiency, waste, and foregone opportunities. These practices can be attributed primarily to shortcomings in the entire system and are by no means the only cause of failures in these three spheres, although they contribute very substantially to such inefficiencies. In fact, Soviet sources have traditionally pointed to the enterprise manager as being the major culprit for failures in the system—that this is gradually changing is discussed in Chapter 12.

Inefficiency is defined here as the improper allocation and utilization of resources that result in poorer production than could potentially be achieved. Improper allocation is inefficient in two ways: (1) It leads to the excess of some types of factors of production at producing enterprises, and (2) it causes the shortages of other types. Enterprises may find that they have excess amounts of some resources, such as machine tools, which stand idle—excess amounts of some factors imply shortages of others, such as manpower, component parts, or raw materials, which prevent utilization of the entire production input factor-mix.

That numerous enterprises—probably a considerable majority—obtain plans that are too easy or too difficult is in large part due to the defective information provided by their managers. Such faulty information feedback leads to inefficiency that manifests itself in idle resources on a national scale in the absence of proper utilization of the over-all production input factor-mix. Inefficiency is compounded by management's constant pursuit of organizational slack, and by the failure of enterprises to supply their customers with needed goods. It is true that some idle resources are required for flexibility purposes, but evidence reveals that in numerous cases there are far more idle resources than are necessary for operational flexibility.

In 1960, investigations at 408 enterprises in 33 regions disclosed 400 million (new) rubles of uninstalled equipment; the value of uninstalled equipment at enterprises throughout the Russian Republic was estimated at 1.8 billion rubles.[64] At the end of 1962, it was estimated that "hoarded excess stocks" of uninstalled equipment stored in enterprise warehouses throughout the country amounted to 900 million rubles.[65] Khrushchev has revealed that as of mid-1963, in the machine-building industry—which is supposed to operate at near maximum capacity during two shifts—24 per cent of all equipment stands idle during the first shift, and 39 per cent during the second. Yet the enterprise managers constantly complain about equipment shortages.[66]

An investigation in 1959 at many plants in various regions revealed excess hoarded stocks of materials totaling 1.5 billion rubles above plan. At the same time it was found that material deficiencies at some of these enterprises totaled 320 million rubles below plan.[67] It is estimated that in the ferrous metals industry, hundreds of millions of rubles of hoarded supplies lie idle in plant warehouses. In 1957, excessive material inventories at enterprises in the Ivanova *Sovnarkhoz* totaled an estimated 7 billion rubles. As of January, 1963, the estimated figure stood at 14.8 billion—far outstripping the growth of output in the region.[68] There is also much evidence that substantial excess manpower exists at numerous enterprises, while others suffer severe shortages in their production programs.[69]

Waste is defined here as output which does not serve a useful purpose, and which represents an irrational misdirection of resources. In an economy of shortages and no unemployment, the production of unusable and unsalable goods that accumulate in warehouses and stores is clearly wasteful. Growth statistics are virtually meaningless when they include figures for wasted output. Much of the waste in the Soviet economy is the direct result of undesirable product-mix and quality practices at industrial enterprises.

During the first half of 1962, output rendered completely unusable because of severe defects totaled 204 million rubles.[70] Bordering on waste, but clearly representing a misdirection of resources, and also causing much inefficiency, is the spoilage and grossly substandard output passed on to consumers. This results in billions of rubles of repair costs and breakdowns. Approximately 14 billion rubles a year are spent on repairs, and most of this is attributed to defective goods.[71] Part of this sum pertains to the repair of consumer durables, but the bulk to breakdowns and repairs at industrial enterprises. Forty per cent of all equipment and machinery failures during operation are attributed to poor quality, defective manufacturing.[72] According to Soviet figures, the proportion of personnel directly engaged in repairing and servicing plant and equipment is nearly double that in U.S. industry.[73]

Waste in the consumer goods sector is even more pronounced and clear-cut. In the past almost any products produced in the Soviet Union could be used by somebody, regardless of their type or quality. In recent years, however, the basic human needs have generally been filled, and consumers have become more reluctant to pay hard-earned money for shoddy merchandise. Hence, the consumer goods sellers' market has begun to show some resistance. It is true that mounting unsalable inventories of consumer goods are largely due to the supply system and to the inability of trade officials to accurately forecast and transmit consumer demand to producers. However, enterprise product-mix and quality practices are also major causes of this situation. In fact, Soviet sources tend to attribute the lion's share of the blame to enterprise managers. If the managers were willing to sacrifice success indicator fulfillment, and hence their premiums, the consumer goods situation would improve substantially. But, understandably, they do not, and unsalable goods continue to mount.

The sales manager of the large Central Department Store in Moscow points out, "A few years ago consumers were willing to accept anything and everything turned out. Things are changing now. The customer no longer merely goes to the store; he goes looking for goods that are well made, attractive, and stylish." [74] He added that unsalable shoe inventories increased by about one million rubles at this store during 1959. In January 1959, the shoe inventory in the entire region was 28.5 million rubles, and 43.8 million rubles as of January 1960. Much of this increase from 1959 to 1960 reflected unsalable goods.

During 1956-61, retail trade in the Soviet Union increased by 62 per cent but stocks of goods at retail outlets more than doubled. As of January 1956, consumer goods inventories in the trade network represented 97 days of retail turnover. As of January 1962, the figure stood at 122 days.[75] At the end of 1962, stocks of consumer goods stood at 20 billion rubles, of which 3 billion rubles were classified as excessive.[76] During the first five months of 1963, as compared to the same period in 1962, overstocked goods in the trade network increased by 600 million rubles. As of July 1963—while aggregate orders from producers were being fulfilled—overstocked clothing totaled 600 million rubles, woolen goods and textiles 350 million, and leather footwear 150 million.[77] Much of this represents unsalable products.

Mounting inventories of unsalable consumer goods have compelled the Soviets to engage in such capitalist practices as price cutting and advertising.[78] In 1962, the state lost more than 200 million rubles from price cuts on unsold consumer goods. But even after the markdowns, 108 million rubles worth of unsalable goods remained on the shelves.[79]

The prevalent resistance of enterprise managers to innovation—to develop and produce new, more durable and better quality products, to introduce new technology, to undertake major improvements in the organization of production—results in a preponderance of foregone opportunities that would substantially increase productivity and output over time. Failure to institute such innovations in the consumer goods sector is also a major contributing cause of mounting stocks of unsalable merchandise. The problems of enterprise innovation are the subject of the next chapter.

Some Comments on Managerial Behavior in the U.S. Economy

Managerial Behavior and the Laws of the Land

Less is known about the intimate aspects of managerial behavior in American industry than in Soviet industry. The American corporation is typically a private entity; whereas the Soviet enterprise is a public entity in the fullest sense of the word. No one has the right to pry into the internal affairs of the American firm except with special cause sanctioned by law. It is true that over the years companies have been required to disclose more and more of their private affairs to public and government perusal—but the large part of their internal operations remain protected from the view of outsiders. Nevertheless, it is common knowledge that American managers often violate the laws of the land to perpetuate their own and/or their company's positions. We learn at times of price-fixing collusion, bribery, price discrimination, income tax evasion, illegitimate rebates, misrepresentation in advertising, patent and copyright infringements, illegal restraints of trade, falsification of financial statements, and so forth.

With the growing complexity of American society, and with greater concern for human welfare, more and more legislation is enacted which restricts the activities of enterprise managers. This means that there are more laws to be broken for the sake of self-interest. However, the American economy still basically remains a "Thou shalt not" system. There are fewer laws, rules, and regulations to be broken in such a system than in a "Thou shalt" economy, where each "Thou shalt" in effect represents some law, regulation, or command.

Conflicts of Interest: Ownership vs. Management

When we look at managerial behavior from the point of view of conflicts of interest between ownership and management in American corporations, the latter often gain at the expense of the former. Self-interest is no doubt as prevalent among American managers as with Soviet managers, but the undesirable practices engaged in at the expense of ownership differ because of the basic differences in the two systems.

Many American managers are probably inclined to reinvest most or all of their company's profits to build up organizational slack, thus securing and perpetuating their own positions, rather than paying out dividends. There are also many ways by which management can profit at the expense of greater company profits. Through various accounting practices—depreciation charges, inventory evaluation, charging costs to capital expenses that should be charged to income, creation of hidden reserves, and so forth—management may calculate company profits to benefit its own claims and desires. Similarly, management may award itself unwarranted bonuses or raises, award other companies subcontracts for personal rather than economic reasons, incur large, unnecessary expenses for travel and entertainment, and so forth. In all of these practices the intent is essentially similar to that of the Soviet manager, who, for personal gain, conceals productive capacity, hoards resources, engages in product-mix and quality distortions, resists innovation, and undertakes illegal procurement activities.

Problems in Managerial Planning and Intrafirm Resource Allocation

There is substantial evidence that in American industry the very act of measuring a given manager's or employee's performance frequently leads to a distortion of effort and information.[80] It is perhaps human nature that when an individual is evaluated, and particularly if he is rewarded on the basis of various quantified performance standards, he may be inclined to strive for modest standards. This may be the case regardless of whether the "success indicator" is a production quota, sales, profit or cost reduction target, or some other standard. In most cases the search for slack tends to be accompanied by biased planning proposals, and varying degrees of deficient information channeled upward to superiors.

The pursuit of slack and the resulting bargaining are likely to be much more intensive in Soviet industry than in most American companies—given the extreme situation of resource uncertainty and inflexibility in the Soviet economy. In the American war economy the intensity may approach the Soviet level. However, even in peacetime, the pursuit of slack and intraorganizational bargaining may be very intensive in a given American enterprise because of several conditions essentially similar to those in the Soviet economy. If there is much inflexibility and red tape in revising plans and providing additional resources as unanticipated conditions dictate, this would tend to intensify the search for slack during the planning process. The same may be true if plans are established in the face of great uncertainty (for example, long-term plans, sales forecasts for certain products) and personnel is held responsible for its ful-fillment, even though it does not have adequate authority to cope with unforeseen circumstances. Finally, if a given organization runs into stormy weather, whether because of the business cycle, market forces, a steel strike or an "economy" drive initiated by new management, per-sonnel would tend to compete more vigorously for scarce resources. This in turn would precipitate much active search for slack and probably considerable bargaining as well.

Many of the forms that the search for organizational slack take in the Soviet enterprise during the planning process may also be found in many American firms—particularly at the plant level. Where bureau-cratic action is required to eliminate organizational slack in Soviet indus-try, market forces generally perform this function in American industry. While market forces and the profit motive tend to keep organizational inefficiency and mistakes within tolerable limits, there is a tendency for organizational slack to grow during boom periods. As resources become less scarce, intrafirm bargaining is apt to become less intensive, and we are likely to find substantial organizational slack built into company plans. This typically may include increased expenditures in advertising, travel, research and development, staff and service activities, elaborate training programs, employee and customer services, and so forth. Many of these expenditures may not be needed to maintain the company's level of profits—in fact, they may be impeding profit performance. On the other hand, with organizational slack, company managers are much more inclined to plan and carry out major innovation measures that may significantly enhance long-term profitability.

In reality, Parkinson's Law is very often not a myth.[81] Company per-sonnel tends to find ways to absorb excessive expense budgets and other allocated resources in unnecessary and often wasteful ways. This is done largely to insure for the same amount of resources in the next period. As the external environment becomes less favorable, resources become more scarce, bargaining becomes more vigorous, and prior slack is dimin-ished. In very stormy weather organizational slack accumulated in better times serves as a cushion and enables the firm to survive. Hence, organi-zational slack absorbs a substantial share of the potential variability in the firm's environment, and in this manner it may play both a stabilizing and adaptive role.

If the internal company environment is such that lower level managers incorporate biases into their planning proposals and provide deficient information to their superiors, we are likely to get a system of arbitrary planning basically similar to that of Soviet industry. This, in turn, typically results in much unproductive time, effort, and expense; and company personnel will continue to behave as it does during the plan-ning process, until such behavior no longer serves a useful purpose. Fortunately, the American firm—even a very large one—is infinitesimally small as compared to the Soviet economy. For this reason higher level administrators have a better insight into the true productive capabilities and resource needs of their subordinate administrative units than do *gosplan* and the *sovnarkhoz* in the Soviet system. Therefore, internal planning errors are not likely to be as grave—even in an environment of arbitrary planning. Moreover, significant planning errors, once they are revealed, can generally be rectified more promptly and effectively in American, as compared with Soviet, industry—given the inflexible and extremely bureaucratic structure of the latter.

In general, it is within the sphere of intracompany planning that American industry resembles Soviet industry, since external market forces do little if anything to assure efficient internal resource allocation. To overcome the lack of an operational internal price system, and to make cost accounting more effective in intracompany operations, various devices are used by many companies. Decentralized product divisions and various other "profit center" departments are created, and often costly intrafirm transfer price systems for goods and services are established. This proves most effective where the price mechanism is used by integrated (in terms of functions) and fairly independent subordinate units, and where no large external economies or dyseconomies are present.

The problem of efficient planning and internal resource allocation is most vexing in connection with staff and service activities, and in non-profit organizations. Here profitability, marginal analysis, and cost accounting have little or no meaning. In absence of objective criteria, arbitrary resource allocation rules must often be resorted to. At times past performance may be the only guiding light—but past performance may not reflect efficient resource utilization. It is probably for these reasons that large arbitrary cutbacks are often made in the budgets of staff and service departments as the firm runs into unfavorable market conditions. For example, one Los Angeles company recently laid off 80 staff personnel—including its entire long-range planning department. Yet a significant increase in profits was realized shortly thereafter. Such drastic action is, of course, easier if the company has had a recent change in top management, as was the case here.

Similarly, when the Soviet enterprise manager finds that his longtime, friendly, *sovnarkhoz* superior has been replaced by a faceless unknown, he may also find himself with a substantially tightened plan.

Undesirable Practices, Performance Standards, and Plan Fulfillment

It is true that the profit motive—as weak as it may be in some American companies—does a reasonably effective job in balancing the attainment of the various short-run objectives of the company. In fact, profitability in a market economy is the best available performance standard—in terms of short-run operating efficiency—since it serves to summarize the effects of a host of competitive forces. However, there has been a growing awareness by many American corporations that emphasis on short-term profit results often serves as an obstacle to innovation and the attainment of other long-term objectives. It is likely that only those firms which have considerable organizational slack dare to venture in major innovation activities where substantial resources and risks are entailed.

Managers below the top management level usually concentrate on these aspects of performance measured and utilized for evaluation purposes, rather than their jobs and responsibilities as a whole. Where profitability cannot be used as a meaningful performance standard, it is often very difficult to devise a norm that combines all the desiderata or subgoals of a given job or department into a composite score for evaluating over-all performance. The literature contains numerous examples of company personnel—both managerial and nonmanagerial—who fulfill their success indicators in undesirable ways.[82] Undesirable practices are probably more prevalent where success indicator fulfillment is difficult, and where there is no all-embracing criterion, such as profit, for evaluating performance.

At the factory level undesirable practices often resemble those engaged in at Soviet enterprises, since the success indicators are often similar. We hear of and/or observe storming activities, efforts to push through defective output, the postponement of maintenance and repairs, falsified results, ceilings on output, the buildup of reserves, and so forth. However, because of market forces and the relatively easy task of controlling such distortions in an American company, regardless of its size, the extent of such distortions does not nearly approach that of Soviet industry. Under wartime conditions we have a somewhat different story, as was pointed out earlier.

Regarding sales, undesirable practices are often resorted to in efforts to fulfill key performance standards. If for instance, the success indicator is total sales revenue, there may be a tendency to concentrate on the sale of the highest priced items without regard for profit margins, to concentrate on good customers at the expense of cultivating potentially good customers, to cut prices unduly, and to use various selling techniques detrimental to the company's reputation and future sales. Much costly policing and control may be required to counteract such tendencies.

In most every sphere of company activity, there is evidence that personnel at times carries out its plans in various undesirable ways. No doubt where unrealistic performance standards are established, the "psychology of losing hope" is likely to emerge, thus causing worse performance than need be.

In bureaucratic government agencies and various other nonprofit organizations a multitude of rules, regulations, policies, and standard procedures are typically required in the absence of market forces and other objective operational guidelines. In such oragnizations there are likely to be more violations and undesirable practices than in private enterprises—there are more things to violate and there is less room for internally "legal" maneuverability. In fact, personnel is likely to find itself in a "Thou shalt" rather than a "Thou shalt not" environment.

Concluding Remarks

It should be pointed out that a study of inefficiency and waste in the American economy—especially during recessionary periods—would undoubtedly reveal some alarming figures. While resource shortages and the supply system are chief causes of productive inefficiency and waste in the U.S.S.R., market flunctuations, ineffective demand, overinvestment, and overproduction are typically major causes in the U.S. However, in both cases poor enterprise performance, in the economic sense, is frequently chiefly due to external constraints beyond the control of the micromanagers. In this connection there might well be significant defects in the macromanagerial structure within which the enterprise managers must operate. Often, greater economic gains may be realized by overcoming these defects rather than concentrating on the improvement of the internal operations of productive enterprises.

Because of its affluence, the American economy can much better afford to put up with waste and inefficiency than the Soviet economy. The U.S. has achieved its enviable affluence because of competitive forces and the pursuit of profits. Rather ironically, affluence—and not only depression—has led to much welfare legislation and probably greater concern for personal security. This, in turn, has reduced the effectiveness of the market price system as an economic regulator, and the profit motive as an economic incentive.

9 • Management and Innovation

Innovation has historically not been a problem in the Soviet economy. In the early period of industrialization, Western technology and products could be copied directly or adapted to Soviet conditions without serious strain. In the formerly simple Soviet economy considerable progress could be made without recourse to very sophisticated innovative techniques. In the consumer goods sector the crudest forms of output served to satisfy the demands of an impoverished population.

In recent years, however, the problem of innovation has gained considerable importance in Soviet aims. Instead of having surplus manpower and productive capacity, labor shortages have become increasingly critical, and innovation in the form of improving productivity is deemed essential. Rising standards of living and somewhat greater consumer choice are leading to mounting inventories of obsolete, unsalable consumer goods valued at billions of rubles. We are here concerned with the development and production of new products at industrial enterprises, the introduction of new technology, as well as other forms of major production process innovation.

The current situation of product innovation and technical progress in the Soviet Union is paradoxical. We cannot help but be impressed with the great Soviet advances in certain top priority and strategic spheres of industrial activity—armaments, satellites, atomic power projects. At the same time Soviet sources voice widespread complaint about product and process innovation at industrial enterprises in general. Western observers in the Soviet Union are amazed at the obsolete and often horrendous consumer goods. The Soviets themselves frequently refer to their shoes as "logs" and their clothing as "funeral garments." [1] Visits to Soviet factories—even those accessible to foreigners—reveal much "antique" machinery and outdated production processes. According to most Soviet sources, the opposition of managers is the major barrier to enterprise innovation. The following background information is pertinent to the subject.

Planning for Enterprise Product Innovation

Every Soviet enterprise personally surveyed has a long-range plan for technical development. This plan is subdivided into annual plans, and

184

for a given planned year it is further broken down into quarterly plans. The long-range plans are not operational and reflect no more than very general innovation goals. For instance, the long-term product innovation goal at a mining equipment enterprise is "the development and production of conveyer machinery that would reduce the manpower needed in the mines." At consumer goods plants the goals are no more than statements of the long-range objectives of their respective branches of industry —"to develop and increase the output of new varieties of high quality shoes (or clothing)."

Product development activities and the full-scale production of new products for customers are indicated in concrete terms only in the annual and/or quarterly plans at producer goods enterprises. At most consumer goods producers, concrete innovation tasks are spelled out only in quarterly plans.

There is no set pattern as to how or where new product ideas originate. Producing enterprises, research and design institutes, higher authorities, or even customers, may initiate product innovation proposals. Product development assignments may come as direct orders from above to a given enterprise, or the enterprise may initiate the undertaking of such assignments. As for full-scale production of new products, this may come about through enterprise initiative or higher directives, often upon the recommendations of research and design institutes. Several managers interviewed pointed out that initiative by enterprises developing the new product is a very common way by which full-scale production comes about, because these enterprises are in the best position to judge whether the new product is perfected, and whether the plant is capable of undertaking production assignments.

Higher authorities almost always approve the quantities of new products to be produced by a given enterprise in a given quarter or year. Central planners in conjunction with the appropriate industrial state committee make the final decisions involving important types of producers goods. Decisions regarding most new types of consumer goods are made by the *sovnarkhoz* in conjunction with the appropriate republican trade organization. If a major consumer good innovation is involved, the approval of various central agencies, such as the All-Union Institute of Clothing, may be required.

Problems and Complexity of Coordination

One would expect that in an economic system based on extensive planning and control the coordination of product innovation activities would be facilitated. But this is far from the case in the vast, complex Soviet economy—the coordination of product innovation activities is a very serious problem in Soviet industry. There is much duplication of effort on a national scale, and much confusion frequently results. As Khrushchev has pointed out, each organization involved in product development tends to bring forth its own designs and technology—"it invents the bicycle itself, so to speak." [2]

Hundreds of industrial research and design institutes participate in innovation activities with industrial enterprises. Most enterprises having more than a few hundred personnel also have their own experimental, development, and design facilities. All of the enterprises visited have such facilities and deal with outside institutes. Most institutes are affiliated with plants in a given branch of industry. They are advisory and participative in nature and do not have any formal authority over enterprises.

Often several—at times more than a dozen—institutes participate in product development activities with a given enterprise, and frequently several suppliers must provide special commodities for such activities. Coordination problems are usually more severe in the development of producer goods, especially machinery, than in consumer goods (particularly nondurables) since generally more participating bodies are involved.

An actual experience cited by Khrushchev reveals the economic consequences of coordination problems and serious time lags in product innovation. At the end of 1962, he visited an artificial fiber plant where he was shown a new experimental machine for the continuous production of viscose rayon. The machine had been developed by a number of research institutes and was manufactured in the Kiev Experimental Workshop in 1960. If the obsolete machines in the fiber plant were replaced with the new ones, the annual output of rayon from the same production area would increase by 1,200 tons, or 22 per cent, at an annual cost saving of 1.5 million rubles. The rise in labor productivity would release 800 workers from hazardous menial tasks. However, for the time being these advantages are present only on paper. By the time production of the new machine for customer use is planned for, perfected and achieved, it will be at least 1965. And at present, new artificial fiber plants are being designed and built to use the obsolete machinery. [3]

A major reason for establishing central state committees for all industrial sectors at the end of 1962 was to improve the coordination of innovation activity. Formerly, the nationwide industrial research and design institutes were not under effective coordinating agencies—many were suborinate to *sovnarkhozy*, others to republican agencies, and still others to central organizations. In 1963, nearly all of these institutes (more than 1,700) have been made subordinate to the appropriate industrial state committees. The research and development facilities at some enterprises have also been placed under the jurisdiction of these committees. The committees have been granted powers over several aspects of enterprise innovation, as discussed in Chapter 2.

Although it is still too early to tell how effective the state committees will prove to be in practice, there are already signs of confusion and ineffectiveness (see Chapter 6). For example, the committees and *sovnarkhozy* are colliding because of conflicting directives regarding innovation issued to industrial enterprises.[4] Somewhat better coordination and enterprise innovation will no doubt result because of the powers granted to the state committees. However, they can only coordinate and control a very limited number of activities and there will probably be a tendency to concentrate on relatively few high priority tasks. The State Committee on Automation and Machine Building alone, now has subordinate to it several hundred institutes and development bureaus at enterprises.

The Process of Enterprise Product Innovation: A Case Example

Managerial officials at a Kharkov enterprise gave this account of the development of a new model of industrial ventilation equipment. This case illustrates concretely the complexities of the process of coordinating enterprise product innovation.

In 1958, an idea for a new type of ventilation machinery originated at the All-Union Sanitary Machinery Institute in Moscow—an affiliate of the Kharkov enterprise. The idea was discussed with the enterprise, a number of supplier and customer enterprises, a number of other institutes, and various central agencies including *Gosplan*. Central authorities gave the go-ahead to undertake product development early in 1960. The Institute for Sanitary Machinery as well as three other institutes prepared drawings and technical data for the design of the new product. Several suppliers provided special materials and components. The Kharkov enterprise made a number of corrections in the data received from the institutes. A few prototypes of the new model were then constructed at the plant. During this stage some components were sent to the different institutes for further testing. Early in 1961 the sample models were assembled and tested at two customer plants where eventually they were to be installed permanently. Some changes were then made in the product at the Kharkov plant with the aid of the institutes.

A visit to the enterprise in June 1961, showed that they were producing an experimental series of 20 models of the new product. Tests would again be carried out at some customer plants on completion of the series, and any remaining bugs would then be ironed out at the Kharkov enterprise. Managers indicated that full-scale production of the new product for customer use was expected to commence sometime in 1962. The enterprise in conjunction with the Institute for Sanitary Machinery would advise the Kharkov *Sovnarkhoz* and central authorities when the new product is perfected. These authorities would then assign certain quantities of the new product to be produced in the enterprise operating plan. The customers would also be assigned. The chief engineer of this plant acknowledged that the process of product innovation is very complex and requires much cooperation.

At the consumer goods plants visited, the process of product innovation is not as complex. None of the plants deal with more than a few institutes. There is, nevertheless, much evidence in Soviet sources of coordination problems in the consumer goods sector.

The example cited shows that coordination problems can cause significant time lags from the inception of a new product idea until full-scale production is undertaken. As will be seen, enterprise management often greatly contributes to time lags, which further aggravate the situation. Unless enterprise managers have an interest in a given innovation, it is extremely difficult to obtain their earnest cooperation.

Managerial Resistance to Product Innovation

Since enterprise initiative and participation are usually required in product innovation activity, management can cause significant time lags from the inception of a new product idea until the product is successfully developed and again from its successful development until full-scale production is authorized. This may be the case whether or not the enterprise has participated in the product's development.

Soviet sources indicate that managers generally oppose product development tasks and the incorporation of assignments to bring out new products in the enterprise's operating plan.[5] An enterprise manager states in *Pravda:* "All enterprise personnel, without exception, are interested in having the plant produce the same machine for the longest possible time without any change whatsoever."[6]

Soviet sources cite numerous examples of severe delays resulting from managerial opposition to product development and many cases of managerial opposition to the planned production of perfected new products: The same type of turret lathe has been made by enterprises in one region since 1925 although many improved lathes have been available to them; an equipment producer has manufactured the same product for years despite the fact the similar equipment—50 per cent more efficient—has long been developed and can be produced at about the same cost. A Soviet economist, affiliated with the Ukrainian Academy of Sciences, agreed during an interview that there has been much managerial resistance to product innovation particularly with the development of capital goods.

Managerial behavior in the consumer goods sector is no different. Many sources reveal that extremely unnecessary delays exist both from the inception of the new product idea until successful development, and particularly from successful development until full-scale production is planned. There are widespread complaints that new consumer products for which there is apparently a significant demand are often intentionally withheld from production by management.

Even when product development assignments and the planned manufacture of new products are incorporated into enterprise operating plans, frequently these planned "obligations" are not fulfilled intentionally. In Soviet reports on the fulfillment of the national economic plans, major complaints typically deal with the nonfulfillment of innovation tasks at industrial enterprises. In Chapter 4 it was indicated that several of the enterprises surveyed—particularly in the consumer goods sector— plan for and produce a sizeable portion of new items. However, many goods classified as "new products" or "product innovations" represent negligible changes in the specifications, colors, styles, or designs of existing products. As one source points out, "The enterprise merely changes a button and management claims an innovation." [7]

It should not be concluded that enterprise managers shun and stifle all product innovation. For example, during Khrushchev's visit to Yugoslavia in August 1963 he stated that "During the 1959-63 period, 13,000 new types of machines, mechanisms and apparatuses were introduced in production in Soviet industry." [8] But back at the Kremlin his condemnations substantially outweigh his plaudits regarding product innovation. He has summed up the situation of managerial opposition to innovation, as follows:

> In our country some bureaucrats are so used to the old nag that they do not want to change over to a good race horse, for he might tear away on the turn and even spill them out of the sleigh! Therefore, such people will hold on to the old nag's tail with both hands and teeth.[9]

The situation is not due to incompetence or mere aberrations. Rather, managers oppose product innovation because of certain conditions present in the economic milieu.

Causes of Managerial Opposition

The principal reason for managerial opposition to product innovation is the premium-success-indicator system. Many Soviet sources assert that product innovation is in conflict with enterprise success indicator results, and hence premium attainment. One source states: "The system of premiums to management for fulfilling the plan has become a great obstacle to the introduction of new machinery." [10]

An enterprise manager complains that for 15 years his plant produced old products and constantly overfulfilled the plan, thus deriving lucrative premiums. Since undertaking the development and manufacture of new products, the plan is no longer fulfilled and premiums are forfeited.[11]

Another enterprise official asks, "Why does the Verkhniye Sergi Plant find it 'unbeneficial' to introduce the manufacture of new bits that would increase the speed of drilling and lower its costs?" and attributes this situation to the probable underfulfillment of success indicators.[12] Still another source cites this example:

> A plant produces aircraft engines with a useful life of 1,500 hours. It is known that it would require not twice as much but only 20 per cent more labor to produce an engine with a useful life of 3,000 hours. Nevertheless, despite the obvious advantages of producing new goods of better quality, no plant or *sovnarkhoz* will do this on its own. The gross output would fall by some 20 per cent.[13]

Khrushchev himself often points out that those managers who avoid product innovation are the ones who are most frequently rewarded. The premium-success-indicator system by itself is not an independent cause of managerial opposition to product innovation. There are certain major underlying reasons for the conflict between innovation and premium attainment: (1) The cost of innovation is not adequately provided for; (2) there are problems of price; (3) there is considerable risk.

Cost of Product Innovation

The total costs involved in enterprise product innovation are not given adequate provision in the enterprise plan. This is more than just a problem of accurately estimating resource needs in the face of uncertainty. Aggregate output, cost and labor productivity targets are generally approved without taking into account the effect innovation activities will have on the fulfillment of these success indicators. Materials, components, equipment, manpower and financial resources for product innovation are typically assigned in some *ad hoc* manner—if at all—during the related operating period and not during the planning process when resource allocations are formally approved. As a result, enterprises frequently find that they do not have sufficient resources to fulfill both product innovation assignments and quarterly success indicators.

In spite of frequent government resolutions and decrees to rectify this situation through earmarked resource allocations for innovation activity, it still persists on a widespread scale. One leading Soviet economist cites the following example which clearly illustrates the present situation:

> Assume that a tractor plant has decided to install pressure lubrication or surface hardening for certain parts. The designer makes the suggestion and the technologist approves it. But management and the planning department

may oppose the idea because it is unbeneficial under the present method of evaluating the enterprise's work. Production costs will go up, the amount of labor required will increase, and labor productivity will drop. Go and prove to the *sovnarkhoz* and *Gosplan* that more personnel, money, materials, equipment, etc. are needed to make these improvements. If you succeed in proving this, there is no place to get the supplies and people since everything has been distributed.[14]

In effect, the present Soviet managerial reward system is designed to give largest bonuses to products which are easiest to produce—which typically are those which have been longest in production. When a new product or process is introduced, workers and supervisors shift to a higher point on a new learning curve. The result is, in the short run, higher production costs and lower rates of output. Eventually the men will learn the new techniques and output will rise again, but failure to recognize this initial inefficiency costs the Soviet economy much in terms of less rapid technical progress and product innovation.

The Problem of Price

The price structure is another obstacle to product innovation, since better enterprise success indicator results can usually be achieved by producing old products which have long-established, fixed prices. Prices usually remain fixed for several years and are rarely adjusted promptly in view of technical progress and other improvements in production. The profit margins on old products typically range from 20 to 30 per cent, and often more than 40 per cent.[15] Provisional wholesale prices for new products are usually established on a cost-plus 3 to 5 per cent basis. Unless the enterprise succeeds in substantially inflating the planned costs for new goods, cost results would almost always be worse with new as compared to old products. The provisional prices are usually revised downward after the production of the new item has been perfected; this greatly increases the reluctance of enterprises other than the initial producer to manufacture new products. Attempts in recent years by the Soviets to establish price subsidy funds for certain types of new products—mainly machinery and equipment—have not proved effective in practice.

In general, the fact that new product prices are determined on a prescribed cost-plus basis does not benefit those enterprises that develop and produce more durable, economic, or aesthetic goods. This situation is clearly reflected in the words of a Soviet design engineer:

The existing system of enterprise indices does not encourage a ball bearing plant to strive to increase the useful life of the bearings it produces. If the life of the bearings is doubled, the demand will be cut in half. This would be very useful for the national economy, but the plant has no stake in it: the price of the bearings is not related to their durability.[16]

The prominent Soviet economist and author Gatoviskii states:

> The price, and thereby, also profit very often make the manufacture of new technology disadvantageous, especially if account is taken of additional outlays, often unforeseen when gearing production to new models, the additional trouble, production risk, etc. . . .[17]

The Problem of Risk

There is an inherent risk that product innovation may adversely affect success indicator performance, because the status quo at the enterprise would usually be at least somewhat upset. Such risk would exist even if an attempt were made to provide adequate resources for enterprise innovation tasks, because it often entails retraining personnel, retooling, as well as changes in methods, procedures, and processes. Many unanticipated problems may emerge, and often considerable spoilage will result. All of these factors divert attention and resources from regular operations and can, therefore, serve as significant obstacles to premium attainment.

In addition to these problems, if management initiates product innovation proposals, there is the risk that higher authorities will not approve them. This could result in much wasted time and effort because of the numerous proposal documents and extensive negotiations with superior authorities which are typically required. One Soviet lawyer points out that there is no dividing line between "negligence and legitimate doing" in Soviet industry.[18] Another source has this to say:

> Frequently a person who never makes mistakes is the man who never shows any personal initiative and never takes risks upon himself; and such people are considered good managers. The whole world will come loose on the head of the innovator who is courageous and not afraid of risk or mistakes which accompany research and change.[19]

A statement which has appeared in a Soviet literary publication vividly illustrates the dilemma of risk and innovation in Soviet industry:

> The system of innovation is unfortunate. Innovation involves risk and, as in all gambling, capital. If you risk, it is easy to lose, isn't that so? But even if the director is given the capital, let him just risk and not win. . . . No, it does not behoove a director to take risks. . . . Suppose your director desires to bring into production a new (plastic) powder. . . . He would have to wait endlessly in ministerial reception rooms. There is a risk here. The risk is not that millions might be lost. He might take up these powders and, God forbid, the quarterly plan will be messed up, and the ministry will show up badly in the statistical report.[20]

It is evident that there is no inducement for enterprise management to take risks or be the first to innovate, since risk taking is not rewarded and, in fact, may lead to adverse consequences.

Managerial Opposition to Technical Progress

One may expect, in view of labor shortages and the absence of unemployment in the Soviet planned economy, that the introduction of new production processes and technology at industrial establishments would be facilitated. This is far from the case. Enterprise managers are reluctant to introduce major technical changes for essentially the same reasons they oppose product innovation. By upsetting the status quo, short-run targets may not be fulfilled and premiums forfeited. Retraining, retooling, ironing out production bugs, and other factors which hinder success indicator performance are usually involved. Often adequate resources are not provided for technological improvement measures, and generally the cost of change is not fully accounted for in the enterprise plan.

The short-run horizon of management is in conflict with any process innovation tasks that will not provide immediate benefits to the enterprise. Since the enterprise does not have an operational long-range plan, the impact of process innovation over time is of little concern to management. Even if such innovation will yield substantial increases in output, labor productivity, and cost reduction in time, this would be of no benefit to management if short-run results suffer. In fact, future enterprise plans would usually be tightened accordingly as favorable results from processes innovation begin to accrue.

If old machines wear out, management usually finds it safer to repair or even rebuild them than to introduce more complicated models and major changes in the production process. Substantial resources for repair and maintenance activity are often obtained since their allotment is based on past expenditures. More than two million personnel and 800,000 machine tools are employed in repair work in Soviet industry. Every third metal-cutting tool and every fourth machine tool operator is engaged in repair work. The materials used in repairing equipment each year could be used to produce an additional 100,000 metal-cutting machines. Often ten or twenty times more is spent on repairing a machine than the costs entailed in producing a new and better one.[21]

Khrushchev looks with some nostalgia at the effectiveness of competitive forces under capitalism with regard to technological innovation, as can be seen from his statement:

> In capitalist conditions the application of new technology in production is spurred by competition. Capitalist firms regularly renew their machine tool equipment in order that they may not go bankrupt. Some firms, for example, do not permit machine tools in their plants to remain in operation for more than ten years, since this equipment wears out and becomes obsolete. And the capitalists know that if they use old equipment they cannot survive in competition with firms that use improved equipment.[22]

Data issued by the Central Statistical Administration in 1963, disclose that 26 per cent of all metal-cutting machines and 27 per cent of all forge-press equipment in use in the Soviet machine-building industry are more than 20 years old. About 8,000 metal-cutting machines and 3,000 forge presses are more than 40 years old. Khrushchev points out that such equipment is "more fit for museum display than for production." [23] Reports on the fulfillment of Soviet economic plans indicate that slow technical progress at industrial enterprises is a widespread, serious problem.

Soviet concern about managerial resistance to process innovation has come to the fore in connection with increased emphasis on automation and mechanization of plant production processes. In view of manpower shortages and ambitious economic plans, the need for technical progress is presently more crucial than ever.

Ineffective Incentives for Enterprise Innovation

Various incentive schemes have been tried by the Soviets to induce enterprise management to innovate both products and processes, but none have met with much success.[24] Up to 1961, there were bonuses available for the production of new products by equipment and machinery producers, based on a 1956 statute. Bonuses to enterprise personnel, including management, were supposed to be contingent on the economic effectiveness (savings) resulting from the use of new machinery and equipment at customer plants. It is evident from Soviet sources and interviews with Soviet managers that this bonus system proved highly ineffective. Whereas premiums for success indicator fulfillment have always been concrete and assured, innovation bonuses have been awarded in an *ad hoc* manner. The size of potential innovation bonuses and the criteria for awarding them have been far from clear to enterprise personnel. Much delay was usually involved in receiving bonuses, and often they were not received at all.

During 1956-61, bonuses for product innovation awarded to personnel at equipment producers constituted only about 1 per cent of total salaries and wages. However, an innovation decree of July 1960 stipulated that, as of 1961, a new bonus fund was to be set up to encourage enterprise innovation by assessing enterprises a certain percentage of their total payrolls. The levy for machine-building enterprises was stipulated as 1 per cent, and 0.3 per cent for consumer goods producers. As before, bonuses for the production of new models by equipment producers supposedly are based on a prescribed percentage of the annual economies to be derived from the new product, as compared to similar old products in use at customer plants. But now earmarked bonus finds supposedly have been established. There are also bonuses available to all types of enterprises for the introduction of new technology and major production process improvements. These bonuses supposedly are based on the annual economies derived from the implementation of the process innovation measures at the enterprise.

Managerial personnel questioned in mid-1961 about the new innovation bonus scheme declared that it was in effect, but could shed little light on how bonus payments are determined. Soviet sources clearly reveal that there still is much confusion in the payment of innovation bonuses and that such bonuses remain ineffective.

The 1960 innovation decree also stipulated that deductions for the Enterprise Fund from planned profits earned would be 10 per cent, rather than the standard 1 to 6 per cent during the first year of production of new machinery and equipment (no other types of producers are affected). Instead of the maximum allowable limit of 5.5 per cent of total enterprise annual payroll, the allowable deduction limit would be from 6 to 7 per cent, depending on the volume of new machinery produced. This reform was not yet in effect at the enterprises surveyed, and more recent Soviet sources give no indication that it has been implemented on a widespread basis. Assuming full implementation, it is unlikely that the new Enterprise Fund provisions would have a significant impact on managerial behavior. Even by doubling its size, this fund would not take priority over the pursuit of premiums, and the higher maximum limits would be of no consequence to enterprises which do not derive profit deductions in excess of the standard allowable limits. That lower profits generally result from the production of new products remains the more important problem.

In the consumer goods sector only negligible bonuses are provided for product innovation. Some monetary rewards are available to enterprise artists, stylists, and designers if their new product proposals are judged the best by the enterprise artistic council. The enterprise as a whole may also be awarded lump-sum bonuses for presenting new items judged the best at branch-of-industry fairs and exhibitions. At two enterprises surveyed which had received such bonuses, the average bonus per employee was about 2 rubles. In addition to the small sums involved, the bonuses for consumer product innovation appear to be rewards for aesthetic rather than operational achievement. Such bonuses do not insure that the enterprise will produce the acclaimed new products in desired quantities or even at all.

In general, incentive compensation for enterprise product and process innovation does little, if anything, to deemphasize premiums as the major determinant of managerial action. It is fallacious to assume that there has been virtually no product or process innovation at Soviet enterprises—considerable innovation has been introduced at some enterprises, and, as was pointed out earlier, in certain strategic sectors of the economy. There may at times be favorable benefits—material or otherwise—for initating and fulfilling innovation tasks. But generally, enterprise managers oppose innovation nevertheless.

Pressure and Problems of Control in Enterprise Innovation

One may justifiably ask why the Soviets have had such great success in atomic power, defense, and space projects. The answer rests, in large part, with the fact that the major causes of managerial opposition normally present in most branches of industry are not present in highly strategic spheres of industrial activity.

A number of Soviet officials interviewed indicated that short-run success indicator results and related rewards have little significance in top priority, strategic projects. Managerial personnel is lucratively compensated by basic salaries and promotions, and demotions are not usually dependent on short-run results. Managers assigned to strategic projects are the leading experts in their fields—if they fail, there is no better source of human skill to turn to. This greatly reduces the problem of risk and personal security. Moreover, the deficient provision of resources rarely exists since the best physical, human, and financial resources are supplied and assured. The fact that there is much national—and indeed international—prestige for accomplishments in strategic spheres of industrial activity also serves as a significant motivating force. Finally, planning, coordination, and control in these spheres receive the direct, constant attention of the highest government, Communist party, and planning agencies.

In the branches of industry under study, when enough pressure is exerted through superior authorities and party channels, and when firm, concrete orders are received from above, the enterprise may have no choice but to undertake innovation tasks or severe sanctions may result. In such cases, management would be inclined to carry out innovation tasks even if premiums were forfeited. For example, managers interviewed at a Kharkov mining equipment enterprise said that during 1960 success indicators were not fulfilled, and premiums were forfeited, because certain product innovation tasks were carried out in accordance with firm directives emanating from central authorities.

Soviet sources do cite many examples of favorable innovation results due to pressure exerted on management by superior authorities and party committees at all levels. In addition, research and design institutes, plant *aktiv* (zealous workers) organized in permanent production councils, production committees, technical councils, and innovator councils, and even the trade unions at times compel managers to innovate.

No doubt if top-level officials place high priority on the development and production of a specific machine tool or consumer good, or on the introduction of a new production process at a given plant, this can generally be accomplished through firm orders and pressure. But the span of attention and control of top-level authorities and party agencies is obviously greatly limited in the vast Soviet economy. Therefore, there would be considerably more innovation if enterprise managers desired to innovate on their own initiative.

It is evident from Soviet sources and interviews with Soviet managers that in most instances no significant penalties are imposed for failure to fulfill innovation assignments. In general, *sovnarkhoz* officials and enterprise party officials are reluctant to compel managers to innovate unless they themselves have received firm orders and are subject to pressure from their own bosses. The personal status of these officials hinges on the same criteria used for evaluating and rewarding enterprise management. For this reason innovation assignments often have little operational significance for enterprise managers.

Conclusions

In a country that claims as one of its major advantages over capitalism public ownership of new discoveries, this advantage is certainly not being significantly exploited. Although enterprise managers have access to information about new products and processes developed and introduced elsewhere, the problems of planning, control, coordination, and managerial opposition all are significant obstacles to innovation.

No competitive forces compel Soviet managers to develop and produce new products or to introduce new processes in order that their enterprises and managerial status may endure. The survival of an enterprise or a manager in his job is not dependent on the size of profits or long-run results. Also, given the price structure and the absence of patent laws, there is no significant gain to the enterprise or its management for beneficial innovation results.

The Soviet manager's sense of mission is not one of causing change—in fact, he is often reluctant to adapt to change. His sense of mission is the fulfillment of short-run success indicators, and the system of premiums may well motivate management to accomplish this. Short-run success indicators are essential for the coordination of the myriad of interdependent units which constitute the planned Soviet economy, but they lead to forfeited innovation accomplishments, many of which, in time, could be of great benefit to society.

Implications for American Industry

Innovation in American industry is not without its imperfections. Sheer complacency or conservatism in quasi-monopolistic or monopolistic companies, the lack of financial resources in smaller companies, commercial secrecy, the buying up of inventions, trade union resistance, and unemployment caused by change are all significant problems present in the American economy.

In spite of these problems, competitive forces, patent laws, and the pursuit of profits encourage and compel American enterprises to innovate both products and processes in order to survive. In addition, many competent American managers are instilled with a sense of mission to cause change. However, with a shift from owner-managers with a flare for entrepreneurship to more security-minded professional managers, many American companies are currently confronted with managerial opposition to innovation.

It is, no doubt, human nature for managers who are evaluated by superiors on the basis of short-run results to try and avoid upsetting the status quo by undertaking innovation activities. Acceptance of innovation obligations creates uncertainties—the risk that such obligations will not be successfully fulfilled. In addition, other, often more important, criteria for evaluating managerial success may suffer in the process.

Probably the great majority of American companies stress short-run results and evaluate divisional, departmental, and individual success monthly, quarterly, and/or annually on the basis of certain performance standards. Evidence clearly indicates that company divisions and other profit-centered administrative units frequently strive to avoid the incorporation of major innovation tasks into their operating plans; or if such tasks are assigned, they are often not fulfilled.[25] In fact, firm pressure from the head office frequently is needed to compel lower level managers to innovate. This is often due—at least to a considerable extent—to the fact that bonuses and promotions are based on short-term profit results. It is further aggravated in many instances by a fairly high degree of short-run executive mobility in many companies, particularly at the division level. This situation is rather similar to innovation problems at Soviet enterprises, although the short-run success indicators are not the same.

The division manager of a large decentralized American company clarifies why they oppose innovation:

> When we drop a product or change a process which we have had for years, it invariably means getting rid of equipment, people, and at times, a complete installation. Emotionally, this is never an easy thing to do particularly when in exchange you must embark into areas which will require a greater amount of risk and hurt your profit picture for several years. Certainly a growing organization must trim its product line and move into new areas, but it would be contrary to human nature to expect those people who must suffer through the transition to welcome such a change.[26]

However, a growing number of highly progressive American firms are recognizing the cost of innovation, in terms of lost production and higher costs. In industries such as aerospace, the notion of learning curves is now well established, and managers are not unduly punished or penalized for making innovations.[27]

The reluctance to innovate by divisional or middle management may also be overcome, at least partially, by providing separate budgets including earmarked resources for innovation activities so that these activities will not hinder short-run success indicator performance. The Soviets are attempting to move in this direction. It may also be feasible for large companies to set up independent research and development units similar to those in the Soviet Union. These units could undertake experimental work, including testing and development, until the major bugs entailed in a given innovation are ironed out. Then the regular operating units could adopt the innovation with a minimum of risk and disruption. In this manner short-run operating results would not be significantly handicapped. The coordination and control problems with such an organizational setup would undoubtedly be much less severe than in the vast Soviet economy.

Perhaps the best way to encourage innovation would be to evaluate and reward managers on the basis of long-run results—three or five years, for example. This would require operational long-range plans, and managers would be evaluated in accordance with the soundness of these plans as well as their fulfillment. In this way, anticipating appraisal of long-range plans would become more important. Such a system would induce managers to look ahead and give greater weight to long-run considerations. Certainly practical problems would undoubtedly be involved: Managers could not be promoted for several years if they were accountable for long-run results. More assured short-run profits may be sacrificed in pursuit of longer run goals. Effective long-run performance standards and forecasts would be difficult to devise. Nevertheless, the gains that could be reaped by looking further into the future might much more than compensate for those problems that may be entailed.

Although some American companies have adopted practices similar to those outlined above, extended use by more may be worth serious consideration.

10 • Management of Personnel

A basic problem in any industrial society is how to motivate employees to work with optimal efficiency. Regardless of whether the enterprises in which people work are state or privately owned, the owners desire higher productivity and greater efficiency in enterprise operations.

In democratic societies persuasion has long replaced coercion as a means of boosting labor productivity. Although it is now generally agreed that the carrot is more effective than the stick, just what variety of carrot exerts the greatest lure is still unresolved. Incentive systems that prove highly effective in the Kaiser Steel Company or the American Motors Corporation may be doomed to failure if adopted by other enterprises.[1] The "Scanlon Plan" yields remarkable results in some enterprises but proves highly unsuccessful in others.[2]

There is much experimentation with incentive systems and other motivational devices in American industry, and the philosophy of personnel administration tends to vary somewhat by company. In recent years, however, there has been a noticeable trend toward greater employee participation in planning and decision-making. As personnel has acquired more education and greater skills, it has been felt that it can contribute more to the company through suggestions and initiative.

The philosophy of personnel administration and human relations in Soviet industry is prescribed by the government as state policy. But in the final analysis, the efficiency and effectiveness of employee performance are chiefly dependent on the day-to-day and face-to-face contact between supervisors and subordinates on the premises. The Soviets rely on three main methods for improving the productivity of the industrial worker. First and foremost, they rely on money, on the assumption that if performance above the required minimum is rewarded with extra pay, the worker gains financially and the economy benefits from increased productivity.

Second, there is great emphasis on worker participation in planning and decision-making, on the premise that those who are actually doing the job are in the best position to estimate their capabilities and needs, and to improve their operations generally. Such participation is also advocated by the regime as a form of pressure on management to make them adhere to state policy and to reveal hidden reserves in plant operations. Here, too, monetary incentives are involved, since workers are paid for suggestions that are adopted if they result in improvements. Both Communist party and trade union officials attached to the enterprise are responsible for organizing and encouraging this participation.

The third technique for stimulating workers to better performance is socialist competition and indoctrination through education, training, publicity, and mass media emanating chiefly from party and union channels. In every plant there are party and union officials responsible for instilling a feeling of moral obligation in the workers to behave in accordance with the wishes of the regime.

Nature of Incentive Compensation [3]

Virtually all enterprise personnel is entitled to some form of additional earnings for performance above the stipulated minimum called for in the plan. Supervisory personnel of producing shops is awarded bonuses—usually monthly—on the basis of similar criteria used for premium payments to top-level enterprise managers. The types of incentive compensation available to nonmanagerial employees depends on the nature of their jobs.

Soviet managers and officials personally interviewed indicated that the number of employees that were compensated for individual piecework results has declined in recent years, especially at plants that have introduced more automated processes. Soviet sources and interviews reveal that the trend in Soviet industry is toward more bonuses to workers for collective results.

At many plants, pieceworkers receive monthly bonuses in addition to their basic piecework earnings, and these bonuses may often amount to 40 or 50 per cent of their total monthly wages. The bonuses to pieceworkers are awarded for a variety of reasons. For example, a shoe factory gives bonuses to cutters for reducing the amount of leather waste in each unit of output. Similarly, bonuses are given for reducing scrap metal at many plants producing machinery and related components. At two plants visited, which turn out consumer goods, pieceworkers are entitled to bonuses of from 20 to 30 per cent—in a few cases even more—of monthly earnings for maintaining high quality output.

Employees not on piecework can also get bonuses for reducing waste and spoilage, conserving fuel and energy, improved repair and maintenance, quality control, and so forth. In fact, every factory worker seems to have the chance of earning some type of bonus for above-average results.

Within broadly prescribed state policy, enterprise management has some independence in determining the specifics of the plant's bonus payment schemes. In many enterprises shop chiefs and department heads can award bonuses to workers in accordance with basic conditions decided on by management. The formal approval of enterprise trade union officials is generally required with regard to bonus payments to workers, and such approval is usually forthcoming. In some cases superior officials above the enterprise stipulate that bonuses should be given for specific results—for instance, the economizing of certain material in short supply. Specific higher orders with regard to bonus payments often result from a state campaign involving a particular type of task or accomplishment sought. In spite of the state's attempts to standardize regulations for worker incentive payments, there does not appear to be a very uniform policy in this connection. In fact, many Soviet sources are urging that enterprise management be granted virtually complete independence over internal incentive schemes for personnel.

Presently, there is considerable discussion among Soviet experts as to which kind of incentive is more effective—collective or individual payments. Those favoring collective incentives argue that this method encourages cooperation, creates higher morale and productivity by fostering the team spirit, and serves as a mechanism for self-control within work groups. Those favoring individual rewards feel that each worker's contributions, efforts, and qualifications are overriding factors to consider. They maintain that incomes are unfairly distributed with collective payments, and that these encourage laziness and job shirkers. Most Soviet sources, however, take the view that a combination of individual and collective incentives works best.[4]

Incentive Compensation and Employee Behavior

Needless to say, no matter what type of incentive is used, the Soviet worker is just as eager as his Western counterpart to secure easy performance standards.

In recent years, there has been a general overhauling of wage rates and a tightening of labor standards throughout Soviet industry, although loose standards are tolerated in a small number of jobs in order to provide adequate pay. Despite official policy, however, loose standards seem to be increasing [5] and are creating problems of deficient labor norms (see Chapter 8). The chief engineer of one equipment plant visited indicated that the average overfulfillment of historical norms in his plant was 150 per cent.

Several plant managers interviewed were asked whether Soviet workers resemble their American counterparts in such matters as adding movements during time and motion studies, putting ceilings on output, ostracizing rate busters, falsifying results, and generally striving for easy standards. The laughter this question aroused showed obviously that managers on both sides of the Iron Curtain have pretty much the same problems to contend with in this area.

Manager-Worker Interaction [6]

In striving for easy performance standards Soviet workers often have allies in their superiors. Because enterprise management, shop chiefs, foremen, and other line bosses also get bonuses for fulfilling and over-fulfilling certain performance standards, there is naturally a tendency— if their targets are easy to hit—not to put so tight a squeeze on subordinates' performance standards. If the enterprise is not successful in obtaining easy targets, superiors right down the line have no choice but to tighten up performance standards.

In general, however, individual and collective performance standards do often vary in terms of their looseness and tightness within a given plant, and this frequently causes uneven results, thus hindering coordination of activities among different shops and work brigades. At times conflicts arise between management and workers, where the former tries to hold back the latter from maximizing incentive compensation by "over-producing," since overproduction may lead to more difficult enterprise success indicator targets in subsequent periods. For example, *Pravda* has reported a case where one workshop wanted to assemble 14 machines per month, but the plan called for only 3 and management slowed down work in the shop, thus affecting shop bonuses.[7] Other similar conflicts arise because management is rewarded quarterly, whereas the other workers are paid bonuses monthly.

As mentioned earlier, in theory the job of enterprise party and trade union officials is to deter managerial abuses and to stimulate the workers to reveal reserves, strive for tighter performance standards, and generally improve plant operations. In practice, however, since these officials are evaluated and rewarded by the same criteria as the management of the enterprise, they tend to go along with both managers and workers in their efforts to obtain easy plans and performance standards (more will be said about this in the next chapter). There are numerous instances where party and to a lesser degree union activities have succeeded in motivating workers to reveal untapped reserves and willingly raise their productivity, but for the most part, these occasions were related to specific programs or one-shot efforts made in response to higher orders. True, too, there are periodic reports of workers who, spurred by a sense of moral obligation, voluntarily uncover reserves and undertake vigorous campaigns to improve plant productivity, but, on the whole, complaints about worker behavior clearly outweigh plaudits.

In spite of problems of employee behavior, the Soviets seem to be convinced that the presence of monetary incentives does liberate more of the worker's productive capacity, and although they have not considered abolishing incentive compensation linked to performance standards, the search for more effective incentive schemes continues.

Moral Stimuli and Socialist Competition

We should not assume that most Soviet workers lack all sense of moral obligation to the state; no doubt most of them take considerable pride in their country and sincerely desire industrial progress. However, it is easy for them to rationalize that by overfulfilling performance standards sanctioned by the state, and thus maximizing incentive compensation, which is also sanctioned by the state, they are acting in the state's interest. They conveniently overlook the fact that their performance standards may have been deficient to begin with.

Attacking this prevailing self-interest from another angle, attempts have been made for some years to stimulate better enterprise results through personnel training programs, which devote just as much—and probably more—attention to indoctrination and the development of the altruistic "Communist worker," as to improving capabilities.[8] Such on-the-job training is conducted throughout Soviet industry mainly under the guidance of the Communist party, but the effectiveness of such "training" clearly leaves much to be desired.

Socialist competition among enterprises is also used chiefly as a moral incentive. During the 1962-63 period, Soviet leaders have placed great emphasis on competitions among workers' collectives to compete for the title of "Communist Labor Brigade," while workers whose performance is not linked to team effort can earn the title of "Communist Shock-worker." [9] The party and union officials attached to each plant have been charged with the task of more actively stimulating workers to earnestly partake in socialist competition on the regional and national levels.

This type of competition is essentially a nonmaterial incentive—though modest monetary rewards are usually given to the winners, and the victors—whether they be enterprises, shops, work teams, or individuals—receive much publicity. It is difficult, of course, to assess the effectiveness of this kind of competition—particularly in view of the emphasis presently being given to it—but one is inclined to suspect that in the great majority of cases, monetary gain is still the key to the individual Soviet worker's performance.

Framework of Employee Participation [10]

The Soviet policy that calls for "participation of the masses" in the management of production, and the harnessing of local initiative, is called "democratic centralism," a term coined by Lenin. This is basically similar to the philosophy of "bottom-up management," "grass-roots budgeting," or consultative direction found in many American companies. The Soviet leaders have given vigorous emphasis to participation of all enterprise personnel in planning and decision-making since the reorganization of industry in 1957, and this emphasis has been further intensified with the 1962-63 industrial reorganization.

In spite of this official state policy, the Soviet rulers, Khrushchev in particular, continue to condemn the tendency of many managers to be autocratic, and to rule by "dictatorial orders and administrative fiat." [11] This problem is undoubtedly also common in many American companies where a policy of consultative direction and participation is advocated.

In Soviet industry the effectiveness of employee participation is limited because the autonomy of enterprise management is very limited in relation to the external environment. In addition, the effectiveness is somewhat handicapped at the outset by the employees' desire for easy performance standards. Often, however, their participation is crucial to Soviet managers if they are to achieve the results required to meet difficult enterprise success indicators established by higher authorities, and the state system of paying for productive suggestions does encourage worker participation, of course.

At each enterprise standardized "participating bodies" spend a great deal of time at meetings, conferences, and councils. Enterprise managers interviewed explained that these bodies are vested only with the right to propose, recommend, and advise management. In cases of conflict, however, appeals may be made to the next higher management level within or above the enterprise, or to plant party and/or union officials who, in turn, may take some action within or above the enterprise.[12]

After the reorganization of 1957, "permanent production conferences" were set up at virtually all industrial enterprises under the general guidance of the plant trade union committee and its chairman. The members of the conference include workers, managerial personnel, party and union officials, and are elected by the various shops and departments. There is an elected chairman, sometimes an outstanding worker; conferences are called at least quarterly and at any other time when an important issue arises.

The main purpose of these meetings is to obtain wide and continuing participation in planning and decision-making, from the drafting stage through the evaluation of results. The enterprise director and his key deputies are supposed to give serious consideration to all proposals and recommendations before any final decision is made. However, if the decision is in opposition to the majority vote, members have the right to appeal to authorities above the enterprise. As a rule, the appeal is made through party or union officials. Several managers interviewed asserted that disagreements between the director and the permanent production conference are seldom taken to higher authorities for adjudication. Instead, such disagreements are worked out within the enterprise, through the director and the conference chairman, or in some cases by the plant's elected arbitration commission.

Diverse topics are covered by these conferences: the shift to a new production line; the introduction of new technology; plant modernization and production quotas. Plant managers interviewed said that many valuable proposals for improving operations and the utilization of resources evolved from these conferences, and that all proposals are carefully studied and many are adopted.

On the other hand, there are frequent complaints that these conferences often do not exert any real influence on management, that much time is wasted, and that employees' recommendations and suggestions are frequently ignored. There is also substantial evidence that personnel often use these conferences to try to obtain easier quotas and looser performance standards.

Technical councils—also called committees or commissions—have been widely established at the enterprise level as a result of a 1958 central decree. These councils, too, are permanent but their members are usually appointed by the director, rather than elected. The director of one equipment plant said that he selected all members solely on the basis of their technical abilities; there were several workers on the councils at the plants visited, all headed by chief engineers.

There are no regular scheduled meetings for these technical councils, but at the enterprises surveyed, the councils met at least quarterly, and sometimes monthly, to deal with problems of both annual and long-range innovation. Typical items on their agenda are the adoption of new products and the phasing out of existing ones, product design and modification, installation of new technology and production processes, elimination or reconversion of existing facilities and equipment, improvement of production organization and existing technology, and shop and plant modernization.

Some Soviet sources paint a glowing picture of the innovations that have been proposed by these technical councils and successfully adopted, but equally reliable sources strongly suggest that enterprise managers and workers alike, more often than not, oppose major innovation. It seems reasonable to suppose that this is so, since major innovations interfere with short-run results and thus reduce incentive pay for most, if not all, enterprise personnel.

As if the above participating bodies are not enough, most enterprises —and all those surveyed—have a "council of innovators" and a "Council of Rationalizers and Inventors." These are sometimes referred to as "social organizations." The innovators are leading workers, or *aktiv*, elected by enterprise personnel on the basis of their technical ability and suggestion contributions. Their major concerns are to initiate proposals for increasing productivity, make better use of resources, and to study new methods and procedures. They also screen proposals to be presented at permanent production council meetings. The Council of Rationalizers and Inventors is part of a nationally elected organization of workers with impressive records for having their suggestions implemented at their plants. This council discusses new suggestions and is also assigned the task of encouraging all workers to initiate proposals for improvement.

Aside from all of these formally organized bodies, there are usually monthly plant and shop meetings of employees. If major problems arise special meetings are called. According to the director of one machinery plant, hundreds of useful suggestions come out of these meetings, but he also conceded that workers sometimes resort to them to propose a reduction of work assignments. Soviet sources concur and complain that workers use these general meetings to try to obtain easy performance standards, and that, altogether, much unproductive time is spent in these discussions.

There can be little doubt that a great deal of time is indeed consumed by meetings and employee participating activities. At the meeting of the Party Central Committee in November 1962, Khrushchev advocated even more participation, more consultative direction on the part of managers, and the establishment of more participating and advisory bodies at industrial enterprises. We cannot know whether he did this because employee participation, on the whole, had been productive or somewhat unproductive. As a result, certain new types of employee participating bodies were set up at many enterprises during 1963, chiefly on an experimental, voluntary basis.[13]

The first of these bodies are the production committees, which undertake many of the same activities as the permanent production conferences but have fewer members, apparently only key workers, engineers, and supervisors. The committees are governed by a bureau—usually containing three to five members and they have continuous contact with the enterprise director and act in an advisory capacity.

The second are called "public or technical norm-setting" bureaus. These are made up of groups of workers and frontline supervisors who are supposed to revise and tighten labor norms in their respective shops. These voluntary norm-setting bureaus are under the direct guidance of shop and plant party and trade union committees, and work jointly with the plant's department of labor and wages, which is formally in charge of norm setting. In some cases these new bureaus have been established on the initiative of the newly formed production committees.

How effective these new norm bodies are in practice is a matter of conjecture. Some sources cite highly beneficial results, while others condemn such participation as being extremely insincere and ineffective because of both managements' and workers' attitudes. Their effectiveness no doubt depends mainly on the over-all environment at a given plant.

Many of the members of the voluntary norm-setting groups are apparently party members or aspiring members, and may, therefore, spur their fellow workers beyond their usual concern for material rewards. For example, the Yegorav Railroad Car Factory has 13 voluntary norm-setting bureaus in various large shops. In a period of about 6 months, the workers themselves are reported to have revised 19,301 labor norms upward.[14] At the Krasnaya Presnaya Plant—the state's largest machine casting enterprise—900 norms were also revised upward in one large shop in a period of a few months. Though labor norms in this shop are still being overfulfilled by 120 to 150 per cent, in the past they were typically overfulfilled by considerably more than 150 per cent.[15]

At some enterprises, voluntary economic analysis groups and bureaus made up of all types of enterprise personnel have been formed. These bodies have taken upon themselves the task of analyzing plant results and disclosing untapped reserves, but their role is strictly advisory in nature.

Employee Suggestion Systems

Now that we have some background on how employee suggestions are elicited at Soviet enterprises, the suggestion system itself and its effectiveness are considered here.

In addition to being paid for an implemented suggestion, the employee may gain prestige and recognition in the National Society of Inventors and Rationalizers, and in the innovation council at the enterprise. If he makes an exceptionally worthwhile proposal, or if he maintains an outstanding suggestion record, his picture may be posted on the plant bulletin board, and may even appear in the newspapers. He may also receive medals and other honors from the state.

But again, first and foremost, the regime recognizes that "money talks." Remuneration for implemented suggestions is contingent upon the amount of savings derived from them. The worker receives an initial lump-sum payment when his suggestion is implemented. This sum may not exceed 25 per cent of his total estimated remuneration for the suggestion, which in turn is based on the total savings it is expected to achieve in one year. The balance of the award is paid on the basis of the actual savings for one year. For rationalizations (improvements) remuneration is based on the best results achieved in either of the two years following implementation; for inventions it is based on the best results achieved in any one of the five years following implementation.

If a joint, rather than an individual, proposal is implemented, remuneration is divided equally. Others who help in the development—

designers, engineers, foremen—are also entitled to a share of the reward. In all cases, however, at least 65 per cent of the total goes to the innovator or innovators.

If an employee's innovation is adopted at other plants, he is entitled to a prescribed reward from the authorities in the region concerned. This obviously begins to get complicated, and Soviet officials interviewed said that it is difficult to keep track of the implementation of all suggestions at all plants. Thus, the innovator does not always get all that is coming to him. However, most enterprises have a bureau of technical information, which keeps other enterprises posted on innovations it is adopting and receives similar data from them. This exchange serves as at least some check on who is implementing or has implemented whose suggestion—at least within the same region.

In May 1959, the Soviet government adopted a statute that provided for an increase of 25 per cent in awards for implemented suggestions. In addition, this statute called for the establishment of bureaus of rationalization and invention at all enterprises to insure that adequate time and analyses are given to employee suggestions. (See the related discussion in Chapter 3.)

It appears that enterprise suggestion systems, in conjunction with the numerous opportunities for employee participation, do motivate many Soviet workers to initiate worthwhile proposals. The number of suggestions that have been made and implemented, and their resulting economies have grown considerably. The rising educational level and increased skills of the labor force probably account for much of this trend, but the even more impressive results since 1959 are more likely due to the increased emphasis on participation, the establishment of cost reduction as an enterprise success indicator, and the conditions set forth in the 1959 statute.

Table III indicates the results of employee suggestion systems for the

TABLE III • *Innovation results for the national economy—1940-1959—rationalization and invention*

	1940	1945	1950	1956	1957	1958	1959
Number of Suggestions Made (in millions)	.591	.387	1.241	2.376	2.503	2.961	3.300
Number of Suggestions Adopted and Introduced (in millions)	.202	.165	.655	1.405	1.537	.1816	2.000
Resulting Economies and Savings from Introduced Proposals (converted to millions of new rubles)	90.4	124.5	497.6	736.1	812.6	972.1	1100.0

Source: Kursakov S., 1960, p. 8, Table 1.

country as a whole for the 1940-59 period. In the first 6 months of 1960, *Pravda* reported, two million suggestions were made, of which 1.3 million were implemented, representing an annual saving of 650 million rubles. The figure for the entire year was probably about double. In 1961, 2.5 million workers submitted more than four million suggestions, of which 2.8 were implemented, providing annual economies of more than 1.7 billion rubles. For 1962, there were 4.2 million suggestions, of which 2.7 million were introduced, amounting to annual savings of about 1.6 billion rubles. In the first 6 months of 1963, about 2.2 million suggestions were made and 1.4 million introduced, resulting in an estimated annual saving of 750 million rubles.[16]

In recent years, more than 5 per cent of the total Soviet labor force have submitted suggestions, and this proportion is growing. From the writings of Soviet economists it would seem that the state's long-range goal is to get 20 per cent of the labor force to put forth worthwhile suggestions. Certainly, to date, the improvement brought about by the suggestion system appears quite impressive—the reported economies are equivalent to between 1.5 and 2 per cent of the U.S.S.R.'s total annual revenues in recent years, and to more than 4 per cent of the total profits earned by all state organizations. It follows that the remuneration to plant personnel for implemented suggestions has also been fairly substantial. From 1956 to 1959, it amounted to from 4.1 to 4.8 per cent of total annual savings achieved.[17]

A personal survey at ten enterprises pinpoints some 1960 figures. The over-all findings are presented in Table IV.

The average remuneration for suggestions at eight enterprises reporting was between 5 and 10 per cent of the average annual wage for one employee, or the equivalent of from two to four weeks' pay. At nine enterprises, the total number of suggestions amounted to about 10 per cent of the total number of personnel. (Since some personnel is not entitled to remuneration for suggestions, this ratio would be higher if it were calculated on the basis of eligible personnel only.) There was considerable variation in the ratios among enterprises, however. At a few plants the ratio of number of suggestions to total number of personnel was around 5 per cent, whereas at the mining equipment plant it was about 25 per cent. At three enterprises the actual number of individuals making suggestions was: (1) silk fabric—100; (2) clothing—168; (3) mining equipment—380. In these three cases, more than 5 per cent of all employees made proposals.

At eight enterprises reporting, the total remuneration paid represented from 7 to 8 per cent of the total economies achieved, almost double the national percentage reported for 1956-59. The survey also found that remuneration for implemented suggestions went mainly to workers,

TABLE IV • *Results of employee suggestions in 1960 for 10 enterprises surveyed.*

Enterprise	Total Number of Industrial Personnel	Number of Suggestions Made	Number Adapted and Implemented	Total Annual Economies (new rubles) from Implemented Suggestions	Total Remuneration to Employees on the Basis of One Year's Economies	Average Remuneration per Implemented Suggestions
Leningrad Machinery	5,100	342	251	320,000	22,500	92
Moscow Machine Tool	5,200	500	300	not reported	not reported	–
Kharkov Mining Equipment	5,000	1,300	789	400,000	36,000	46
Kharkov Air Conditioner	5,500	296	200	165,000	12,000	60
Kharkov Ball Bearing	5,000	561	333	420,000	22,000	66
Leningrad Shoe	12,000	1,026	630	375,000	27,000	43
Moscow Silk	2,000	184	133	110,000	11,000	96
Moscow Watch	6,300	not reported	not reported	225,000	not reported	–
Kharkov Clothing	3,350	195	103	128,000	8,900	55
Kharkov Book	2,000	120	108	46,000	3,400	31

rather than managers or technical personnel assigned to innovation activities. Clerical employees, too, were responsible for a number of adopted suggestions.

Thus far we have been dealing with averages, but, actually, there seems to be a marked variation in the size of individual awards. The larger awards probably go, year after year, to many of the same individuals who possess a special talent for and interest in innovation, and these workers often draw more from this source than their basic pay.[18] In 1960, for instance, one worker at a Leningrad machinery plant visited developed a new precision measuring instrument, for which he received the equivalent of nearly three months' base pay. What is more, other plants were planning to use his invention as well, so by now, he must have made an even tidier sum. An employee of one of the laboratories of the Moscow Silk Factory submitted a suggestion that was implemented in 1959. The innovation, which resulted in savings in the processing of silk, was subsequently introduced at other plants in the region, and by mid-1961, the laboratory worker had totaled up the equivalent of five months' basic pay. People of this type, or *aktiv,* as they are called, are probably constantly making valuable suggestions and participating prominently in enterprise planning.

On the other hand, there is a good deal of evidence that a large number of suggestions produce only negligible savings. One Soviet source estimates that the savings and related remuneration are not even calculated for about 50 per cent of all suggestions at many plants. In 1959, in the Leningrad region, the savings resulting from 23.3 per cent of all implemented suggestions were not even calculated.[19] In such cases the innovator may receive an *ad hoc* token payment.

It seems highly possible that employees often weigh the effect their suggestions may have on performance standards and therefore on regular incentive compensation. If the idea is likely to lead to more difficult performance standards in the future, they may find it prudent to forfeit the award rather than upset their chances of regular incentive pay, to say nothing of upsetting their co-workers in the bargain. Workers in Soviet industry probably face less risk of working themselves out of their jobs than in the West, but even so they seem to have a saying that is roughly the equivalent of "Don't rock the boat." Significantly, a number of enterprise managers interviewed mentioned that workers have a tendency to hoard suggestions that promise substantial improvement.

But the workers are not the only ones who drag their feet; sometimes management creates the real bottleneck. The boss's ego may come into play; a foreman or other supervisor may discourage or sit on suggestions for fear that they make him look incompetent. However, it is probably more difficult for the Soviet manager to stifle employee suggestions than it is for his American counterpart, since there are numerous channels of appeal open to the worker and many platforms from which he can propose his ideas. More important than ego, though, is the fact that, with few exceptions, managerial personnel are as keen about easy targets and performance standards as the workers are. So, just as workers may hoard good suggestions, managers will shelve them until a more auspicious time.

Very likely many suggestions that would produce economies above the amount required for maximum incentive compensation are stifled, and, conversely, they may be stifled if management thinks that enterprise success indicators cannot be met even if all potential savings from suggestions are realized. In both cases, the motive is to try to insure easily attainable targets in the next operating period.

At a ball bearing plant visited, although 428 suggestions were approved in 1960, only 333 were implemented; thus, the plant had a reserve source of economies in almost 25 per cent of the suggestions made that year. At a clothing factory, out of 163 approved suggestions, only 103 were implemented; here, 37 per cent of the proposals were held in abeyance. Probably not all the shelved suggestions were hoarded specifically for use at a more auspicious time for management, but no doubt many were. One Soviet source discloses that the result of an investigation at the enterprises in the Sverdlovsk region showed that the number of employee suggestions approved as worthy, but not yet implemented as of November 1957, stood at 19,000.[20]

Despite all the negative aspects of the Soviet suggestion system, however, there seems to be no doubt that, in conjunction with the numerous channels for employee participation, it does encourage a great many people to submit worthwhile proposals. Certainly, very respectable savings from this source have been achieved, both at individual enterprises and on a national scale.

Employee Suggestion Systems in Capitalist Countries

Employee suggestion systems proved highly effective in American industry during World War II. With overemployment and concentration on the war effort, the obstacles common to suggestion systems largely disappeared. In normal times, those companies which assure job security, obtain top management, employee, and union support, and provide for and widely encourage employee participation tend to derive highly favorable results from suggestion systems, whereas other firms may experience varying degrees of ineffectiveness.

The National Association of Suggestion Systems (NASS) was founded in 1942 to assist member companies and agencies in the United States and Canadian industry, commerce, and government in the improvement of their suggestion programs. The Association has grown from the original group of 35 members in 1942 to a membership of over 1,200 in 1963.

The number of suggestions submitted per 100 eligible employees at NASS member firms has shown an upward trend, increasing from 25.6 in 1955 to 30.5 in 1960. Total dollars of award steadily increased during the 1955-60 period—total awards in 1960 represented a 42 per cent increase over 1955. The average award for 1960 was $33.48 as compared to $30.22 in 1955. Table V presents data on suggestion system results for 1961-62 based on the reports submitted by 216 NASS member firms.[21]

TABLE V • *National Association of Suggestion Systems statistical data (216 firms reporting).*

Statistical Data for Year		1961	1962
1. Average Number of Employees:	Total Number	6,771,630	6,867,066
	Number Eligible	6,028,715	6,119,054
2. Suggestions Received:	Total Number	1,942,931	2,451,302
	Number per 100 Eligible Employees	32	40
3. Employees Submitting:	Total Number	385,626	517,065
	Number per 100 Eligible Employees	20	27
4. Suggestions Processed:	(a) Total Number Completed	1,779,648	2,422,848
	(b) Number of these Awarded	462,129	514,880
	% Awarded of Those Completed $\frac{(b)}{(a)}$	25.5	21.3
	Number Awarded per 100 Eligible Employees	8	8
5. Award Payments:	(a) Total Dollars Paid	$16,244,477	$18,457,034
	Average Award $\frac{5\ (a)}{4\ (b)}$	35.15	35.85
	Highest Individual Award Paid	56,031	15,360

These data clearly indicate that those companies which establish an effective suggestion system environment derive results just as favorable —if not more favorable than those realized at Soviet enterprises. There are, of course, differences in the conditions, eligibility, and general reporting procedures regarding suggestion systems in American and Soviet industry, and even to a small degree among various NASS members. However, the data clearly do indicate growing popularity of suggestion systems and greater emphasis on employee participation by NASS member companies.

There are organizations similar to NASS in England and West Germany. It is significant to note that data submitted by member firms in these countries indicate considerably poorer per capita suggestion system performance and results than in North American industry. The German results, in turn, lag substantially behind the British results.[22] The reason for inferior performance in these countries—particularly Germany—can probably be largely attributed to the widespread philosophy and application of autocratic direction by managers, as opposed to consultative direction.

Concluding Remarks

It is evident that despite the great stress placed by the Soviet regime on indoctrinating workers to gain their cooperation, they apparently recognize that material incentives and not moral stimuli are the most potent motivating force. The desire for personal gain is universal and cannot be eliminated or underestimated. In this respect, at least, the Communist view tallies with the capitalist view.

The great emphasis on financial incentives is, of course, hardly surprising in an economy where the standard of living still lags far behind that of the advanced Western countries. More unexpected and far more significant is the fact that the Soviet system offers the individual worker the opportunity to exercise a considerable degree of initiative and ingenuity, if he chooses to do so.

It is an accepted fact in American industry that monetary gain is but one factor in the attainment of desired performance from employees. The hierarchy of human needs—physiological or economic, psychic and social—is seemingly significant in practice as well as in theory. Human motivation in industry encompasses the entire enterprise environment—the individual's satisfaction with his work group and job, work group and superior-subordinate interaction, and human relations in general. Few studies have been made and little is known about these other factors of human motivation in Soviet industry.

With rising living standards and the fulfillment of basic physiological needs, monetary incentives may well become less potent as a motivating force in the Soviet economy. Even now Soviet man can not be thought of as merely "economic man," and psychic and social needs are becoming more important. While enterprise employees generally change jobs because they can obtain better pay and/or housing elsewhere, in many instances, they now relocate because they are unhappy with their superiors and the "human" environment at their place of employment. Soviet managers are now being criticized because they "don't know the needs and moods of the people." [23] It can be predicted with confidence that human relations skill and ability will become increasingly important for the successful Soviet manager.

11 • Controls Over Enterprise Management

We have seen that the Soviet state uses plans, directives, educational indoctrination, moral stimuli, rewards and fines in its attempt to induce enterprise managers to act in the best interests of the regime. In spite of these devices, undesirable managerial behavior persists as a widespread, serious problem in the Soviet Union. One may wonder what the various control, inspection and checking agencies are doing to permit such undesirable behavior and deviations from the intentions of the party and government. For the Soviet enterprise manager is confronted with the most extensive and costly managerial control apparatus in the world.

Within the enterprise, his industrial superiors, party and trade union officials are vested with the right to investigate enterprise activity—outside there are scores of party, union, financial and banking representatives. Of course perfect, or even nearly perfect, control over enterprise management is not possible in the vast Soviet economy. There are limitations pertaining to spans of attention and control, time, inadequately trained control officials whom management can outwit, and so forth. But perhaps the most significant control problem concerns the motives, attitudes, and actions of those officials who are in the best position to exert effective control over enterprise managers—notably administrators of the *sovnarkhoz* and its branch administrations, and the party committee chairman of the enterprise.

Higher Authorities—The *Sovnarkhoz*

Higher industrial authorities—the appropriate *upravleniye* of a given *sovnarkhoz* in particular—obviously constitute the major source of control and supervision over enterprise management. These authorities have clear-cut powers; moreover they are supposedly the best equipped, because of training and skill, to handle this task competently. Although these officials are hindered from performing their functions adequately because of the deficient information they receive from enterprise managers, their motives and behavior more often than not significantly further reduce the effectiveness by which they exert control over enterprise managers.

The personal status of the administrators of the *sovnarkhoz* and its branch administrations hinges on aggregate enterprise results. They are evaluated by the same criteria as enterprise management—the *sovnarkhoz* for gross output, cost reduction and labor productivity performance for the region as a whole, and the *upravleniye* for similar results in the particular branch of industry. Soviet sources and personal interviews strongly suggest that gross output is of paramount importance in this connection.

It is not clear whether *sovnarkhoz* executives are paid premiums on the same basis as enterprise management, although there are indications that they are entitled to some type of bonus. An official of the Leningrad *Sovnarkhoz* and a Soviet planner interviewed were rather hazy with regard to *sovnarkhoz* bonuses. The official was evasive and the planner said that it was quite possible that *sovnarkhoz* executives receive bonuses under the same conditions as enterprise managers. In any event, it is safe to assume that *sovnarkhoz* officials wish to insure the fulfillment of their success indicators, since this would enhance the satisfaction of their personal goals. Their localistic practices, discussed previously, clearly confirm this, and it is not surprising to find that *sovnarkhozy* frequently render assistance to subordinate managers in the latters' attempts to provide for enterprise success indicator fulfillment. This is based on the nexus of common interests and "a family atmosphere" which exists between enterprise managers and their *sovnarkhoz* superiors.

During the Planning Process

During the planning process the *sovnarkhoz* officials are inclined to defend enterprise planning proposals in negotiations with republican and central authorities, as pointed out in Chapter 5. This, in turn, increases the chances of obtaining easy plans for the *sovnarkhoz* and its branch administrations. There is also much evidence that *sovnarkhozy* vigorously and successfully defend management's efforts to insert items in the enterprise plan which are not compatible with the wishes or requirements of customers in other regions and trade organizations. This is usually done by claiming that the enterprise will not possess proper resources to produce the desired goods.

Sovnarkhoz officials, in cases where they have direct authority over norm setting, frequently establish and/or approve deficient utilization norms for subordinate plants—particularly with regard to materials in short supply. For example, one *sovnarkhoz* approved a norm of 583 kilograms of rolled steel to be used in the fabrication of a certain type of machine for 1960. The average amount actually consumed in this process by subordinate plants in 1959 was 542 kilograms.[1] Another *sovnarkhoz* approved a norm of 150 kilograms of fuel for the production of one ton of steel by its enterprises for 1960. The planned norm for this process in 1959 was

141.5 kilograms, and the actual expenditure of fuel was only 138.1 kilograms.[2]

Cases are cited where *sovnarkhozy* intentionally establish easy cost reduction, labor productivity, and gross output targets for enterprises. This would most likely occur if the *sovnarkhoz* itself has received an easy plan.

In addition to various forms of direct, active participation with enterprise managers in undesirable practices, *sovnarkhoz* officials often aid managers during the planning process by inaction or "shutting their eyes" to such practices. Even when various state inspectors report hoarded resources and other adverse practices to the *sovnarkhoz*, frequently no corrective action is taken. Undoubtedly, the *sovnarkhoz* keeps in mind reports of excess resources, should other plants in the region need them in the future; yet substantial excess resources are often maintained by plants within the region with the knowledge of *sovnarkhoz* officials. In fact, the *sovnarkhoz* itself generally exhibits strong hoarding tendencies and often engages in illegal procurement. Frequent reports also show that *upravleniye* officials collude with subordinate enterprises in their hoarding practices and try to prevent excess resources from being redistributed to other *upravleniye* within the same *sovnarkhoz*.[3]

Other forms of assistance to enterprise management resulting from *sovnarkhoz* inaction include the nonassignment of beneficial innovation tasks and a general toleration of undesirable practices such as price inflation, faulty labor classification, deficient norms, overstating needs, understating capacity, and so forth. Such practices are often condoned up to a point, as long as there are no serious adverse consequences for other enterprises in the region.

However, there usually would be a change in the attitudes and actions of *sovnarkhoz* officials when under pressure from central authorities through a tightening up of their own draft plans. At such times they, in turn, would bring pressure to bear on subordinate enterprises by tightening up their plans, thus opposing management's interests. This situation of "pressure as the result of pressure" is common in American companies. A given manager is often inclined to support and even vigorously defend the budget requests and other planning proposals of his direct subordinates in negotiations with his own superiors. But when head office tightens up the plans submitted by lower level managers, there is no choice but to tighten up plans all the way down the line.

Plan Fulfillment

The *sovnarkhozy* apparently exert fairly effective control over enterprise product-mix and quality distortions when output is destined for users in the same region. But they seriously fall down on the job where output is for extraregional customers, even more so when consumer goods are involved. If such a customer is clearly of high priority in the state's eyes, *sovnarkhoz* control over output distortions would tend to be effective. But in such cases the enterprise itself would be very reluctant to engage in such distortions, assuming that management's interpretation of priorities coincides with that of the *sovnarkhoz*. Of course, in some instances the enterprise cannot fulfill delivery commitments even for top priority customers because of inadequate resources.

The *sovnarkhoz* would probably overlook management's attempts to fulfill enterprise success indicators by ignoring planned "obligation" pertaining to innovation, plant modernization, training of personnel, and the like. However, if firm orders are received by *sovnarkhoz* officials from their own superiors regarding a specific innovation task or other measure to be fulfilled by a subordinate enterprise, effective control is likely to be exerted. In general, the *sovnarkhoz* would have to assess what planned tasks can be sacrificed at subordinate enterprises without resulting in serious penalties imposed by its own bosses.

There are many examples of *sovnarkhozy* reducing enterprise targets without valid reason—particularly those of important plants—during the operating period in order to provide for overfulfillment of plans in the statistical report. For example, a number of enterprises in the Tula region requested decreases in their planned labor productivity targets during 1963. The requests were granted and the labor productivity target for the region as a whole was reduced from a planned increase of 8.9 per cent to 7.6 per cent. The actual increase in labor productivity realized was 9.9 per cent, thus reflecting plan fulfillment of 102.3 per cent.[4] Through such practices management often reaps lucrative premiums, and in many cases enterprise managers are awarded unwarranted and illegal premiums.[5]

Sovnarkhozy engage in a variety of other undesirable practices that benefit both themselves and their subordinate enterprises. For instance, not uncommonly they split the manufacture of simple products among a number of enterprises. Each plant buys semifabricates from the plant next preceding in line, and performs simple and often highly similar operations on these goods, which then are sold to the next plant thereby doubling or tripling gross output results.[6]

The formation of larger *sovnarkhozy* through amalgamations in 1963— involving the large majority of existing regions—has in many instances served to double or triple the number of branch administrations within a given *sovnarkhoz* as well as the number of enterprises under a given *upravleniye*. While the creation of larger *sovnarkhozy* may somewhat reduce the problems arising from localism and the pursuit of self-efficiency, it is very possible that such gains will be offset by problems arising from overburdened spans of control in some, or many, instances.

Communist Party Control Over Management

Every industrial enterprise has a Communist party committee elected from the body of personnel who are party members. Larger plant shops also have elected party committees. The enterprise committee is headed by a secretary who is responsible to higher party agencies, and who usually holds this job full time at larger enterprises. At some plants he may perform industrial duties as well, but he would rarely be a member of the top management staff. At a few of the enterprises surveyed—even one with 5,000 employees—the party secretaries combined their party duties with plant employment.

The enterprise party committee is entrusted with the task of stimulating and mobilizing personnel to carry out the plan and all higher directives, and of checking on, counteracting, and reporting any irregularities at the enterprise.[7] Some sources assert that the effectiveness of party control at enterprises is reduced because the powers of the party seccretary are not clearly spelled out. In effect, he can do virtually anything, anytime, in an attempt to insure that the regime's interests are being met.

The director, who is almost always a party member himself, is supposed to consider seriously all party proposals and advice, but he has the authority to make the decisions regarding all matters within the enterprise. The party secretary can, however, appeal any decision to higher party or industrial agencies, or the central government—even to Khrushchev himself. If an appeal is undertaken, the director may wield just as much, or even more, influence with superior authorities—particularly if his is an important enterprise—and he may, therefore, prove victorious against his party opponent.

It seems that at many enterprises there is a tendency to divide the managerial functions, as we understand them, between management and the party committee—the former being chiefly concerned with the technical aspects of planning, control, organization, and training, and the latter with the motivation and education of personnel, human relations, and various social issues. In many instances, the party secretary and his committee members are deeply involved in housing and other welfare problems, arbitrating conflicts among personnel, and human relation problems in general. The party plays the key role in organizing "Comrade Courts" at enterprises whose members sit in judgment on worker violations such as pilfering, drunkenness, absenteeism, and laziness. These courts try to correct this socially undesirable behavior of delinquent employees.

Assuming that the party secretary desires to exert effective control over undesirable managerial practices, evidence strongly suggests that more often than not he is no match for management because of inferior industrial training, experience, and technical skills.[8] A number of Soviet managers personally interviewed indicated that while the advice and "constructive criticisms" of plant party officials are "always carefully considered," the wishes of these officials are at times not adhered to since management has a better knowledge of the technical implications entailed.

The presence of a zealous party secretary undoubtedly serves as a significant constraint over undesirable management activity, but it would seldom eliminate all such activity. There are many examples of enterprise party activities which have resulted in better utilization of resources, beneficial innovation, better output quality, and so forth. In many instances enterprise party committees establish commissions of plant employees—usually party members—to control quality and product-mix distortions, the introduction of new technology, and the fulfillment of various other tasks assigned by superior agencies. However, such control activities only prove highly effective when they pertain to specific campaigns, programs, and one-shot efforts in response to concrete higher orders and pressure, rather than on a continuous basis.

Probably the major obstacle to effective control over management by the enterprise party secretary is due to the fact that his personal status and success hinge on the same criteria used in evaluating and rewarding management. Not only is he evaluated in terms of enterprise success indicator performance, but he also receives bonuses under precisely the same conditions that management is awarded premiums. Full-time party secretaries receive both their basic salaries and bonuses from superior party agencies. Those who combine the job of party secretary with regular employment are entitled to any incentive compensation that pertains to their industrial work, as well as to bonuses from the party agencies for party work.[9]

Why the Soviets follow such a policy is open to question. It clearly violates the organizational principle of separation—a person responsible for controlling and checking on the activities of a given administrative unit should be independent from this unit and should not be evaluated and rewarded by the same criteria. The Soviet policy regarding the enterprise party secretary is analogous to an American company in which quality control officials, or staff men responsible for checking on the activities of line managers, are evaluated and rewarded by the same success criteria applicable to the personnel being controlled. Under such conditions—whether at an American or Soviet enterprise—patterns of collusion are quite likely to emerge between those being controlled and the "controllers." Conceivably, the Soviets fall into this trap because of their traditional philosophy that aggregate plan fulfillment is deemed of utmost importance, without considering the possibility that the plan may be unsound to begin with.

Given the Soviet success criteria situation, in a majority of cases the interests of enterprise management and the party secretary possibly coincide. There is much evidence that enterprise party officials connive with managers in their attempts to obtain an easy plan, and knowingly let managers get away with undesirable practices in plan fulfillment.[10] In many instances the party secretary pulls strings to get more resources for the enterprise, better housing, and so forth.

The party secretary would be more inclined to oppose the enterprise director when the director is not in the good graces of superior authorities, for instance when the enterprise has not been fulfilling its success indicators. In fact, reports of party secretaries initiating disciplinary measures against management more often than not point out that the enterprise involved has a poor plan fulfillment record. A recent case involving a Leningrad shoe factory serves to illustrate this point.[11]

The management of this enterprise had not received any premiums for the four previous quarters. The director, at the initiative of the party secretary, was brought to trial for "shoes of poor quality, for maintaining substandard output . . . for regularly causing material damage to customers, and still greater moral damage to the state." It was pointed out that the director had ignored the advice and complaints registered at enterprise party meetings, and that poor performance was not due to inadequate supplies since the plant had been provided with resources to "produce elegant and durable goods." The penalty imposed on the director was not too severe—six months of corrective labor and a deduction of 15 per cent of his salary.

The party secretary in this case probably opposed the director for another reason in addition to his record of plan nonfulfillment. This enterprise had been under widespread criticism by consumers and retail outlets for its poor quality shoes. Since an intensive state campaign was, and still is, being waged against shoddy consumer goods, the director made a good scapegoat for appeasing the public. It is in such situations that the party secretary has the best chance of successfully opposing the director, thereby receiving plaudits for his own effort.

A director who continually secures easy plans and obtains premiums for his enterprise is likely to be regarded as a successful manager, thus making him more secure in his position. Under such circumstances the nexus of common interests between management and the party secretary would stand less chance of being disrupted.

There are reports where even district and regional party officials defend undesirable managerial practices at enterprises in their area since they, too, are judged by the results of enterprises under their jurisdiction. To cite one specific example [12]—a shipbuilding enterprise was investigated by an inspector of the Russian Republic Commission of State Control who was in collusion with the enterprise party secretary. In part, the following irregularities were found: (1) inflated supply requests and hoarded materials, (2) theft of supplies, (3) surplus labor, (4) disorders in accounting and statistical records, (5) illegal bonuses, (6) building boats as bribes for private persons.

The enterprise party secretary reported the director to a superior party agency. The director charged that the secretary was trying to "undermine" his authority and the workers sided with the director. The party secretary was reprimanded and dismissed. A brigade leader at the plant later wrote a letter to the newspaper revealing the various actions of the director, and this employee was dismissed.

The director gained the sympathy and defense of higher party officials and one of them stated, "Suppose you were trying to run an enterprise such as a shipyard. Do you think you could do it without violating the laws?" An official of the district party bureau later commented:

> Like the peasant's hut of old, life at the shipyard is divided into two parts, white and black. The white consists of the high percentage of plan fulfillment, bonus awards to personnel, the paved roads, the workers' cottages, the appearance of prosperity. The black consists of inflated supply orders, trickery, deception of clients, work done on the side, the lack of ethics. . . .

Despite his activities, the director was evidently not removed. This is no doubt an extreme case; however, it does serve to illustrate that management's position seems to be most secure when the enterprise maintains a good plan fulfillment and premium record.

Much of the pressure brought to bear on enterprise management through the party hierarchy emanates from the national level. If firm, concrete orders flow down this hierarchy, the enterprise may have no choice but to abide by these orders. It is through such orders and party pressure that enterprises are often compelled to innovate. However, there is a definite limit to the number of concrete orders superior party agencies can issue to enterprises and have successfully fulfilled, since they are not familiar with local conditions and detailed plant operations. By the time many central party directives reach specific enterprises, they are translated into imprecise statements. Moreover, effective control over all such directives issued is an impossible task.

At the November 1962 plenum of the Central Committee of the Communist Party, Khrushchev introduced two significant changes in the party central apparatus with the aim of achieving better control over enterprise management.[13] In 1963, the party apparatus at all levels above the enterprise has been divided into industrial and agricultural committees. Formerly, higher party agencies tended to focus most of their attentions on agricultural problems. An attempt has been made to place on the industrial committees those party officials most competent to deal with industrial problems. This subdivision was made in the hope that it would result in a better concentration of skills and effort and more vigorous pressure and control in connection with enterprise activities. Probably some improvement will be realized from this party reorganization, although it may not be substantial.

The second reform has entailed the establishment of a central Party-State Control Committee under the Central Committee of the Communist Party and the U.S.S.R. Council of Ministers.[14] This committee has subordinate agencies and inspectors located in all areas of the country responsible for performing supercontrol functions. They are charged with investigating whether party and government directives are being carried out at industrial enterprises, as well as any irregularities that may arise. This control apparatus replaces the highly ineffective Commission of State Control, a government organization which was staffed largely with nonparty members. The staff of the new party-state control agency is considerably larger than that of the defunct organization. In fact, Khrushchev points out that out of some 10 million party members in the Soviet Union, about 2.5 million are now engaged full time in controlling the activities of somebody or some organization.[15] Whether the costs entailed in maintaining such an army of controllers is more than offset by the benefits realized is a matter of conjecture.

The party-state control apparatus—with its larger and assumably more conscientious staff—will probably exert somewhat more effective control over enterprise activity than the former state control apparatus. However, the new agencies will still be faced with the serious limitations of time, adequate attention, and sufficient numbers of properly trained personnel. Moreover, it was very difficult for the previous agencies to discover irregularities at enterprises on their own initiative—usually a lead or signal was required. In most instances such leads came from persons within the investigated enterprise or at other organizations who were involved in a dispute with the management of the enterprise investigated. There was also a tendency to investigate plants that were not fulfilling their plans rather than those that were. Even when state control inspectors reported undesirable managerial practices and other irregularities to the appropriate *sovnarkhoz* and/or party officials, frequently no corrective action was taken. The party-state control agencies will undoubtedly be confronted with all of these problems and limitations, but perhaps to a lesser degree than the former agencies. There are already some complaints that the new control agencies are not performing their functions effectively.[16]

Those enterprises having secure managers, and where content personnel and party secretaries are consistently rewarded for plan fulfillment, would probably be the least likely to be investigated by external party agencies. Ironically, management may find itself in this desirable position because it has successfully capitalized on undesirable practices.

The Trade Union

Soviet trade unions are organized on an industrial basis, and their membership includes both workers and managers in the given branch of the economy. The trade union hierarchy extends downward from its acme, the Central Council of Trade Unions, through republican, regional, and local agencies. Every industrial enterprise has a trade union committee headed by a chairman who is subordinate to superior union agencies. Within the enterprise there are also committees in the larger workshops.[17]

The structure of Soviet trade unions is nominally democratic with elected committees at each level, and with the central council elected at national conferences. However, the Communist party is in virtually full control of all union activity, and usually puts up the candidates for election. In many—if not most—instances, elected union officials are party members. In general, the unions function under the direct guidance and with the aid of the party. Hence, the unions have little independence to express workers' interests if they are in conflict with the wishes and policies of the party or government.

The formal powers of Soviet trade unions were expanded in 1957-58, and again in 1962. The rights of the enterprise union committee and its chairman are spelled out more concretely than is the case for the party committee.

At the enterprise, union officials are deeply involved in welfare matters —safety, sanitation, working conditions, social security benefits, housing, recreation. They also play an important role in the settlement of disputes between individual workers and management. The factory union committee advises management and grants formal approval with regard to labor standards, piece rates, classification and grading of personnel, distribution of incentive compensation, and dismissal of employees.

The union is responsible for organizing various forms of socialist competition at the enterprise to make workers work harder and better. The approval of the plant union committee is required in connection with the over-all enterprise plan. All plan indices, as well as matters pertaining to working conditions, safety, and so forth, are incorporated into a collective agreement signed by both the director and the trade union chairman before the plan is submitted to higher authorities.

The effectiveness of trade union control over management probably depends largely on the attitude of the enterprise party secretary. If the secretary is favorably disposed toward management, the union chairman may deem it best not to oppose management. There are occasional reports of management preventing the election of "unfriendly" persons to union posts and overthrowing antagonistic plant union officials with the aid of the party secretary, and at times even with the help of higher union and party officials or the *sovnarkhoz*.

In general, however, the chairman of the enterprise union committee would probably identify with the interests of management since he, like the party secretary, is evaluated and paid bonuses on the basis of enterprise success indicator performance. Hence, it is not surprising to come across frequent complaints that plant union officials are in collusion with management, that they do not exert any real influence, and that they take no action when their advice and complaints are ignored by management.[18]

Where conflicts do arise with management that cannot be resolved within the enterprise, the union chairman can appeal to superior union agencies or the *sovnarkhoz* directly, or through the party secretary. Enterprise managers and union officials personally interviewed indicated that most disputes are worked out at the plant. Apparently disputes brought to higher authorities for adjudication by plant union officials usually involve welfare and social matters, rather than technical issues. It seems that in most cases no corrective action is taken when reports of enterprise irregularities are brought to the attention of superior union agencies. At times a persistent enterprise trade union chairman must take his grievance to the Central Council of Trade Unions before an investigation is even initiated.

One factory director interviewed summed up the relationships among management, the party, and the trade union at the enterprise level as "the coexistence of three forces with nearly all matters of conflict settled at the enterprise." This statement probably holds true in the large majority of cases.

Other Controls Over Management

There are two other state organizations exerting control over enterprise management which warrant mention: the State Bank (*Gosbank*) and the Ministry of Finance.[19] The nearly 8,000 Gosbank offices situated throughout the country exert monetary control—"control by the ruble"— over industrial enterprises. The local branch of the bank has the duty of scrutinizing all enterprise payments, checks, and receipts to see that they conform to the plan and to the various state financial regulations. This type of control is facilitated because virtually all of the enterprise's funds must be kept in the bank, and the bank is the only source of short-term credits.

Such state bank control certainly keeps financial distortions from getting seriously out of hand, particularly since bank officials are not caught up in the nexus of common interests with enterprise management and have no direct interest in enterprise success indicator performance.

However, control by the state bank agencies is not entirely effective, and management can and does circumvent banking controls to serve its own interests.

Because of this lack of direct interest in enterprise operations, banking agencies restrict control activity to those matters which impinge directly upon their own affairs. Therefore, control over enterprises by the banks is carried on in a fairly aggregate manner—payrolls, payments to suppliers, receipts from customers, use of working capital, bank loans, and investment funds are generally not subject to very detailed control. Even if the bank wished to exert its full control powers, detailed control over the expenditure of funds by enterprises is an extremely difficult and time-consuming task. In addition, bank employees are typically bogged down with internal work because of the constant interference and barrage of memos forthcoming from superior banking agencies.

The central reports prepared by the banking agencies are often completed too late to take corrective action, and even when bank officials reveal irregularities existing at enterprises such action is frequently not taken. There are also indications that banking officials at times fail to exert proper control and show favoritism because of personal relationships with enterprise managers. Soviet managers—just like their American counterparts—may see fit to cultivate friendly relations with bank officials through small gifts, special favors, and various other forms of *blat*.

The Ministry of Finance, through its local offices and inspectors, is another important cross-checking agency. The inspectors audit enterprise books and accounts, noting particularly any failures to earn expected profits or, where applicable, to pay the proper amount of sales tax. They are supposed to report infractions and search out inefficiencies. No doubt the presence of such inspectors serves as a significant constraint over the extensiveness of records falsification. But, here too, the control officials usually restrict their activities to those matters which impinge directly on their own affairs—in this case, to make sure that the state is getting all of its profits and taxes according to regulations.

The Soviet leaders are showing increasing awareness that armies of control personnel, as well as the various other devices used to compel enterprise managers to behave as the state wants them to, are not sufficient to curb undesirable managerial practices. Such practices will persist as long as they continue to serve a useful purpose for the people who have created them. It is evident that a substantial curtailment of undesirable practices in Soviet industry can only be brought about by restructuring the "rules of the game" within which enterprise managers must operate.

IV · PROSPECTS

12 · Soviet Industry in Transition

It is clear that the Soviets are encountering severe difficulties in structuring their economy to provide enterprise managers the proper incentives to obtain desired results. What appears to be needed is major structural reform rather than the continuous piecemeal reforms or periodic campaigns which have become a way of life in the Soviet economy. Problems of inefficiency, waste, and opposition to innovation are approaching a crisis. This is acknowledged and widely discussed by the Soviets, and new industrial reforms are being sought and worked out.

What is perhaps most striking is that the debates prevalent among Soviet experts, and several of the changes under study and being implemented, are much less trammeled by dictates of traditional ideology than ever before. In fact, the problems inherent in the system are causing the Soviets to consider seriously the adoption of various administrative practices from the capitalist world that were formerly labeled as "petty bourgeois" elements of decadent capitalism—the most notable one being the profit motive.

During the Stalin era, Marxist-Leninist economic doctrines had hardened into dogma; the Soviet economic system was more a matter of faith than rationalism. Criticism of the master, or even penetrating thought about the defects of the system in use, was positively discouraged. Present day Soviet leaders are beginning to realize that in many respects modern industry in any society has a uniform prescription for sound management—that is, both macro- and micromanagement.

At the present stage of Soviet economic development, blind adherence to Communist ideology greatly impedes the achievement of desired economic results. When theology in economics breaks down, the dogma must be discarded. What counts most in the East-West competition for economic supremacy is workability and results. Ironically, it now appears that if capitalist techniques will best serve the Soviet cause, the Soviets are now willing to utilize them. This is reflected by Khrushchev's statements at the November 1962 plenum of the Central Committee of the Communist Party:

> There was a time—I am speaking of the period of the cult of the individual —when the idea was intensively propagated that everything that was ours

was absolutely ideal and everything foreign was just as absolutely bad. . . .
We should remember V. I. Lenin's directive that we be able, if necessary,
to learn from the capitalists, to adapt whatever they have that is sensible
and advantageous.[1]

Fortunately for his followers, Lenin said and wrote enough to provide
quotations for any circumstance that might arise.

Let us examine the more dramatic reforms being considered and introduced by the Soviets with the view of improving the performance of
enterprise managers, and thereby national economic results.

Managerial Incentives and Enterprise Success Indicators

In the last few years there have been a host of proposals dealing with
new success indicators and managerial incentives to be used for evaluating and rewarding enterprise preformance. The large majority of these
proposals do not call for significant changes in the Soviet economic
system; nor would they do much, if anything, to improve the situation.
For example, several Soviet experts urge that widespread use be made of
value added, standard processing costs, and machine productivity as success indicators in various branches of industry. Other experts advocate
the adoption of success indicators that could possibly lead to better
enterprise results, but fail to show how they can be implemented effectively in practice—for instance, quality and durability of output, detailed
product-mix according to customer requirements, and innovation results.

Soviet economists, planners, and industrial executives tend to de-
nounce shortcomings in the system and suggest remedies without, however, exploring all the ramifications of their proposals. This is chiefly
due to their inexperience with equilibrium economics—equilibrium analysis requires consideration of not just the immediate effects of certain
actions, but also secondary and tertiary effects as well. Failure to consider all related consequences is also present in the most publicized and
dramatic proposals for reform which constitute the now famous Liberman Plan.

Evsey Liberman—prominent Soviet economist, professor at the pres-
tigious Kharkov Engineering-Economics Institute, and official of the
Kharkov *Sovnarkhoz*—has advocated certain reforms regarding industrial
enterprises which have received much attention in the West, and which
have been and still are the subject of great debate in the Soviet Union.[2]
Liberman's proposals revolve around the adoption of a profit motive in
conjunction with greater decentralization of authority to enterprise
managers. The Liberman Plan has been the subject of much discussion
and considerable controversy since its publication in *Pravda* and the
Ekonomicheskaya Gazeta toward the end of 1962, although some of his
current proposals previously appeared in specialized Soviet journals as

early as 1955. However, Liberman's recommendations for radical reform were kept from public view and widespread discussion until Soviet leaders gave the green light to seriously consider the adoption of some type of profit motive in Soviet industry.

This came at the 22nd Congress of the Communist Party in October 1961, when Khrushchev stated:

> We must elevate the importance of profit and profitability. In order to have enterprises fulfill their plans better, they should be given more opportunities to dispose of their profits, to use them more extensively to encourage good work of their personnel, and to extend production.[3]

The regime has rationalized that profit in the Soviet system is not the same as in a capitalist system. True, in both cases profit at the enterprise level represents a surplus from operations. But the Soviets claim that on a national scale, profit benefits their entire population, whereas in capitalist countries profit winds up only in the hands of the relatively few capitalists. In the former case profit is a means to an end—a better life for all—in the latter, it is an end in itself for the owners of enterprises.

Liberman's plan would eliminate all existing targets now established for the enterprise by superior authorities except aggregate output, major items of the product-mix, and delivery schedules to be met. This would provide for more local autonomy at the enterprise level because several targets heretofore handed down from above would now be decided upon only at the enterprise—labor productivity, production costs, payroll, total number of personnel, profit, a substantial portion of capital investment, and most innovation measures. Apparently, the enterprise would still be assigned the bulk of necessary supplies to accomplish its job, but Liberman fails to be explicit on this point.

Profitability, expressed as the ratio of total profit divided by total fixed and working capital, would be the key enterprise success indicator. Profit results would depend on actual sales to customers, but still on the basis of fixed prices. The objective is to induce enterprises to utilize more efficiently their equipment and inventories and to be more concerned with customer requirements and consumer demand, because by producing and selling more with the same resources, a higher return would be realized. Managers would be rewarded depending on the rate of return of their enterprises. For any premiums to be paid, the three sets of targets still approved by superior authorities would have to be met.

A manager would propose his own rate of return for each year at the outset of the enterprise's long-range plan. The higher the profitability target proposed, the bigger the potential performance premium he would be paid if the target is achieved. Monetary rewards would be greater if targets are overfulfilled, but considerably more substantial premiums would be earned by bidding high at the outset and then accomplishing the task. The system would be basically similar to the rules for contract bridge. However, some premiums could still be earned even if the target is not met as long as actual profitability exceeds the prescribed "profitability norm."

Profitability norms would be established for an individual enterprise, and where possible for groups of comparable enterprises, by higher authorities for the duration of the long-term plan period and for each planned year within this period. These norms would represent the minimum level of profitability that must be earned by a given enterprise for any premiums to be awarded, and would be established taking into account technical conditions, nature of output, and the price structure. It is anticipated that management would be encouraged to plan for profitability in excess of the prescribed norm in order to derive greater rewards. In all cases the actual rewards paid out would depend on a prescribed ratio between the profitability norm, the profitability target proposed by the enterprise, and actual profitability realized for a given period. This ratio would be spelled out prior to the long-term planned period, and the rules will remain unchanged for the duration of this period. By establishing profitability norms several years in advance, there need be no fear that the targets will be raised if the enterprise does very well in one year. Since good work will not be penalized with higher profitability norms the next period, management would have every incentive to raise its sights and no reason to hold back its productive efforts.

The "norms" would also vary according to the proportion of new products produced by the enterprise. Since the introduction of new products usually entails initial costs and unforeseen problems, the profitability norms against which the plant is being measured will be lowered when new products are being introduced, on the presumption that this will induce enterprises to develop and produce new products. In cases where enterprises have the right to initiate provisional wholesale product prices, price inflation would be kept in check by customers who would now have a direct interest in their own profitability results.

The enterprise would retain and have more control over a much greater share of profits earned, thus providing for substantially more decentralized investment. In this manner it is hoped that management will desire to introduce new technology, improve production processes, and expand production by investing a large portion of retained profits in order to increase future profitability. The regulations governing the rates of profit retention and broadly prescribed uses of profit at the enterprise would also be spelled out several years in advance.

To insure a united effort in the profit drive, Liberman proposes a comprehensive profit-sharing system at industrial enterprises. Where possible, incentive compensation paid to departments, collectives, and individuals within the enterprise would be based directly on contributions to over-all enterprise profitability. Management would be given virtually complete independence over the use of the bonus fund to stimulate production and efficiency in the most expedient manner. It may use it for salary bonuses, new housing, and so forth.

In short, Liberman predicts that his reforms will motivate managers to desire and initiate plans that are sound rather than easy and thus more stable and efficient, and that as a result, artificial shortages would disappear. Under present conditions, enterprise management has an incentive to hold excess resources of all types; under the proposed system there would be every incentive to minimize such holdings. Since profits would be calculated only on goods actually sold—returned and stored goods would not be reflected in total revenues—this would deter poor quality output, product-mix distortions, and the overstocking of warehouses. Moreover, management would be encouraged to give adequate attention to product and technological innovation, as well as other long-term improvement measures.

As might be expected, the endorsement of the Liberman Plan was somewhat less than unanimous. Liberman found his greatest support among the more liberal faction of Soviet economists, and understandably, from enterprise managers who have long desired greater authority in their external dealings and to carry out their administrative functions. His more moderate critics favored some features of the plan but voiced concern about the internal inconsistencies of his proposals. His adversaries, while exercising remarkable restraint, insisted that the plan, if adopted, would undermine the basic nature of the Soviet economy. Some argued that Liberman's proposals were too radical and that his reliance on profitability would be tantamount to capitalism.[4] The proposed system was received sympathetically, if not favorably, by Khrushchev at the November 1962 party plenum. However, no final decision was made regarding its adoption, although experiments are now being conducted in the use of profit as a success indicator at a number of different enterprises in various regions.[5]

It is significant to note that in 1958 the Czechs implemented a system that was basically similar to the Liberman Plan. During the 1958-61 period, the new system appeared to be working considerably better than the former system and this was reflected by better economic performance.[6] It is very possible that this contributed to widespread interest in the Liberman Plan by the Soviets. However, the Czechs ran into serious difficulties during the 1962-63 period, and this has undoubtedly reduced the likelihood that the Liberman Plan—or perhaps even a modified version of it—will be widely implemented in the Soviet economy in the foreseeable future.

Many of the problems that would evolve if Liberman's proposals were to be implemented in Soviet industry are quite obvious. Since the enterprise would have complete independence over its own payroll, manpower and cost plans, and could undertake many investment projects, serious disproportions on a national scale could emerge accompanied by serious fluctuations in economic activity. Resources might drift from high priority sectors which promote economic growth into lower priority sectors where there is a pent-up demand for output. Considerable unemployment of manpower and other resources could emerge in some sectors, while severe resource shortages could plague others. There would be serious imbalances between wages and national income and consumption. In fact, the whole system of financial planning on a national scale, including the state budget, would be seriously undermined.

Since profitable enterprises would be in a position to invest substantial funds, such decentralized investment activities would cause critical dislocations and disproportions throughout Soviet industry. Many high priority projects would be sacrificed in favor of more "profitable" projects which are less desirable in the eyes of the state but which would serve to increase enterprise profitability. Uncompleted projects would also prove a very serious problem. Because important supplies would continue to be allocated to plants, equipment and other commodities needed to undertake and complete decentralized investment projects would frequently not be available to the enterprise. In their haste to finish investment projects in order to expand plant operations, poor quality workmanship and subsequent breakdowns would also create serious problems at numerous enterprises. Problems pertaining to decentralized investment proved to be among the most critical in Czechoslovak industry.

The Liberman Plan would fail to encourage enterprise managers to initiate realistic but ambitious plans as long as the situation of supply uncertainty persists. Although supply problems were not as acute in Czechoslovak industry, enterprises not fully secure about the provision of adequate resources continued to strive for modest plans after 1958.

Enterprises would continue to fulfill their success indicators, including profitability, in undesirable ways if need be. They would still engage in product-mix and quality distortions, inflate prices, sacrifice innovation tasks and other measures beneficial for the long run, and so on. This is evident from the Czech experience, as well as the limited experiments being conducted with the use of profit as a success indicator at Soviet enterprises.

At present, a customer receiving defective merchandise has no inducement not to accept it—such merchandise may be better than nothing. The proposed profitability scheme also does not offer an alternative to hapless customers, except that completely useless supplies would undoubtedly be rejected since the customer enterprise's rate of return would be needlessly lowered. Soviet experts agree that variations in profits in light of the product-mix produced can not be avoided. The product-mix and quality problem would remain critical, but Liberman's supporters hopefully claim that enterprises would not make profitable but un-needed and unsalable items since such output would always be refused by customers. Given the inflexibility of the supply system and the exist-ing lack of effective controls over output distortions, this is a mere aspi-ration. The problem would remain most acute in connection with the delivery of consumer goods to the wholesale trade organizations whose officials are not evaluated on the basis of sales to ultimate consumers.

Under the Liberman Plan enterprise managers would still be con-fronted with much interference from above, and most of the bureaucratic encumbrances with which they must deal today. Superior authorities would still determine the basic questions of what to produce, how much, and for whom, since they would continue to approve total output, product-mix, and delivery targets. This system also implies that supply inputs—and hence, how to produce—would be largely determined for the enterprise as well. With all of these constraints, can profit maximization be a meaningful goal in terms of economic efficiency?

Bureaucratic action, subjectivity, bargaining, and bickering would per-sist in conjunction with the "profitability norms," as well as the other targets approved by superior authorities. This, too, is evident from both the Czechoslovak experience and the experiments being conducted in Soviet industry.

The establishment of meaningful profitability norms for individual enterprises, or even for groups of comparable enterprises, would be a very costly and time-consuming venture. There is much room for admin-istrative discretion and bargaining. The profitability norms must be flexible and take into account technical progress, extent of plant opera-tions, plant location, makeup of the product-mix, share of new products, and, of greatest significance, the price structure. Since profitability norms and prices would continue to be planned from above, why should profit-ability performance be significantly better than other success indicators such as cost reduction? Deficiencies and illogicalities in the pricing system would be present in this system of profitability. Only at those enterprises producing a standardized, homogeneous type of output which does not change over time, would profitability be likely to represent a meaningful measure of efficiency.

Although there is much opposition to the Liberman Plan, the dis-satisfaction with the existing system of managerial incentives and success indicators is virtually unanimous. There is also unanimous agreement that price reforms are urgently needed, and this subject will shortly be discussed at greater length.

It appears that perhaps the majority of all those who have commented on Liberman's proposals are not opposed to the adoption of some measure of profitability as one, but not necessarily the only, enterprise success indicator. Some feel that profitability should be used only in those industries producing a stable line of homogeneous output—for example, the extractive industries. Many feel that actual sales to customers should be reflected somewhere in the system of success indicators. Several experts voice the opinion that different combinations of success indicators should be used for individual enterprises and/or groups of comparable enterprises. The nature of the indicators would be determined in view of those aspects of performance deemed most important by the state. It is felt that by establishing common success indicators for groups of comparable enterprises, "competition" for better results would be stimulated. But here again the use of varied success indicator systems would be very costly and time-consuming to administer, while bargaining and distortions would still persist. Most of the experts agree that rewards should be based on operational long-range plans, and that such rewards should also encourage the enterprise to initiate sound plans. But neither of these conditions can be met given the existing system of supply allocation.

With all of the recommendations for reform, there has been little indication as to how the various proposals can be effectively implemented in practice. As of mid-1964, the fate of the Liberman proposals—in total and individually—has not yet been decided. It is very possible that some measure of profitability will be used as a success indicator in at least some industries. When and how extensively profitability will be used as an important enterprise success indicator depends chiefly on how rapidly and effectively price reforms are carried out.

Profitability, Price Reform, and Decentralization

The majority of Soviet influentials—including Khrushchev and even many of Liberman's opponents—have gone on record as favoring greater decentralization of authority at the enterprise level. They are in accord that this is necessary in light of the extreme bureaucratic encumbrances and inflexibilities with which the manager must deal. A resolution was adopted at the November 1962 party plenum charging appropriate authorities with the task of analyzing the whole question of managerial authority and the drafting of laws expanding the powers of enterprise managers.[7] As yet there has been no available report on the outcome of this resolution. Exactly how, and to what degree, authority is to be further decentralized and delegated to local managers remain extremely sticky and complex problems.

Under existing conditions partial decentralization clearly does not seem to be the answer. Even when authority is decentralized to the *sovnarkhoz* level, imbalance and localism emerge as serious problems. Lower levels in the industrial hierarchy do not possess proper information about the economy as a whole or of economies outside their own artificially imposed boundaries; nor are they much concerned about such matters. In absence of genuine market relations, only the center is in a position to tell what is needed on a national scale, but it lacks adequate information about local conditions and has great difficulty in translating its requirements into precise and enforceable orders. Moreover, the central planners are becoming more and more overwhelmed by the growing complexities of the task of linking millions of interconnected production and resource allocation decisions.

The problems of imbalance and localism that occur with decentralization result in a tendency to recentralize many of the powers extended to regional economic agencies. In turn, overcentralization results in substantial inefficiency and waste on a national scale. Hence, partial decentralization without objective criteria for economic decision-making is not feasible in the present day Soviet economy; a high degree of decentralization would be even less feasible. On the other hand, complete centralization is not plausible given the sheer volume of work in conjunction with the problems of deficient information, success indicators, and managerial behavior.

In capitalist industry substantial decentralization of authority even within a single company is feasible since the market price system provides effective guidelines for decision-making, the profit motive provides for a reasonably effective driving force, and competition serves as a checking force in terms of economic efficiency. In order to grant more authority to Soviet enterprise managers and in order to use profitability as a meaningful success indicator, objective criteria for decision-making are essential for desired results.

With greater decentralization, and in any system of profitability, prices are critical. Clearly, any reward system linked to profitability must be established, taking into full account the ability of a given enterprise to make profits in light of the price structure. Prices that reflect relative scarcities and factor costs are also essential if enterprises are to be called on to make independently basic economic decisions. If prices are too high, enterprises would make profits without effort. Since factories are producing chiefly for assigned customers who badly need the items, demand factors are not particularly meaningful in the Soviet Union at present; nor would they be if profitability were to be the key enterprise success indicator given the existing features of the Soviet economic system. It was pointed out earlier that wholesale prices for goods are quite inflexible, being set at infrequent intervals by the planners on the basis of average costs (plus a small profit margin) for an industrial sector that produces the item in question. The prices for some heavy industry commodities are actually subsidy prices; in such cases they do not reflect actual costs even when they are initially set.

Soviet experts—including most proponents of the Liberman Plan—realize that before a meaningful profit motive scheme can be adopted, and before greater decentralization of authority can take place, the pricing system must undergo a complete overhaul. This entails more than mere revisions in fixed wholesale prices which have begun in 1962; it means fundamental reforms in the price structure itself. The experts agree that prices must be reviewed and revised on a timely basis and must be "simultaneously flexible and stable." This calls for a system which enables revision of prices on the basis of current rather than historical conditions, and how this is to be done is far from clear. This type of price fixing would place new responsibilities on the planners, since errors here could easily vitiate the entire plan if there is to be greater decentralization.

In general, there is much disagreement on how best to deal with the pricing problem.[8] The numerous proposals for price reform fail to show clearly how they would be implemented—economic, political, social, and technological considerations must be taken into account. Moreover, the discussions on pricing are tempered with ideology as the experts attempt to rationalize their proposals in terms of Marxist theory. A workable solution to the pricing problem is also hindered since Soviet economics has only come to life since 1956 after a prolonged period of intellectual stagnation. Stalin completely stifled the development of operational economic theory. Given this situation, it is very difficult to come to grips with such concepts as marginal and equilibrium analysis or scarcity prices.

Most of the experts agree that prices in most instances should reflect production costs, but what should be included in these costs is a matter of controversy. Some favor price subsidies for certain goods while others do not. Some of the outspoken economists even go further. They assert that if prices are ever to approach more realistic levels, an outright charge —in effect, interest—must be imposed for the use of capital. They claim that a direct scarcity charge for capital not only would result in better investment decisions economically but would also deter managers from maintaining idle plant capacity. It is conceivable that the Soviets will eventually adopt concepts of interest, and perhaps even rent, in their system of economic accounting. Many economists assert that depreciation charges should be made on uninstalled and idle equipment in order to discourage hoarding at enterprises. This type of reform seems likely to be enacted in the foreseeable future, but by itself, it will do little to improve the situation.

It has been advocated by many of the experts that prices should be linked to the quality and durability of products; in the case of certain producer goods, such as equipment, prices should reflect their effectiveness or productivity at user plants. They also desire "windfall" profits on new products during the first year of their production, while prices on old products would be lowered each year. They feel that such a system would encourage enterprises to develop and produce new and better products.

Some experts favor having one wholesale transfer price for each product, but for evaluation purposes a different bookkeeping price would be established for each producer in light of technical conditions. A few even call for a system of intraenterprise transfer prices accompanied by a comprehensive system of internal profit-and-loss accounting.

Apparently only a handful of Soviet economists realize that a truly operational price system, based on administrative decisions rather than a market mechanism, requires mutual consistency in terms of relative costs among interindustry transfer prices, because the costs of factor inputs are reflected in the cost of output. It is highly questionable whether such a price system can be designed without a market mechanism. If it cannot, the basic question of how to produce in the most economic sense could not be solved effectively. Theoretically a market mechanism could perhaps be simulated through input-output analysis and linear programming with the use of computers. In reality, the problem is immense because of the number of individual prices and computations entailed. For example, in the American railroad industry alone there are some 43 *trillion* separate prices (rates).

Many Soviet experts are calling for a system of rational prices which reflect relative scarcities. They realize that prices may have to deviate somewhat from costs for the proper distribution of goods and to stimulate the right product-mix. Some of them point out that wholesale prices may also have to fluctuate with consumer demand. However, none overtly recommend an extensive system of genuine market relations to solve the pricing problem; although some suggest that for various goods in plentiful supply, there should be competition among enterprises for orders placed where production costs are lowest. In general, the experts are counting on advances in computer technology and scientific planning techniques—mathematical techniques, econometrics, linear programming, economic cybernetics—to solve the pricing problem, and we will return to this topic later.

If a market mechanism in conjunction with a high degree of decentralization at the enterprise level emerges in the Soviet economy within the next decade, it will probably occur in the consumer goods and agricultural sectors. It is conceivable that use will also be made of a market mechanism for a limited number of plentiful producer goods. A market mechanism is now used in the collective farm sector, but here resource inputs are minimal. Whether a market mechanism can ever be used on a substantial scale without deflecting resources from centrally planned sectors and the growing number of high priority projects is a matter of conjecture. At present there is a quasi-market mechanism in use for consumer goods and state farm produce at the retail level—retail prices are adjusted by adjusting turnover taxes in order to clear the market. But this has no bearing on the activities of industrial enterprises.

It is not possible to predict with any degree of confidence whether and how soon the Soviets can design an extensive rational price system without using a market mechanism. The key unknowns in this connection are threefold: If prices are not provided by a market, can they be usefully derived from a pseudomarket with an electronic computer and sophisticated mathematical techniques? Is a price theory derived from equilibrium analysis relevant to an economic system in which the scales are deliberately weighed by the planners? Are marginalism and the concepts of factor and opportunity costs only meaningful where there is a continuous process of adjustment to market pressures, where, so to speak, water can find its own level? [9]

Other Communist countries—notably Czechoslovakia, Poland, and Hungary—which have granted more authority to enterprise managers, and which attempted to use some measure of profitability as a key enterprise success indicator, have run head-on into the pricing problem.[10] Consequently, much of the authority decentralized to the enterprise level subsequently had to be recentralized.

Yugoslavia has found a workable solution for its economic problems by making extensive use of the market price system, and by granting enterprises considerable authority and independence. Yugoslavia, with its so-called "market socialism," is truly a cross between a "Thou shalt" and a "Thou shalt not" economy.[11] This country has proved that genuine market relations, competition, and the profit motive can serve as fairly effective economic regulators even under a system of state-owned enterprises.

It is true that there are more constraints on enterprise operations than in most capitalist systems. There is also, of course, greater control exerted over some industries than others in Yugoslavia. Many products are subject to complete price control, there are price maxima on many others, and there are comprehensive regulations governing the use of enterprise profits, investment, taxes, depreciation and interest charges. These economic regulations must be juggled and revised from year to year—something that would be very difficult to do in the vast Soviet economy—and higher authorities at times find it necessary to delve into the nonregulated affairs of industrial enterprises. At the same time, however, the majority of products are not subject to price controls, and most enterprises do determine in large part what to produce, how much of each item, for whom, and how to produce. Wide use is made of sales promotion, brand names, licensing, copyrights, and patents, and there is also an antitrust law to deal with monopolistic practices.

This system emerged in the early 1950's, and the trend has been one of greater decentralization of authority at the enterprise level. While national income grew by only 2 per cent annually during the 1948-52 period, the annual figure during 1953-56 was more than 8 per cent, and for 1957-61 nearly 13 per cent.[12] These impressive growth rates have been accompanied by substantial increases in living standards. In 1962, the growth rate fell somewhat and a few of the old methods of central planning reappeared. However, this seems to have been merely a modification of the decentralization trend rather than a reversal of it.

Because of Yugoslavia's impressive economic performance, some Communist countries—notably Czechoslovakia, Poland, and Hungary—are considering the adoption of a similar economic system. The Poles in particular—led by their world-renowned economist Oskar Lange—seem to favor some brand of market socialism, but with more sophistication in their pricing methods.[13]

What of the Russians? Is there a likelihood that they will adopt an economic system similar to that of the Yugoslavs? The answer at this time appears to be a definite no. It is highly improbable that the Soviet Communist party—with its traditions and vested interests dating back several decades—will allow such a system on obvious ideological grounds. In addition, market socialism would clearly undermine the leadership position of the party, as well as the entire system of central planning and control. One hears little about party control in Yugoslav industry, and there would be no need for the giant party control apparatus in Soviet industry under market socialism.

Top-level Soviet government officials and planners—also having a long tradition of vested interests—would also tend to oppose any form of "Titoism" since their jobs and status would be in jeopardy. The number of persons employed by federal economic and administrative agencies in Yugoslavia declined from 43,500 in 1948 to 8,000 by 1955. The staff of the central planning commission now numbers less than one-third in comparison with the early 1950's.[14] Most of the central planners, economists, and industrial officials laid off entered lower level economic organizations, including industrial enterprises, and many needed to go through special training programs. Such drastic measures would be extremely difficult, if not impossible, to impose in the Soviet Union, where the basic features of its economic system and its accompanying bureaucracy and vested interests have been in effect for decades.

Finally, some brand of market socialism is highly unlikely because Russia is a leading world power with many economic priorities and overcommitted economic resources. National security, arms and space races, foreign aid programs, the desire for self-sufficiency in many economic sectors, a top priority objective to triple the size of the chemical industry by 1970 through a massive 42 billion ruble investment program, and various other pressures and priorities that plague the Soviets do not significantly plague the Yugoslavs—or for that matter the Czechs, the Poles, or the Hungarians. The Soviets are clearly not now in a position to drastically change their economic system by allowing the market and consumer sovereignty to direct economic activity extensively.

What, then, can the Russians do to substantially improve their economic system? They fully realize that major structural reform is urgently needed since the present system is a serious bottleneck to meaningful economic growth and technical progress. One of the possible answers seems to be the electronic computer in conjunction with the development of scientific planning techniques.

Centralization, Decentralization, and the Development of Scientific Planning Techniques

To say that the Soviet economy has outgrown its technology of planning and control is a gross understatement. Techniques which were designed for implementing an earlier set of needs and requirements have now become outdated and highly inadequate in the context of a new set of conditions.

According to one Soviet expert, the task of planning Soviet industrial production is some 1,600 times more complex now than it was in 1928, but planning methods have remained largely unchanged. A prominent Soviet mathematician predicts that unless the planning system is drastically reformed, the amount of planning work will have to be 36 times greater by 1980—this will require the services of the whole adult population of the U.S.S.R. An article published in a leading Soviet economic journal in December 1962 claims that the size of the apparatus of planning and control has increased by roughly 50 per cent within the last seven years. Another source reports that the number of employees of supply organizations alone above the enterprise level, increased by some 100,000 during the years 1958-62.[15]

Greater decentralization of authority certainly seems to be imperative, indeed inevitable. Although market socialism is ruled out, this does not necessarily rule out greater decentralization of authority to enterprise managers. At the same time there are clearly limits as to how far and how quickly decentralization can and will be carried out, even though somewhat greater decentralization may be favored by those in a position to bring it about.

Most of the Soviet leaders and experts seem to be placing more and more faith in electronic computers in conjunction with scientific planning techniques as a panacea for economic ills. They see in such tools and techniques a means for devising an operational price system and more efficient planning and control. Khrushchev himself was allegedly responsible for the introduction of electronic computers in Soviet planning.[16] Limited use has been made of mathematical methods and computers in national economic planning since the early 1960's. In September 1963, an interdepartmental scientific council charged with the task of introducing mathematical planning techniques and computer technology on a widespread basis has been set up under the State Committee for Coordinating Scientific Research of the U.S.S.R. Council of Ministers.[17]

In American industry computers and various sophisticated mathematical planning techniques—referred to by such terms as econometrics, operations research, and management science—are used primarily for microdecision-making by individual firms. A variety of problems are solved through these techniques—for example, inventory levels, flow of goods, plant location, devising optimum combinations of factor inputs and outputs. Within the framework of existing technology a vast number of calculations can be undertaken and a considerable amount of data can be processed in a short period of time. The market price system and marginal analysis serve as ingenious computing aids.

In the Soviet Union, marginal analysis has only recently been receiving the attention of Soviet economists, and since the Soviets do not have an operational price system to work with, a chief aim is to develop one with the help of computers and mathematical techniques. Moreover, the aim is to use such tools and techniques for macroeconomic decision-making on a national scale, rather than merely for microdecision-making. This means that the amount of data and calculations required will be infinitely greater than is the case for decision-making in a single firm. Hence, the Soviets clearly have a long, rough road ahead of them if they are to make substantial advances in the use of computer technology and scientific techniques for national economic planning. Perhaps significantly, computers are one of the major items on the U.S. export ban list to Russia and other Communist nations.

Most of the would-be Soviet reformers now eulogize electronic computers and have high expectations concerning their potential as a tool of economic planning. There are, however, differences of opinion regarding the degree of centralization or decentralization that computers will permit. Only a handful of ivory tower model-builders—comprising mathematicians and engineering professors—envisage a system of extreme centralization through computerization of the whole economy. This lunatic fringe of pure technocrats advocates and foresees a system of detailed physical planning, preferably without the use of money prices, and decontaminated from human frailties.[18] They ignore the problems of human motivation and behavior, success indicators, innovation, administration, and economics.

Eventually, they claim, the computers themselves, on the basis of algorithms prepared in advance, will provide each enterprise and *sovnarkhoz* with the optimum variant of the plan—human decisions will not be needed in selecting the optimum—and then the computers will analyze and appraise its fulfillment by *sovnarkhozy* and enterprises. This will entail a uniform, nationwide cybernetic system of centralized economic planning and control in which an enterprise will play merely the passive role of supplying information and obeying the planners. Ultimately, the computers are to take over more than just the planning near the top: the lower levels of the economy are to be dehumanized as well. Within the next two decades, one model-builder argues, the proliferation of automated factories will further facilitate and strengthen complete central planning. Such factories will be carrying out programs fed into them by computers—without human interference—since built-in feedback loops will provide them with the ability to adapt themselves to changing circumstances.

What is entailed in designing such an electronic leviathan? It was pointed out in Chapter 1 that the job of planning, coordinating, and controlling national economic activity can be mathematically likened to the square of the number of different commodities produced and the number of productive units. This thesis is also presented by some of the Soviet model-builders, although they explicitly mention only the number of commodities. By Soviet estimates there are presently some twenty million specific types of items making up the nation's detailed product-mix, and this figure would increase substantially with expansion of the chemical, electronics, machine tool, consumer goods, and various other industries. There are also presently some 200,000 Soviet industrial establishments, not to mention the hundreds of thousands of other organizations.

It is obvious that a virtually infinite number of decisions and calculations would have to be undertaken by the computers if a system of complete centralized planning and control is ever to evolve. It is improbable that such a system can be designed for decades, in fact generations, if at all. Even assuming that such a system could eventually be designed, the ruling party group and top-level government officials would never let the computer and formula experts supplant them and human judgment in running the economy. Hence, not only technical necessity but also opposition by the regime rules out a computer-run economy, and indeed places a limit on the degree of computer centralization that will be allowed even in the long run.

A more moderate and larger group of reformers—made up largely of economists—see in linear programming, input-output matrices, and computers a way to speed up plan construction and to permit the preparation of alternative plans. They are also deeply concerned with price reform, and with these tools they hope to devise a system of pricing parameters to be used as the key criterion in economic decision-making.[20] Some of these experts argue that only a Soviet-type economy, in which the ends to be served by the economy can be defined by a supreme political authority, provides the opportunity to apply modern econometric techniques on a nationwide scale. It is asserted that rational factor of production and product prices can be derived through linear programming with the aid of computers, essentially from and through an optimizing calculation in relation to the general requirements of the plan. This clearly calls for a marginal approach. Their aim is to develop a mathematical model of the economy which allows the central planners to determine the final output pattern and then rationally allocate resources to achieve the output targets. They emphasize that a system of planning through linear programming does not aim at profit maximization, at least not at the enterprise level.

Such a system, it is claimed, would be compatible with either far-reaching centralization or greater decentralization than exists at present. Since prices would serve as an adequate guide to choices between alternatives, more decentralization of authority to enterprise managers would be facilitated, if this were to be desired by the regime. Some of the reformers in this group think that it would be feasible for *sovnarkhozy* and even enterprises, to do the main computations, within a framework laid down in Moscow. They are mainly concerned with price reform and not as much with who is going to apply their optimal valuations. They are also not concerned with problems of deficient information, success indicators, sellers' markets, and managerial behavior, all of which must be satisfactorily resolved before such a system could be proved effective. Certainly the computer and scientific planning techniques alone cannot eliminate these serious problems.

There are other definite limits as to how quickly and extensively this proposed system could be implemented effectively in practice. Clearly, input-output analysis with the aid of computers can move prices closer to market scarcity in both theory and practice than nonoperational Marxist theory and the crude balancing process now in use. However, only a limited number of variables can be dealt with effectively in the compilation of the national economic plan for any one year. If fairly comprehensive central planning is desired, the matrix would have to be gigantic to supplant the present set of aggregate material balances compiled at the center alone. To derive a system of rational prices, prices must be continually adjusted in a mutually consistent manner until a state of equilibrium is reached. Numerous alternatives as to how to produce in the most economic sense must be considered in any measure of truly scientific economic planning. Adjustments and refinement would be required once the plan was implemented, probably on a month-to-month basis.

The actual computing stage would be only a minute part of the whole programming process in such a system. Sufficient and accurate data must be collected and communicated to the planners rapidly—something that the existing Central Statistical Administration apparatus is not yet in a position to do. The pertinent information must be recorded and translated into machine language, the computational jobs must be scheduled and set up. Once the data are processed, they must be broken down and retranslated into usable form before they are forwarded to the decision-makers.

In a dynamic economy, if such a system is to prove truly effective, modification in the program would be required each period to take into account technical progress, investment decisions, changing input-output relationships, growth of output, changing product-mixes, and so forth. Assuming fixed technical coefficients significantly limits the dynamic potential of programming, even within one sector, let alone on a national scale. Undoubtedly, the planners would be confronted with much imprecision and unpredictable changes in parameters. It would be hardly possible to define with the necessary clarity the aims of the program on a national scale, or in very disaggregate terms, or what it is that should be optimized. Finally, many of the essential elements of the plan are in fact dependent on the calculations for which they are to serve as a base.

Experience with linear programming in the much smaller and less complex Polish economy suggests that it cannot entirely replace the material balances techniques of central planning. Econometric techniques can aid in national economic planning, but they apparently cannot be its sole basis.

It seems safe to conclude that scientific planning techniques and electronic computers will not substantially improve Soviet economic planning for some years. Certainly modest improvements can be realized even in the short run, but selectivity in the choice of variables to be treated through mathematical techniques and computers is necessary. The design of an operational model and a rational price system for the economy as a whole is clearly a very long-range task. It is probable, however, that rational prices and efficient resource allocation criteria governing a limited number of major commodities will be devised in the foreseeable future; this number will undoubtedly grow in time. As more goods become subject to rational prices, greater decentralization of authority to enterprise managers in the industries affected seems likely.

But those industries which are least amenable to central planning because of rapidly changing conditions and the need for flexibility—for example, chemicals, electronics, machine tools, consumer goods—are the ones in which a rational system of fixed prices will be most difficult to design. All in all, advances in scientific planning techniques and computer technology would be compatible with increased decentralization, especially if rational price fixing and timely information feedback for strategic control purposes are facilitated.

It is conceivable that eventually the Soviet economy will evolve into a system in which central investment planning and pricing parameters will serve as guidelines for substantial decentralized decision-making by enterprise managers. Under such a system only a limited number of key commodities would be allocated by the planners. However, if such a system ever does evolve, it would not be for many years, because the regime is not likely to devolve large portions of its powers to professional managers at any one time. Hence, substantial decentralization—if it does occur—will not occur overnight; rather it would occur as a slow evolutionary process with recentralizing tendencies no doubt emerging in the interim. In general, decentralization will probably be greater in some industries than others, and to some extent this is presently the case.

Even the most ardent advocates of decentralization—notably Liberman and his proponents—would leave the decisions on economic objectives with the central planners but decentralize down to the enterprise level the decisions on how to attain the ends thus selected. Let central planners set the ends, exclaims Liberman, and leave the enterprise free to decide the means. The decentralizers acknowledge that a price reform would have to precede such a change in the system. For this reason they favor any advance in computer technology and planning methodology that would enable greater decentralization of authority to enterprise managers. However, they are primarily concerned with administrative efficiency and managerial incentives rather than with macroeconomic problems. Pure Titoism, or the abolition of current central planning, is not overtly expressed by the reformers—although some are probably in favor of such a system.

Although the Russians are having great difficulty in devising an economic system that adequately combines central planning with local decision-making and initiative, such a system is crucial at this stage of Soviet economic development. Those sectors least amenable to centralized planning and control are becoming increasingly important in Soviet life. Here flexibility and local initiative are essential because of rapidly changing conditions. The dilemma involves retaining enough power at the center to successfully undertake priority tasks without sacrificing the flexibility needed at the fringe.

Improvements in the Supply System

Just as important as all of the problems here discussed are those pertaining directly to the supply system. It is true that if fixed prices were to express relative scarcities, there would be less need for supply rationing through administrative allocation, more self-policing, less illegal procurement, and fewer undesirable managerial practices in general. However, as was noted above, such price fixing on an extensive scale is clearly a long-term project; but substantial improvements in the supply system are essential in the short run if the critical problems of inefficiency, waste, and opposition to innovation are to be alleviated to a high degree.

A number of Soviet reformers—led by the prominent economist Nemchinov—advocate the gradual conversion of supply allocations into a system of state trade, with enterprises buying their supplies as required from producers, wholesalers, and local warehouses.[21] They are not too clear about the practical steps to be taken. Apparently, they want a system based on commercial purchasing and market prices for commodities that are plentiful, and supplier selection on the basis of fixed prices for many other commodities that are not acutely scarce. However, the bulk of these reformers accept the present basic features of planning, including the centralization of major decisions on resource allocation.

Enterprises are currently allowed to procure various types of commodities and services independently, and their number has been increasing slightly in recent years. Presently, more supply warehouses and stores are being opened in many regions which will enable enterprises to freely buy more goods, but at fixed prices. In some regions special offices are being established to buy unneeded commodities from enterprises and sell them to more needy plants.[22] However, with all of these activities only a limited number of commodities—mostly minor in nature—are involved.

If enterprises are to be allowed to freely procure goods on a substantial scale—whether this be on the basis of fixed or market prices—the regime would have to change its national planning policy. In this connection the overcommitment of national resources would have to end, and there would have to be a slowdown in planned economic growth, resulting in more flexibility and greater planned excess capacity and reserves throughout Soviet industry. By sacrificing statistical economic growth, there would be less arbitrary planning and undoubtedly better balanced desiderata attainment at the enterprise level. With greater supplier selection and more flexibility in plant operations, the problems of output distortions and delivery failures could be substantially reduced, and enterprises would also be somewhat less inclined to resist innovation. If actual sales revenue and/or some measure of profitability were to be used as enterprise success indicators—even without an extensive system of true scarcity prices—this, too, would probably improve the supply situation and render supply contracts more effective.

While a deliberate cutback in economic growth in conjunction with planned excess capacity is alien to the Soviet engineering perfectionists' mentality regarding centralized economic planning, they may have no choice but to modify their system in this manner within the next few years. The dilemma then would be to choose those sectors in which economic growth is to be sacrificed. Heavy industry, and perhaps space and defense activity, would seem to be the most likely candidates. Such a change in national planning policy seems to be the only way by which the supply situation can be substantially improved, at least within the not too distant future, and there is little doubt that such an improvement would provide for more meaningful economic growth and development, a rise in real welfare, and somewhat more enterprise innovation, even though statistical growth would decline.

Another way of meeting some of the problems of supply and the sellers' market is the merger movement underway among industrial enterprises. This movement entails both vertical and horizontal integration, and the amalgamated enterprises are called "firms." Some years ago in the Soviet Union, enterprises were joined together in combines and trusts, but this was done only in a relatively small number of conspicuous cases. The present merger movement began in the Ukraine at the end of 1961, and since then hundreds of firms have been established in other parts of the country as well. A similar merger movement undertaken by the Czechs in 1958 has proved quite successful, and the Soviet movement is very likely to become widespread.[23] In fact, it may eventually become the dominant form of enterprise organization in Soviet industry. There is currently much experimentation regarding the organizational structure of the newly created firms, and the managers of these firms are being given more authority over their organizing function. Several sources are calling for greater powers with regard to the other managerial functions in these firms as well, and it is conceivable that these powers will soon be granted.

In vertical integration, it can be expected that many types of supplies will become more dependable—perhaps at the expense of specialization and economies of scale in some instances. Clothing plants are being merged with various types of fabric producers, leather producers with shoe factories, chemical producers with various types of raw material suppliers, and so forth. In both vertical and horizontal integration, it is anticipated that the much larger amalgamated firms will acquire more bargaining power with external suppliers, thus providing for greater cooperation and more effective lateral communication. Horizontal integration is also expected to provide for economies of scale and more efficient internal operations. There are already reports of substantial amounts of material and equipment being transferred from newly merged firms to more needy enterprises, and various other types of economies being realized.[24] Hence, a desire for maximum economies of scale in all industrial societies tends to pull diverse organizational frameworks in the same direction.

The localistic tendencies of *sovnarkhozy* and their pursuit of self-sufficiency are also problems that must be dealt with if substantial improvement in the supply system is to be realized. The Soviets continue to have great difficulties with interregional dealings among widely scattered enterprises having conflicting interests. There is a strong bias under Soviet conditions in the direction of some system of territorial self-sufficiency, for this would appeal to both the local interests, by easing supply problems, and to central authorities, by reducing planning complexities. If an effective span of control combined with a high degree of self-sufficiency can be developed on a territorial basis, this would probably improve conditions considerably. Clearly the existing system of some 40-odd *sovnarkhozy* does not seem to be the answer. It is with this aim of self-sufficiency in mind that the councils and planning commissions have been established in 18 major economic regions (territories) in 1963, with each large region encompassing a number of existing *sovnarkhozy*.[25]

These new bodies are to work on long-range territorial development plans beginning with the 1966-70 national plan, although some of them have apparently begun such work already. They are to advise *Gosplan* U.S.S.R., and, in the case of the Russian and Ukrainian territories, the republican *gosplans*, on investment decisions, the location of new plants and industries, research activity, specialization, and various other matters having long-term implications. Input-output balances are to be worked out for each of these 18 territories. By breaking the economy up into more manageable units, this could also facilitate the application of scientific planning techniques and electronic computers in economic planning.

The Soviets foresee the day when, because of the location of new enterprises and industries, the various economic territories will become highly developed and reasonably self-sufficient. Under such a system central decisions would probably only pertain to such strategic considerations as national defense, major investment projects, transportation, and certain highly important commodities. But this is strictly a long-range venture, and climatic, geographical, and physical conditions all serve as constraints on the degree of self-sufficiency that can be realized in the various territories. Moreover, in the interim localistic tendencies in the larger economic regions may be stimulated, although over time the repercussions on a national scale would probably be much less severe than they are today. It would be sheer conjecture to predict how rapidly and effectively territorial development will progress so as to curb adverse localistic practices—it may well be a decade, or even longer, before substantial progress is realized.

Possible Reforms in the Consumer Goods Sector

A number of reforms have been advocated which have as their chief aim the creation of greater sensitivity and concern regarding consumer demand on the part of consumer goods producers. Some sources propose that trade activities be integrated into the *sovnarkhoz* apparatus, thus making producers, wholesale trade agencies, and retail outlets directly subordinate to the same higher authorities. Conversely, other sources recommend that consumer goods producers be integrated into the trade and retail complex. Many sources propose that factories should sell directly to retail outlets, thus eliminating the wholesalers. There are as yet no indications that major steps in any of these directions are to be taken, although some minor ones appear likely.

In a very limited number of experimental cases *sovnarkhozy* and producers have recently opened up their own stores or taken over their existing retail outlets. In some cases, large consumer goods producers are exclusively supplying retail stores with various items of their product lines directly, rather than through wholesalers. For example, the large Progress Shoe Firm in Lvov has its own stores in Lvov and Moscow which carry only its own products.[26] A large textile shop in Moscow is now supplied directly by the nearby Sverdlov Silk Fabric enterprise.[27] This type of arrangement would appear to be feasible only for certain types of products, and where producers, preferably in the same city, are large enough to exclusively supply the retail stores.

The head of the State Committee for Light Industry, comrade Tarasov, recommends the creation of a widespread network of integrated production-retail sales organizations for various types of consumer goods extending far beyond the area of production.[28] Apparently many *sovnarkhozy* and producers are in favor of opening up their own stores and/or in supplying retail outlets directly. It is conceivable that such an arrangement will become more widespread in the future, however, whether this would significantly improve the quality and variety of consumer goods is open to question. Why should the producers be particularly concerned about consumer demand, given the present system of success indicators? It would be unfair to judge them on the basis of retail sales as long as they have no authority over retail prices.

On the other hand, such a setup could lead to better communication in the transmission of consumer demand to the producer, and would probably result in somewhat greater effort on his part—for noneconomic reasons—to produce in accordance with consumer demand. Most managers no doubt take considerable pride in the reputation of their enterprises and in the brand names of their products. For this reason they would be more concerned about satisfying the consumer if their enterprises were to be the exclusive, direct suppliers of various retail outlets. In the final analysis, however, the grim history of shoddy consumer goods in the Soviet Union cannot be substantially overcome until the producers are provided with more adequate resources, in terms of both quantity and quality. This condition would still hold true even if a market mechanism is eventually introduced in the consumer goods production sector.

Summary

It is obviously impossible to predict with confidence the role of enterprise management in the Soviet economy of tomorrow, or the shape of things to come in general. Even if we had at our disposal all the data available to the Soviet rulers and their staffs of experts, this would not be possible; they, themselves, do not know the answers. Some of the reforms are fairly certain to be implemented; others are less certain; still others are highly uncertain. Some of the reforms under study, if implemented, could only lead to substantial improvements in the long run, while others could perhaps improve conditions somewhat in the next few years.

There is no doubt that central authorities will continue to determine national economic objectives and key economic policies. They will continue to plan and control all aspects of economic activity deemed strategic or highly significant for the accomplishment of national goals. In this connection, they will continue to make the major investment and resource allocation decisions for the different economic sectors, and guide the proportionate development of these sectors.

Within these general constraints there is still a wide range of possibilities regarding the degree of centralization or decentralization of economic decision-making. However, there are clearly limits to the degree of centralization or decentralization that will be permitted by the regime, both in the short run and in the more distant future. These limits are dictated by ideological, economic, technological, and political considerations, as well as vested interests.

Within the next few years enterprise managers will probably acquire somewhat greater authority and independence over their administrative functions and in their external dealings, more so in large integrated firms. Before a significant amount of decentralization can take place and hence, before enterprise managers can have a major voice in what to produce, how much of each item, for whom, or even how to produce, a fairly extensive system of scarcity prices must be developed. And only then could an effective profit motive be introduced on a widespread basis at the enterprise level. If a market mechanism emerges in Soviet industry in the next decade it will probably only be in the consumer goods sector, and perhaps in connection with a limited number of other commodities in plentiful supply.

How rapidly and extensively a rational system of fixed prices can be developed depends on advances in computer technology and various sophisticated mathematical techniques. Such tools and techniques could do much to make planning and control more efficient in the Soviet economy, but only modest progress can be expected in the next several years. This is strictly a long-term project, as are the design of operational long-range plans at the enterprise level, and the development of a nation-wide network of reasonably self-sufficient economic regions. All of these factors could eventually do much to improve the supply system, heighten technical progress and innovation, and reduce waste and inefficiency in the Soviet economy.

The Soviets may soon find it necessary, perhaps even beneficial, to establish less ambitious national economic plans and to refrain from overcommitting economic resources. By planning for a slower rate of statistical growth in conjunction with greater flexibility and planned excess reserves in the economy, this would probably do much to improve the supply situation, encourage more innovation, as well as reduce inefficiency and waste. Enterprises would be inclined to pursue their ultimate objectives in a more balanced manner. If the Soviets do make this change in their national planning policy, there will probably be cut-backs in heavy industry, and perhaps in defense and space activity as well.

A number of more modest reforms may be introduced in the short run which could somewhat improve matters. Enterprises are likely to be allowed to freely procure a growing number of commodities that are not in short supply. The enterprise merger movement will continue to become more widespread, thus improving the supply situation and allowing greater economies of scale for many of the newly created firms. If more consumer goods producers operate their own stores or sell directly to retail outlets, this could lead to somewhat greater interest and effort on their part to satisfy consumer demand.

In short, the adoption and extensive implementation of several of the reforms discussed in this chapter would undoubtedly improve managerial performance and national economic results. Modest improvements are likely to be realized in the foreseeable future, but substantial improvements are only likely in the long run. All in all, the Soviets clearly have an arduous, rocky road ahead of them and are certainly not to be envied.

• Conclusion

The intellectual ferment in the Soviet Union shows clearly that the problems of inefficiency, waste, and opposition to innovation in production are serious, widespread, and as yet unresolved. As Soviet citizens become more affluent, the grim industrial history of shoddy consumer goods, ill-fitting clothing, and unusable commodities becomes more distressing. The problem of supplying factories with proper equipment, components, and raw materials grows increasingly critical as production rises, becomes more complex, and requires higher tolerances not only in quality but also in delivery schedules.

So far the Soviets have not been able to devise a system that effectively combines central planning with local decision-making and initiative. They are encountering severe difficulties in structuring their economy to provide enterprise managers the proper incentives to obtain desired results. This problem will become increasingly acute as the Soviet economy continues to grow more complex, and as the base level on which meaningful economic growth is measured becomes higher. Adherence to Communist theology and the difficulties encountered in developing an integrated and workable plan are leading to serious operational problems.

When theology in economics breaks down, much of the dogma has to be discarded. The stakes—in terms of demonstrating the superiority of the Communist system—are too high to allow for failure through blind adherence to faith. Hence, significant shifts occur in the rules of the game in the Soviet economy. Ironically, the measures being considered and adopted are, to a considerable extent, converging toward capitalist techniques. The alternative systems of decentralization of authority, profitability, enterprise mergers, operational long-range enterprise plans, more rational prices, marginal analysis, interest charges on capital, computer technology, mathematical planning techniques, and various other reforms may turn out to be more workable for economic results. However, the absence of a genuine market price mechanism, a capitalist profit motive, and competition impedes efficient resource utilization, the satisfaction of customer needs, consumer demand, and innovation.

The Soviet Union has run head-on into the allocation problem without an effective, self-regulating price system. The elaborate, yet fairly automatic feedback mechanism in a capitalist economy tends to prevent any unit of the system from going substantially out of control. But Marxist enterprises lack this control. If the planners miscalculate—even slightly—there is usually no way to apply corrective action unless and until the plan is revised. This is not a trivial point. In spite of all the defects of any modern capitalist state, literally billions of prices are—through the market—automatically interrelated in a manner too complex for any man, planner, or computer to grasp. The system is never in balance, and never will be, but at least it leans always toward a dynamic equilibrium. Capitalist states have a real advantage in being able to ignore this allocation problem to a considerable extent in the competition between rival economic systems, particularly when relatively advanced economies are involved.

In any capitalist society, shortages, poor quality, erratic deliveries, and similar problems tend to be dealt with quite effectively through the market price system. Prices of scarce goods and services rise; enterprise managers and entrepreneurs see the possibility of profitable opportunities—and scarce goods become available. Surpluses are underpriced, leading to losses, withdrawals, and eventual elimination of the problem.

It is true that in any capitalist country this adjustment process is modified by various political, social, and economic factors, which tend to make some adjustments difficult. Monopolistic and oligopolistic market structures, for example, may prevent rapid adjustments of the sort previously described. Perhaps significantly, the most difficult allocation problems in capitalist countries arise when, for reasons of social welfare, prestige, military security, politics, or venal self-interest, the law of supply and demand is violated. American agriculture, shipbuilding, and ocean shipping are examples.

But where the pricing system is effectively used as an allocation tool, it does its job extremely well. One seldom hears of the U.S. being short of a given auto part, a certain type of machine tool, or a particular size of suit, but the U.S.S.R., struggling to grow without pricing allocation, constantly is beset with this type of problem.

The difficulty in a planned economy of the Soviet type is that industrial or ultimate consumers have no real say in the planning process. The major decisions on what, how much, for whom, when, and how to produce are necessarily made by some central planning authority. If, as in the Soviet Union at present, the planners are faced with staggering problems of information distortion and technical complexity, the planning process works badly. Indeed, it is rather surprising that it has worked as well as it has; yet it is quite likely to work less effectively in the future.

Attempts to modify the planning process may well be doomed to failure —at least in terms of comprehensive central planning. It is possible that some improvements can be made in the elimination of inaccurate information and possibly in managerial motivation. But given the basic features of the Soviet system, the basic problem will always remain—namely, how to systematically integrate the incredibly complex industrial structure in a meaningful way so that enough of everything is produced at the right time. It does not suffice to deal in gross quantities in this kind of problem; an extraordinary amount of detail must be included. To date, there is no feasible means of achieving such detailed planning for an entire economy, although advances in both data processing and economic analysis will undoubtedly make possible much more refined work than could be accomplished previously.

Lacking such detailed plans, the Soviet technocrats must necessarily rely on enterprise managers to do such work for them. Because of this reliance, managers must be motivated to accomplish the desired results. As with most individuals, self-interest and the desire for recognition, prestige, power, and income are motivating forces.

A major problem has been that, lacking an automatic adjuster or equator of general and personal interests, the Soviets have been unable to devise a suitable way to reward managers for "correct" behavior. Indeed, without a meaningful price system and profit motive, it becomes very difficult to decide on what constitutes correct behavior. The problem is not so much one of determining over-all aggregate goals—rather, as we have seen, it is one of framing rational, consistent behavior rules for micromanagers, who lack objective economic criteria for socially desirable decision-making.

This Soviet problem contains lessons for all countries that have some nationalized enterprises. Nationalization carries with it an intellectual mystique all its own, and discussion of public ownership is typically conducted in advance on a rather grandiose level. The details can be left to the technicians after the firms become state owned. But the Russian experience with enterprise level planning indicates clearly that these details assume more and more importance as the economy becomes more complex. Without adequate criteria for measuring economic performance, it becomes very difficult to make the system work.

The problems of efficiency measurements of public firms have been discussed extensively in other European countries facing similar problems, although practical solutions have not yet been devised. Indeed, in the 1950's, England denationalized segments of the steel and motor trucking industries which had been nationalized several years before. Denationalization in the auto industry has recently occurred in West Germany. In France, national economic planning—*"Le Plan"*—is carried out in a spirit of cooperation between government and private industry, and is limited to capital investment and is not strictly compulsory. In most Western countries, including the United States, the so-called "extreme liberals" are no longer talking about nationalizing anything. Nationalization may well have ended with the takeover of certain basic industries—for example, utilities, railroads, banks—which produce a homogeneous good or service, and which are relatively susceptible to state administration.

In the Soviet Union, abandoning the market price system did not solve the problems of economic performance; it merely created another kind of efficiency measuring problem which grows more critical as the Soviet economy advances. Solution of this problem may well be the most urgent economic task facing Russia—indeed the entire Communist bloc—in the next decade.

A final comment might be added in view of over-all Soviet economic policy. The major advantage to leaders of a Marxist state is that aggregate demands can be decided at the top, not by consumers. The result in Russia in the past 40 years has been a steady pressure for more investment at the expense of consumption. The consumer never was important in Communist calculations—a fact which has influenced the tone and flavor of life in Russia since the revolution. One result has been rapid economic growth over the past several decades—although this growth rate has been equaled and surpassed at times by non-Communist countries. But one wonders what the over-all results might have been if Russia had followed a capitalist course.

The major emphasis in this book has deliberately been on the environment and constraints of the Soviet industrial enterprise and its management to clearly show that in the Soviet Union major gains could best be achieved by changing the external environment of the enterprise. Some marginal gains could be achieved by working within the enterprise: improving the qualification of personnel, bettering the performance of managerial functions, and so on. But such internal gains are obviously small compared to possibilities inherent in properly reforming the external structure of control, regulation, and guidance of enterprise managers. For the Soviets themselves, such major structural changes are clearly painful, since, in many cases, they may well involve capitalist heresies and bureaucratic empire dismemberment. However, the Soviets' overwhelming desire for grandeur in the modern world, may give them little choice in the matter.

If and as the Soviet economy approaches the American economy in terms of volume and diversity of industrial output, technical complexity, and scope and complexity of market relationships, the structure of the two economies may well turn out to be much more similar than initially contemplated. Increasingly similar industrial organization calls for an increasingly similar type of manager on whom economic well-being largely depends.

V · APPENDICES

A • Sources of Information

This study is based on information obtained from Soviet and Western written sources, as well as data derived from personal interviews conducted in the Soviet Union in 1960 and 1961. In total, approximately 100 Soviet planners, economists, academicians, workers, Communist party, trade union, domestic trade and industrial officials, including managerial personnel at 16 enterprises, were interviewed. In addition, interviews with similar persons in Czechoslovakia and Poland in 1961 have provided supplemental information about problems inherent in planned economies. In some instances the Czech and Polish officials interviewed were more candid about various sensitive topics than their Soviet counterparts, and this has provided a deeper insight into certain Soviet problems.

This writer's first trip to the Soviet Union in 1960 was undertaken with a tourist visa. Consequently only little pertinent information was obtained with respect to this study. The second trip, in May and June 1961, was highly productive since a special visa had been acquired. Previously made contacts with various Soviet officials, greatly facilitated the arrangement of personal interviews and visits to enterprises.

In some cases visits to industrial enterprises extended beyond one day, and with only a few exceptions they lasted at least four hours. All the Soviet enterprises surveyed are in the Russian or Ukrainian Republics, which together account for the bulk of Soviet industrial production.

Qualified interpreters, highly familiar with industrial and economic terminology, were provided in cases where interviewees were not fluent in English. This writer's oral use of the Russian language is not too strong. Certain structured questions and common topics were discussed at most of the enterprises surveyed. Other topics were discussed in depth at different enterprises.

The study draws heavily on information obtained from 12 of the Soviet industrial enterprises surveyed, and these are listed on Table II, Chapter 7. Several of these enterprises gave this writer access to their plans, organization charts, and various other technical, accounting, statistical, and policy documents. About half of the enterprises are engaged in the production of machine tools, equipment, and related components. The others are consumer goods producers manufacturing such items as shoes, clothing, textiles, silk fabrics, watches, and books. The findings presented in this study are, however, generally applicable to most other types of Soviet industrial enterprises as well.

Much use has also been made of current Soviet newspapers, journals, and government documents. These sources are often very candid and critical about the more sensitive problems of industry and management. In fact, they frequently name the organization or individuals who have engaged in undesirable activities, thus making evidence of this nature concrete and credible. By combining interview data with current secondary sources some pertinent, meaningful conclusions evolve.

B · Map and Description of New Economic Regions

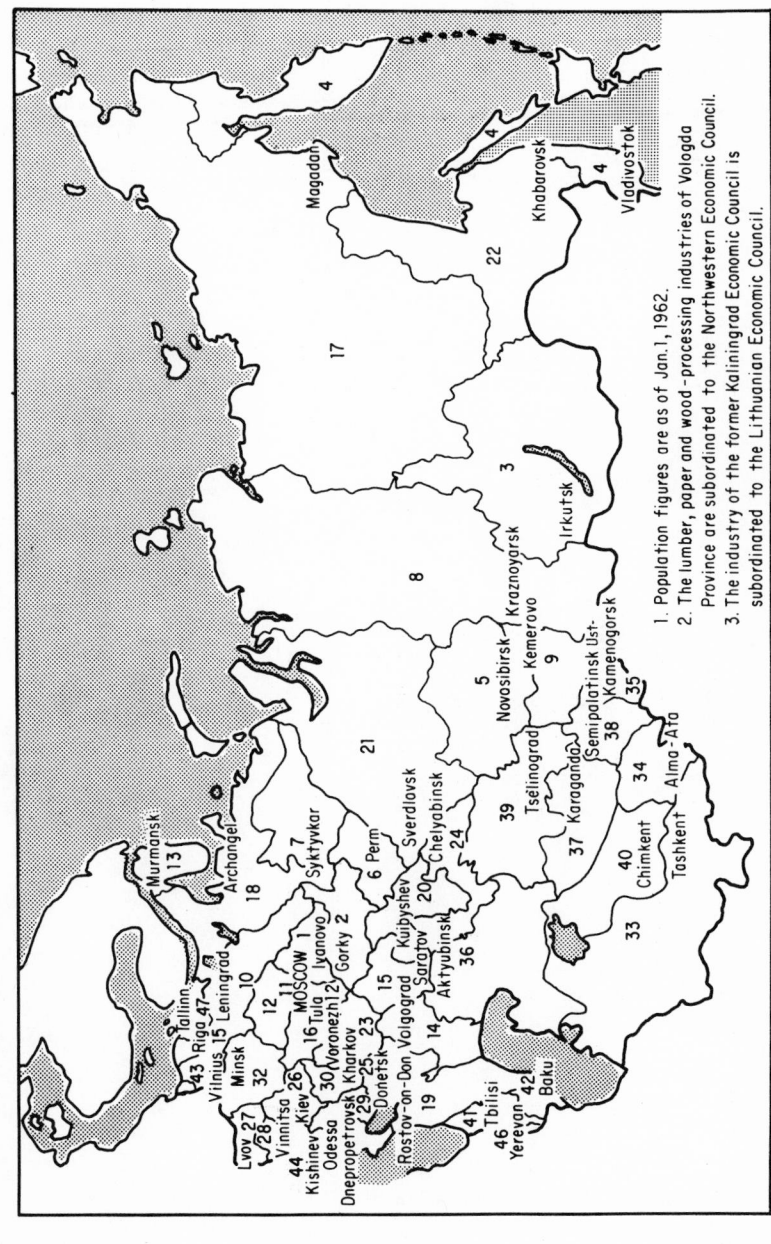

1. Population figures are as of Jan. 1, 1962.
2. The lumber, paper and wood-processing industries of Vologda Province are subordinated to the Northwestern Economic Council.
3. The industry of the former Kaliningrad Economic Council is subordinated to the Lithuanian Economic Council.

Murmansk 13
Magadan 4
4
Vladivostok
Khabarovsk 4
22
17
3
Irkutsk
8
Kraznoyarsk
5
Novosibirsk
Kemerovo 9
Tselinograd
Semipalatinsk Ust-Kamenogorsk 35
38
Karaganda 34
Alma-Ata
37
40
Chimkent
Tashkent
33
39
24
Chelyabinsk
20 Sverdlovsk
6 Perm
Syktyvkar 7
Archangel 18
O
21
Kuibyshev
Saratov 36
Aktyubinsk 14
Volgograd 15
Rostov-on-Don 19
Donetsk 23
Kharkov
Dnepropetrovsk 25
Odessa 30 Voronezh 2
Kiev 26
Kishinev 44
Vinnitsa 28
Lvov 27
Vilnius 15 Leningrad
Riga 47
Tallinn
43
Minsk 32
12 10
Tula 1 Ivanovo
MOSCOW 16
Gorky 2
Tbilisi 46
Yerevan 42
Baku
41 45

Translation from *The Current Digest of the Soviet Press*, published weekly at Columbia University by the Joint Committee on Slavic Studies, appointed by the American Council of Learned Societies and the Social Science Research Council. Copyright 1963; by permission.

No.	Name of Region	Location of Economic Council	Makeup of Region	Territory (thou. sq. km.)	Total Pop. (mil.)	Urban Pop. (mil.)	Leading Branches of Industry
1.	Upper Volga	Ivanovo	Vladimir, Ivanovo, Kostroma and Yaroslavl Provinces	149.4	5.1	3.1	Light, chemical, machine-building, food, building materials
2.	Volga-Vyatka	Gorky	Gorky and Kirov Provinces; Mary, Mordvinian and Chuvash Autonomous Republics	263.2	8.3	3.6	Machine-building, lumber, chemical, light
3.	East Siberian	Irkutsk	Irkutsk and Chita Provinces; Buryat Autonomous Republic	1,550.7	3.9	2.3	Lumber, nonferrous metallurgy, coal, food, machine-building, building materials
4.	Far Eastern	Vladivostok	Maritime Territory; Sakhalin and Kamchatka Provinces	725.3	2.3	1.7	Fishing, lumber, coal, oil, nonferrous ore mining, machine-building
5.	West Siberian	Novosibirsk	Novosibirsk, Omsk and Tomsk Provinces	634.6	4.9	2.6	Machine-building, chemical, lumber, food
6.	Western Urals	Perm	Perm Province; Udmurt Autonomous Republic	202.8	4.4	2.6	Machine-building, lumber, chemical, oil

260

No.	Name of Region	Location of Economic Council	Makeup of Region	Territory (thou. sq. km.)	Total Pop. (mil.)	Urban Pop. (mil.)	Leading Branches of Industry
7.	Komi	Syktyvkar	Komi Autonomous Republic	415.9	0.9	0.5	Coal, oil, lumber, building materials
8.	Krasnoyarsk	Krasnoyarsk	Krasnoyarsk Territory; Tuva Autonomous Republic	2,572.1	3.0	1.6	Nonferrous metallurgy, coal, lumber, building materials, machine-building
9.	Kuznetsk Basin	Kemerovo	Altai Territory; Kemerovo Province	357.2	5.8	3.4	Coal, ferrous metallurgy, machine-building, food
10.	Leningrad	Leningrad	Leningrad, Novgorod, Pskov and Vologda Provinces	242.2	7.8	5.3	Machine-building, chemical, ferrous metallurgy, lumber, light, food
11.	Moscow City	Moscow	Moscow	—	6.3	6.3	Machine-building, light, chemical, food
12.	Moscow	Moscow	Kalinin, Moscow, Ryazan and Smolensk Provinces	220.8	9.4	4.8	Light, machine-building, chemical, food, building materials
13.	Murmansk	Murmansk	Murmansk Province	144.9	0.6	0.6	Fishing, nonferrous metallurgy, chemical
14.	Lower Volga	Volgograd	Astrakhan and Volgograd Provinces; Kalmyk Autonomous Republic	234.1	2.9	1.7	Machine building, food, ferrous and nonferrous metallurgy, oil and gas, building materials
15.	Volga	Saratov	Penza, Saratov and Ulyanovsk Provinces	180.7	4.9	2.3	Machine-building, light, food, oil and gas, chemical, building materials

No.	Name of Region	Location of Economic Council	Makeup of Region	Territory (thou. sq. km.)	Total Pop. (mil.)	Urban Pop. (mil.)	Leading Branches of Industry
16.	Oka	Tula	Bryansk, Kaluga, Orel and Tula Provinces	115.1	5.4	2.5	Machine-building, food, ferrous metallurgy, chemical
17.	Northeastern	Magadan	Magadan Province; Yakut Autonomous Republic	4,302.3	0.8	0.5	Mining
18.	Northwestern	Archangel	Archangel Province; Karelian Autonomous Republic	759.7	2.0	1.2	Lumber, machine-building
19.	Northern Caucasus	Rostov-on-Don	Rostov Province; Krasnodar and Stavropol Territories; Dagestan, Kabardino-Balkar, North Ossetian and Chechen-Ingush Autonomous Republics	355.1	12.5	5.6	Oil, gas, coal, food, machine-building, building materials, chemical
20.	Central Volga	Kuibyshev	Kuibyshev Province; Bashkir and Tatar Autonomous Republics	265.3	8.9	4.4	Oil, chemical, machine-building, food, building materials
21.	Central Urals	Sverdlovsk	Sverdlovsk and Tyumen Provinces	1,630.1	5.4	3.7	Ferrous and nonferrous metallurgy, machine-building, lumber

No.	Name of Region	Location of Economic Council	Makeup of Region	Territory (thou. sq. km.)	Total Pop. (mil.)	Urban Pop. (mil.)	Leading Branches of Industry
22.	Khabarovsk	Khabarovsk	Amur Province; Khabarovsk Territory	1,188.3	1.9	1.4	Lumber, food, machine-building, mining
23.	Central Black Earth	Voronezh	Belgorod, Voronezh, Kursk, Lipetsk and Tambov Provinces	167.7	7.9	2.4	Machine-building, food, ferrous metallurgy, chemical, building materials
24.	Southern Urals	Chelyabinsk	Kurgan, Orenburg and Chelyabinsk Provinces	282.8	6.1	3.7	Ferrous and nonferrous metallurgy, machine-building, oil and gas extraction
25.	Donetsk	Donetsk	Donetsk and Lugansk Provinces	53.2	7.0	6.0	Coal, ferrous metallurgy, machine-building, chemical, building materials
26.	Kiev	Kiev	Kiev, Zhitomir, Cherkassy and Chernigov Provinces	110.8	7.6	3.0	Machine-building, food, light, building materials
27.	Lvov	Lvov	Lvov, Volhynia, Transcarpathian, Ivano-Frankovsk and Rovno Provinces	88.8	6.3	2.0	Food, machine-building, light, lumber, coal, gas and oil extraction
28.	Podolsk	Vinnitsa	Vinnitsa, Khmelnitsky, Ternopol and Chernovtsy Provinces	69.4	5.7	1.2	Food, sugar, light

No.	Name of Region	Location of Economic Council	Makeup of Region	Territory (thou. sq. km.)	Total Pop. (mil.)	Urban Pop. (mil.)	Leading Branches of Industry
29.	Dnieper	Dnepropetrovsk	Dnepropetrovsk, Zaporozhye and Kirovograd Provinces	83.2	5.7	3.5	Ferrous metallurgy, machine-building, chemical, food
30.	Kharkov	Kharkov	Kharkov, Poltava and Sumy Provinces	34.8	5.8	2.8	Machine-building, food, light, gas
31.	Black Sea	Odessa	Odessa, Crimea, Nikolayev and Kherson Provinces	110.8	5.4	2.8	Machine-building, food, light
32.	Belorussian	Minsk	Belorussian Republic	207.6	8.3	2.9	Machine-building, food, light, lumber, chemical
33.	Central Asian	Tashkent	Uzbek, Kirgiz, Tadzhik and Turkmenian Republics	1,273.4	15.2	5.6	Light, food, nonferrous metallurgy, oil and gas, chemicals
34.	Alma-Ata	Alma-Ata	Alma-Ata Province	227.6	1.6	0.8	Food, light, machine-building
35.	East Kazakhstan	Ust-Kamenogorsk	East Kazakhstan Province	97.3	0.8	0.4	Nonferrous metallurgy, food, building materials
36.	West Kazakhstan	Uralsk	West Kazakhstan Territory	729.6	1.2	0.5	Oil, ferrous metallurgy, chemical
37.	Karaganda	Karaganda	Karaganda Province	394.7	1.3	1.0	Coal, ferrous and nonferrous metallurgy, machine-building, building materials

No.	Name of Region	Location of Economic Council	Makeup of Region	Territory (thou.sq. km.)	Total Pop. (mil.)	Urban Pop. (mil.)	Leading Branches of Industry
38.	Semipalatinsk	Semipalatinsk	Semipalatinsk Province	179.6	0.6	0.3	Light, food
39.	Virgin Land	Tselinograd	Virgin Land Territory	600.0	3.4	1.1	Mining, food
40.	South Kazakhstan	Chimkent	South Kazakhstan Territory	492.2	2.0	0.8	Chemical, nonferrous metallurgy, food, light
41.	Georgian	Tbilisi	Georgian Republic	69.7	4.3	1.9	Food, ferrous metallurgy, light, machine-building
42.	Azerbaidzhan	Baku	Azerbaidzhan Republic	86.6	4.1	2.0	Oil and gas, chemical, food, light, machine-building
43.	Lithuanian	Vilnius	Lithuanian Republic; Kaliningrad Province	65.2 / 15.1	2.9 / 0.6	1.2 / 0.4	Food, light, lumber, machine-building
44.	Moldavian	Kisinev	Moldavian Republic	33.7	3.1	0.8	Food, light, building materials
45.	Latvian	Riga	Latvian Republic	63.7	2.2	1.3	Food, light, machine-building, lumber
46.	Armenian	Yerevan	Armenian Republic	29.8	2.0	1.0	Chemical, nonferrous metallurgy, food, building materials, light
47.	Estonian	Tallinn	Estonian Republic	45.1	1.2	0.7	Food, shale, light, machine-building, lumber

• Glossary

Aktiv The most active and zealous members (usually workers) of an organization.

Blat The use of personal influence, special favors, and bribes to obtain special treatment or illegal favors.

Fond Acquisition document for the procurement of centrally allocated Supplies.

Gosplan State Planning Commission (Committee).

Gost All-Union Technical Standards.

Naryad Warrants indicating terms of supplier-customer agreements.

Orgtekhplan Plan of technical-organizational measures; part of the *tekhprom-finplan* of the industrial enterprise.

Sovnarkhoz Regional Economic Council

Tekhpromfinplan Technical-industrial-financial plan of the industrial enterprise. In essence the operating plan.

Tolkach Pusher, fixer, expediter, usually an unofficial supply agent.

Upravleniye Branch-of-industry administration which constitutes part of a Regional Economic Council.

Zayavka A statement of supply needs. In essence an application form.

• References

Introduction

1. See, for example, the quantitative data on Soviet economic performance presented in A. Bergson and S. Kuznets, eds., *Economic Trends in the Soviet Union* (Cambridge: Harvard University Press, 1963). W. Nutter, *Growth of Industrial Production in the Soviet Union* (Princeton, N.J.: Princeton University Press, 1962).

Chapter 1

1. For a related discussion see J. Galbraith, *The Affluent Society* (Boston: Houghton Mifflin Company, 1958), Chap. ix.

2. An example of a national goal statement in a developed economy is found in the Report of the Commission on Money and Credit, *Money and Credit* (Englewood Cliffs, N.J.: Prentice-Hall, Inc., 1961), pp. 9–45.

3. For excellent standard sources on the functions of management common to any type of productive organization, see H. Koontz and C. O'Donnell, *Principles of Management,* 3rd ed. (New York: McGraw-Hill Book Company, 1964); W. Newman, *Administrative Action,* 2nd ed. (Englewood Cliffs, N.J.: Prentice-Hall, Inc., 1963); W. Newman and C. Summer, *The Process of Management* (Englewood Cliffs, N.J.: Prentice-Hall, Inc., 1961).

4. This type of comparative analysis of economic systems is covered in many studies. See George N. Halm, *Economic Systems* (New York: Holt, Rinehart & Winston, Inc., 1960) for a comprehensive, clear survey of the problem. See also W. Leeman, *Capitalism, Market Socialism and Central Planning* (Boston: Houghton Mifflin Company, 1963).

5. See the Report of the Commission on Money and Credit, *op. cit.,* pp. 9–45, for an unofficial but authoritative statement of American economic goals.

6. For a simple and relevant discussion of this point, see Paul A. Samuelson, *Economics,* 6th ed. (New York: McGraw-Hill Book Company, 1964), particularly Chaps. iii, iv, vii, and viii. An excellent analysis of the ideologies of the present day American economic system can be found in R. Monsen, *Modern American Capitalism* (Boston: Houghton Mifflin Company, 1963).

7. However, only in the past few decades have capitalist countries succeeded in controlling major economic fluctuations to any extent. This control and the analysis leading to it are largely due to the work of John M. Keynes. See Alvin H. Hansen, *A Guide to Keynes* (New York: McGraw-Hill Book Company, 1953), for a discussion of this type of macroeconomic analysis.

8. Cf. Halm, *op. cit.,* Chap. iv.

9. Market corrections depend in part on the degree of market concentration in the industry. Monopolies and oligopolies can often resist adjustments more successfully than firms in more competitive markets. See John F. Due and Robert W. Clower, *Intermediate Economic Analysis,* 3rd ed. (Homewood, Ill.: Richard D. Irwin, Inc., 1961), pp. 185–294, for an extended discussion of firm behavior under various com-

petitive conditions. Union pressure, government regulations, and technical constraints may also tend to make rapid adjustments difficult.

10. Samuelson, *op. cit.,* p. 77.

11. Hence, the notion of "satisficing" rather than maximizing in managerial decision-making has emerged in recent years. Cf. H. Simon, *Administrative Behavior,* 2nd ed. (New York: The Macmillan Company, 1961), p. xxv and Chaps. iv. and v.

12. Cf. A. Berle and G. Means, *The Modern Corporation and Private Property* (New York: The Macmillan Company, 1932); A. Berle, *Power Without Property* (New York: Harcourt, Brace & World, Inc., 1959), esp. Chap. xi.

13. This concept of contributions and inducements evolves from Chester Barnard's concept of organizational equilibrium; see his *Functions of the Executive* (Cambridge: Harvard University Press, 1938, 1962). See also H. Simon, *op. cit.,* Chap. vi; W. Newman and T. Berg, "Managing External Relations," *California Management Review* (Spring 1963), pp. 81ff.

14. Such conflicts of economic and noneconomic issues are debated at great length by economists and others. See, for example, Paul A. Samuelson, *op. cit.,* particularly pp. 36–55, 109–78, 399–443, 488–512, 549–76, and 697–720.

15. For an intriguing discussion on a capitalist economic system with absolutely free competition see L. Von Mises, *Human Action: A Treatise on Economics* (New Haven: Yale University Press, 1949).

16. Cf. Halm, *op. cit.,* Chaps. x, xviii, and xix. For an excellent historical study on the emergence of the Soviet economic system see N. Jasney, *Soviet Industrialization, 1928–1952* (Chicago: University of Chicago Press, 1961).

17. *Ibid.*

18. See the interesting discussion on Walrus in John F. Due and Robert W. Clower, *Intermediate Economic Analysis,* 3rd ed. (Homewood, Ill.: Richard D. Irwin, 1961). See also W. Leontief's major study, *The Structure of the American Economy, 1919–1939* (New York: Oxford University Press, 1951).

19. See the related discussion in M. Dobb, *Soviet Economic Development Since 1917* (New York: International Publishers, 1948).

20. For a comprehensive examination of the Soviet price system see M. Bornstein, "The Soviet Price System," *American Economic Review* (March 1962), pp. 64ff.

21. G. Grossman, "The Soviet Economy," *Problems of Communism* (March–April 1963), p. 41.

22. *Planovoe Khoziaistvo,* No. 3 (1963), 13.

23. N. Buzulukov, in *Problems of Economics* (October 1959), p. 27. In 1955, of 206,000 industrial enterprises, some 20,000 of them employed roughly 75% of the industrial labor force. About 89% of the enterprises employed less than 500 personnel. See N. Spulber, *The Soviet Economy* (New York: W. W. Norton & Company, Inc., 1962), p. 54.

24. L. Gatovskii, "The Role of Profit in a Socialist Economy," *Soviet Review* (Summer, 1963), p. 19.

Chapter 2

1. Following the 1957 reorganization, about 75% of the national industrial product was being produced by enterprises subordinate to *Sovnarkhoz.* This output was being produced chiefly by 20,000 large plants.

2. A small number of consolidated firms (see Chapter 12), trusts, and combines are directly responsible to the *sovnarkhozy* head offices rather than to the *upravleniye.* Many of the very small industrial establishments are under the jurisdiction of local industry, but even these are now being absorbed by *sovnarkhozy.* Khrushchev points out that as of the end of 1962, the *sovnarkhoz* apparatus accounted for 89% of national

industrial production. See *Current Digest of the Soviet Press (CDSP)*, XIV, No. 47 (1962), 8.

3. For a discussion on the effects of the 1957 reorganization see A. Nove, *The Soviet Economy* (New York: Frederick A. Praeger, Inc., 1961), esp. Chap. vii.

4. N. Dewitt, *Education and Professional Employment in the U.S.S.R.* (Washington, D.C.: Government Printing Office, 1961), pp. 486–87.

5. See A. Nove, "The Industrial Planning System: Reforms in Prospect," *Soviet Studies* (July 1962), pp. 1ff.

6. A list of State committees as of the end of 1961 can be found in *Pravda* (December 9, 1961). Only those industrial committees dealing directly with defense activity have had clear-cut decision-making powers.

7. The proceedings of the November 1962 plenum and the decrees on the reorganization of industry are translated in *CDSP*, XIV, Nos. 46, 47, 48 (1962).

8. A comprehensive discussion on existing central agencies is presented in a lengthy editorial in *Planovoe Khoziaistvo* (April 1963).

9. For elaborated discussions on these 18 territories see *CDSP*, XV, Nos. 17 and 43 (1963).

10. For discussions on the duties and organization of the 47 new *sovnarkhozy* see *Ekon. Gaz.* (February 2, March 9, September 14, and October 5, 1963); editorial, *Izvestia* (August 17, 1963).

11. A. Zolotov, *Ekon. Gaz.* (February 2, 1963), pp. 11ff.

12. For a comprehensive treatment of the Ministry of Trade apparatus, see M. Goldman, *Soviet Marketing* (New York: Free Press of Glencoe, Inc., 1963).

Chapter 3

1. Cf. R. Bauer and B. Tschirwa, "The Illiberal Education of Soviet Managers," *Prod* (July 1958), p. 4.

2. N. Dewitt, *Education and Professional Employment in the U.S.S.R.* (Washington, D.C.: Government Printing Office, 1961), p. 501, Table VI–52.

3. *Ibid.*

4. Cf. V. I. Lenin, *Selected Works,* Vol. VI (New York: International Publishers, n.d.), pp. 332–33.

5. For a more thorough discussion of Soviet education as it relates to management development see Dewitt, *op. cit.,* particularly Chaps. iii to vi; D. Granick, *The Red Executive* (New York: Doubleday & Company, Inc., 1961), Chap. iv.

6. Cf. the following highly interesting and pertinent sources: N. Adfeldt, "Management Personnel and the Science of Administration," *Ekon. Gaz.* (September 29, 1962), p. 7; also translated in *Current Digest of the Soviet Press (CDSP)*, XIV, No. 40 (1962), 3–4; V. Gvishiani, "Administration is Above All a Science," *Izvestia* (May 19, 1963), p. 2; partially translated in *CDSP*, XIV, No. 20 (1963), 25ff.

7. Cf. editorial in *Planovoe Khoziaistvo* (November, 1962); K. Plotnikov, "E. Liberman: Right or Wrong," translated in *Problems of Economics* (April 1963), pp. 25–26.

8. V. Lisitzin, *Ekon. Gaz.* (October 26, 1963), pp. 7–8.

9. For a discussion of the concept of parallel departmentation see W. Newman and J. Logan, *Business Policies and Management* (Cincinnati: South-Western Publishing, 1959), pp. 517–18.

10. For a discussion of the concept of functional authority see W. Newman and J. Logan, *op. cit.,* pp. 490ff.

11. Many standard American textbooks in management theory present criteria and operational guidelines which aid in efficiently organizing and grouping activities. See, for example, H. Koontz and C. O'Donnell, *Principles of Management,* 3rd ed. (New York: McGraw-Hill Book Company, 1964), Chaps. xiii, xiv, and xvi; W. Newman,

Administrative Action, 2nd ed. (Englewood Cliffs, N.J.: Prentice-Hall, Inc., 1963), Chaps. ix, x, xvi, and xvii.

12. Industrial enterprises in other Communist countries have similar ultimate objectives prescribed by the state. Cf. J. Kornai's book on Hungarian industry, *Overcentralization in Economic Administration* (London: Oxford University Press, 1959), pp. 121ff.

Chapter 4

1. Much of the data presented in this chapter has been obtained from personal interviews. An interesting historical survey of the authority of Soviet enterprise managers is also presented in G. Von Wrangel, "Die staatlichen Industrie-Manager in der Sowjetunion," *Osteuropa* (March 1963), pp. 113–27.

2. Cf. V. Laptev, "Planning and the Authority of the Enterprise," *Voprosy Ekonomiki,* No. 6 (1963), 26ff; *Ekon. Gaz.* (January 5 and October 26, 1963). This is also evident from a book by the Soviet economist B. Riabinskii, *Planning and Economies of Metallurgical Enterprises* (Moscow: State Scientific-Technical Publishing House, 1963).

3. M. Weitzman *et al.,* "Employment in the U.S.S.R.," in *Dimensions of Soviet Economic Power* (Washington, D.C.: Government Printing Office, 1962), p. 635.

4. V. Gvishiani, *Izvestia* (May 19, 1963), p. 2; also partially translated in *The Current Digest of the Soviet Press (CDSP),* XV, No. 20 (1963), 25ff.

Chapter 5

1. Paul A. Samuelson, *Economics* (New York: McGraw-Hill Book Company, 1961), p. 826.

2. These observations are based on personal interviews as well as recent Soviet sources. Cf. the series of articles translated in *CDSP,* XV, No. 22 (1963).

3. An interesting discussion on the material balancing process can be found in N. Spulber, *The Soviet Economy* (New York: W. W. Norton & Company, Inc., 1962), Chap. ii.

4. See H. Levine, "Recent Developments in Soviet Planning," in *Dimensions of Soviet Economic Power* (Washington, D.C.: Government Printing Office, 1963), pp. 47ff; editorial, *Planovoe Khoziaistvo* (April 1963).

5. Apparently for 1962 *Gosplan* U.S.S.R. drew up balances for and allocated 19,000 commodities as compared to some 8,000 to 14,000 in previous years. See A. Nove, "Prospects for Economic Growth in the U.S.S.R.," *American Economic Review* (May 1963), p. 546.

6. Cf. sources cited in fn. 2, Chapter 4, above.

7. Data on the number of centrally planned commodities in recent years are found in Levine and Nove, *op. cit.*

Chapter 6

1. Data on capital investment in industry for 1961 can be found in M. Kahn, "The Soviet Economy in 1961," in *Dimensions of Soviet Economic Power* (Washington, D.C.: Government Printing Office, 1962), pp. 229ff.

2. *Pravda* (August 10, 1955); J. Berliner, "Managerial Incentives and Decision-Making, a Comparison of the United States and the Soviet Union," in *Comparisons of the United States and Soviet Economies,* Part I (Washington, D.C.: Government Printing Office, 1960), p. 358.

3. See, W. Nutter, *Growth of Soviet Industrial Production* (Princeton, N.J.: Princeton University Press, 1962), pp. 222–24. According to recent CIA figures the over-all Soviet economic growth rates for 1962 and 1963 were only 2.5%; *Business Week* (January 18, 1964), pp. 30–31.

4. Berliner, *op. cit.*, p. 358.

5. A. Vedishev, "Three Years of Work under New Conditions," *Problems of Economics*, III, No. 9 (1961), 53.

6. Kahn, *op. cit.*, p. 223.

7. *Pravda* (November 20, 1962); translated in *The New York Times* (November 21, 1962), p. 13.

8. See the discussion in the *Economist Intelligence Unit Three-Monthly Economic, U.S.S.R.* No. 41 (May 1963) (London: Spencer House), pp. 1–2.

9. S. Nestorova (Director of Plant), *Current Digest of the Soviet Press (CDSP)*, XV, No. 26 (1963).

10. Cited in A. Nove, *The Soviet Economy* (New York: Frederick A. Praeger, Inc., 1961), p. 202.

11. *Ekon. Gaz.* (February 23, 1963), p. 37. Many other concrete examples can be found in E. Lokshin, "Improving Material and Technical Supply of the U.S.S.R. National Economy," translated in *CDSP*, XIII, No. 11 (1961), 19ff.

12. Editorial, *Planovoe Khoziaistvo* (April 1963).

13. Cf. *Izvestia* (November 27, 1963); *CDSP*, XV, No. 48 (1963), 35; *Ekon. Gaz.* (February 23 and March 16, 1963).

14. V. Laptev, *Voprosy Ekonomiki*, No. 6 (1963), 26ff.

15. *Ekon. Gaz.* (February 9, 1963), pp. 38ff.

16. V. Pushakarev, *Ekon. Gaz.* (January 15, 1962), p. 8.

17. V. Dyken, *Ekon. Gaz.* (January 1, 1962), p. 5. Also translated in A. Nove, "The Soviet Planning System," *Soviet Studies* (July 1963), p. 6.

18. V. Agranovskii, *Ekon. Gaz.* (June 10, 1960), p. 3.

19. Lokshin, *op. cit.*, pp. 19ff.

20. M. Stephev, *CDSP*, XIV, No. 50 (1962), 17ff.

21. E. Klemov, *Ekon. Gaz.* (February 16, 1963), pp. 16–17.

22. *CDSP*, XV, No. 35 (1963), 36.

23. *Izvestia* (August 17, 1963).

24. *Ekon. Gaz.* (February 16, 1963), pp. 16–17.

25. Numerous concrete examples of supply failures were revealed at a consumer goods conference held in July, 1963; see *CDSP*, XV, No. 26 (1963), 5ff.

26. G. Menchikov, *Ekon. Gaz.* (March 9, 1963), p. 31.

27. Cf. Lokshin, *op. cit.*, pp. 19ff.

28. *CDSP*, XIV, No. 47 (1962); translated from *Pravda* (November 20, 1962).

29. *Ekon. Gaz.* (February 9, 1963), p. 39.

30. V. Dymshits, *CDSP*, XV, No. 14 (1963), 13–14.

31. *Izvestia* (August 17, 1963).

32. *Ekon. Gaz.* (October 12, 1963), p. 6.

33. *Ekon. Gaz.* (February 9, 1963), p. 38.

34. Cf. *Ekon. Gaz.* (October 26, 1963), pp. 24ff. E. Johnson, "Planning and Contract Law," *Soviet Studies* (January 1961).

35. E. Klenov, *Ekon. Gaz.* (February 16, 1963), p. 17.

36. The Enterprise Fund is discussed in Chapter 7 of this book. See I. Oblomskaia, "Concerning the Enterprise Fund," *Problems of Economics*, II, No. 2 (1960), 34ff.

37. *Izvestia* (September 6, 1963), p. 3.

38. *CDSP*, XV, No. 17 (1963); translated from *Pravda* (April 26, 1963).

39. *Ibid.*

40. *Ibid.*

41. For an intriguing discussion on *"blat"* and the *"tolkach"* in Soviet industry, see J. Berliner, *Factory and Manager in the U.S.S.R.* (Cambridge: Harvard University Press, 1957), Chaps. xi and xii.

42. *Ekon. Gaz.* (May 15, 1960).

43. *Izvestia* (September 4, 1960), p. 6.

44. "Tractors and Pushers," *Ekon. Gaz.* (February 16, 1963), p. 17.

45. M. Zhebrak, *CDSP*, XIV, No. 28 (1962), 24–25.

46. The decree is translated in *CDSP*, XIV, No. 7 (1962), 4.

47. These and other examples are found in *Ekon. Gaz.* (February 23, 1963), pp. 37ff.

48. See W. Nutter's comments on A. Nove's article, and Nove's reply in *American Economic Review* (May 1963), pp. 572–75.

49. Cf. A. Khavin, "Problems of Manpower Distribution," translated in *CDSP*, XIII, No. 33 (1961); R. Fakiolas, "Problems of Labor Mobility in the U.S.S.R.," *Soviet Studies* (July 1962), pp. 16ff.

50. *Trud* (February 8, 1963), p. 2; translated in *CDSP*, XV, No. 6 (1963), 35.

51. "Restless Russians," *Wall Street Journal* (September 12, 1963), p. 1.

52. *Ibid.*

53. For an enlightening account of American wartime economic planning by two experts who played a key role in setting up and implementing the system, see D. Novick and G. Steiner, *Wartime Industrial Statistics* (Urbana: University of Illinois Press, 1949).

Chapter 7

1. *Pravda* (March 4, 1962); *New York World-Telegram and Sun* (March 5, 1962), p. 2.

2. L. Alter, *Current Digest of the Soviet Press (CDSP)*, XIII, No. 30 (1961), 26ff.

3. See D. Granick, "Soviet American Management Comparisons," *Comparisons of the United States and Soviet Economies*, Part I (Washington, D.C.: Government Printing Office, 1960), 145.

4. *Factory and Manager in the U.S.S.R.* (Cambridge, Mass.: Harvard University Press, 1957), esp. Chaps. iii and iv.

5. *Ibid.*

6. *Ibid.*, p. 322.

7. This claim is made by a Hungarian economist; see J. Kornai, *Overcentralization in Economic Administration* (London: Oxford University Press, 1959), p. 133. Liberman's article appeared in *Voprosy Ekonomiki*, No. 6 (1955).

8. The success indicator reform is presented in *CDSP*, XI, No. 50 (1959), 18–20. Quite frequently Soviet reforms are not implemented to the same extent or in precisely the same manner as indicated in written sources.

9. Cf. H. Shaffer, "What Price Economic Reforms," *Problems of Communism* (May–June 1963), p. 21.

10. L. Gatovskii, "The Role of Profit in a Socialist Economy," *Soviet Review* (Summer 1963), pp. 19–20.

11. *Ibid.*, p. 14.

12. Almost unbelievable examples are presented in I. Oblomskaia, "Concerning the Enterprise Fund," *Problems of Economics*, II, No. 12 (1960), 36ff. A. Zaytsev, "Problems of Material Incentives in Government Owned Enterprises," *Problems of Economics*, II, No. 3 (1959), 35ff.

13. Actual uses of the Enterprise Fund at plants surveyed differ somewhat from the regulations stipulated in written sources. The written sources claim that at least 20% is used for expanding and improving plant and production, at least 40% for housing improvements, and up to 40% for bonuses, social security, and welfare benefits. See *CDSP*, XII, No. 27 (1960), 13ff.

14. Ye Manevich, *Voprosy Ekonomiki*, No. 5 (1961).

15. A. Bachurin, "Problems of Profitability at Industrial Enterprises," *Problems of Economics*, II, No. 11 (1960), 29–30.

16. *Pravda* (December 11, 1962), pp. 6–7.

17. A discussion on incentives for socialist competition can be found in *Partiinaya Zhizn* (March 1960), pp. 71–72. See also *CDSP*, XV, Nos. 17, 18, 44 (1963).

Chapter 8

1. N. Antonay, *Current Digest of the Soviet Press (CDSP)*, XIV, No. 37 (1962), 19.

2. V. Andreyev, *CDSP*, XIV, No. 29 (1962), 27.

3. The concept of "organizational slack" as used in American industry has been defined as the difference between total resources and total payments required to maintain the coalition of the various participants essential for the firm's survival and growth. See R. Cyert and F. March, *A Behavioral Theory of the Firm* (Englewood Cliffs, N.J.: Prentice-Hall, Inc., 1963), pp. 36ff.

4. *CDSP*, XV, No. 17 (1963), 4–5.

5. S. Bunkov, *Izvestia* (July 6, 1961), p. 3.

6. A. Zakharyan, *Pravda* (June 23, 1961), p. 2.

7. E. Lokshin, *CDSP*, XIII, No. 11 (1961), 30.

8. G. Menchikov, *Ekon. Gaz.* (March 9, 1963), p. 31; *Izvestia* (July 21, 1961), p. 3.

9. O. Antonov, *op. cit.*, pp. 15ff.

10. Cf. M. Laptev, *Voprosy Ekonomiki* (June 1963), pp. 26ff.

11. *CDSP*, XV, No. 17 (1963), 4–5; translated from *Pravda* (April 26, 1963).

12. Cited in G. Schroeder, "Soviet Industrial Labor Productivity," *Dimensions of Soviet Economic Power* (Washington, D.C.: U. S. Government Printing Office, 1962), p. 160.

13. I. Spiridona, *Izvestia* (May 5, 1961).

14. *Ekon. Gaz.* (October 5, 1963).

15. Cf. Z. Atlas, *Ekon. Gaz.* (October 16, 1961), p. 30.

16. V. Mitin, *Pravda* (February 4, 1960), p. 4.

17. Cf. *Pravda* (October 12, 1962), p. 3; and the account by a Soviet plant engineer in *CDSP*, XIV, No. 41 (1962), 16.

18. O. Antonov, *CDSP*, XIV, No. 21 (1962), 15.

19. Cf. *Ekon. Gaz.* (March 16, 1963), pp. 8–9.

20. I. Reidi, *Pravda* (February 20, 1962), p. 2.

21. M. Zykov, *Sovetskaya Torgovlia*, No. 6 (1960), p. 24.

22. See the interesting discussion in P. Hanson, "The Assortment Problem in Soviet Retail Trade," *Soviet Studies* (April 1963), pp. 347ff.

23. A. Korilkov, *Ekon. Gaz.* (October 16, 1961), p. 30.

24. *Pravda* (August 9, 1960), p. 2.

25. I. Maevskii, "Further Improvements of Economic Planning," *Problems of Economics*, III, No. 2 (1961), 24.

26. The decree is found in *Pravda* (May 25, 1961).

27. Cited by A. Dulles in "What Drives the Soviet Manager," *Harvard Business School Bulletin* (August 1961).

28. M. Kaser, "The Reorganization of Soviet Industry," in *Value and Plan*, G. Grossman, ed. (Berkeley: University of California Press, 1960), p. 231.

29. For example, one machinery factory in the Urals typically turns over to its superiors each planning period 17,000 sheets of documents relating to its material requirements; J. Montias, "Planning with Material Balances in Soviet Type Economics," *American Economic Review* (December 1959), p. 978. A recent source cites the case of a factory whose supply documents for ballbearings weighed 200 kilograms and were sent to 14 agencies; *Ekon. Gaz.* (March 30, 1963), p. 7.

30. N. Umnova, translated in *CDSP*, XII, No. 15 (1960), 24.
31. These and other similar examples are presented in I. Fofanov, "Some Problems in Stimulating Production," *Problems of Economics*, II, No. 6 (1959).
32. B. Miroshnichenko, "Problems of National Economic Planning," *Problems of Economics*, IV, No. 2 (1961).
33. Ye Manevich, *CDSP*, XIII, No. 33 (1961), 10ff.
34. E. Liberman, "Planning Production and Standards of Long-Term Operations," *Problems of Economics* (December 1962), pp. 16ff.
35. Numerous examples of distortions caused by success indicators can be found in A. Nove, *The Soviet Economy* (New York: Frederick A. Praeger, Inc., 1961), Chap vi; and O. Antonov, *CDSP*, XIV, No. 21 (1962), 14–15.
36. Cf. L. Gatovskii, *Problems of Economics* (Summer, 1963), pp. 19–20; J. Berliner in *Comparisons of the United States and Soviet Economies*, Part I (Washington, D.C.: Government Printing Office, 1960), pp. 358–59; *Pravda* (July 20, 1960), p. 2.
37. Cf. *Pravda* (September 3, 1963), p. 2; *Ekon. Gaz.* (February 23, 1963), p. 37; E. Lokshin, *op. cit.*, pp. 29ff.
38. P. Hanson, *op. cit.*, pp. 351ff.
39. G. Dikhtiar, "Soviet Trade in the Period of Full Scale Communism," *Problems of Economics* (August 1962), p. 47.
40. *Izvestia* (May 6, 1961), p. 4.
41. *CDSP*, XIV, No. 21 (1962), 14–15.
42. I. Senin, *Pravda* (December 11, 1962), pp. 6–7.
43. Editorial, *Ekon. Gaz.* (October 5, 1962).
44. *Ibid.* (November 23, 1963).
45. *Ekon. Gaz.* (July 16, 1963), pp. 16–17; *CDSP*, XV, No. 26 (1963), 5.
46. *Izvestia* (August 31, 1963), p. 2.
47. G. Karweina, *Neue Illustrierte* (January 13, 1963).
48. G. Dikhtiar, *op. cit.*, pp. 47–48.
49. *Ekon. Gaz.* (November 23, 1963).
50. See the related discussion in P. Hanson, *op. cit.*, pp. 347ff.
51. *Ekon. Gaz.* (March 16, 1963), pp. 8–9.
52. Cf. *Izvestia* (December 4, 1961, and May 25, 1962); *Ekon. Gaz.* (July 16, 1963), pp. 16–17.
53. Cf. *Izvestia* (August 27, 1961, and September 8, 1963).
54. A. Berg, *CDSP*, XV, No. 42 (1963), 27.
55. An example is the Leningrad Electrical Equipment enterprise which typically produces about 55–60% of its monthly output during the last 10 days of the month; *CDSP*, XIII, No. 23 (1961), 23.
56. *Izvestia* (September 1, 1963).
57. *Ibid.* (September 6, 1963).
58. As cited in H. Swearer, "Khrushchev's Administrative Reforms," *Challenge* (April 1963), p. 18.
59. Cf. *Ekon. Gaz.* (February 16, 1963), pp. 16–17.
60. Cf. B. Miroshnichenko, *op. cit.*, pp. 13ff; *Pravda* (October 12, 1962), p. 3.
61. See B. Balassa, *The Hungarian Experience in Economic Planning* (New Haven, Conn.: Yale University Press, 1959), pp. 144–45.
62. J. Kornai, *op. cit.*, pp. 130–31.
63. Translated in *CDSP*, XIV, No. 45 (1962), 17.
64. *Ibid.*, XII, No. 43 (1960), 23–24.
65. *Pravda* (December 11, 1962), pp. 6–7.
66. *Ibid.* (May 22, 1963).
67. *CDSP*, XI, No. 44 (1959), 3ff.
68. *Ekon. Gaz.* (March 9 and February 23, 1963).

69. See fns. 23 and 24 of this chapter. See also *CDSP*, XIII, No. 33 (1961), 7ff.
70. *Pravda* (December 11, 1962).
71. F. Tabeyev, *CDSP*, XV, No. 15 (1963), 31.
72. A. Berg, *op. cit.*, p. 27.
73. G. Schroeder, *op. cit.*, p. 160.
74. *Izvestia* (February 21, 1960), p. 2.
75. G. Dikhtiar, *op. cit.*, p. 48.
76. M. Goldman, "Economic Controversy in the Soviet Union," *Foreign Affairs* (April 1963), p. 511.
77. *CDSP*, XV, No. 26 (1963), 5.
78. Cf. D. Phelps, "Soviet Marketing, Stronger Than We Think," *Harvard Business Review* (July–August 1961); M. Goldman, "Marketing, a Lesson for Marx," *Harvard Business Review* (January–February, 1960).
79. *CDSP*, XV, No. 26 (1963), 5–8.
80. Cf. R. Likert, *New Patterns of Management* (New York: McGraw-Hill Book Company, 1961), particularly Chap. xiii; G. Strauss and L. Sayles, *Personnel* (Englewood Cliffs, N.J.: Prentice-Hall, Inc., 1960), pp. 322ff; W. Newman and C. Summer, *The Process of Management* (Englewood Cliffs, N.J.: Prentice-Hall, Inc., 1961), pp. 175–76; R. Cyert and J. March, *A Behavior Theory, op. cit.*, Chap. iv.
81. "Work expands to fill the time (or money) available for its completion," C. Parkinson, *Parkinson's Law* (London: John Murray, Publishers, Ltd., 1961), pp. 9ff.
82. See sources cited in fn. 80 of this chapter. See also M. Dalton, *Men Who Manage* (New York: John Wiley & Sons, Inc., 1959), Chap. iii; W. Moore, *The Conduct of the Corporation* (New York: Random House, 1962), esp. p. 115; F. Jasinsky, "Use and Misuse of Efficiency Controls," *Harvard Business Review* (July–August 1956); P. Blau, *Bureaucracy in Modern Society* (New York: Random House, 1956).

Chapter 9

1. Cf. *Izvestia* (October 24, 1962).
2. Translated in *Current Digest of the Soviet Press* (*CDSP*), XIV, No. 47 (1962), 3ff.
3. *Ibid.*
4. Cf. *Pravda* (April 26, 1963).
5. Extensive documentation to this effect can be found in B. Richman, "Managerial Opposition to Product Innovation in Soviet Union Industry," *California Management Review* (Winter 1963), p. 11ff.
6. *Pravda* (October 3, 1962).
7. Cf. *Izvestia* (August 30 and August 31, 1963).
8. *Pravda* (August 22, 1963).
9. *Ibid.* (July 2, 1959).
10. *Izvestia* (May 29, 1962).
11. *Pravda* (October 3, 1962).
12. Translated in *CDSP*, XIV, No. 21 (1962), 14–15.
13. *Izvestia* (November 21, 1961).
14. E. Liberman, *Ekon. Gaz.* (November 10, 1962), pp. 10–11.
15. See L. Gatovskii, "The Role of Profit in Socialist Economy," *Soviet Review* (Summer 1963), pp. 19–20.
16. *Izvestia* (May 25, 1962).
17. L. Gatovskii, *op. cit.*, p. 20.
18. *Izvestia* (May 15, 1960).
19. Editorial, *Ekon. Gaz.* (November 23, 1963).
20. As cited by A. Nove in *The Soviet Economy* (New York: Frederick A. Praeger, Inc., 1961), p. 169.

21. These figures are translated in *CDSP,* XV, No. 15 (1963), 31; and *CDSP,* XV, No. 17 (1963), 3ff.

22. Translated in *CDSP,* XIV, No. 47 (1962), 3ff.

23. *Pravda* (April 26, 1963).

24. For a detailed discussion on innovation incentives in Soviet industry see B. Richman, *op. cit.*

25. For substantial evidence based on many personal interviews with American company managers, see E. K. Warren, *Long Range Planning in Decentralized Corporations* (unpublished doctoral dissertation, New York: Columbia University, 1961).

26. *Ibid.,* pp. 103–104.

27. Cf. H. Asher, *Cost-Quantity Relationships in the Airframe Industry* (Santa Monica, Calif.: Rand Corporation, 1956).

Chapter 10

1. See *Time Magazine* (May 3, 1963), p. 95; D. Jones, *Wall Street Journal* (December 13, 1962), and *Wall Street Journal* (March 4, 1963), p. 12.

2. See *Group Wage Incentives; Experience with the Scanlon Plan* (New York: Industrial Relations Counselors, Inc., 1962).

3. For a more detailed discussion and extensive documentation with regard to this topic, see W. Galenson, *The Soviet Wage Reform,* Institute of Industrial Relations, Reprint No. 172 (Berkeley: University of California, 1961); B. Richman, "Employee Motivation in Soviet Industry," *Annals of Collective Economy* (October–December 1963).

4. See the discussions in B. Sukharevskii, "On Improving the Forms and Methods of Material Incentives," *Problems of Economics* (April 1963), pp. 3ff; V. Grishin (Chairman, Soviet Central Council of Trade Unions), *Current Digest of the Soviet Press* (*CDSP*), XV, No. 17 (1963), 27–29; N. Garetovskii, *Finansy SSSR,* No. 3 (1963), pp. 8ff.

5. Cf. G. Kosiachenko, "Important Conditions for Improvement of Planning," *Problems of Economics* (April 1963), pp. 21ff.

6. For a thorough general discussion on worker-management disputes and channels of appeal available for worker grievances, see E. Brown, "Interests and Rights of Soviet Industrial Workers and the Resolution of Conflicts," *Industrial and Labor Relations Review* (January 1963), pp. 254ff.

7. *Pravda* (March 7, 1959).

8. A thorough account of on-the-job training at Soviet enterprises can be found in M. Paramov, *Metodika Provedenia Zaiaty, Ekonomicheskikh Seminarakh* (Moscow: Moskva Rabochii, 1962).

9. V. Grishin, *op. cit.,* and in *CDSP,* XV, No. 44 (1963), 5ff; N. Khrushchev, *CDSP,* XV, No. 18 (1963), 15ff.

10. For a more complete account of employee participation in Soviet industry, see B. Richman, *op. cit.; Izvestia* (August 8 and August 31, 1963); G. Von Wrangel, "Die staatlichen Industrie-Manager in der Sowjetunion," *Osteuropa,* No. 2 (1963), 13ff; S. Stepanov, *Kommunist* (June 1963), pp. 23ff.

11. Cf. *CDSP,* XIV, No. 47 (1962), 13; *Time Magazine* (August 30, 1963), p. 22.

12. See E. Brown, *op. cit.*

13. See V. Grishin, *CDSP,* XV, No. 17 (1963), 27–29; V. Manushin, *Ekon. Gaz.* (January 5, 1963), pp. 14–15.

14. G. Popov, *CDSP,* XV, No. 37 (1963), 25–26.

15. I. Nikiforov (Director of Krasnaya Presnaya Plant), *CDSP,* XV, No. 18 (1963), 33–34.

16. Figures obtained from *Pravda* (July 13, 1960; January 23, 1962; January 26, 1963; and July 19, 1963).

17. S. Nekhoroshev, "The Economic Nature of Remuneration for Invention and Rationalization Suggestions," *Problems of Economics*, II, No. 4 (1959), 37ff.

18. Cf. the cases cited in S. Nekhorshev, *op. cit.*

19. *Ibid.*

20. S. Stepanov, "Role of Inventors and Innovations," *Problems of Economics*, I, No. 4 (1958), 77–78.

21. The data have been obtained from the annual statistical reports issued by the *NASS* head office in Chicago. These reports also present detailed results for individual member organizations. Other pertinent information regarding suggestion systems also can be obtained from *NASS*.

22. *Ibid.*

23. Cf. *CDSP*, XIV, No. 50 (1962), 18–19; *Pravda* (December 8, 1962), p. 2.

Chapter 11

1. *Current Digest of the Soviet Press (CDSP)*, XI, No. 44 (1959), 14.

2. B. Miroshnichenko, "Problems of National Economic Planning," *Problems of Economics*, IV, No. 2 (1961), 16–17. This source cites other similar examples.

3. Cf. *Ekon. Gaz.* (March 9, 1963), p. 31.

4. Editorial, *Ekon. Gaz.* (October 5, 1963).

5. *Ibid.* (November 23, 1963), p. 3.

6. Cf. *CDSP*, XV, No. 21 (1962), 14–15.

7. For a highly informative account of the role of the party in Soviet industry, see J. Hough, *The Role of the Local Party Organs in Soviet Industrial Decision-Making* (Cambridge, Mass.: Harvard University, unpublished doctoral dissertation, 1961).

8. Cf. *Pravda* (May 12 and October 16, 1963).

9. A description of the system of rewards for enterprise party secretaries can be found in *Partiinaya Zhizn*, No. 6 (March 1960), 71–72; and *CDSP*, XI, No. 39 (1959), 25.

10. Cf. *Pravda* (July 14, 1962; August 14, 1962; May 23, 1963; and October 15, 1963). Editorial, *Ekon. Gaz.* (October 5, 1963).

11. Cited in *Izvestia* (August 27, 1961), p. 3. It is interesting to note that I interviewed this enterprise director shortly before his downfall.

12. This case is translated in *CDSP*, XII, No. 15 (1960), 24ff.

13. *CDSP*, XIV, Nos. 46 and 48 (1962).

14. *CDSP*, XV, No. 17 (1963), 3.

15. Cf. *Pravda* (April 5, 1963).

16. For an informative, comprehensive account of the role of trade unions in Soviet industry, particularly at the enterprise level, the following two articles by Emily Brown are highly recommended: "Interests and Rights of Soviet Industrial Workers and the Resolution of Conflicts," *Industrial and Labor Relations Review* (January 1963), pp. 254ff; "The Local Union in Soviet Industry," *Industrial and Labor Relations Review* (January 1960), pp. 195ff. It is also worthwhile reading the report by V. Grishin (Chairman of the Central Council of Trade Unions), translated in *CDSP*, XV, No. 44 (1963), 5ff.

17. See the sources cited in the above footnote as well as: *Pravda* (July 14 and August 14, 1962); *CDSP*, XIV, No. 28 (1962), 24.

18. For an enlightening, though not entirely up-to-date, discussion and analysis of these organizations regarding enterprise control, see J. Berliner, *Factory and Manager in the USSR* (Cambridge, Mass.: Harvard University Press, 1957), Chap. xvi. For a current discussion see *Ekon. Gaz.* (November 30, 1963), pp. 13–15.

Chapter 12

1. Translated in *Current Digest of the Soviet Press (CDSP)*, XIV, No. 47 (1962), 4

2. Liberman's own articles containing his proposals are translated in *CDSP*, XIV, Nos. 36 and 46 (1962); and *Problems of Economies* (December 1962). Readers are also urged to read two articles on the Liberman Plan by Western authors: M. Goldman, "Economic Controversy in the Soviet Union," *Foreign Affairs* (April 1963); and A. Nove, "The Liberman Plan," *Survey* (April 1963).

3. Cited in L. Gatovskii, "The Role of Profit in a Socialist Economy," *Soviet Review* (Summer 1963), p. 19.

4. Responses to the Liberman Plan can be found in *CDSP*, XIV, Nos. 37–46 (1962). Also of great interest are the seven articles in response to Liberman translated in *Problems of Economics* (April 1963).

5. Cf. P. Karagedov, *Voprosy Ekonomiki* (August 1963), pp. 64–75.

6. See B. Richman, "Managerial Motivation in Soviet and Czechoslovak Industries; a Comparison," *Journal of the Academy of Management* (Summer 1963), pp. 107ff. This article examines Czech industry up to 1962. Because of poor economic results in 1962, the Czech 1961–65 5-year plan was abandoned. The 1962 plan called for a 9.4% increase in industrial growth, while the actual figure was only 6.2%. The interim 1963 plan called for only a 1% increase. The major cause of failures has been the great amount of uncompleted investment projects which have absorbed large amounts of resources. See *Three-Monthly Economic Review*, Eastern Europe-North, No. 29 (March 1963), (Economist Intelligence Unit, Spencer House, London). In personal correspondence with Yale economist John Montias, who is an expert on the Czechoslovak economy, he points out that gross industrial output actually declined by 0.5% in 1963.

7. *Pravda* (December 1, 1962); translated in *CDSP*, XIV, No. 48 (1962), 17.

8. Discussions on the Soviet price system can be found in Gatovskii, *op. cit.*, p. 14ff. Three enlightening articles are translated in *Problems of Economics* (December 1962). The reader is also urged to read the discussion and analysis presented in A. Nove, *The Soviet Economy* (New York: Frederick A. Praeger, 1961), Chaps. viii and x.

9. These points are also brought out by Nove, *op. cit.*, p. 287.

10. For an enlightening article by two Polish economists on pricing problems in Communist countries, see A. Wakar and J. Zielinski, "Socialist Operational Price Systems," *American Economic Review* (March 1963), pp. 109ff.

11. For a comprehensive treatment of Yugoslav industry see A. Waterston, *Planning in Yugoslavia* (Baltimore, Md.: Johns Hopkins Press, 1962).

12. *Ibid.*, p. 1.

13. Cf. W. Grampp, "New Directions in the Communist Economies," *Business Horizons* (Fall 1963), p. 32. See also R. Vicker, "Marxists, Inc.," *Wall Street Journal* (April 3, 1964), p. 1.

14. Waterston, *op. cit.*, pp. 28–33.

15. These figures with related Soviet documentation are found in L. Smolinski and P. Wiles, "The Soviet Planning Pendulum," *Problems of Communism* (November–December 1963), pp. 31–32.

16. Cf. *Izvestia* (March 25, 1963), p. 2.

17. *Ibid.* (September 13, 1963), p. 3.

18. The case of the extreme centralizers with related documentation is found in Smolinski and Wiles, *op. cit.*, pp. 26–27.

19. *Ekon. Gaz.* (May 4, 1963), p. 4.

20. Cf. L. Kantorovich, *Ekon. Gaz.* (November 10, 1962); A. Berg, *Pravda* (October 24, 1962). The ideas and work of this group of reformers are also discussed and analyzed in A. Nove, *op. cit.*, pp. 240–41, and Chap. xi; and in an article by the same

author, "Prospects for Economic Growth in the USSR," in *American Economic Review* (May 1963).

21. Cf. V. Nemchinov, *Pravda* (September 21, 1962); *CDSP,* XIV, No. 38 (1962).

22. Cf. G. Menchikov, *Ekon. Gaz.* (March 9, 1963), p. 31.

23. See B. Richman, *op. cit.,* pp. 107ff. This article contains extensive documentation on the Soviet Merger Movement.

24. Cf. *CDSP,* XV, No. 47 (1963), 32–33.

25. See sources cited in fn. 9, Chapter 2, above.

26. *Izvestia* (September 13, 1963), p. 4.

27. P. Hanson, "The Assortment Problem in Soviet Retail Trade," *Soviet Studies* (April 1962), pp. 356ff.

28. *Izvestia* (September 13, 1963), p. 4.